Argumentation in Everyday Life

To Sara

Argumentation in Everyday Life

Jeffrey P. Mehltretter Drury
Wabash College, USA

Los Angeles | London | New Delhi
Singapore | Washington DC | Melbourne

FOR INFORMATION:

SAGE Publications, Inc.
2455 Teller Road
Thousand Oaks, California 91320
E-mail: order@sagepub.com

SAGE Publications Ltd.
1 Oliver's Yard
55 City Road
London EC1Y 1SP
United Kingdom

SAGE Publications India Pvt. Ltd.
B 1/I 1 Mohan Cooperative Industrial Area
Mathura Road, New Delhi 110 044
India

SAGE Publications Asia-Pacific Pte. Ltd.
18 Cross Street #10-10/11/12
China Square Central
Singapore 048423

Printed in the United States of America

Library of Congress Cataloging-in-Publication Data

Names: Drury, Jeffrey P. Mehltretter, author.

Title: Argumentation in everyday life / Jeffrey P. Mehltretter Drury.

Description: Los Angeles : SAGE, [2021] | Includes bibliographical references and index.

Identifiers: LCCN 2018040587 | ISBN 9781506383590 (paperback: alk. paper)

Subjects: LCSH: Debates and debating. | Logic. | Reasoning.

Classification: LCC PN4181 .D78 2021 | DDC 808.53—dc23 LC record available at https://lccn.loc.gov/2018040587

This book is printed on acid-free paper.

Executive Publisher: Monica Eckman
Acquisitions Editor: Lily Norton
Editorial Assistant: Sarah Wilson
Production Editor: Jyothi Sriram
Copy Editor: Laurie Pitman
Typesetter: Hurix Digital
Proofreader: Jeff Bryant
Indexer: Kathy Paparchontis
Cover Designer: Candice Harman
Marketing Manager: Henry Allison

19 20 21 22 23 24 10 9 8 7 6 5 4 3 2 1

BRIEF CONTENTS

APPENDICES

DETAILED CONTENTS

PART III • CONTESTING ARGUMENTS

Chapter 8 • Generating Productive Clash   **175**

Chapter 9 • Evaluating Arguments & Cases   **195**

PART IV • APPLIED ARGUMENTATION AND DEBATE

PREFACE

As an undergraduate student, I was exposed to the world of competitive intercollegiate debate, and, in my second semester, I became a scholarship debater. Much like Division I athletes, I received free tuition to compete against other colleges on the policy debate circuit. Unlike Division 1 athletes, my battles were primarily verbal rather than physical. Armed with the idealism of my youth and various library databases on the World Wide Web (which was a novel thing at the time), I discovered and advocated what I claimed to be permanent solutions to the world's problems. Across my four years, I resolved the 60-year standoff with North Korea, I protected Africa from the threats of deforestation one semester and AIDS the next, I remedied the long history of racial discrimination in the United States, and I prevented an arms race in Southeast Asia that risked global nuclear war. If these claims seem exaggerated, it's because that was the nature of the system in which competitive policy debate occurred: advocate policies that save the most lives and, when all else fails, just make sure your advocacy doesn't result—hypothetically speaking—in global nuclear war.

Through my experience, I learned that skills in argumentation and debate are a double-edged sword. They have the potential to be both empowering and constraining, both productive and destructive. Indeed, on the empowering and productive side, I gained skills in critical thinking, confident public speaking delivery, thinking on my feet, and effectively consuming massive amounts of information in a short amount of time. But, I also picked up some bad habits: jumping to immediate conclusions, combativeness guided by the goal of victory, viewing debate as a zero-sum game where there is only one winner and many losers, and a reliance on other people's ideas as indisputable "evidence" for claims.

I suspect my experience extends to the virtues and vices of argumentation in everyday life. In your experience, you probably believe that reason and logic should guide human conduct when appropriate conditions are fostered. And, in your experience, you probably recognize the value of skills in critical thinking, argument construction and refutation, and oral communication. But, in your experience, you have probably seen debate lead to intractability, intolerance, anger, and resentment. And, in your experience, you may be concerned that current societal practices of debate and argumentation can occasionally harm the nation, family relationships, and friendships more than they help.

The challenge, then, becomes finding ways to argue in a constructive manner. *Argumentation in Everyday Life* seeks to offer just that: to teach you how to productively engage in argumentation, debate, and critical thinking. What defines an argument or a debate? What role should argumentation and debate play in resolving difficult problems? What makes an argument or a debate "good"? How can you construct, comprehend, and contest arguments in ways that enhance rather than detract from your goals and finding the best outcome? These are just some of the questions we will answer in the following pages.

While the book tackles many topics, there are two important caveats about its scope:

1. ***Argumentation in Everyday Life* focuses on argumentation in Western society,** drawn primarily from examples in the United States. Argumentation and debate exist in virtually all cultures but the specific features, norms, and expectations differ across cultures. Because a single book could not capture all of these unique differences, the focus here is on debate in Western society, and it will become clear that, with rare exception, the examples are all drawn from everyday argumentation in the United States. If you're seeking a cross-cultural study of argumentation, this book is not for you.

2. ***Argumentation in Everyday Life* does not offer a panacea** to personal, professional, and societal problems. Argumentation and debate play an important role in our everyday lives but not all problems require debate (or even arguments for that matter). When you're thirsty, arguments may not help and will likely exacerbate the problem so you should just have a drink instead. When people are suffering from illness, oppression, or homelessness, arguments may not help so you may need to give money, time, or some other resource instead. When you're angry at someone, arguments may not help so you may need to express yourself non-argumentatively or just walk away. If you're seeking a manual that prescribes argumentative cures to all the problems that ail us, this book is not for you.

So what *can* you expect from the book? As a beginner's guide to argumentation, it explores the various possibilities for using argumentation in everyday life. It introduces concepts, theories, and strategies to help you gauge when the situation is right to use argumentation and debate for productive gains. You don't need any prior training in argumentation or debate to profit from the content, but, at times, you may be concerned that the material is quite formal or technical. Like any skill, however, the more you practice, the easier it becomes. That's why the book includes numerous features to help you practice and apply the content. The book also addresses argumentation in the real world. Despite my background in the specialized realm of competitive debate, this book strives to help you translate the formal content into your daily experience as both an advocate and an audience member.

This book offers unique resources to help you navigate this complex terrain of argumentation. Here are a few of the noteworthy features:

"The Debate Situation"

This book contributes the idea of the "the debate situation," a birds-eye view of any given debate (or exchange of arguments between two or more people) organized around three necessary components: arguments, issues, and the proposition. The visual model of the debate situation illustrates how these features work together in guiding a debate, and it lays the groundwork for understanding and generating arguments.

Easy to Use Standards for Evaluating Arguments

A second contribution of *Argumentation in Everyday Life* is that it combines a prominent argument model (named after logician Stephen Toulmin) with a standards-based approach (the ARG conditions) to test the quality of an argument. The ARG conditions are three questions an advocate should ask of an argument in determining whether or not it is rationally persuasive. These questions are best served by research but don't necessary require it, and thus they provide a useful posture for critically assessing the arguments you encounter.

Emphasis on Context

Argumentation in Everyday Life emphasizes multiple contexts of argumentation (the "everyday life" element of the title). Your daily life involves numerous personal, professional, and public experiences, and you inhabit numerous roles. Since each of these realms and roles require argumentation and debate, it doesn't make sense to consider one at the expense of the others. Consequently, the book uses examples from and theoretical discussions about a variety of situations. This broad scope helps you connect the lessons more fully to your everyday life and encourages you to grapple explicitly with dilemmas arising in these different contexts.

Emphasis on Choice and Empowerment

Finally, *Argumentation in Everyday Life* approaches argumentation and debate as a series of choices you must make. These choices exist as both arguer and audience member and they range from whether to engage in the first place to the stance you have toward your co-arguers to when, where, and how to advance your arguments. Theoretically, everything is debatable and you could critique everyone's ideas on every topic. Consequently, one major challenge becomes *choosing* which arguments to address and how to address them. This book offers strategies to help you find your voice and make argumentation an empowering skill.

Each chapter incorporates multiple features designed to assist your learning and connect it to your life:

Key Terms, Definitions, and Glossary: A list of key terms is at the end of each chapter. The definitions of these terms are emphasized on the page they are first introduced and included in Appendix III: Glossary.

Everyday Life Examples: Each chapter features at least one "Everyday Life Example," a case study that illustrates the lessons or content from that chapter in action. These will come from a variety of contexts to show the utility of the material.

Find Your Voice Prompts: Beyond illustrating how others have used the concepts, you will encounter brief thought experiments to help you apply the ideas to your own life. These are subjective prompts that encourage you to reflect on your own experiences and hone your connection to and understanding of the topic.

Build Your Skill Prompts: Whereas Find Your Voice prompts are largely subjective, Build Your Skill prompts tend to be objective applications that test how well you have learned the information. They offer a chance to apply the material to additional examples that you can check against the answers in Appendix II.

Application Exercises: The conclusion of each chapter offers two exercises for more extensive engagement with the material. These might be assignments your class instructor could use or something you complete on your own to facilitate more extensive understanding and application of the material.

As you embark on the journey through this textbook, I have tried to make it accessible, engaging, and valuable. If I've done my part correctly, the book will challenge you to engage in self-reflection, slow down in your argumentation, and internalize the lessons. It is my ultimate hope that this book empowers you to find your voice and create positive change through argumentation in everyday life.

—*Jeffrey P. Mehltretter Drury*

Wabash College

ACKNOWLEDGMENTS

This textbook necessarily draws inspiration and material from a variety of other sources that have influenced my study of argumentation and debate over the past 20 years. Many of the concepts, strategies, examples, and exercises are adapted from my encounters with others in the small pedagogical community of argumentation and debate. I owe much of my knowledge of policy debate and debate strategy to my mentors at Northern Illinois University, including M. Jack Parker, Dorothy Bishop, and John Butler. At the University of Wisconsin-Madison, Robert Asen helped refine my thinking about argument forms and conditions for cogency, and I have benefitted from collaboration with and materials by Pamela Conners and Maegan Parker Brooks.

The staff at SAGE has been a huge help. Thanks to Karen Omer for taking a chance on me and providing excellent guidance in the early stages, Matt Byrnie for helping me improve the table of contents, Sarah Wilson for navigating with me the challenges of copyright and permissions, and Terri Accomazzo for being a tireless editor, answering my numerous questions throughout the writing and revision processes.

I give my sincere thanks to the following reviewers, who offered valuable feedback on my proposal and manuscript: Susan P. Millsap, Otterbein University; Christopher Leland, Azusa Pacific University; Suzanne J. Atkin, Arizona State University; Benjamin Krueger, Northern Arizona University; Catherine Wilson, University of Louisiana at Monroe; and Carroll Nardone, Sam Houston State University.

The "everyday life" component of the book would be much less interesting were it not for the generous permission of the following people to use their material: Maria Guido and John Kahlil for *Scary Mommy*; Zzzmessi1 and Ghost_of_John_Galt from Reddit; James Harrison; the American Psychological Association; CMG Worldwide on behalf of Lou Gehrig's estate; WalletHub; Gallup; Richard Dillio and the Entertainment Software Association; Gregory Mankiw; John Gau; Peter Adeney (aka Mr. Money Mustache); Taylor Mali; and the U.S. Substance Abuse and Mental Health Services Administration.

I am grateful to my students and colleagues at Wabash College. My students throughout the years have inspired me and sparked ideas for some of the examples you'll find throughout the book. Special thanks to Collin Bell, Wabash College class of 2017, who kindly offered a student perspective on some of the chapters, and to Jennifer Y. Abbott and Todd F. McDorman, who encouraged me and gave me helpful advice from their own textbook writing process. I am also grateful to Wabash College's John J. Coss Faculty Development Fund for covering licensing costs and the dean of the College for financially supporting my research sabbatical to write the book.

I thank my family—Barb Drury, Jill and Bryan Huntsman, David Drury, Joe and Kathy Mehltretter, and Rachel and Ryan McElaney—for believing in me and taking an interest in the book's progress. Their support drove me to make the book the best it could be. Finally, Sara has been my rock and biggest fan since day one. It's because of her encouragement that I contacted SAGE with my book idea in the first place, because of her initiative that I wrote it in Edinburgh, Scotland, and because of her love that I dedicate the book to her.

A FRAMEWORK FOR ARGUMENTATION AND DEBATE

PART I

INTRODUCTION
TO ARGUMENTATION
AND DEBATE

Argumentation, or the process of forming and communicating claims based on supporting information, is a fundamental aspect of everyday life.

Take a moment to reflect on the various opportunities for argumentation as you go about your daily business: You look at the nutritional information on cereal boxes to determine which is healthiest for breakfast. You go to work or school and debate important ideas with colleagues and friends. You weigh the pros and cons of a working lunch before deciding to take a full lunch break. As the work day winds down, you pull up your social media feed and read argumentative posts on important (and frequently not-so-important) topics. You turn on the TV after you come home and are bombarded by advertisements offering reasons to buy the products.

All of these moments have, at their core, argumentation. Whenever you reach a conclusion about something based on reasons, whenever you challenge another person's reasons or conclusions, whenever you consider the benefits and drawbacks of action, you are engaging in argumentation. As Edward Z. Rowell, a professor of rhetoric, observed back in 1932: "Argument is a part of the real business of living. It serves us in our daily tasks, in our perplexities, in our disputes, in our search for truth, and in the promotion of our interests."[1] You probably agree that argument's role hasn't changed much in the last century.

The prevalence of argumentation in everyday life means you surely have cultivated argumentation and debate skills through the process of living. But one lesson of argumentation and advocacy is that we can always pursue self-improvement and learn more than we currently know. Thus, you can gain a lot by studying theories and concepts of argumentation, especially since many of them are tried and true, having first been identified more than two millennia ago in ancient Greece or Rome. If you have no formal

ARGUMENTATION: The process of forming and communicating claims advanced by support

3

experience with argumentation and debate, don't worry, this book is also for you. It is designed to give you practical tools to use in your daily life.

This first chapter justifies the importance of your journey into the world of argumentation and debate. We'll define some key terms—argument, debate, and controversy—and consider the current state of argumentation. We'll then explore the importance of honing your argumentation skills to improve your personal, professional, and public lives. Finally, we'll explore a few aspects relevant to your lived experience of argumentation and debate: audiences, co-arguers, presumption, burdens of proof, and spheres of argument. By the end of this chapter, you should have a working understanding of the nature, value, and situations of argumentation in everyday life.

ARGUMENT, DEBATE, AND CONTROVERSY

ARGUMENT: A claim advanced by support

In the English language, people often use the word "**argument**" to mean at least three different things: an object, an action, and a controversy. As an *object*, arguments are products that people construct and advance through communication. This is the meaning behind the statement, "I disagree with your argument that Coke is better than Pepsi." As an *action*, argument may mean an exchange of reasons on a topic among communicants. This meaning is evident, for example, when someone says, "We had a heated argument about which soda [or "pop"] is better." Finally, sometimes we mean the general **controversy**, or many debates happening all over the place, such as the statement, "Congress's consideration of a soda tax reinvigorated the argument over sugary beverages in the United States."

CONTROVERSY: Prolonged argumentation at the societal level spanning space and time

People commonly use all three senses of the word but having multiple meanings for "argument" in this book would create confusion. To avoid this, we will use the word *argument* exclusively to mean the object, or product, of argumentation. Specifically, our starting definition of an argument is a claim advanced by support. When referring to the action-based meaning, we'll use the word **debate**: the exchange of arguments on a topic. And, the word *controversy* will refer to the prolonged argumentation at the societal level spanning space and time.

DEBATE: The exchange of arguments on a topic

Here's an example to illustrate how we will distinguish argument and debate:

Me: You should clean the dishes *(claim)*

You: Why?

> Me: You should clean the dishes *(claim)* because it's your turn *(support)* *(argument)*
>
> You: I disagree *(claim)* because you are the one who dirtied all the dishes currently in the sink *(support)* *(argument)*

(debate)

In later chapters, we'll explore these terms in greater depth but it's important to note that argumentation, debate, and controversy are not reserved to formal settings between two people who have timed segments for their content. The everyday nature of argumentation means that you frequently argue as a student, family member, employee, consumer, citizen, friend, and a whole host of other roles you occupy. You encounter, evaluate, employ, and engage arguments every day. In many cases, you may not even recognize the presence of arguments because they are so ingrained in your experience; you may instictively process or disregard the information and move on with your day. And, arguments come in all shapes and sizes: in verbal, audio, and visual formats, in questions and statements, in formal writing and casual conversation.

Additionally, debate is not limited to ceremonial, argumentative occasions but occurs in many forms such as conversation, heated yelling, text messaging, and online posts. Debate also occurs in a hypothetical sense when we produce argumentative writing that imagines the reader holding a counter-perspective and accounts for arguments against our position. All reason-based advocacy, then, uses argumentation and offers the potential for debate.

Despite the frequency of argumentation and debate in everyday life, most people are not formally taught how to argue in an effective, ethical, and eloquent manner. Few K-12 schools teach argumentation as a formal skill akin to reading, writing, and arithmetic. While many colleges and universities require public speaking of all students, courses in argumentation and debate tend to serve smaller populations. And the debating societies that were once breeding grounds of articulate communicators have been eliminated altogether or become so technical that an outside observer would hardly recognize them as contests in argumentation.

Consider your own education in argumentation:

Where and how did you learn to argue? It's possible you learned some argumentation skills in school but you've probably honed them primarily through experience based on trial and error.

When did you learn to argue? Your training in argumentation probably began at a very young age. A toddler who says "no" to a parent's request is not advancing a full argument but is certainly advancing a claim. As you grew older, you learned that you need a reason or two for those claims to get others to agree.

From whom did you learn to argue? If you had an argument coach who taught you these skills, consider yourself a lucky individual. Most of us learn argumentation and debate from observation: how parents or guardians debate with one another, how siblings and friends respond when things don't go their way, how teachers and leaders argue ideas, how the mass media communicate claims, etc.

If most people learn to argue informally through their life experiences that might explain why current argumentation practices are often disappointing. Books such as *The Assault on Reason* by former Vice President Al Gore or *The Argument Culture: Moving from Debate to Dialogue* by linguistics scholar Deborah Tannen contend that public discourse in the 21st century has prioritized competition, fearmongering, and personal interests over rational and productive conversation.[2] Some authors, such as social psychologist Jonathan Haidt in *The Righteous Mind*, take the argument further by claiming that humans are biologically predisposed to non-rational impulses and must exert substantial energy to use rational argumentation.[3]

The messages that surround you on a daily basis likely illustrate the inadequacy of contemporary argumentation. The mass media and press often pay lip service to the importance of argumentation while relying on polemics and drama that accentuate rather than resolve disagreements. Politics, business, and interpersonal relationships are often no better. In politics, "compromise" is a dirty word while personal attacks, inflexibility, and competition abound. *Saturday Night Live* recognized this prevalent political culture of argumentation in the 2016 presidential campaign when, during a mock debate between Hillary Clinton (Kate McKinnon) and Donald Trump (Alec Baldwin), McKinnon and Baldwin broke characters. They noted that what passes for debate these days is often personal insults yelled at one another, with McKinnon observing that "the whole election has been so mean."[4]

The situation is not much better on college and university campuses across the United States. Once considered bastions of free thought and expression, campuses today seem happier to avoid contentious disagreement by instituting "free speech zones" or "safe spaces," reducing or canceling controversial speakers, and conferring legitimacy on all ideas and perspectives. These elements may be important and useful in isolation and in particular circumstances, but they also limit when and where students can engage in open argumentative expression. If everyone is entitled to his or her own opinion, then debating those opinions with reasoned evidence is inappropriate and potentially offensive. If some speakers are denied a voice, then we may not learn how to productively respect all perspectives. And if safe spaces segregate us from those with whom we disagree, then we all remain shackled by our existing and sometimes flawed beliefs. Historian Mark Lilla observed in a *Wall Street Journal* article that historical shifts in social identity have hastened this trend, explaining that "classroom conversations that once might have begun, *I think A, and here is my argument*, now take the form, *Speaking as an X, I am offended that you claim B*. What replaces argument, then, are taboos against unfamiliar ideas and contrary opinions."[5]

This reality is not helped by the echo chamber of social media, in which the curation of messages on Facebook, Twitter, and other outlets is designed to reinforce our existing beliefs. According to Michael J. Socolow, a professor of journalism, the inability or unwillingness to "properly read a social media feed" means that "some very smart people are helping to spread some very dumb ideas."[6] In particular, he noted the lack of support for claims—that is, the lack of a full argument as we've defined the term—to be a significant tell for "fake news" and cautioned people against immediately believing what they read, *especially* if it conforms to your existing worldview.

If any of this describes your own experience, please know that it's not entirely your fault. The inability to argue is cultivated early in life. NoRedInk, an online learning platform widely utilized in U.S. school districts, recently conducted a study of more than 200,000 middle and high school students from all 50 states. More than half of the students couldn't distinguish a claim from support, couldn't identify when support fails to advance an argument's claim, couldn't spot weak evidence, and couldn't detect imprecise, misleading language.[7] NoRedInk founder, Jeff Scheur, credited these results to limited hands-on experience with argumentation, noting that students "need strong modeling. They need practice."[8]

Although this landscape may seem bleak, Scheur's statement provides a ray of hope for budding arguers. This book provides exactly the kind of modeling and practice that can help you cultivate the skillful art of argumentation. The title indicates the book's emphasis on improving the culture of argumentation in everyday life rather than training you for technical debate. While some of the material may seem specialized at first, it's designed to give you adaptable tools for numerous situations. Before starting down this path, though, it's beneficial to more fully consider the value of our journey.

WHY STUDY ARGUMENTATION?

The study of argumentation has a long history, dating as far back as 500 BCE. In ancient Greece, Rome, and China, scholars of the art of rhetoric recognized that people can hone habits of mind and speaking through training and practice. This tradition has endured over time, through the Roman Empire, dark ages, renaissance, industrial revolution, and into the present day. People in all eras understood the need for pursuing reason and truth through argumentation.

But changing times provoke different needs, desires, and pursuits. Has our online, social media environment brought us to a post-argument culture? Is the study of argumentation still relevant in the 21st century? First, reflect on your personal incentive through the Find Your Voice feature on this page. Then, we'll explore at least three broad reasons acquiring argumentation and debate skills should be important to you.

Skills Are Empowering

First, learning skills in argumentation and debate is empowering because you cultivate the tools to find and use your voice. It's often easier to retreat to the safety of our electronic devices than it is to confront challenging topics face-to-face.[9] The real world, however, demands that we talk honestly and openly with others to cultivate ideas, reach judgments, and take action. When disagreements inevitably arise, argumentation becomes a primary tool for addressing them rather than deluding ourselves that they will go away if we ignore them. Building your argumentation and debate skills, then, can empower you to more effectively advocate your ideas and engage the ideas of others. Research shows that training in argumentation and debate can boost your confidence and improve your speaking and writing.[10] Yes, debate will involve risks and surprises, but this excitement is the very reason debate can have such a profound impact.

FIND YOUR VOICE
STUDYING ARGUMENTATION

Effective arguers emphasize what their audience stands to gain from agreeing with them. You, as *my* audience, should take a moment to reflect on what you might gain from learning the skills taught in this book. What concrete, personal goals motivate your effort to improve your argumentation skills? Establishing these motivations now and keeping them in your mind might help sustain your learning down the road.

These skills translate directly into leadership. Erika Anderson, author of *Leading So People Will Follow*, argues that passionate leadership relies, in part, on the ability to "make a clear case without being dogmatic."[11] Learning argumentation and debate skills can help foster your own leadership on the controversies that surround you. It's often the case that our intuition and conviction may underlie and occasionally override our argumentation so these skills are necessary to balance the non-rational and rational sides.

Beyond honing your own ability, argumentation skills empower you to be a more critical audience member. John Dewey, an education philosopher and proponent of strong public argumentation, defined **critical thinking** as "active, persistent, and careful consideration of any belief or supposed form of knowledge in the light of the grounds that support it, and the further conclusions to which it tends."[12] Putting this in our book's language, Dewey essentially defined critical thinking as active, persistent, and careful consideration of arguments.

Critical thinking requires energy, focus, and time, and it doesn't stop once you reach a decision; even if you accept an argument as true, critical thinking involves constantly questioning it as you encounter new information.

Of course, if you don't know what criteria to use in critically evaluating an idea, then you can't be expected to do so. Luckily, training in argumentation and debate gives you such tools and improves critical thinking.[13] Empowerment means you can take these skills with you when you encounter arguments in society. Peer pressure, mass mediated messages, political propaganda, and other manners of argumentation exert the most power when we consume rather than critically engage them. The more you stop and reflect on these messages, the more you'll weaken their hold over your mind. You must often decide for yourself where you stand on important topics and argumentation skills give you the autonomy to do so and help you evaluate how well arguers use information to advance their own agendas.

CRITICAL THINKING: Active, persistent, and careful consideration of arguments

Skills Are Productive

Second, learning skills in argumentation and debate is productive insofar as the skills help individuals and communities make better decisions and achieve their goals. When people understand how arguments work, they can more quickly and successfully weigh evidence to reach a conclusion. If we want others to make reasoned decisions, then we ought to train ourselves in what counts as reasoned decision-making.

Argumentation and debate skills are also a productive part of societal change. The example of 1960s civil rights leader Malcolm X is instructive. Even though he justified "any means necessary" in bringing about civil rights, it's telling that he *chose* debate as his preferred means of activism.[14] He believed debate was a powerful method of revealing a situation's truth and of fostering change. His efforts, along with the argumentation efforts of other advocates for civil rights in the 1960s, are testament to the productive power of argumentation and debate.

The ability to argue in a productive manner is also a desirable trait in any employee, romantic partner, or friend. In the workforce, for example, the Association of American Colleges & Universities (AAC&U) noted that "more than nine in ten employers (91 percent) say they value [critical thinking, communication, and problem-solving skills] more than a potential employee's undergraduate major."[15] There are a few reasons why employers might prefer the mastery of these skills rather than of a subject matter. First, they make you more self-sufficient, not relying on your boss or colleague to hold your hand through every obstacle or anxiety. Second, they promote the *process* rather than *content* of tackling challenging topics. Many employers will provide training for important job-based skills, but it is harder to teach employees so-called "soft skills" (e.g., how to communicate ideas, think critically, or argue cogent arguments).[16] Third, these skills make you a more pleasant and productive group member, open to using the available information rather than being aggressively inflexible. Ultimately, argumentation skills help you better manage your personal and professional lives where you spend most of your time and energy each day.

Skills Are Democratic

Third, learning skills in argumentation and debate is democratic by helping you meet your responsibility to public life. Because argumentation involves choice—of whether and what to communicate—it necessarily engages ethics and community values (see Chapter 3). Training in argumentation can make you more sensitive to the interests and viewpoints of different audiences, enabling you to appropriately adapt your messages, consider multiple perspectives, and work through competing ideas while valuing everyone's voice. This might be why the AAC&U report observed that these skills help "prepare graduates to live responsibly in an increasingly diverse democracy and in an interconnected global community."[17]

The democratic virtue exists regardless of the argumentation's outcome. In the very process of debating others, you communicate a lot about what you personally value, how you understand your role, and what worth you afford them. For instance, a simple interruption of a co-arguer conveys that stating your own ideas is more important than listening. You may recall the eye roll seen 'round the world, delivered by CNN host Anderson Cooper in May 2017 during a televised interview with Kellyanne Conway, one of President Trump's counselors. It became a viral sensation in animated GIF and meme formats and sparked a wave of discussion about the virtue or vice of rolling one's eyes. Regardless of your own stance on the controversy, Conway felt it belittled her ideas and her worth as a person.[18] Cultivating skills in argumentation and debate makes you more aware of these reactions and promotes accountability when you slip up.

The above reasons all underscore that argumentation occurs with specific people and in specific situations. Learning the skills of argumentation and debate, then, requires you to recognize how contextual factors might guide and shape your involvement. We'll first consider audiences and co-arguers before turning to three general spheres, or contexts, of argumentation.

AUDIENCES AND CO-ARGUERS

You may have noticed that our definition of debate—"the exchange of arguments on a topic"—doesn't specify *who* is debating. This doesn't mean that the people involved in the argumentation don't matter. On the contrary, there is always an audience for argumentation. Even U.S. founders such as Alexander Hamilton, whom we credit with writing philosophical statements that have stood the test of time, wrote their material "in the midst of controversy" with a desire to "convince people through appeals to their reason."[19]

FIND YOUR VOICE
AUDIENCES AND CO-ARGUERS

Take a moment to reflect on the debates you have in a typical day. With whom do you usually debate? Are those co-arguers also the audience members? If not, for whom do you usually debate? You probably don't have "typical" audiences and co-arguers but rather encounter many different debate relationships throughout each day. The more skilled you become, the easier it is to recognize and adapt to your various audiences.

AUDIENCE: The people to whom arguers speak and from whom arguers seek assent

CO-ARGUER: The people with whom arguers exchange arguments

Rather, the definition's vagueness allows room for a variety of audiences and co-arguers. By **audience**, we mean the people who we want to agree with our arguments. **Co-arguers**, on the other hand, are those with whom we debate, or exchange arguments. They are the people whose arguments we must address and surmount to earn the audience's assent.

Consider the various combinations of audiences and co-arguers. One common scenario is for the audience to comprise different people than co-arguers, as represented in scenarios such as political candidate debates. It's likely that you participate in debates of this nature in the classroom, workplace, or on social media platforms. Often, however, the audience for your arguments *is* your co-arguer, such as when exchanging text messages or emails to resolve an interpersonal conflict. Sometimes a person who starts as an audience member may become a co-arguer, for instance if someone challenges a statement that you didn't intend to be controversial. Sometimes your audience and co-arguers are imaginary rather than actual, such as when producing a written document that argues your ideas while addressing counter-arguments. And, sometimes you alone may be the arguer, co-arguer, and audience, such as when you generate a pro-con list for yourself or write an argumentative message to someone that you never send.

Once you've determined your audience, you should then consider two questions that help you understand your argumentation in relation to that audience. These questions apply to any advocacy situation, although they tend to be more useful for formal argumentation occasions (e.g., a presentation for your boss) as opposed to informal ones (e.g., a debate among friends at 2 a.m. about which of the four houses at Hogwarts is best).

PRESUMPTION: The expected outcome of a proposition absent a debate

The first question you should ask is: Where does **presumption** lie in the debate? To presume something is to expect it based on probability. Chaim Perelman, a rhetoric and argumentation scholar, explained presumption as "what normally happens and . . . what can be reasonably counted upon."[20] Presumption refers to the expected outcome of a proposition absent a debate. Rhetorical scholar Richard Whately explained that presumption "must stand good till some sufficient reason is adduced against it."[21] For instance, presumption in our Hogwarts debate likely favors Gryffindor; it's what most people would want absent a debate. Presumption will always lean toward one side of a debate, but it may change as you change your audience or as a controversy develops. For instance, in many parts of Europe presumption still favors smoking in public spaces. This used to be the case in the United States as well, but that presumption has flipped since the early 2000s.

Presumption has a strong impact on the debates we have. For debates in the courtroom, for instance, jurists are told that presumption favors the defense; the accused is innocent until proven guilty beyond a reasonable doubt. For debates about action, presumption often favors the *status quo*, or the current state of affairs in the "present system"; as change-averse people, we assume no action necessary unless we are convinced otherwise. As you can imagine, however, presumption will often depend on the audience and co-arguers. When advocating student loan forgiveness before students, presumption will likely favor the policy whereas advocating it before college administrators will likely favor the *status quo* or stricter requirements for loan forgiveness.

Presumption helps you answer a second important question: What is my **burden of proof** in the debate? The burden of proof refers to an arguer's responsibility to sufficiently demonstrate a claim. All arguers face a burden of proof but what it means to "sufficiently demonstrate" a claim will depend on the situation, presumption, and the audience(s) and co-arguer(s). For instance, the burden of proof is greater when arguing *against* presumption than it is when arguing *for* presumption. Additionally, the burden of proof is usually greater for arguers who have less power than the audience (e.g., a student trying to convince a professor of something).

We'll spend more time with these concepts in later chapters, but they are important terms to introduce now because they often guide the very framework of a debate. Given the diversity of scenarios for debate, understanding audiences, co-arguers, presumption, and burden of proof can be crucial to your participation and effective arguers should spend time reflecting on these elements. You should also recognize how these factors exist within particular spheres of argumentation.

BURDEN OF PROOF: An arguer's responsibility to demonstrate a sufficient case on the proposition

SPHERES OF ARGUMENT

There are virtually limitless circumstances for argumentation and debate but this doesn't mean that the strategies, tactics, and procedures are different for all of them. Rather, there are patterns to argumentation depending on the situation and participants. You could probably piece together some patterns based on your own experience: argumentation at home over the dinner table likely follows a consistent pattern that differs from the pattern at a club meeting or the pattern in Tweets or the pattern for papers you write for class. And if you're anything like my students, you probably feel like the patterns for argumentation in one subject (say, biology) completely differ from those in another (say, history).

These differences point to the concept of **spheres of argument**, or metaphoric spaces where argumentation occurs. G. Thomas Goodnight described argument spheres as "branches of activity—the grounds upon which arguments are built and the authorities to which arguers appeal."[22]

Such spheres are not physical locations, such as the house or the store, but figurative arenas that are activated when groups of people use specific argumentation norms. Consider the parallel to a church: Most faith traditions argue that a church exists not in a physical structure but in the community of people who assemble and behave in a particular religious manner (prayer, singing, etc.). Similarly, an argument sphere exists when a group of people assemble and behave in a particular argumentative manner. This means that an argument sphere can emerge anywhere, including cyberspace.

ARGUMENT SPHERE: a metaphoric realm of argumentation characterized by predictable patterns

Three broad spheres—personal, technical, and public—usefully explain different patterns of argumentation. We'll consider each kind of sphere before exploring an Everyday Life Example displaying how spheres shape argumentation and debate.

Personal Spheres

PERSONAL SPHERE: A realm characterized by informal argumentation of limited scope among individuals

If you have ever debated a family member about who gets the last cookie in the box or who has to complete a chore, you've enacted argumentation in a **personal sphere**. Personal spheres involve informal argumentative exchanges in which the participants largely determine their own procedures and guidelines. Because most personal spheres don't specify such guidelines (e.g., what kind of evidence is appropriate; who gets to speak for how long and when; how debate is resolved and concluded), participants often need to make up the rules as they go and adapt as appropriate. Presumption will vary in these debates but the burden of proof tends to be the lowest in personal spheres.

Beyond the informal nature of this realm, personal spheres are characterized by consequences that don't extend much, if at all, beyond the individuals engaged in the debate. That is, the resolution of the debate is of personal importance. Debates about topics such as who gets to hold the remote control or what to eat for dinner are largely consequential for only those participating in the debate (and a few others who may be affected by its outcome). Ultimately, personal spheres exist whenever we debate topics related to our lives and the lives of our family and friends.

Consider the decision of whether to become vegetarian. A personal sphere debate involving you and your family members might discuss some of the following topics: What is the financial cost to going vegetarian? How easy is it to find delicious and nutritious meatless food? What does your religion say about meat-eating? How will vegetarianism impact your general health and levels of energy throughout the day? These questions are of strong consequence to your own life but the significance largely stops there. You may also ask the broader societal impact of meat eating on the environment or on the animals themselves but personal sphere argumentation tends to focus more on how the outcome impacts you directly. As for procedures, there are not very strong guidelines for when, where, or how you should argue the answers to these questions.

Technical Spheres

TECHNICAL SPHERE: A realm characterized by formal argumentation within a specialized community

If you have ever written a paper for a class or a memo for a job that required you to use a particular format, you've enacted **technical sphere** argumentation. Technical spheres tend to be rule-driven and specialized, using logical forms and vocabulary appropriate to each arena. Most of the time, technical sphere argumentation is governed by institutional structures or groups who enforce those guidelines.

For instance, creating a resume is an argument—it offers evidence for your "profile" claim—that should be adapted to the technical sphere of the (kind of) workplace to which you're applying. Even if the format looks slightly different from one resume to the next, you can probably predict that there will be supporting information about a person's education, work experience, and skills. Resumes that violate these guidelines in egregious ways tend to be discounted. Of course, there are many technical spheres that may require different things on a resume—applying for a job in the education field requires different kinds of information and arguments than applying for a job in art or science. To outside observers, these rules may seem cumbersome or confusing but those who are part of the technical sphere often recognize how these conventions ensure consistency and quality. This explains why the papers you write for different classes follow different rules; each field of study comprises a different technical sphere following a different argumentation pattern.

Technical spheres tend to involve experts whose arguments are relevant to a specific knowledge community. The consequences of and audience for technical sphere argumentation extend beyond those involved in the debate but are limited to the community in which the debate occurs. For instance, a company's Board of Directors may debate a budgeting decision that impacts the company's employees but matters very minimally for the public at large. Similarly, a person's resume may get forwarded up the ladder but the outcome of the debate over the person's credentials is limited to the company and applicants.

Let's revisit the decision of eating meat. Dieticians comprise a technical sphere debating ideas that differ substantially from personal sphere debates on this topic. For instance, dieticians have pursued whether meat eating correlates to risk of various forms of cancer.[23] Arguments on this topic address specialized subjects such as polymorphism in enzymes (FADS2) and rely on strict research methods such as experimental or lab design to isolate factors. The goal is for other members of this technical community to build on and utilize the research with the eventual hope of finding a truth to share with the public at large.

The technical sphere of dieticians differs from the technical sphere of philosophers. In 2015, for example, a debate occurred in the pages of the *Journal of Agricultural and Environmental Ethics* about whether humans should grant animals "moral status," thus rendering meat eating unethical.[24] This argumentation relied not on experimental design and isolating causal relationships but rather on the logical sequence from premise to conclusion, drawing value judgments based on the definition of terms and the sentient nature of animals. Here, again, the argumentation addressed a specific community and used the particular argumentative norms appropriate to that community.

Outside of scholarly research, there are other technical spheres that debate the topic of meat eating: restaurant owners discussing whether the sale of meat products makes sense for their company mission and profits; animal welfare organizations strategizing for how to best raise awareness and generate action; religious institutions offering justifications for restrictions they place on eating meat. In each case, resolving the debate may be important to society at large but it represents technical sphere argumentation because it is focused primarily on the community to which the arguers belong and it utilizes the specialized guidelines and norms of that community.

Public Spheres

If you have ever commented on a news article through social media or debated the consequences of a national policy proposal with a friend, you've enacted **public sphere** argumentation. In a public sphere, people transcend their status as private individuals to consider their role as engaged members of society, often in the role of citizen. Jürgen Habermas, a prominent theorist of public spheres, explains that "a portion of the public sphere comes into being in every conversation in which private individuals assemble to form a public body."[25]

Public sphere argumentation often strives to generate public opinions about topics of general concern that, ultimately, produce communal knowledge and societal change. The consequence of public sphere argumentation, then, exceeds that of both personal and technical spheres and tends to involve more diverse considerations.

PUBLIC SPHERE: A realm characterized by community-oriented argumentation of societal scope

Public spheres are more formal than personal spheres but less specialized than technical ones. For instance, a family friend's struggle with discrimination may be enough of a basis for arguing in a personal sphere the nature of racism today but it may not justify your arguments in a public sphere for how the nation should address civil rights. At the same time, public sphere debate often requires translation from technical spheres, such as lawyers explaining the parameters of current civil rights laws, to a general audience.

Although argumentation norms may differ from one public sphere to the next, public spheres often uphold a few core argumentation principles. First, public sphere argumentation frequently promotes a *common good* rather than personal interests. Arguers certainly pursue their own benefit but public spheres tend to prioritize thinking beyond oneself to consider the public consequence of an argument. Because public spheres involve people outside your personal or professional network, there is a higher likelihood of encountering people who disagree with your ideas or have different values than you. Board members of a company may make technical decisions based on profit motive behind closed doors, for instance, but once they go public with their ideas they must justify them to people who care very little about the company's profits. Thus, finding common ground and shared values becomes part of the argumentation process.

Beyond the common good, public spheres often prioritize *equality of access*. In an ideal society, every person would participate in debates about topics of common concern. This is in stark contrast to technical spheres, which have gatekeepers and strict guidelines for entry, and personal spheres, which draw conversational boundaries based on access, familiarity, and trust. Proponents of social media often appeal to this equalizing factor in celebrating the virtues of these platforms; everybody has the power to share their ideas and participate in discussion. Although public spheres often fall short of the ideal insofar as exclusions exist based on various traits such as language, income, biological sex, race, ability, or education,[26] arguers in a public sphere often strive to promote an inclusive environment that affords everyone the opportunity to participate.

Third, public spheres tend to promote *freedom of speech*. Especially in the United States, censorship, demagoguery, and propaganda violate democratic principles and arguers often encourage freedom of speech and thought because they believe that the best ideas will prevail through open debate. Freedom of speech also means that all controversies are worth discussing, especially those they make us uncomfortable. Labeling some topics such as domestic violence or mental illness as "private" concerns best dealt with in personal spheres undermines the power of public sphere argumentation to tackle complex problems that affect society.

Returning to our example of meat eating, public sphere debates look quite different than both personal and technical sphere debates. Public spheres address concerns about cost, cancer, and conscience but there are more diverse (societal) considerations at play, including environmental impact, public health, and bullying.[27] Additionally, debates occur across many platforms such as newspapers, websites, social media, popular culture programming on television and radio, and even songs. For instance, the band Goldfinger's 2002 song "Open Your Eyes" addressed numerous public sphere concerns, including the meat industry's manipulation of people, the environmental and moral impact of meat eating, and the profit motive of factory farms.[28] This song represents public sphere argumentation because it addresses the general public rather than a personal or specialized community and it focuses on the common good by transcending concerns from personal or technical spheres.

BUILD YOUR SKILL
SPHERES OF ARGUMENT

Similar to our meat-eating example, consider for the controversies below how the topics and patterns of argumentation might be similar and different across the three spheres:

A. Rising student loan debt in the United States

B. Opioid abuse among American youth

C. Mass murder of civilians in Syria

D. The discriminatory nature of the Washington Redskins name

Interaction of Spheres

Table 1.1 summarizes the personal, technical, and public spheres of argument. They often exist independently but they can also conflict with or complement one another. The following are some examples of this interaction:

- Students at Marjory Stoneman Douglas High School in Florida took their technical sphere debates about gun control into the public sphere following a mass shooting in February 2018 that killed 17 community members. Specifically, after students had debated gun control in class and as part of the debate team the prior semester, they used their knowledge to create a social movement organization and spark a national conversation on the topic. The *Miami Herald* noted that the students "have been praised for their composure and well-articulated arguments," thanks in large part to their training in argumentation and debate.[29]

- Concerns about climate change started in a technical sphere when scientists measured atmospheric carbon dioxide and discussed concerns about the "greenhouse effect."[30] By publishing reports and working with various government institutions, the controversy entered the public sphere. Debates over climate change continue to this day despite decades of technical sphere evidence.

- Public sphere debates about immigration became a personal sphere struggle in 2017 for the Beristains of South Bend, Indiana, when Roberto Beristain was detained and eventually deported for illegally entering the United States 15 years earlier. His wife, who voted for President Trump, believed that the administration would only deport "bad hombres" rather than "get rid of all the people."[31] Trump's immigration policy addressing the common good of the national public sphere seemed unrelated to the private lives of the Beristains until they were personally affected.

TABLE 1.1 ■ Spheres of Argument		
Sphere	**Mode of Argumentation**	**Scope of Immediate Consequence**
Personal	Informal	The participants in the debate
Technical	Formal & Specialized	The particular knowledge community
Public	Open & Democratic	The "public" community or society at large

The above cases illustrate how debates in one sphere may bleed into or implicate others. The nature of these interactions can tell us a lot about the evolution and, in some cases, the resolution of a controversy because we are able to chart how they develop across time and space. This knowledge underscores the different kinds of evidence and norms that help ideas gain or lose favor with particular audiences.

The interactions can also tell us about the health of the various spheres. When Goodnight outlined the spheres in the 1980s, he expressed concern that "the public sphere is being steadily eroded by the elevation of the personal and technical groundings of argument."[32] Other scholars were less concerned about the rise of technical elites. In response, for instance, Charles Arthur Willard argued that public controversies require expertise from technical spheres while noting that "every expert's span of authority is narrower than most public problems," requiring "an overlap of specialized discourses."[33] Various experts should guide public discussion for Willard because average citizens lack knowledge on most topics. John Dewey and journalist Walter Lippmann also famously debated in the 1920s this conflict between public and technical spheres. Questioning whether or not "the American people" can be trusted to govern, *The Phantom Public* by Lippmann argued that experts should guide society while Dewey's *The Public and its Problems* prioritized education of average citizens to ensure self-rule.[34]

To further explore this interaction between spheres, we'll consider a post from *Scary Mommy* by Maria Guido addressing the vaccine controversy in the United States. This is a useful Everyday Life Example because a parent's choice to vaccinate children relates to all three spheres and because the post represents everyday argumentation through online forums. *Scary Mommy* is a website that provides pregnancy and parenting advice, describing itself as "a massive vibrant community of millions of parents, brought together by a common theme: Parenting doesn't have to be perfect."[35]

FIND YOUR VOICE
PUBLIC VS. TECHNICAL SPHERES

Consider your view on whether the people can and should govern. What role should public opinion play in determining solutions to public problems?

What role should experts play? When the two disagree, how should individuals, organizations, and politicians resolve the conflict?

As you read Guido's post, consider how the personal, technical, and public spheres are each represented: According to Guido, what questions and concerns motivate argumentation in each sphere? Which sphere's argumentation does Guido prioritize as most important to the controversy? Finally, consider which sphere *you* think should take priority and why?

Identifying the arguments from the different spheres helps arguers better recognize the competing concerns that animate any given controversy, especially since we often need to manage considerations from all three spheres. Guido began with the public sphere—bill SB277 in California—but then included the personal, scientific, and public concerns motivating the proposed law. Box 1.1 illustrates this complexity, offering one example of how public controversies often have origins in other spheres.

Everyday Life Example 1.1

Maria Guido, "California Set to Pass One of the Toughest Mandatory Vaccine Laws in US," *Scary Mommy* **(blog), June 25, 2015.**[36]

1 Schoolchildren in California may be required to be vaccinated unless there is a medical reason not to
2 do so, thanks to a law that cleared another hurdle today, as the State Assembly approved it by a vote
3 of 46–30.

4 Bill SB277 would change the law so that only parents of children with medical reasons to refuse
5 vaccinations will be allowed to opt out of vaccines for their kids before they enter daycare or the
6 school system. As it stands now, religious and personal beliefs can exempt students.

7 The bill was crafted in response to a large Measles outbreak that originated at Disneyland in
8 December 2014. There is a disproportionate amount of unvaccinated children in southern California,
9 thanks in part to the "Personal Belief Exemption" that allows parents to opt out of vaccines easily.
10 Hopefully not any more.

11 From *NPR*: "If it passes out of the Legislature, the bill would then move to the desk of Gov. Jerry
12 Brown. The governor hasn't indicated whether he'll sign the bill, but a spokesman said via email that
13 Brown 'believes that vaccinations are profoundly important and a major public health benefit and any
14 bill that reaches his desk will be closely considered.'" In other words: this bill is passing.

15 If signed into law, California will be the biggest state with such a mandate in place. There are only
16 two other states *in the country* that don't allow for philosophical or religious exemptions to vaccines:
17 Mississippi and West Virginia. *Vox* has a comprehensive graphic of school vaccine exemptions by
18 state. 19 states still allow philosophical exemptions. 48 states allow religious exemptions. Well, 47
19 when this law passes.

20 When it comes to personal belief exemptions, there is no medical basis for the vaccine paranoia. The
21 vaccine-autism link has time and time again been proven non-existent. There is no scientific evidence
22 that backs refusing or delaying vaccines.

23 Vaccines are essentially the biggest medical miracle of the 20th century. Measles was considered
24 eliminated in 2000, because the U.S. has a highly effective vaccination program and a strong public
25 health system for detecting and responding to cases and outbreaks. It came back in full force when
26 parents got wrapped up in the hysteria—and started believing celebrities instead of scientists.

27 Choosing whether or not to vaccinate your child is not a personal choice—it's a public health issue.
28 Let's hope California will serve as an example and other states without strict vaccine laws in place
29 will follow suit.

Source: Maria Guido, "California Set to Pass One of the Toughest Mandatory Vaccine Laws in US," Scary Mommy (blog), June 25, 2015, http://www.scarymommy.com/california-set-to-pass-one-of-the-toughest-mandatory-vaccine-laws-in-us.

BOX 1.1: SPHERES AND THE VACCINE CONTROVERSY

The major concerns raised in Guido's post correlated to the spheres:

- *Personal Sphere:* Religious and personal belief exemptions (lines 6, 9-10); anti-vaccine hysteria promoted by celebrities rather than scientists (lines 25-26)

- *Technical Sphere:* Bill SB277 cleared hurdle following California State Assembly vote (lines 2-3); Bill SB277 moves to Governor's desk for signature (lines 11-12); no scientific evidence that vaccines are harmful or linked to autism (lines 20-22); vaccines are "medical miracle" (lines 23-25)

- *Public Sphere:* Law in response to Disneyland measles outbreak (lines 7-8); Governor's belief that vaccinations are "a major public health benefit" (line 13); laws regulating vaccines across the country (lines 15-19); public health responsibility (lines 27-29)

Mapping the spheres also helps arguers better distinguish information from opinion and better weigh conflicting values among the spheres. Acknowledging a wider array of concerns is especially important when public and technical arguments challenge our established personal beliefs. In this case, Guido promoted the arguments from technical spheres (science) and public spheres (responsibility to public health) above personal spheres (hysteria), culminating in the forceful claim that "choosing whether or not to vaccinate your child is not a personal choice—it's a public health issue." Ultimately, being able to recognize and resolve these conflicts is part of effective argumentation.

Summary

This chapter has demonstrated how learning argumentation and debate skills will benefit your personal growth, professional influence, and public engagement insofar as the skills are empowering, productive, and democratic. You should now have a stronger sense of the world of argumentation in two ways: (1) by being able to define key terms such as argument, debate, controversy, presumption, and burden of proof; and (2) by understanding contextual considerations as they relate to co-arguers, audiences, and spheres. The three spheres of argument—personal, technical, and public—are a particularly helpful concept you can use to analyze and engage controversies in everyday life.

Application Exercises

Exploring Technical Spheres in Higher Education: Look at the assignment sheets for major writing assignments in classes you are or have taken. According to those prompts, what counts as "good" argumentation? What norms must you follow to engage that technical sphere? How are the norms for argumentation similar to and different from courses in the same department? How are the norms for argumentation similar to and different from courses in different departments?

Engaging Public Sphere Argumentation: Read articles or posts from two different sources (e.g., Townhall.com and Huffingtonpost.com; *New York Times* and *Chicago Tribune*) discussing the same controversy and answer the following questions:

1. Who is the audience for each article, what presumption are they likely to have, and how does the article attempt to meet its burden of proof in convincing that audience?

2. As examples of public sphere argumentation, do the articles emphasize the common good, equality of access, and freedom of speech? Which qualities do the articles demonstrate in their *enactment* or *performance* of the argumentation?

3. Do the articles summarize arguments from other spheres? If so, what do these arguments tell us about the nature of the controversy and the priorities that audience members should have when attempting to resolve the controversy?

Key Terms

Argumentation 3

Argument 4

Controversy 4

Debate 4

Critical Thinking 8

Audience 10

Co-Arguer 10

Presumption 10

Burden of Proof 11

Argument Spheres 11

Personal Sphere 12

Technical Sphere 12

Public Sphere 13

Endnotes

1. Edward Z. Rowell, "Prolegomena to Argumentation," Part IV, *Quarterly Journal of Speech* 18 (1932): 591.

2. Al Gore, *The Assault on Reason* (New York: The Penguin Press, 2007); Deborah Tannen, *The Argument Culture: Moving From Debate to Dialogue* (New York: Random House, 1998).

3. Jonathan Haidt, *The Righteous Mind: Why Good People Are Divided by Politics and Religion* (New York: Vintage Books, 2013).

4. Kate McKinnon, "Hillary Clinton/Donald Trump Cold Open–SNL," *Saturday Night Live*, YouTube video, 9:23, November 6, 2016, https://youtu .be/hxH6bKNPBIA.

5. Mark Lilla, "The Liberal Crackup," *Wall Street Journal*, August 11, 2017, https://www.wsj .com/articles/the-liberal-crackup-1502456857. See also: George F. Will, "Trump and Academia Actually Have a Lot in Common," *Washington Post*, January 27, 2017, https:// www.washingtonpost.com/opinions/ trump-and-academia-actually-have-a-lot-in-common/2017/01/27/34123034-e3fc-11e6-a453-19ec4b3d09ba_story.html.

6. Michael J. Socolow, "How to Prevent Smart People From Spreading Dumb Ideas," *New York Times*, March 22, 2018, https://www .nytimes.com/2018/03/22/opinion/face-book-spreading-ideas.html.

7. Valerie Strauss, "The Work of 213,284 Kids Was Analyzed. These Are the Writing and Critical-Thinking Skills that Stumped Students," *Washington Post*, October 24, 2017, https://www.washingtonpost.com/news/answer-sheet/wp/2017/10/24/the-work-of-213284-kids-was-analyzed-these-are-the-writing-and-critical-thinking-skills-that-stumped-too-many-students.

8. Jeff Scheur, quoted in Strauss, "The Work of 213,284 Kids Was Analyzed."

9. Sherry Turkle, *Reclaiming Conversation: The Power of Talk in a Digital Age* (New York: Penguin Press, 2015), 34–36.

10. Judith A. Sanders, Richard L. Wiseman, and Robert H. Gass, "Does Teaching Argumentation Facilitate Critical Thinking?" *Communication Reports* 7.1 (1994): 27–35.

11. Erika Anderson, "Passionate Leaders Aren't Loud—They're Deep," *Forbes*, June 11, 2012, https://www.forbes.com/sites/erikaandersen/2012/06/11/passionate-leaders-arent-loud-theyre-deep/.

12. John Dewey, *How We Think* (Boston: D.C. Heath & Co., 1910), 6.

13. Mike Allen, Sandra Berkowitz, Steve Hunt, and Allen Louden, "A Meta-Analysis of the Impact of Forensics and Communication Education on Critical Thinking," *Communication Education* 48 (1999): 18–30.

14. Robert James Branham, "'I Was Gone on Debating': Malcolm X's Prison Debates and Public Confrontations," *Argumentation and Advocacy* 31 (1995): 117–137.

15. Association of American Colleges & Universities, *Step Up and Lead for Equity: What Higher Education Can Do to Reverse Our Deepening Divides*, 2015, p. 11, http://www.aacu.org/sites/default/files/StepUpLeadEquity.pdf.

16. Mara Leighton, "4 Soft Skills LinkedIn Says Are Most Likely to Get You Hired in 2018," *Business Insider*, April 18, 2018, http://www.businessinsider.com/best-resume-soft-skills-employers-look-for-jobs-2018-4.

17. Association of American Colleges & Universities, *Step Up and Lead for Equity*, p. 11.

18. Olivia Beavers, "Conway Links Anderson Cooper's Eye Roll to Sexism," *The Hill*, May 11, 2017, http://thehill.com/homenews/media/332895-conway-links-anderson-coopers-eye-roll-to-sexism.

19. Ron Chernow, *Alexander Hamilton* (New York: Penguin Books, 2004), 250.

20. Chaim Perelman, *The Realm of Rhetoric*, trans. William Kluback (Notre Dame, IN: University of Notre Dame Press, 1982), 25.

21. Richard Whately, *Elements of Rhetoric* (Nashville, TN: Southern Methodist Publishing House, 1861), 110.

22. G. Thomas Goodnight, "The Personal, Technical, and Public Spheres of Argument: A Speculative Inquiry into the Art of Public Deliberation," *Journal of the American Forensic Association* 18 (1982), 216.

23. Kumar S. D. Kothapalli, et al., "Positive Selection a Regulatory Insertion–Deletion Polymorphism in FADS2 Influences Apparent Endogenous Synthesis of Arachidonic Acid," *Molecular Biology and Evolution* 33 (2016): 1726–1739; Yessenia Tantamango-Bartley, et al., "Are Strict Vegetarians Protected Against Prostate Cancer?" *American Journal of Clinical Nutrition* 103 (2016): 153–160; J. Godos, et al., "Vegetarianism and Breast, Colorectal and Prostate Cancer Risk: An Overview and Meta-Analysis of Cohort Studies," *Journal of Human Nutrition and Dietetics* 30 (2017): 349–359; A. M. J. Gilsing, et al., "Vegetarianism, Low Meat Consumption and the Risk of Lung, Postmenopausal Breast and Prostate Cancer in a Population-Based Cohort Study," *European Journal of Clinical Nutrition* 70 (2016): 723–729.

24. Timothy Hsiao, "In Defense of Eating Meat," *Journal of Agricultural and Environmental Ethics* 28 (2015): 277-291; Stijn Bruers, "In Defense of Eating Vegan," *Journal of Agricultural and Environmental Ethics* 28 (2015): 705-717; Bernard E. Rollin, "The Inseparability of Science and Ethics in Animal Welfare," *Journal of Agricultural and Environmental Ethics* 28 (2015): 759-765; László Erdös, "Veganism Versus Meat-Eating, and the Myth of 'Root Capacity': A Response to Hsiao," *Journal of Agricultural and Environmental Ethics* 28 (2015): 1139-1144; Timothy Hsiao, "A Carnivorous Rejoinder to Bruers and Erdös," *Journal of Agricultural and Environmental Ethics* 28 (2015): 1127-1138.

25. Jürgen Habermas, "The Public Sphere: An Encyclopedia Article (1964)," trans. Sara Lennox and Frank Lennox, *New German Critique* 3 (Autumn 1974): 49.

26. Nancy Fraser, "Rethinking the Public Sphere: A Contribution to the Critique of Actually Existing Democracy," *Social Text* 25/26 (1990): 56-80.

27. On this last point, see Matt Frazier, "10 Things I Wish I Knew Before I Went Vegan," *Huffington Post,* September 26, 2013, http://www.huffingtonpost.com/matt-frazier/vegan-diet_b_3996646.html. Although the article focuses on veganism, the discussion of jokes and loneliness easily apply to vegetarianism as well.

28. Goldfinger, "Open Your Eyes," *Goldfinger: Official Band Site,* http://goldfingermusic.com/music/open-your-eyes-goldfinger/track/open-your-eyes.

29. Kyra Gurney, "Last Fall, They Debate Gun Control in Class. Now, They Debate Lawmakers on TV," *Miami Herald*, February 23, 2018, http://www.miamiherald.com/news/local/education/article201678544.html.

30. "A Brief History of Climate Change," *BBC News*, September 20, 2013, http://www.bbc.com/news/science-environment-15874560.

31. Helen Beristain, quoted in Joseph Dits, "Wife of Granger Restaurant Owner Facing Deportations Says She Regrets Voting for Trump," *South Bend Tribune*, March 25, 2017, http://www.southbendtribune.com/news/local/wife-of-granger-restaurant-owner-facing-deportation-says-she-regrets/article_65151376-10b7-11e7-ba7c-6783f924ac92.html.

32. Goodnight, "The Personal, Technical, and Public Spheres of Argument," 205, 206.

33. Charles Arthur Willard, "McWorld and the Tweed Jihad," *Argumentation and Advocacy* 33 (Winter 1997): 131.

34. Walter Lippmann, *The Phantom Public* (New York: Harcourt Brace, 1925); John Dewey, *The Public and its Problems* (Denver: Swallow, 1927).

35. "About Scary Mommy," *Scary Mommy* (blog), http://www.scarymommy.com/about-scary-mommy.

36. This reprint omits hyperlink references. Maria Guido, "California Set to Pass One of the Toughest Mandatory Vaccine Laws in US," *Scary Mommy* (blog), June 25, 2015, http://www.scarymommy.com/california-set-to-pass-one-of-the-toughest-mandatory-vaccine-laws-in-us.

2

THE DEBATE SITUATION

The fast food restaurant Arby's has positioned itself in recent years around the quality and quantity of its meats. When the inventor of Hawaiian pizza, Sam Panopoulos, passed away in 2017, Arby's responded to the reignited controversy about putting pineapple on pizza by releasing a brief video showing a choice between a pineapple and an Arby's slider sandwich. True to the video's title—"It's not a meat. How is this even a debate?"[1]—a hand pushes away the pineapple and grabs onto the slider. This video prompts the question: What does it take for a debate to exist? According to Arby's, a debate requires choosing from two or more viable options. Hence, there was no debate because the choice to go with the meats was obvious.

For our purposes, choice is not enough to make a debate. Think about debates you've had with others. What are common characteristics across them? What, in your mind, indicates something is a debate rather than another communication event such as conversation, discussion, or dialogue? You could probably pinpoint various features that define a debate because you have built expectations over time for what the concept means.

Our definition of debate—"the exchange of arguments on a topic"—indicates two important qualities: (1) that there are arguments exchanged by a person or people and (2) that those arguments serve a central purpose in the debate by addressing a topic. In Chapter 1, we explored how audiences, co-arguers, and spheres offer some guidance concerning the rules of engagement. Here, we will explore structural features common to debates across all spheres, audiences, and co-arguers.

This chapter organizes this information around the **Debate Situation**, or the interaction of arguments and issues on a proposition concerning some controversy.

Whereas debate is a process, a debate situation is an entity that can be observed through the tangible arguments people advance. Like debates, debate situations can occur in speaking or in writing, across time and space, and through a variety of argumentative means. Basically, a debate situation exists any time there are three major components in relation to a controversy:

DEBATE SITUATION: The interaction of arguments addressing issues relevant to a proposition about a controversy

23

- Arguments

- A Proposition

- Issues

We'll look at each element in turn to consider how it provides the groundwork for debate. We will then turn to the logistics of how argumentation occurs in a debate situation and, finally, conclude with two Everyday Life Examples. Learning these concepts will be the foundation for subsequent topics. By the end of this chapter, you should be able to place the everyday arguments you encounter in relation to their debate situations.

ARGUMENTS

Arguments are perhaps the most obvious feature of a debate situation. We tend to communicate this element most explicitly and the presence of arguments often signals that we are in a debate. In Chapter 1, we defined the minimum requirement for an **argument**: a claim advanced by support. So what do we mean by claims and support?

Claims

CLAIM: A statement that you want your audience to accept

Claims, sometimes called "conclusions," are the assertions that you want others to accept. They often serve as the endpoint of a (sub-)argument and may be signaled by the use of the word "therefore." By their nature, claims are controversial and open to dispute; otherwise the claim would be support or not part of an argument at all.

Although claims can always be phrased as statements, arguers don't always state them in this format. Sometimes a claim might be implied in a question (e.g., "do you really want to eat that donut?") or stated indirectly (e.g., "I wish I had a tasty donut like that"), requiring inference and interpretation to suggest a claim (e.g., "you should give me your donut").

Any given claim can be classified as a fact, value, or policy claim:

FACT CLAIM: A descriptive claim characterizing truth or falsity

1. **Fact Claim:** Fact claims are descriptive claims about truth or falsity, but they are not necessarily true or false in a verifiable sense. Fact claims assert how something *is* in the world even if the claim is not "proven." Scientific discoveries are fact claims because they *argue* for a new way of understanding something. Here are some examples of fact claims: "Life begins at conception"; "There is no connection between vaccines and autism"; "Our company's poor marketing is costing us profits." Each of these describes the world even though the statement is debatable for some audiences.

VALUE CLAIM: An evaluative claim asserting a judgment about something

2. **Value Claim:** Value claims are evaluative claims that assert a judgment about something, often in relation to the moral or aesthetic qualities of an object. Some examples of value claims: "Abortion is immoral"; "Parents who don't

vaccinate their children are negligent"; "Marketing is crucial to our business profile." We know that each example is a value claim because it evaluates rather than describes the world and understanding each claim requires some sort of criterion or benchmark for determining the value: What does it mean to be immoral, negligent, or crucial?

3. **Policy Claim:** Policy claims are deliberative claims that propose some agent take some action. Because policy claims are argumentative, they often consider a hypothetical world by imagining an action that hasn't yet taken place. Here are some policy claims: "You should not get an abortion if you get pregnant"; "Parents should vaccinate their children"; "Our company should hire a marketing firm." Each of these indicate an action and an agent who should implement that action.

POLICY CLAIM: A deliberative claim proposing some agent take some action

Distinguishing the kind of claims is important because it often indicates the appropriate support and responses that one might choose.[2] For instance, debate about a value claim will likely center on the criteria (e.g., what constitutes "negligent" parenting?) whereas debate about a policy claim will likely center on the consequences of action (e.g., are there more pros than cons to vaccinating children?).

As we explore the nature of the debate situation, we'll use a running example around the claim "I should attend college," a claim you may have considered explicitly at some point in your life. This claim is controversial because there are numerous reasons against pursuing this action and numerous alternative actions you might pursue instead. Thus, we have the seeds of a debate but need support as the second required element of an argument.

Support

Support for an argument comprises the reason or reasons for the claim; it is the starting point or foundation for an argument. Support explains *why* the audience should accept the claim, often signaled by the word "because."

SUPPORT: The reason(s) for a claim

Support might sometimes be called "evidence," "data," or "premises"—these are generally synonymous—but "support" is preferable because it is a broader term that better captures how an arguer can reach a claim through a variety of supporting means. We'll discuss this more in Chapter 5.

A simple argument form, then, looks like the representation in Figure 2.1. We diagram the claim at the far right because it is the end-point of this argument.

Arguments may also contain numerous pieces of support. A more complex but still basic argument might look like Figure 2.2, with the arrows indicating how supporting statements advance, or lead to, claims.

Your claim tends to become more agreeable for members of your audience as you increase the quantity and quality of (relevant) support for it. In addition, support that is agreeable to members of the audience enhances their likelihood of adhering to your claim. Consider the

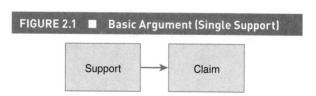

FIGURE 2.1 ■ Basic Argument (Single Support)

Support → Claim

FIND YOUR VOICE
IDENTIFYING EFFECTIVE SUPPORT

What are good reasons that justify attending college? What are poor reasons that you or others have advanced? As you answer these questions, you may discover that it depends on the sphere, audience(s), and co-arguer(s). Your family members likely have different concerns than your friends, which may differ from your own priorities. Financial considerations may drive some people's decision whereas others are more concerned with educational outcomes. There are literally dozens of factors you could (and perhaps did) consider.

FIGURE 2.2   ■   Basic Argument (Multiple Support)

FIGURE 2.3   ■   Basic Argument for Attending College

questions posed in the Find Your Voice as they relate to our example claim.

To convince yourself and others that you should attend college, you might note that college offers long-term job security. This statement on its own doesn't seem very disagreeable and, despite knowing there are many educational and social reasons to attend college, you decide a vocational reason is most persuasive for your family and friends. So, it serves as reasonable support for the more controversial claim that you should attend college. We now have an argument, depicted in Figure 2.3.

These two pieces—a claim and support—are the minimum requirements for an argument to exist and often the only parts that are spoken or written. However, fully understanding an argument requires adding some elements to our basic model.

The Toulmin Model of an Argument

This section outlines an argument model named after its creator, logician Stephen Toulmin. The Toulmin model, depicted in Figure 2.4, offers an abstract rendering of how arguments move from support to claim that is adaptable to the arguments we generate and evaluate in everyday life.

WARRANT:
The inferential statement that justifies the claim on the basis on the support

The Toulmin model adds a number of significant features that we'll briefly explore here and return to in later chapters. First, the warrant visually connects the support to the claim. To warrant means to justify. So, the warrant states how the support justifies or authorizes the claim.

Indicated by the word "since," you can think of a warrant as an inferential leap that, once supplied, should explain how the support is relevant to the claim.

The argument about attending college has an inferential leap at play, an implied statement that explains how we move from "a college degree offers long-term job security" to "I should attend college." What statement might justify this movement? The warrant is something approximating, "people should do things that protect their future." When we add the warrant, the argument becomes: "A college degree offers long-term job security. *Since people should do things that protect their future*, therefore I should attend college." The reasoning now makes more sense, but it requires some critical thinking and interpretation to get here.

Sometimes the warrant may not be readily agreeable to co-arguers or members of the audience. In these cases, you may need to offer **backing**, which serves as support for the warrant. Rather than considering a specific application, backing explains why the warrant is *generally* acceptable.

BACKING: Support for the warrant of an argument

You can think of backing as a second level of "why:" "Why is the support justified for this claim" is one level that gets at the warrant, and "why is this a good warrant" is the second level that gets at the backing.

Returning to our example, do you agree with the warrant that you should do things that protect your future? If so, what backing might you provide? One option might be to explain that people will spend more years as an adult post-college than they will in college. Adding the backing would produce this argument: "A college degree offers long-term job security. Since people should do things that protect their future *on account of them spending more years as an adult post-college than they will in college*, therefore I should attend college." As you can see, this is the same argument with which we began but it better captures how the support leads to the claim.

Of course, there are often conditions when the general warrant does not apply. Most arguments have exceptions for which the arguer must account. Toulmin used the word **rebuttal** for these conditions of exception,[3] but other scholars sometimes call them a reservation.

REBUTTAL: Conditions in which the warrant does not apply

FIGURE 2.4 ■ The Toulmin Model of an Argument

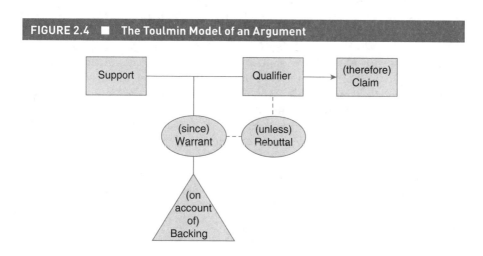

Rebuttals, indicated by the term "unless," rarely undermine the claim entirely but rather limit the scope of the claim so that it doesn't apply to all cases. It's important to note that rebuttals focus on the *warrant*, not the *claim* of the argument. There may be many reasons you should reject a claim but that's more a matter of refutation (see Chapters 8-10) than rebuttal.

So, when might the warrant that you should do things to protect your future not apply? It makes sense if you're young and healthy, but it is less applicable if you're suffering from a terminal illness. It turns out, then, that there is at least one condition in which you should not do things to protect your future. You could likely generate others. Here's our revised argument: "A college degree offers long-term job security. Since people should do things that protect their future on account of them spending more years as an adult post-college than they will in college, *unless I have a terminal illness*, therefore I should attend college."

The more rebuttals to an argument, the weaker the claim becomes. This doesn't mean you should refrain from arguing the claim entirely. Rather, you might add a **qualifier,** our final element of the model. A qualifier is a word or phrase that indicates the scope and force of a claim.

Terms such as "definitely," "probably," "likely," or "possibly" are all qualifiers because they tell us how certain we are of the claim. Understanding arguments also requires understanding how aggressively the arguer advances the claim; we demand a lower burden of proof for "probable" claims than for "certain" claims.

Given the exception of terminal illness that we identified, and given that I don't want to assume whether you have a terminal illness, we should limit the scope of our claim. In the final analysis, then, our argument is as follows: "A college degree offers long-term job security. Since people should do things that protect their future on account of them spending more years as an adult post-college than they will in college, unless I am suffering from a terminal illness, *probably* therefore I should attend college." Mapped onto our Toulmin model, it would look like Figure 2.5.

This model can be especially helpful when you are faced with more complex arguments than a single support-claim structure. Your rationale for attending college might involve multiple supporting statements or reasons. For instance, you might develop the statement that a college degree offers long-term job security by using a statistic from a 2014 study by the New York Federal Reserve stating that college graduates will earn $1 million more than high school graduates in their lifetime.[4] You might also cite the Pew Research Center report that those with a college degree are three times less likely than high school graduates to be unemployed (12.2 percent compared to 3.8 percent).[5] Beyond job security, you should probably note that college offers valuable and diverse education. All of these additional statements, as diagrammed in Figure 2.6, have made a single argument a bit more formidable to dissect.

Notice that the point about long-term job security is actually a sub-argument that includes a claim and support. And, both support statements there have a further piece of support. We know this because each arrow in the diagram represents a different sub-argument (comprising a claim and support). We call it an **argument chain** when a statement serves as a claim in one sub-argument and support for a subsequent one

QUALIFIER: A word of phrase indicating the force of the claim

ARGUMENT CHAIN: The claim of one argument supports a subsequent claim

FIGURE 2.5 ■ Toulmin Model Example

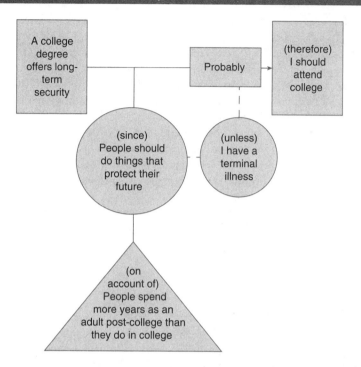

FIGURE 2.6 ■ The Case for Attending College

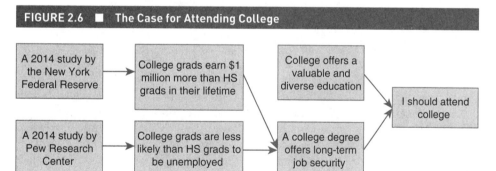

And when multiple argument chains converge to support a single, overarching claim, we call this a **case**. Put another way, a case represents all the substantive arguments an advocate establishes to support his or her stance and serves as an advocate's *offense* in a debate (see Chapters 5-7 for more about case-building). You cannot persuade an audience in a debate without a case, just as you cannot claim victory in a sporting match without offense.

CASE: A strategic and comprehensive series of argument chains that an arguer communicates on a proposition

We see this term used in everyday argumentation when people say things like "Trump's case for [China tariffs] is stronger than the one he made for his steel and aluminum ones" or published articles titled things like "The Case for Reparations."[6]

Understanding a full case would require you to determine the warrants, backing, rebuttals, and qualifiers for each of the arguments represented in the diagram. So, for instance, you'd need to identify why college graduates earning $1 million more than high school graduates in their lifetime authorizes the sub-claim that a college degree provides long-term job security. This warrant would likely be something like "earning potential is an indicator of job security." You'd also need to consider why the 2014 New York Federal Reserve study warrants the sub-claim that college graduates earn $1 million more in their lifetime (namely, because the New York Federal Reserve is a trustworthy source). Anytime you see an arrow in the diagram, there's an implied warrant and backing that moves the argument from support to claim, inviting the audience to accept the final claim that you should attend college. This final claim—the proposition—is the second constituent of a debate situation.

A PROPOSITION

PROPOSITION:
The main claim over which an entire debate occurs

Figure 2.6 indicates that some claims are more important to the overall debate situation than others. In this case, the claim "I should attend college" is of primary importance while two other claims—"a college degree offers long-term job security" and "college provides a valuable and diverse education"—are in subordinate positions. The diagram reveals how the entire structure builds up to the claim that "I should attend college." This ultimate claim is called the **proposition**, or sometimes the "resolution," and it serves as the focal point of a debate.

Because a proposition is a claim, the reasons for it are not part of the proposition itself. In written argumentation such as newspaper editorials or scholarly essays, the thesis statement is often equivalent or related to the proposition.

Typically when two people enter into a debate situation, one person argues in favor of the proposition while the other person argues in opposition to it. The person in opposition determines his or her advocacy by adding the word "not" to the proposition. For instance, if you and you friend were debating whether you should attend college, your proposition would be "I should attend college" and your friend's oppositional stance would be "you should *not* attend college." This also applies to fact (e.g., "our company's poor marketing is *not* costing us profits") and value (e.g., "marketing is *not* crucial to our business profile") claims.

You should note three important qualities of debate propositions:

1. **A proposition focuses the debate**, even if the proposition is not stated explicitly. Consider televised presidential debates. Although they cover a range of domestic and foreign policy topics, each candidate's arguments build to a single proposition: You should vote for me. This statement guides the debate and every argument implicitly or explicitly demonstrates that your

vote would pay dividends. Hence, while arguments in a debate situation may cover numerous topics, or what we will call "issues," a single proposition likely guides them.

2. **A proposition could be a fact, value, or policy claim**. You could imagine having an entire debate over a fact proposition, such as "fraternity and sorority hazing reduces student retention." At other times, our motivation for debate might center on propositions of value, for example that "the hazing process is harmful to students." Or even about policy: "Our college should crack down on hazing of students during pledgeship." None of these would produce a better or more advanced debate. Rather, as noted earlier, the kind of proposition will influence the nature of the debater's arguments and how the debate evolves.

3. **You should think of a proposition as an invitation**. When you assert a proposition, you are inviting others to join your debate situation. Just like party invitations, if you state your proposition incorrectly or too open-ended, the wrong crowd might show up to the debate. Additionally, if you leave out important information, it's possible no one accepts your invitation at all. A proposition, then, should be tailored to one's specific purpose in having a debate and advocates should carefully word the propositions they advance.

The metaphor of invitation is important because it means that identifying a proposition often depends on the negotiation between the intent of the arguer and the perception of the audience. Take a moment to consider the three scenarios in the Build Your Skill feature. Each scenario lends itself to one dominant proposition, but it is possible to generate at least two for each.

The ambiguity of propositions isn't a bad thing in itself, but it does mean that you may need to first figure out the primary proposition—what content the debate can reasonably address—before turning to the arguments. I'm sure you have been in debates when you don't even remember what you're arguing about. Essentially, you and your co-arguer(s) have lost or forgotten the proposition. Ultimately, then, propositions are crucial to focus and organize the arguments within the debate. We'll spend a little more time with policy propositions because they are the most common type you will encounter in your personal, professional, and public life.

Policy Propositions

Dedicated to the best course of action, policy propositions are best worded using the following format: *[agent] should [action]*. The word "should" implies a future action and focuses the debate on whether it would be beneficial for the agent to perform the action. Alternative words than "should" imply a very different kind of debate; for example, the statements "we could go to the local Mexican restaurant for dinner" or "we can go to the local Mexican restaurant for dinner" invite debate about whether you have the ability to go there, not whether it's worthwhile to do so.

BUILD YOUR SKILL
IDENTIFYING PROPOSITIONS

Identify at least two propositions that could organize your participation in the debate for each of the following argument scenarios:

A. Your significant other remarks, "I hate that we always just hang out. We haven't been on a date in at least a month."

B. Your mom asks you, "What exactly are you planning to do with a degree in communication?"

C. When you approach a garbage can, it is marked in big letters that read "LANDFILL."

Photo by Jeffrey P. Mehltretter Drury, from San Diego Zoo Safari Park, 2014

To invite productive and meaningful debate, you should craft your policy propositions with wording that is:

1. **Active.** Policy propositions should use active phrasing to specify *who* will enact the proposed policy. The agent could be a person, organization, or institution but it is a necessary component. The proposition that "NCAA Division I college athletes should be paid" may sound good in theory but it's in passive voice and, as a result, it gets more complicated. Who should pay the athletes—the colleges, the NCAA, the government? As you can imagine, a debate that "the NCAA should pay Division I athletes" would entail different arguments than a debate that "U.S. colleges and universities should pay their Division I athletes." An active voice makes for a stronger invitation.

2. **Affirmative.** Policy propositions should avoid the word "not" because this creates confusion for the other side. Recall that opposition in a debate is determined by inserting the word "not." If you propose something like, "the U.S. Federal Government should not allow the sale of assault rifles," the opposition to this proposition would produce a double negative statement ("the U.S. Federal Government should not not allow the sale of assault rifles"). For clarity's sake, you should phrase the proposition as "the U.S. Federal Government should ban the sale of assault rifles."

3. **Controversial**. Policy propositions should represent a call for change and be open to debate. Consider something like, "the U.S. Federal Government should continue funding the military." This proposition supports the *status quo* rather than advocating change. Moreover, would you be willing to debate the other side—to advocate that "the U.S. Federal Government should not continue funding the military"? There won't be many takers. This is just one (perhaps extreme) instance of policy propositions that aren't controversial or have been resolved.

4. **Precise**. Policy propositions should concretely identify both the agent and action. See if you can spot why this imprecise proposition is a bad invitation: "Our company should change its parental leave policy." The word "change" says nothing about the actual proposal. In fact, this proposition to change the policy would be agreeable to both those who believe that the parental leave policy should be *more* flexible and those who believe it should be *less* flexible; the imprecise wording would yield false agreement from those holding diametrically opposed positions. A more precise proposition—for example, "our company should increase the length of our parental leave policy"—makes a stronger and more focused invitation to debate.

5. **Singular**. Policy propositions should advocate a single action, albeit this action might be comprehensive or multi-faceted. Bad policy propositions take on too much by offering multiple, unrelated actions or agents. A proposition such as "our company should extend the length of parental leave and apply it equally to domestic partners" really demands two debates, one about the length and one about the scope of the current policy. It's possible that an audience member might agree with one part but not both and so advancing them simultaneously could create confusion or could even lose supporters who would otherwise agree with part of the proposition.

6. **Objective**. Finally, policy propositions should avoid inflammatory or loaded phrasing that implies a correct, moral answer. Recall that propositions are a kind of claim; they should never offer reasons for the claim. Beyond that, objectivity requires you to eliminate any adjectives that aren't part of a proper noun. For instance, it's sufficient to say "our company should extend parental leave to domestic partners" rather than "our *benevolent* company should *equitably* extend parental leave to domestic partners." The latter phrasing has already charged the debate in favor of the proposition and, as a result, is likely to get less participation by those who disagree. The more objective phrasing is a better invitation to debate.

These six guidelines enable advocates to advance understandable policy propositions. Returning to the proposition "I should attend college," is it worded effectively to organize a policy debate? It would meet most of the criteria but could be more precise: "I should attend college x," "I should attend a residential liberal arts college," "I should take classes at a local community college," "I should attend a state university far away from home." You can practice identifying flaws in the wording of policy propositions with the Build Your Skill prompt.

BUILD YOUR SKILL
TESTING POLICY PROPOSITIONS

For each proposition below, identify which of the six guidelines for wording policy propositions that it violates:

A. Cigarette companies should not advertise on TV.

B. The United States should change its destructive healthcare policy.

C. The Internet should be regulated.

D. We should order pizza or burgers for dinner tonight.

E. Our organization should become more diverse.

F. If you like it, then you should have put a ring on it.

Once arguers have determined a proposition and (some of) the arguments about it, they can use issues to structure the debate content.

ISSUES

ISSUE: A neutral, yes/no question representing a point of disagreement on a proposition

An **issue** is a neutral, yes/no question that represents a point of clash, or disagreement, in a debate. Issues serve as organizing elements that help arguers understand how the arguments relate to one another and to the proposition.

You might also think of issues as representing the sub-topics you would want addressed or questions you would want answered before you're willing to decide for or against a proposition.

We can clarify the concept of issues by returning to our example proposition. When you considered attending college, there were likely dozens of questions you needed to answer before deciding. Some might be: Can I afford it? Is college the right learning environment for me? Will a college degree help me attain my ideal career? Is there an alternative I should seriously consider? The list could go on and on and it would be tailored to your particular needs and interests. Each of these questions theoretically has both a "yes" and a "no" answer that you need to consider and weigh (keep in mind, issues are yes/no *questions* but the *answer* to the question might be "yes," "no," "maybe," or "I don't know"). This means that each of these could become an issue, or point of disagreement, that guides a debate about whether you should attend college.

But, you can't consider all of the issues and eventually need to move forward. So, suppose your friend participates in your process by offering two reasons you should not attend college. First, college is cost prohibitive, at more than $50,000 across four years and, second, college prevents you from getting a hands-on education that you can get by joining the workforce right away. We now have four argumentative claims, two for and two against the proposition, as outlined in Table 2.1.

TABLE 2.1 ■ The Arguments about Attending College	
Pros	**Cons**
1. A college degree offers long-term job security	1. College is cost prohibitive
2. College offers a valuable and diverse education	2. College prevents a hands-on education

After listing the claims in Table 2.1, we should consider if any claims for attending college address the same issue as the claims against it. You mention job security but your friend doesn't. Your friend addresses the cost of college but you don't. These issues are part of the debate situation, but you and your friend have not, at this point, debated them. It appears that the only issue that you both debated is related to the second claim in each column: Will I gain a valuable education in college? You claim "yes" while your friend claims "no." Put another way, we have competing claims in response to the same issue.

It means that there are three main issues in this debate situation:

1. Does a college degree offer long-term job security?

2. Does college offer a valuable education?

3. Is college cost prohibitive?

Each of the above questions corresponds to a "yes" and a "no" argument and, hence, the issues capture the major points of disagreement. As noted earlier, these are just some of the issues you might consider when debating whether to attend college.

Arguments serve as the answers to the issues but you still need to weigh the issues against one another to determine their relative worth. For example, regardless of the answers, is it more important to consider long-term earning potential or short-term costs in deciding whether to attend college? Is cost more or less important than educational experience? A debate gets resolved by weighing both the arguments and the issues that are part of it.

To further clarify the meaning and value of issues, keep in mind the following qualities:

1. **Most debates will involve numerous issues, each connected to the major sub-claims in the debate situation**. Returning to the example of presidential debates, candidates demonstrate the proposition that "you should vote for me" by answering questions addressing numerous issues. For example, one issue in the 2016 campaign was "should the United States build a wall between the U.S. border and Mexico's?" Trump argued "yes" while Clinton argued "no."

2. **Issues are rarely stated verbatim**. Neither Trump nor Clinton stated the issue directly in question format but, based on their argumentative claims, we could infer the issue being debated. Indeed, most of the time, the best way to determine the issues is to list the major claims for and against a proposition

and convert them to yes/no questions, as we did earlier. The more you practice identifying the issues in a debate, the easier the process becomes.

3. **Productive debates occur when debaters address common issues**. Going back to Table 2.1, recall how some arguments didn't have responses. It would be difficult to resolve the debate if it stopped there because the first claims for the two sides each addressed a different issue. For a productive debate, your friend would need to address job security, and you would need to tackle the cost. If you and your friend only argue the issues you respectively raised, then your arguments are like two ships passing in the night; there's no clash and little gets accomplished. We'll discuss clash in more detail in later chapters.

4. **Some issues are more important to the proposition than others**. When we vote for a president, some of the questions they answer in the debate are more important than others to our choice. Similarly, some things matter more to deciding whether to attend college than others. The audience also plays a role here. Understanding the relative importance of issues helps you better tailor your arguments by guiding the sub-topics you should address. Since the importance of issues is arguable, debate will take place not just at the level of content (what the audience should think) but also at the level of issues (what the audience should think *about*).

In sum, issues are implied questions that parallel competing claims to provide structure and focus in a debate. They represent the sub-topics related to the overall proposition that advocates address in attempting to resolve the debate.

THE DEBATE SITUATION

Figure 2.7 illustrates the complete debate situation. The arguments work through the issues to affirm or oppose the proposition. This model features three issues but there is no limit to the number of issues a debate situation should involve and each debate situation will have as many issues as the participants choose to raise. This diagram also shows that each issue has a "yes" and a "no" argument whether or not the arguers raise them.

So, let's return to the debate concerning the proposition "I should attend college." Each side in the debate had two major claims and a few pieces of support and those arguments, as we noted earlier, addressed three different issues. It's possible, then, to map this content onto the debate situation, as depicted in Figure 2.8. The elements in parentheses represent arguments in the debate situation that theoretically exist even though you and your friend did not explicitly argue them.

Seeing this structure should reveal that the existing debate on the proposition is underdeveloped and would need to involve more issues and arguments than represented there. The areas in parentheses are the first place to start by considering how you might establish them through research and analysis. Beyond those, you would also likely raise other issues and generate attendant arguments. Seeing the structure here reveals both strengths to the existing debate situation as well as the gaps that exist.

To assist your skill in detecting the debate situation in everyday life, this chapter concludes with two examples. The first example is from the movie *Monty Python and*

FIGURE 2.7 ■ The Debate Situation

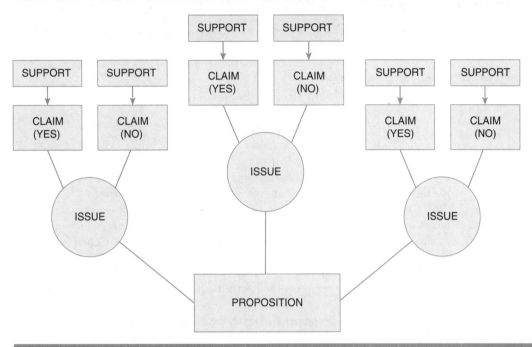

FIGURE 2.8 ■ The Debate about Attending College

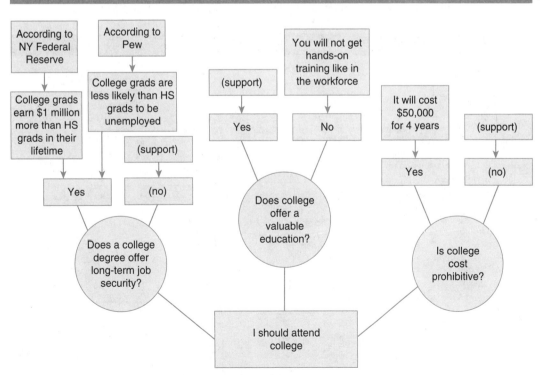

the Holy Grail.[7] Peasants have accused a fellow villager of being a witch, and they present an argumentative case demonstrating this proposition. This is a useful example for beginning advocates because it includes the complete debate situation, explicitly revealing through Sir Bedevere's questions the issues guiding the arguments. As you read the debate, identify the proposition, its type (fact, value, or policy), the issues, and the arguments. Then, refer to Figure 2.9 for a diagram of the debate situation.

Figure 2.9 captures the major issues and arguments addressing the proposition that the woman is a witch. This proposition is a fact proposition because it makes a descriptive claim that is either true or false. The diagram shows how the advocates used argument chains to support their stances (although the figure truncates the sub-arguments about wood being something you burn and about ducks floating in water like wood). Because argumentation often relies on perception, Figure 2.9 is just one possible interpretation or organization of the content; the process relies on judgment rather than finding a "right" answer even though some interpretations are more on target than others. We'll spend more time with interpreting arguments in Chapter 4.

FIGURE 2.9 ■ The Debate about the Witch

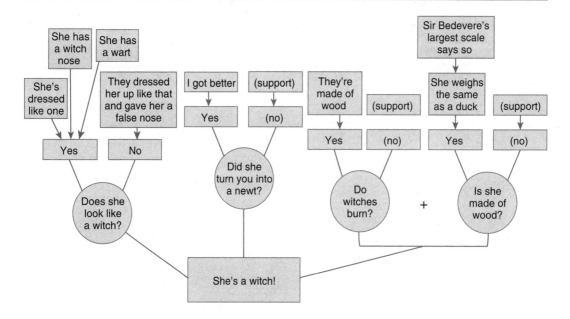

Everyday Life Example 2.1

Monty Python and the Holy Grail, 1975[8]

Peasant1: We have found a witch, may we burn her?

Sir Bedevere: How do you *know* she is a witch?

Peasant2: She looks like one.

Sir Bedevere: Bring her forward.

Woman: I'm not a witch! I'm not a witch!

Sir Bedevere: Er, but you are dressed like one.

Woman: They dressed me up like this.

All: No, we didn't, no.

Woman: And this isn't my nose, it's a false one.

Sir Bedevere: Well?

Peasant1: Well we did do the nose.

Sir Bedevere: The nose?

Peasant1: And the hat, but she is a witch!

Sir Bedevere: Did you dress her up like this?

Peasant1: No! Yes. A bit. But she has got a wart!

Sir Bedevere: What makes you think she is a witch?

Peasant2: Well, she turned me into a newt!

Sir Bedevere: A newt?

Peasant2: I got better.

Peasant3: Burn her anyway!

Sir Bedevere: Quiet. There are ways of telling whether she is a witch.

Peasant1: Are there? Well then tell us!

Sir Bedevere: Tell me, what do you do with witches?

Peasant3: Burn'em!

Sir Bedevere: What do you burn apart from witches?

Peasant1: More witches!

Peasant3: Wood!

Sir Bedevere: So, why do witches burn?

Peasant2: Cuz they're made of . . . wood?

Sir Bedevere: Good. So, how do we tell whether she is made of wood?

Peasant1: Build a bridge out of her!

Sir Bedevere: Ahh, but can you not also make bridges out of stone?

Peasant1: Oh yeah.

Sir Bedevere: Does wood sink in water?

Peasant3: No. It floats!

Peasant1: Let's throw her into the bog!

Sir Bedevere: What also floats in water?

Peasants: Bread! Apples! Very small rocks! Cider! Grape gravy! Cherries! Mud! Churches! Lead!

King Arthur: A Duck.

Sir Bedevere: Exactly. So, logically. . .

Peasant1: If she weighs the same as a duck . . . she's made of wood!

Sir Bedevere: And therefore. . .

Peasant3: A witch!

Sir Bedevere: Very good. We shall use my largest scales.

Source: Monty Python and the Holy Grail, directed by Terry Gilliam and Terry Jones (1975; Culver City, CA: Columbia TriStar Home Entertainment, 2001), DVD.

You perhaps noticed a plus sign on the diagram. This indicates that two supporting ideas—witches burn because they are made of wood and she is made of wood because she weighs the same as a duck according to Sir Bedevere's largest scale—are both necessary to reach the claim. Put another way, you cannot demonstrate she is a witch by *only* demonstrating that witches burn because they are made of wood or by *only* demonstrating that she is made of wood. In this kind of scenario, we say that the argument has **linked support** because both statements are required and connected to justify the claim. Contrast this with the argument about her appearance. There, three supporting

LINKED SUPPORT: Two or more support statements that are both required to warrant the claim statements independently demonstrate she is a witch; you could conclude she was a witch based on the clothing or based on the nose or based on the wart but all three together make the argument stronger. These are called **convergent support** because they function separately but converge to bolster the claim.

Beyond identifying the claims and support, the diagram also identifies the issues that guide the determination of whether she is a witch. Recall that not all issues are of equal importance in a debate. The first two issues—"does she look like a witch?" and "did she turn you into a newt?"—were, for Sir Bedevere, insufficient to demonstrate the proposition and thus the debate hinged on whether the woman was made of wood. Curiously, however, the woman only disputes the claim that she has the physical characteristics of a witch, leaving the other issues unaddressed. As indicated in the diagram, it would have been wise of her to refute the arguments that suggested she was made of wood. There might also be additional ways of determining whether she's a witch that were omitted from the debate entirely. This example illustrates how the debate situation provides a birds-eye view of what happens in a debate.

In addition to revealing how *both sides* of the debate are structured in relation to the major issues and arguments, the debate situation is also useful for constructing or interpreting a single argumentative case. Our second Everyday Life Example will demonstrate this value by examining Franklin Delano Roosevelt's famous speech requesting a Congressional declaration of war on December 8, 1941, in response to the bombing of Pearl Harbor. Although Roosevelt's audience was members of the Congress, the speech clearly resonated with the national public and has stood the test of time, evident when communication scholars rated it the fourth best speech of the twentieth century and the highest rated policy speech by a president.[9] As you read Roosevelt's speech, identify the proposition, its type (fact, value, or policy), the issues, and the arguments. Then, refer to Table 2.2 for a chart outlining the case.

Roosevelt's speech is more complex than the *Monty Python* example because he provides only one side of the debate situation, he doesn't identify the issues explicitly, and he uses a stylistically rich prose format. Because Roosevelt's style is more common in everyday argumentation than Sir Bedevere's, being able to provide structure to a complex case of this nature is a useful skill. To assist your interpretation, Table 2.2 catalogues the proposition and the major issues and arguments that supported it. The table format is an alternative to the diagrams earlier in the chapter.

Roosevelt concluded his speech with a clear policy proposition that followed most of the guidelines discussed earlier in the chapter. He identified the agent and he offered a precise, singular, affirmative, and controversial action. The one flaw is Roosevelt's use of the adjectives "unprovoked and dastardly," which violate the objectivity criterion by stacking the debate in his favor. Roosevelt's placement of his proposition is typical insofar as most propositions are located at the beginning or end of an argumentative case. While he ended the speech with his proposition, he began it with some factual information to set the stage for his request. These lines don't seem argumentative *per se* and, thus, are omitted from Table 2.2. However, the rest of Roosevelt's content is included.

Beyond the arguments, Table 2.2 indicates that Roosevelt raised six issues to help members of the Congress determine whether to declare a state of war with the Empire of Japan. As with the witch example, not all issues in Roosevelt's speech were of equal importance. Even just a casual glance at Table 2.2 shows that Roosevelt dedicated most argumentative effort to supporting the claim that the United States can prevail in the

Everyday Life Example 2.2

Franklin D. Roosevelt, "War Message," December 8, 1941[10]

1   Mr. Vice President, and Mr. Speaker, and Members of the Senate and House of Representatives:

2   Yesterday, December 7th, 1941—a date which will live in infamy—the United States of America was
3   suddenly and deliberately attacked by naval and air forces of the Empire of Japan.

4   The United States was at peace with that nation and, at the solicitation of Japan, was still in
5   conversation with its government and its emperor looking toward the maintenance of peace in the
6   Pacific. Indeed, one hour after Japanese air squadrons had commenced bombing in the American
7   Island of Oahu, the Japanese Ambassador to the United States and his colleague delivered to our
8   Secretary of State a formal reply to a recent American message. And while this reply stated that it
9   seemed useless to continue the existing diplomatic negotiations, it contained no threat or hint of war
10   or of armed attack.

11   It will be recorded that the distance of Hawaii from Japan makes it obvious that the attack was
12   deliberately planned many days or even weeks ago. During the intervening time, the Japanese
13   government has deliberately sought to deceive the United States by false statements and expressions
14   of hope for continued peace.

15   The attack yesterday on the Hawaiian Islands has caused severe damage to American naval and
16   military forces. I regret to tell you that very many American lives have been lost. In addition,
17   American ships have been reported torpedoed on the high seas between San Francisco and Honolulu.

18   Yesterday the Japanese government also launched an attack against Malaya.

19   Last night Japanese forces attacked Hong Kong.

20   Last night Japanese forces attacked Guam.

21   Last night Japanese forces attacked the Philippine Islands.

22   Last night the Japanese attacked Wake Island.

23   And this morning the Japanese attacked Midway Island.

24   Japan has, therefore, undertaken a surprise offensive extending throughout the Pacific area. The
25   facts of yesterday and today speak for themselves. The people of the United States have already
26   formed their opinions and well understand the implications to the very life and safety of our nation.

27   As Commander in Chief of the Army and Navy I have directed that all measures be taken for our
28   defense.

29   But always will our whole Nation remember the character of the onslaught against us.

30   No matter how long it may take us to overcome this premeditated invasion, the American people in
31   their righteous might will win through to absolute victory.

32   I believe that I interpret the will of the Congress and of the people when I assert that we will not only
33   defend ourselves to the uttermost but will make it very certain that this form of treachery shall never
34   again endanger us.

35   Hostilities exist. There is no blinking at the fact that our people, our territory, and our interests are in
36   grave danger.

37   With confidence in our armed forces—with the unbounding determination of our people—we will gain
38   the inevitable triumph—so help us God.

39   I ask that the Congress declare that since the unprovoked and dastardly attack by Japan on Sunday,
40   December 7th, 1941, a state of war has existed between the United States and the Japanese Empire.

Source: Franklin D. Roosevelt, "138 - Address to Congress Requesting a Declaration of War with Japan," December 8, 1941, *The American Presidency Project*. ed. John T. Woolley and Gerhard Peters, 1999-2017, http://www.presidency.ucsb.edu/ws/index.php?pid=16053.

TABLE 2.2 ■ The Debate Situation in FDR's "War Message"

Proposition: The U.S. Congress should "declare that since the unprovoked and dastardly attack by Japan on Sunday, December 7th, 1941, a state of war has existed between the United States and the Japanese Empire" (lines 39-40)

Issue	Claim	Support
Was the attack on Pearl Harbor a surprise?	Yes, the attack was a surprise	United States was at peace with the Empire of Japan (line 4) The United States was in diplomatic negotiations with Japan (lines 4-6) The United States received a reply from the Japanese Ambassador that had no hint of attack (lines 7-10)
Was the attack on Pearl Harbor deliberate?	Yes, the attack was deliberate	The distance between Hawaii to Japan required preparation (lines 11-12) The Japanese government sent false statements and expressions of hope for peace (lines 12-14)
Was the attack on the United States?	Yes, the United States was at risk	The attack caused severe damage to U.S. naval and military forces (lines 15-16) The attack caused the loss of many American lives (line 16) U.S. ships have been torpedoed on the high seas (lines 16-17)
Did the attack expand beyond the United States?	Yes, the attack was throughout the entire Pacific area	The Japanese government attacked Malaya, Hong Kong, Guam, the Philippine Islands, Wake Island, and Midway Island (lines 18-23)
Will the United States prevail in the war?	Yes, the United States will prevail	FDR, as Commander in Chief, has taken measures to defend the nation (lines 27-28) No matter how long it takes, the righteous might of the people will gain victory (lines 30-31) The will of the Congress and the people support the President's effort (lines 32-33) The nation has Confidence in its armed forces and the determination of the people (lines 37-38)
Do hostilities exist?	Yes, hostilities exist	The U.S. people, territory, and interests are in grave danger (lines 35-36)

fight. He then spent substantial time establishing that the attack was a surprise and that the attack targeted the United States and its people. There was not much support for the claim that hostilities exist (perhaps because "the facts of yesterday and today speak for themselves" [lines 24-25]). The Find Your Voice feature encourages you to critically consider Roosevelt's choices in relation to his audience. Mapping his speech onto the debate situation helps us better understand the structure of the case and prepares us to evaluate and respond to it.

FIND YOUR VOICE
ASSESSING ROOSEVELT'S CHOICES

Did Roosevelt address the best issues given his audience? Did it make sense for him to provide the most support for the claim that the United States will prevail in the war? What crucial information did he omit that the audience should know? These are just some questions you might consider in assessing Roosevelt's case.

Summary

The debate situation—the combination of arguments, issues, and a proposition—should help you organize the arguments you encounter in everyday life by showing how the various claims and support fit together in relation to issues on a proposition. The examples of deciding to attend college, *Monty Python and the Holy Grail*, and Roosevelt's "War Message" show this value in slightly different but equally useful ways.

Ultimately, putting a structure and framework onto a debate or even a single argumentative case gives you greater control of the debate situations you encounter. It also reveals the issues and arguments at play in a debate as well as those that none of the advocates chose to raise. Ultimately, the debate situation provides a snapshot of the landscape of arguments as you work toward reaching decisions in everyday life.

Application Exercises

Generating Relevant Issues: Because issues are a challenging concept, follow this prompt to hone your understanding of how issues function in a debate:

1. Identify a properly worded policy proposition you strongly support. Be sure to test it against the criteria outlined in the chapter.

2. Generate as many issues as you can—at least a dozen—relevant to that proposition. Recall that the issues should be yes/no questions and should capture (hypothetical) points of disagreement about that proposition.

3. Rank order the five most important issues to *you* regardless of your answer to the issue. Then consider how you could convince other people that those are most important to deciding the proposition and resolving the debate.

Mapping Debate Situations: Select a recent blog post, editorial, or letter to the editor from a newspaper on a topic of interest to you (make sure it's an opinion article rather than a news story, and it should be 750-1,500 words). Read the article and identify the various features of the debate situation like we did with Roosevelt's speech:

1. Identify the proposition the author of the article is advocating. When possible, use the language of the article. If it is a policy proposition, be sure to follow the guidelines for wording policy propositions.

2. Identify the major claims or reasons for that proposition. Use the paragraph breaks and section headings as a guide to the sub-argument structure developing the overall case.

3. From each claim, identify the issue being debated as well as the support for it. It might help to construct a representation similar to Figure 2.8 or Table 2.2.

4. Evaluate the article by considering (1) how well the chosen issues and arguments are tailored to the audience and (2) whether there are additional issues and arguments the author should have raised for that audience.

Key Terms

Debate Situation 23

Arguments 24

Debate 24

Claim 24

Fact Claim 24

Value Claim 24

Policy Claim 25

Support 25

Warrant 26

Backing 27

Rebuttal 27

Qualifier 28

Argument Chain 28

Case 29

Proposition 30

Issues 34

Linked Support 39

Convergent Support 40

Endnotes

1. Arby's, "It's Not a meat. How Is This Even a debate," Facebook video, 00:11, June 12, 2017, https://www.facebook.com/arbys/videos/10155509445741812.

2. Wayne E. Brockriede and Douglas Ehninger, "Toulmin on Argument: An Interpretation and Application," in *Contemporary Theories of Rhetoric: Selected Readings*, ed. Richard Johannesen (New York: Harper & Row, 1971), 241-255.

3. Stephen E. Toulmin, *The Uses of Argument*, updated ed. (New York: Cambridge University Press, 2003), 93.

4. Jaison R. Abel and Richard Deitz, "Do the Benefits of College Still Outweigh the Costs?" *Current Issues in Economics and Finance* 20.3 (2014): 4.

5. Pew Research Center, "The Rising Costs of *Not* Going to College," February 2014, 3, http://www.pewsocialtrends.org/files/2014/02/SDT-higher-ed-FINAL-02-11-2014.pdf.

6. Eric Levitz, "Trump Is Preparing More Than $30 Billion in Anti-China Tariffs," *New York Magazine*, March 13, 2018, http://nymag.com/daily/intelligencer/2018/03/trump-readies-more-than-usd30-billion-in-anti-china-tariffs.html; Ta-Nehisi Coates, "The Case for Reparations," *The Atlantic*, June 2014, http://www.theatlantic.com/features/archive/2014/05/the-case-for-reparations/361631.

7. The author thanks Jessica Kuperavage for inspiring the idea to use this scene for teaching argumentation.

8. *Monty Python and the Holy Grail*, directed by Terry Gilliam and Terry Jones (1975; Culver City, CA: Columbia TriStar Home Entertainment, 2001), DVD.

9. Stephen E. Lucas and Martin J. Medhurst, eds., *Words of a Cenutry: The Top 100 American Speeches, 1900-1999* (New York: Oxford University Press, 2008).

10. Franklin D. Roosevelt, "138 – Address to Congress Requesting a Declaration of War with Japan," December 8, 1941, *The American Presidency Project*. ed. John T. Woolley and Gerhard Peters, 1999–2017, http://www.presidency.ucsb.edu/ws/index.php?pid=16053.

3

ARGUMENTATION ETHICS & STANCES

In 2004, comedian John Stewart made a now famous appearance on the CNN television program, *Crossfire*. Framed as a "debate" show, *Crossfire* featured discussions with people representing stark positions on the right and left of the political spectrum. The hosts, Paul Begala and Tucker Carlson, invited Stewart on the show to promote his new book, *America: A Citizen's Guide to Democracy Inaction,* but Stewart used the appearance to challenge the hosts for "doing theater when you should be doing debate."[1] Stewart claimed the hosts failed to live up to their "responsibility to the public discourse" by serving as "partisan hacks" who were "hurting America." According to Stewart, the hosts touted their respective party lines rather than being citizens who generated creative solutions to societal problems. When CNN President, Jonathan Klein, canceled *Crossfire* in 2005, he cited Stewart's appearance as partially responsible for his decision. According to the *New York Times*, Klein remarked that he "agree[d] wholeheartedly with Jon Stewart's overall premise" about the need to move away from "head-butting debate shows."[2]

Stewart's critique seemed rooted in a particular set of **argumentation ethics**, or guidelines for moral conduct when arguing, evident when he discussed the hosts' "responsibility." Ethics, broadly conceived, address questions of right and wrong or moral and immoral behavior. Argumentation ethics, then, guide how arguers ought to generate and exchange arguments as moral members of a community.

Related to ethics, Stewart also critiqued Begala and Carlson for their **argumentation stance**. Whereas ethics address your individual conduct in constructing and communicating arguments, stances are a relational feature of the debate situation concerning your interaction with others. Argumentation scholar Wayne Brockriede defined stances as comprising arguers' "attitudes toward one another, their intentions toward one another, and the consequences of those attitudes and intentions for the act itself."[3]

Chapter 2 discussed the "what" of argumentation by addressing the components of any given debate situation. Ethics and stances, on the other hand, refer to the "how" of argumentation by addressing the approach and manner in which people argue. As

ARGUMENTATION ETHICS: Guidelines for moral conduct in argumentation

ARGUMENTATION STANCE: An arguer's attitude and intention toward co-arguers and audiences

such, ethics and stances are a normative dimension to argumentation and debate, offering guidelines for how we should conduct ourselves.

Because of their normative nature, ethics and stances both address the tension between freedom and responsibility. They rely on the freedom of the arguer, meaning you may choose whatever stance you like and whether to heed ethical guidelines. But those choices have consequences for yourself and others. Thus, you also have certain responsibilities as a community member. As you will discover in this chapter, the same content could produce different results if it is advanced using a different ethical guideline or a different stance. And our ethics and stances influence our credibility; if you often violate ethical guidelines, others may be unwilling to debate with you or not trust you. Beyond the outcomes or effectiveness of argumentation, ethics and stances also address the obligations you have in the very act of arguing. That is, we should heed ethics or adopt a particular stance because it is the right thing to do.

It is important to address ethics and stances now, near the start of your skill-building journey, because they occur before you even translate ideas into a spoken or written argument. To help you make more informed choices, this chapter will first explore some ethical guidelines for argumentation and debate while raising some challenging questions for today's pluralistic society. We will then turn to three common argumentation stances and their consequences. The content in this chapter is designed not to give you a "right" answer but to encourage reflection on how you ought to argue with others in everyday life. By the end of this chapter, you should be able to make informed choices concerning ethics and stances when deciding how to argue.

ARGUMENTATION AND DEBATE ETHICS

As noted in the previous section, our freedom to say and do what we want often conflicts with our obligation to do the right thing. Ethics are especially important in situations when doing the right thing (or not) has a direct impact on other people. You have likely encountered ethics in a variety of contexts—there are ethics of academic honesty when writing papers for classes, ethics of the road when driving, and ethics of gaming when playing online with others, to name a few. The same is true of argumentation and debate.

It's often the case that an *effective* argument (one that achieves your goal) or an *appropriate* argument (one that fits the audience, sphere, or situation) may not be an *ethical* argument (one that follows guidelines for moral conduct). For example, appealing to guilt when getting your friends to do something might gain their adherence and may follow the norms of conduct for a personal sphere but it might not be an ethical tactic. Similarly, breaking into your co-arguer's workplace to steal their strategy documents might give you the upper hand in a debate and may be a quid-pro-quo form of counter-attack but that doesn't make it the ethical choice and, as we learned during Watergate, it may be illegal.

Although ethics are important to argumentation, there is not a universal ethical code. Ethics may differ depending on culture, community, and nation. Moreover, just as spheres of argument have different norms for appropriate and effective argumentation, they also have different norms for ethical argumentation. You may know people who think that name calling is perfectly ethical and good-humored when arguing in a personal sphere

FIND YOUR VOICE

IDENTIFYING ETHICAL GUIDELINES

Before reading the guidelines this chapter proposes, reflect on your own experience. What ethical guidelines have you tended to follow? Why? Where did you learn or cultivate these guidelines? Have there been times when a co-arguer violated your personal guidelines for ethics? If so, how have you responded? Being aware of ethics helps build your personal character and enables you to more effectively respond to those who may follow different guidelines than you.

with friends but, even if that's the case, those same people likely avoid that argumentative tactic in technical spheres such as the classroom or workplace. This ethical contrast was illustrated in the early years of *Saturday Night Live* when Dan Aykroyd and Jane Curtin would present a Weekend Update segment called "Point/Counterpoint." They would speak in a tone of voice you'd expect for a public affairs program but engage in name-calling and personal insults, epitomized by the statement Aykroyd commonly used to begin his counterpoint: "Jane, you ignorant slut." The humor of the skit derived entirely from the violation of ethical principles for that sphere; the satire reinforced the ethical norm.

Ethical criteria also differ within personal, technical, and public spheres. Presidential debates are a telling case. In the United States, presidential candidates have no *a priori* ethical guidelines apart from turn-taking and equitable time.[4] Serbia specifies these same guidelines for its presidential debates but also expressly prohibits interruptions by other candidates while Nigeria goes further to proscribe certain kinds of arguments, noting for instance that "direct attack on the personality of candidate will not be allowed and we will strive to ensure that the highest sense of decorum is maintained by the candidates."[5] Argentina, which staged the country's first presidential debates in 2015, offered even more robust ethical guidelines for its candidates: transparency, equality, construction of a public good, good faith, and freedom.[6] The ethical guidelines differ even though they are all public sphere debates involving presidential candidates.

Despite a lack of consensus concerning *which* ethical guidelines to follow, most people would agree that argumentation and debate should follow some. Stop here and use the Find Your Voice feature to consider your personal guidelines for argumentation ethics. Following that, this section proposes five guidelines for consideration in Western societies. We use the label "guideline" to emphasize that there may be exceptions in certain situations rather than viewing them as inflexible rules that must be applied equally in all cases. As we explore each guideline, use the explanation to consider why and when it might be worthwhile.

Ethical Guideline 1: Honesty

Honesty is one guideline for ethical argumentation. Honesty is a broad category that involves numerous behaviors. Honesty demands accurate representations of information. Making up statistics, taking information out of context, or misquoting sources are all dishonest acts, and hence unethical. So is plagiarism, or using other people's ideas as your own. Even when plagiarism happens unintentionally (e.g., forgetting to properly cite our research), it still demonstrates a lapse in ethical judgment.

Honesty also may require you to be candid and direct rather than passive aggressive or beating around the bush. Implying rather than stating claims may be an unethical act when used to manipulate others. People may also conceal their true intentions when arguing or may emphasize their arguments as other-oriented when they are really promoting self-interest. In your own experience, you can likely tell when people are misrepresenting their intentions. This may be ethical if they frame it as a win-win situation (your interests and theirs are satisfied), but it may be unethical if they are dishonest in their motives.

Honesty sounds like a good guideline in theory but the actual practice is more complex, as the following questions reveal:

- Does honesty still apply when it would physically or mentally harm another? Consider parents who conceal information from children to protect their interests. Under what conditions is this ethical or unethical? Should parents always answer a child's question with honest arguments?

- Does honesty also apply to argumentative omissions? If you know information that will harm your case and you intentionally refrain from sharing it, are you being dishonest? If the goal of debate is to come to the best decision on the proposition, then it seems important that audience members and co-arguers are provided all possible information that might help reach that decision but some people don't deem sins of omission unethical.

- Does honesty require arguers to recognize counter-arguments and the quality of support? Is it unethical to cherry pick evidence? For instance, President Trump claimed in his first press conference on February 16, 2017, that "I don't think there's ever been a president elected who, in this short period of time, has done what we've done." He supported this claim, in part, by noting "a new Rasmussen poll just came out just a very short while ago, and it has our approval rating at 55 percent and going up."[7] This support was true—the poll did capture this approval rating—but there were 10 other polls around the same time that gauged his approval between 39 and 48 percent.[8] Clearly, Rasmussen was an outlier, so was it dishonest for Trump to rely on this support?

Ethical Guideline 2: Respect

Respect, like honesty, is also an ethical choice that includes many sub-considerations. One common element is to treat your audience and co-arguers as equals whose time, presence, and ideas you value. Actions such as name calling, personal attacks, or a lack of preparation all compromise the respect you have for others in a debate situation. These are unethical because they dehumanize your co-arguers and audience members.

Respect also involves being aware of other cultures and perspectives. At a basic level, the style of debate common in Western societies—direct statements, linear progression, confident and concrete language, eye contact—does not translate to all cultures. In Japan, for instance, many arguers are more circular and indirect in their reasoning, using analogies and stories to develop implied claims.[9] It might be disrespectful to enter a debate situation with people from a different culture and expect them to conform to your own style.

Additionally, being respectful means avoiding discriminatory behavior toward other individuals and cultures. Language that demeans a person or group of people is unethical even if the people aren't present to hear it. This applies to arguments grounded in racism, sexism, heterosexism, ableism, ageism, and other qualities of social identity such as religion or socioeconomic status. Regardless of their impact on the effect of your argument, their very utterance is morally concerning.

Finally, respect also extends to audience members and co-arguers. Listening attentively and giving arguers a fair opportunity to communicate their ideas is often an ethical act. But, it goes beyond just sitting silently waiting until your turn to pounce; it includes a good faith effort to engage and a willingness to give someone the benefit of the doubt. Assuming the intentions of others may be unethical, particularly to the extent that it leads to prejudice and bias.

The mutual respect among arguers and audience members can create some ethical challenges:

- Does respect limit how you can respond to arguers who disrespect others? Consider a scenario in which someone gets flustered in a debate with you and responds to your argument by saying "that's retarded." This response is disrespectful to people with disabilities but it might be equally disrespectful for you to critique (i.e., personally attack) the speaker for saying that. How should you handle violations of this guideline while maintaining it yourself?

- Does respect require due diligence in preparing for the consequences of your argumentation? For example, Danish newspaper *Jyllands-Posten* chose to publish political cartoons depicting the Muslim prophet Muhammed in 2005. Meant as an argument against self-censorship, this decision was met with an international backlash among Muslims for not respecting the cultural view that visual depictions of the prophet are blasphemous. The newspaper defended its action by touting the principle of free speech but many felt it was unethical for disrespecting another culture and the ensuing riots and protests resulted in lost lives.[10] Should the newspaper have known the consequences of these arguments and, if so, should they have refrained from publishing them?

Ethical Guideline 3: Consistency

A third ethical guideline for argumentation and debate is consistency. To contradict oneself—to advance a claim at one point in time and then advance an opposite or modified claim at another point in time—may be immoral, especially if it (intentionally) confuses or misdirects others. To preach one thing and practice another is also a violation of ethical consistency, as is calling on your audience members to take a particular action but failing to do so yourself. Hypocrisy is a cardinal sin of debate that undermines an argument and casts doubt on the ethics of the arguer.

In contemporary politics especially, accusations of "flip-flopping" are commonly used to critique someone's character. In the 2004 election campaign, President George W. Bush and Senator John Kerry both attempted to exploit this perception. In the first presidential debate, Bush contrasted his leadership on the Iraq War with Kerry's, arguing "The only thing consistent about my opponent's position is that he's been inconsistent. He changes positions. And, you cannot change positions in this war on terror if you expect to win." Kerry responded by arguing that Bush was inconsistent with his policy toward North Korea, declaring Bush's policy to allow North Korea to obtain nuclear weapons as "one of the most serious, sort of, reversals or mixed messages that you could possibly send."[11] Setting aside the fact that these personal attacks are likely unethical themselves (see the previous guideline about respect), Bush and Kerry both addressed consistency as a virtue that makes for ethical argumentation.

However, consistency as an ethical guideline also brings with it some difficult questions:

- Does consistency mean you can't change your mind? Recall that one of the benefits of debate is that it helps people expose error and find the best ideas. Consistency, however, suggests you should be steadfast in your beliefs. How do we determine if and when inconsistency is unethical rather than a sign of mature growth and development?

- Does consistency mean people must always argue what they personally believe? One of the joys of argumentation is that it allows people to play with ideas, to take different perspectives, and even argue things they don't personally believe. Consistency, as a virtue, would imply that these actions are unethical. If it *is* ethical to play devil's advocate or take another side of a controversy, must the arguer offer a disclaimer stating so?

Ethical Guideline 4: Accountability

A fourth guideline is accountability, or being responsible for your argumentation. Accountability is particularly challenging online, where anonymity shields individuals. While eliminating such anonymity is unrealistic, you might promote your own accountability in this environment by asking yourself if you'd still advance the argument with your name and picture attached to it. If not, you probably should refrain from doing so.

Accountable arguers don't always avoid mistakes but are willing to take responsibility when they do. When you contravene ethical guidelines or harm others with your argumentation—whether intentional or not—accountability means you admit your fault, apologize, and strive to avoid the same mistake. For instance, it is likely that something you've posted through social media has, at some point, offended someone else. In such cases, accountability means you should apologize for your conduct and make amends. *VICE* emphasized the need for accountability in our online lives through their humorous article, "The Five Stages of Getting Publicly Shamed on the Internet." According to the article, Stage 4 is "the carefully worded statement" meant to quell the storm.[12]

While accountability is generally a good policy, we might test the scope of this guideline:

- Does accountability mean that violations of ethics are always in the eye of the beholder? To what degree does intent matter when it comes to ethical violations? For instance, if you unknowingly use erroneous support or if you unintentionally offend someone, must you still take responsibility for those arguments? Given that some people are more sensitive to particular ethical guidelines than you might be, who decides when you've violated them? We'll consider these questions explicitly with our Everyday Life Example later in the chapter.

Ethical Guideline 5: Courage

Courage is a final ethical guideline. Courage may seem at first a personal choice rather than a matter of ethics. However, courage (or a lack thereof) can have moral implications. People are often bullied or isolated if they violate norms or advance unpopular arguments. While persecution is unethical itself, courage suggests it might be just as unethical for someone to bend to the pressure from others. To be courageous, then, means you have the resolve and strength to argue in the face of adversity.

New Jersey Governor Chris Christie offers a compelling example of courageous argumentation in response to Hurricane Sandy in October 2012. More than two months after Hurricane Sandy reached the eastern seaboard, the U.S. House of Representatives had still not passed a relief package.[13] When the House postponed the vote until after the holiday recess on January 15, Christie delivered a speech critiquing Republican leaders—members of his own party—for delaying the aid package. Christie argued "the House of Representatives failed that most basic test of public service and they did so with callous indifference for the suffering of the people of my state." Later, he asserted: "Shame on you. Shame on Congress."[14]

This was an ethical choice because Christie stood up for democratic values in the face of adversity and argued what he believed was right rather than staying silent for the sake of popularity or party unity. Some conservatives criticized Christie for dividing the Republican Party, and this speech may be the reason Christie was not invited to the 2013 Conservative Political Action Conference (CPAC).[15] Christie likely knew ahead of time that he would be ostracized for his actions but upheld honesty and courage, claiming "I'm a guy who tells the truth all the time."[16]

Courage can create some ethical challenges in its own right:

- Does courage foster recklessness? Aristotle argued that any quality taken to its extreme raises concerns. An excess of courage, then, could cause argumentative recklessness in which people don't censor their thoughts at all. How should arguers balance a desire to speak their truth with the need for self-censorship?

The five guidelines above offer a framework for ethical argumentation that you can use in a variety of contexts. While these ethical guidelines are useful for everyday life, the bullet points throughout the section have indicated how they might engender some challenging applications. The Build Your Skill feature offers additional opportunities to consider trade-offs between ethics and effectiveness. Then, consider the first Everyday Life Example in this chapter that further explores the difficulties of ethical argumentation.

BUILD YOUR SKILL
EXPLORING ETHICAL GUIDELINES

For the following scenarios, consider what ethical guidelines might be violated. Then, consider how you would personally respond and why.

A. As you leave class, you hear your co-arguers discussing their strategy for an upcoming debate against you. Knowing that you won't get caught, is it ethical to stay outside the door and listen to them?

B. You find statistics in one source that really help support your argument but you also find a source that questions the research methods used to gather those statistics. Is it ethical to use the statistics at this point?

C. Your friend presents a case to you about the poor quality of your significant other. You believe your friend lacks credibility because you know his girlfriend has a history of cheating on him. Is it ethical to advance this counter-argument?

Everyday Life Example 3.1

Adria Richards's Tweets

Richards's Tweets (March 17, 2013): "Not cool. Jokes about forking repo's in a sexual way and 'big' dongles. Right behind me #pycon." [3:32 p.m.][18]

"Can someone talk to these guys about their conduct? I'm in lightning talks, top right near stage, 10 rows back #pycon" [3:34 p.m.][19]

"Code of Conduct #pycon https://us.pycon.org/2013/about/code-of-conduct/" [3:40 p.m.][20]

Source: Twitter/@adriarichards

Everyday Life Example 3.1 also illustrates some challenges of following ethical guidelines in everyday life. In March 2013, Adria Richards was listening to a presentation at a tech conference when two men behind her engaged in sexual innuendo through tech jargon. She was offended and felt afraid,[17] so she took their picture and Tweeted it with a shaming statement. Read three of her tweets and consider if and how ethics are implicated.

One of the two men in the photo was fired from his job, which he credits to the tweet, and posted a statement to *Hacker News* about the situation (including an apology) under the pseudonym "mr-hank."[21] This situation led many people to address Richards—with both support and condemnation—through her Twitter account and various online discussion forums. When someone targeted Richards's employer through a DDoS attack, she also was fired from her job. She blames mr-hank and commented to journalist Jon Ronson that mr-hank "was saying things that could be inferred as offensive to me, sitting in front of him. I do have empathy for him, but it only goes so far." She elaborated that, "If I had a spouse and two kids to support, I certainly would not be telling 'jokes' like he was doing at a conference. Oh, but wait, I have compassion, empathy, morals and ethics to guide my daily life choices."[22]

The situation raises some challenging questions for a multicultural and interconnected world:

- Was Richards decision to post her argument to Twitter courageous? Honest? Respectful?

- Was it unethical for mr-hank to make sexual jokes to a male friend and, if so, on what grounds? What expectation of privacy do and should our arguments have? To what degree should mr-hank be accountable to someone who is not the intended audience for his argument?

- Was mr-hank's decision to post his statement to *Hacker News* courageous? Honest? Respectful?

- Is the public shaming of Richards a taste of her own medicine or unethical argumentation? If unethical, on what grounds? (To assess this, you might consult Richards's tweets and read some of the comments to them.)

The ethics of social media arguments are especially important for a few reasons. First, they can have substantial reach and repercussion, being difficult to sweep away. Through the Library of Congress and the Internet Archive, many posts live on forever even if you delete them from your account. Second, social media tends to be truncated arguments and, thus, may rely on ideas and depictions that are oversimplified or unflattering. Especially when representing other people, you should carefully consider the consequences of your arguments. And, third, social media represents a bizarre confluence of personal, professional, and public spheres. Our debates often mimic personal sphere debates with few rules for engagement but our networks likely involve people from all three spheres. As a result, we may be less cautious or thoughtful than we should be.

Ultimately, argumentation and debate ethics require you to not just heed moral principles but to pause and consider the potential effects of your arguments. The next section explores how these consequences are also affected by argumentation stances.

ARGUMENTATION STANCES

Argumentation stances refer to the attitude and intention an arguer chooses to adopt toward others. We will explore three main stances: competitive, manipulative, and cooperative. These are not, by any means, the only options but they capture three common stances individuals use when arguing. How do you know what stance you or someone else is using? To help you answer this question, our exploration of each stance will consider its goal and tactics.

As described below, the three stances represent extremes of each kind. Keep in mind that an arguer may not embody a particular stance in its entirety. When arguers don't go to the extremes, they hint at their stance based on how they approach the debate situation and how they enact their argumentation, as Everyday Life Example 3.2 will illustrate near the end of the chapter.

Competitive Stance

Read the following front page headlines from September 27, 2016, and try to guess what they are characterizing: "Fight Night" (*USA Today*); "Showdown" (*Philadelphia Enquirer*); "A Pitched Battle" (*Columbus Dispatch*); "A Testy Opening Round" (*Los Angeles Times*); "Clashing Visions over Nation's Future" (*Chicago Tribune*); "A War of Words" (*Seattle Times*); "Clash of Styles" (*Dallas Morning News*); "Two Debaters on the Attack" (*Boston Globe*); "Candidates Press Pointed Attacks in Acerbic Debate" (*New York Times*); "Trump, Clinton Trade Fierce Blows" (*The Wall Street Journal*); and "Hesitant at Start, Clinton Sought to Leave Trump Out Cold" (*New York Times*). By the end of the list, it should have been evident that these headlines all describe the first debate on September 26 between presidential candidates Donald Trump and Hillary Clinton.

COMPETITIVE STANCE: Arguers pursue self-interest by overpowering their co-arguer(s) and audience(s)

All of the headlines reflect a **competitive stance** toward argumentation. In this stance, arguers use arguments instrumentally to achieve their goals by defeating co-arguers and gaining submission from the audience.

The *goal* of debate from a competitive stance is for an arguer's ideas to prevail by overpowering others. Competitive argumentation tends to view debate as a zero-sum game: If one person's ideas prevail, the other person loses. In some extreme cases, the goal for debating is nothing other than debating and showing your linguistic power (you know, those people who like to argue for the sake of arguing).

There are numerous *argumentation tactics* that may signal a competitive stance:

- **Coercion and verbal force**. A competitive stance is often an effort to exert power. Arguers might use tactics of force that prevent others from communicating, such as interrupting, shouting down speakers, or outright censorship. A competitive stance might also involve verbal aggression, such as a raised voice, name calling, or combativeness and divisiveness.

- **Treating others as objects or means to an end**. A competitive stance frequently views audience members and co-arguers as objects to be overcome or as means to an end. This tactic may be somewhat innocuous, evident in a simple disregard for perspective taking, but it might also involve outright hostility towards the viewpoints of others. At its worst, a competitive stance might dehumanize other people through verbal abuse designed to achieve the arguer's goals.

- **Close-mindedness**. A competitive stance typically involves arguments with strong qualifiers (e.g. claims that are "certain" or "obvious") and arguers demonstrate little or no openness to new ideas and risk of self. Arguers using this stance tend to have a response to every possible counter-argument and they rarely listen to and integrate information that challenges their ideas.

- **Lack of respect for rules and ethics of engagement**. A competitive stance tends to view debate as warfare, leading some arguers to believe that anything goes. Motivated to destroy their enemy, they care little for guidelines of decorum or ethics. If rules *are* established, competitive arguers may try to find loopholes or exemptions or even change those rules during the debate. A competitive stance may seek to deny others fair or equal footing to participate.

At this point, it should be evident that a competitive stance is pretty common in everyday life even if it isn't taken to the extreme.[23] Just consider the language people often use to describe argumentation and debate: We characterize debate as a "battle" between diametrically opposed "sides." We "attack" others' arguments and employ "strategies" comprised of "offensive" and "defensive" tactics. We seek to "destroy" their ideas. It's likely that you yourself have used language like this to characterize debates you've had with friends and family members.

Political candidate debates in the United States are a good example of a competitive stance because, as rhetorical scholar David Zarefsky has explained, "the focus in political debates is on winning by not losing, or by cleverly scoring a hit against the opponent." What is more, Zarefsky notes that the viewing audience at home is complicit insofar as their main concerns are: "Were there any major gaffes or blunders? Were there any great one-liners or sound bites? If not, the debates are dismissed as inconsequential."[24] In this stance, argumentation becomes an instrumental tool for achieving victory. This explains why the headlines at the start of this section all signaled debate as competition or warfare.

At the extreme, a competitive stance is quite problematic and would lead arguers to violate numerous ethical guidelines: respect for others, honesty, courage, and accountability. This is arguably why many commentators raise concerns about competitive debate programs, such as *Crossfire*, and about the overall state of public argumentation in society.

Manipulative Stance

Whereas a competitive stance employs force, a **manipulative stance** employs trickery. In this stance, arguers use arguments instrumentally to achieve their goals by manipulating co-arguers and audience members into agreement.

The audience is victimized by both competitive and manipulative arguers but the relationships between the stances are different; competition involves overpowering others to eliminate choice while manipulation involves ensnaring others who provide willing assent.

The *goal* of debate from a manipulative stance is for an arguer's ideas to prevail by beguiling others. Manipulative argumentation approaches debate not as competition or warfare but as opportunity. Argumentation becomes a means to an end that benefits the interests of the arguer. Brockriede characterizes this stance as "seduction" and observes that it provides an *illusion* of the "right to choose" while in reality limiting or eliminating this choice.[25]

Numerous *argumentation tactics* may accompany a manipulative stance, some of which parallel a competitive stance:

- **Misuse of support**. A manipulative stance frequently misrepresents or withholds support to make a claim appear stronger or more appealing. Additionally, a manipulative stance might ground claims in irrelevant support, such as appeals to ignorance (i.e., a lack of contrary evidence), popularity, credibility, or tradition. While these may be appropriate in some cases, they often misdirect the audience's attention. Additionally, bullshit, as a mode of discourse, often falls under a manipulative stance. Bullshitters aren't liars per se because they are indifferent to the truth, saying whatever will further their goals in the moment.[26]

MANIPULATIVE STANCE: Arguers pursue self-interest by misleading their co-arguer(s) and audience(s)

- **Appeals to emotions and credibility**. A manipulative stance might entice others through appeals to the emotions or to the credibility of the arguer. A few common appeals are flattery, or excessive praise, of the audience and appeals to fear that override critical thinking. Emotional and character appeals do, of course, have a place in argumentation and not all of them are manipulative. However, a manipulative stance involves arguers who knowingly and intentionally exploit others' emotions to get their way.

- **Close-mindedness**. As with a competitive stance, a manipulative stance also involves being close-minded with little or no openness to new ideas and little risk of self. Manipulative arguers won't likely impose their position through force, but they may change the subject when challenged, evade answering tough questions, pass the blame to others, and talk their way out of factual contradictions and inconveniences.

- **Lack of respect for rules and ethics of engagement**. As with a competitive stance, a manipulative stance also shows disregard for certain rules and ethical guidelines. Arguers using this stance might blatantly disregard such rules, particularly concerning honesty and respect, or strive to bend them.

A manipulative stance may be less common than a competitive one but it is still fairly widespread in everyday life. You could likely recall some instances in which you have used this stance yourself, perhaps through appeals to fear or guilt. This stance pervades personal spheres because we are more invested in those relationships (so we avoid the forcefulness of a competitive stance), but we are still selfish beings who want to achieve our goals. Beyond personal spheres, a manipulative stance could also be evident in technical spheres like the courtroom—what the Broadway musical *Chicago* called the "razzle dazzle" of oral arguments—or public spheres like national politics.

Advertising frequently exemplifies a manipulative stance through tactics that intentionally deceive consumers. One common argumentative maneuver in advertising involves advancing, as Richard Williford explains, "bewildering claims" that are "supported by restrictions found in tiny print at the bottom of the ads."[27] This is especially concerning for advertising aimed at children, who don't have the capacity to think critically about the arguments. Arguers using this stance care little for these misrepresentations because the focus is on their own interests.

As with a competitive stance, a manipulative stance likely would violate numerous ethical guidelines, chief among them honesty, respect, and accountability. For these reasons, it is best to avoid a manipulative stance.

Cooperative Stance

COOPERATIVE STANCE: Arguers pursue mutual-interest by treating their co-arguer(s) and audience(s) as equals

Unlike the force of the competitive stance or the deceit of the manipulative stance, a **cooperative stance** promotes a multilateral relationship among arguers and audiences to foster choice. This stance considers argumentation and debate a means of learning and seeks to find the best answer, even if that means the arguer abandons his or her original position.

Josina Makau and Debian Marty note that arguers using this stance "recognize that their views can only be enlightened by as comprehensive and open an exchange as is possible."[28]

The *goal* of debate from a cooperative stance is to ensure the best ideas prevail. Cooperative argumentation approaches debate as a communal act designed to test ideas, explore truth, and arrive at solutions. This is not to say that the two other stances never find their way to the "truth" but rather that a cooperative stance is motivated by this endeavor. From this stance, argumentation may also be an end in itself: a ritual of community affirmation and involvement. From this view, the goal isn't to argue for the sake of arguing but to argue for the sake of the community and personal empowerment. For example, many white women in the 1800s signed petitions against slavery not only because they expected their argumentation to bring about emancipation but also because it was a means of female political empowerment.[29]

A cooperative stance may be signaled by numerous *argumentation tactics*:

- **Open-mindedness and risk of self**. A cooperative stance frequently involves openness to others' ideas. Participants using this stance are more likely to promote learning and personal transformation as a result of debate. There is, of course, a difference between vulnerability and weakness; to risk oneself requires in many cases more strength and courage than being rigid in your beliefs.

- **Empathy and understanding**. A cooperative stance involves treating others as individuals with unique perspectives, interests, experiences, and ideas. Empathy, or sharing the feelings of others, is one tactic in a debate that might signal a cooperative stance. Especially in public spheres, competitive and manipulative stances rarely serve as *civic* acts of participation because the focus is so strongly on the individual. Using a cooperative approach more fully emphasizes the controversy's relationship to all community members.

- **Respect for rules and ethics of engagement**. A cooperative stance tends to promote fairness and equality in a debate, making sure the rules are followed. Cooperative arguers also demonstrate concern with ethics to a higher degree than those using a competitive or manipulative stance because they are not primarily motivated to win.

- **Faith in co-arguers and audience members**. A cooperative stance often places faith in others to follow the rules, be empathetic, and demonstrate open-mindedness. It's important to note here that the focus is on faith—conviction without proof—rather than mere belief. Cooperative arguers confronted by competitive or manipulative arguers may get rattled but are unlikely to lose their faith in the potential of their fellow humans.

You should not be surprised that a cooperative stance is, in many cases, a more productive mode of argumentation than the other two. Returning to the opening anecdote of Jon Stewart's appearance on *Crossfire*, it becomes clearer now that he was asking the hosts to use a cooperative rather than competitive stance, to replace dichotomous and contentious argumentation with a more generative approach to controversies.

TABLE 3.1 ■ Argumentation Stances		
Stance	**Goal**	**Common Tactics**
Competitive	Prevail through force	• Coercion and verbal force • Treating others as objects or means to an end • Close-mindedness • Lack of respect for rules and ethics of engagement
Manipulative	Prevail through deceit	• Misuse of support • Appeals to emotion and credibility • Close-mindedness • Lack of respect for rules and ethics of engagement
Cooperative	Find the best outcome	• Open-mindedness and risk of self • Empathy and understanding • Respect for rules and ethics of engagement • Faith in co-arguers and audience members

In the present day, science offers one place where arguers often use a cooperative stance.[30] Many scientists are bound by the empirical world and must provide evidence for their claims. Argumentation, then, becomes a way of testing and sharing ideas among peers, not for selfish gain but for the benefit of the community. As such, most scientists are transparent about their methods and conclusions, not manipulatively concealing information. And, many scientists are open to the possibility that their discoveries are wrong or incomplete, risking their own beliefs for knowledge's sake.

Despite its productive nature, cooperative argumentation is not very common in everyday life. You may perhaps recall some experiences in which you used this stance, such as when resolving a conflict with a significant other or family member, but those instances are likely fewer and farther between your uses of competitive and manipulative stances.

Table 3.1 summarizes the three stances. As you consider how these stances function in everyday argumentation, you might keep in mind the following observations:

- **The three stances are not mutually exclusive**. It might be the case that an arguer uses the goal of one but the tactics of another, such as taking perspectives not to learn from others but to win. This mixture of stances makes it more challenging to debate others because you might not know their intentions and, thus, often need to be vigilant even when the tactics seem pure.

- **The three stances are not exhaustive**. Although they represent common stances to argumentation, there are other approaches that arguers might pursue. For instance, people who are paid to argue (e.g., a public relations specialist, a

FIND YOUR VOICE
ARGUMENTATION STANCES

Consider scenarios in which you might use each of the three stances. Are competitive and manipulative approaches ever the best choice? If so, in what spheres or situations? Also consider what and how much you're willing to risk when you argue. In what spheres or situations should you be vulnerable to change? The more aware of the choice of stance you have, the more productive your argumentation can be.

marketing executive, a speechwriter) may not fit any of the categories because they aren't pursuing their own personal gain through force or deception but also aren't risking their own belief.

- **The three stances are not always matched by co-arguers**. Using a particular stance doesn't mean your co-arguer will follow suit and sometimes you might need to address your co-arguer's stance as part of the debate. Cooperative arguers might be especially vulnerable to those using the other two stances. When faced with a stance that tries to take advantage of you, arguers often need to find strategies (such as critical thinking) to defend themselves or shift the arguer to be more cooperative.

Our Everyday Life Example in this section will illustrate how a cooperative stance enhances a debate's productivity. For this example, we'll consider an exchange from the Reddit bulletin board, "Change My View" (CMV). On CMV, people post statements they believe to be true and invite others to change their view. If an arguer is successful, the original poster (OP) will award a delta (Δ), the mathematical symbol for change. The topics are quite varied, from "toe socks are silly and probably not comfortable" to "it is impossible for the human race to overcome bigotry" to "18 wheelers shouldn't be allowed on the road."

The goal of CMV aligns quite nicely with the goal of cooperative stance arguers: "CMV is a sub-reddit dedicated to the civil discourse of opinions, and is built around the idea that in order to resolve our differences, we must first understand them. We believe that productive conversation requires respect and openness, and that certitude is the enemy of understanding."[31] It's also important to note that OP's are supposed to be open to change, as outlined in Submission Rule B.[32] Responders, on the other hand, are not required to have such openness. Their main rules are that they "must challenge at least one aspect of OP's stated view (however minor), or ask a clarifying question," "don't be rude or hostile to other users," and "refrain from accusing OP or anyone else of being unwilling to change their view."[33] Community members can enforce these rules but all participants have the freedom to use any stance they wish.

Included below is a debate between Zzzmessi1 and Ghost_of_John_Galt on the policy proposition that "sports should not have a place in American universities." As you read the debate (copied directly from the website), identify the stance each arguer is using by considering which tactics and goals from Table 3.1 seem evident.

Everyday Life Example 3.2

Zzzmessi1 and Ghost_of_John_Galt, "CMV: Sports should not have a place in American universities," 2017[34]

1	**Zzzmessi1 (OP)**: I believe that sports in America should be similar to the club system that exists
2	in Europe. Collegiate sports distract from the fact that the focus of any institution of higher
3	education should be education.
4	Many universities in America use sports as a way of building a brand that is based little on
5	academics or campus life outside of sports. With the high tuition prices we have now, this level
6	of branding, especially from public colleges, pressures students to take on large amounts of
7	debt in order to join this sports culture.
8	In addition, sports have diverted students' time within college to watching games and joining the
9	parties associated with them. This can often come at the expense of academics or professional
10	skills.
11	The larger role of sports in an institution can also divert resources away from these
12	academic programs in favor of "big" sports like basketball and football that can often be
13	unprofitable. This mixing of sports and academics creates a conflict of interest that can
14	interfere with athletes' academic life, as it is in the interest of the schools to keep them
15	eligible at all costs. This should not be a concern for universities, especially taxpayer-funded
16	public universities.
17	While I do admittedly enjoy collegiate sports, they have turned into an industry that has very
18	little to do with education, as recent attempts to unionize by NCAA players shows.
19	**Ghost_of_John_Galt**: Of the top 10 unis in the world, the US has six.
20	Link [https://www.timeshighereducation.com/world-university-rankings/2017 /world-
21	ranking#!/page/0/length/25/sort_by/rank/sort_order/asc/cols/stats]
22	Of the remainder, Oxford and Cambridge also have sporting programs and I can't be bothered
23	googling the other 2.
24	Given that, what makes you think that sport is a negative in terms of distraction from education?
25	**Zzzmessi1**: I wasn't aware that those two have programs, but my main issue with college
26	sports is how they've become a large industry that schools consider necessary to building
27	their brand. Sports contribute little to the overall brand of Oxford and Cambridge, while
28	they seem completely involved in schools like Alabama and North Carolina. The level of
29	entanglement between colleges and sports creates a distraction because many students
30	are now choosing schools based on big sports programs, rather than academic quality
31	and fit.
32	**Ghost_of_John_Galt**: But your OP didn't limit it to Alabama and North Carolina. It was all US
33	universities. Given the lack of correlation between sports and poor academic performance, why
34	should they have 'no place' in any US university, merely because Alabama maybe concentrates
35	too much on sport?
36	**Zzzmessi1**: The problem goes deeper than just the few schools I named as examples. Almost
37	every non-liberal arts school has sports teams that schools use as an attraction for students
38	who now consider sports a necessary component of the typical college experience. In order to
39	compete for these students, colleges need to have programs in "big" sports. As for the situation
40	in Europe, colleges very seldom rely on sports to create their brands.

41	**Ghost_of_John_Galt**: But it clearly doesn't harm the academic results of certain schools, yes?
42	But you still think it has 'no place'?
43	Let's turn this around - what evidence do you have that it harms US universities, given their
44	stellar worldwide results?
45	**Zzzmessi1**: From what I've found, the correlation between sports and decreased academic
46	performance is minuscule, at most. I see that the problems with sports are more or less
47	byproducts of party culture that would continue to exist without sports in the US. Thanks for
48	pointing this out. Δ
49	**Ghost_of_John_Galt**: Thanks mate! Have a wonderful day/evening.

Source: Zzzmessi1 and Ghost_of_John_Galt, "CMV: Sports Should Not Have a Place in American Universities," Change My View, Reddit, May 20 2017, https://www.reddit.com/r/changemy-view/comments/6ccukh/cmv_sports_should_ not_have_a_place_in_american.

The exchange intimates two of the three stances but largely represents a cooperative approach. A manipulative stance is least evident insofar as the arguers don't use deception or trickery. However, the participants hint at a competitive stance when they display certainty (lines 2-18, 26-31, 41-42) and respond to each and every argument with a counter-argument. Ghost_of_John_Galt seems more competitive than Zzzmessi1 by using the OP to trap Zzzmessi1 in potential shifts or contradictions (lines 32-33, 41-44).

Nevertheless, both arguers generally utilized a cooperative stance, albeit through different tactics. Ghost_of_John_Galt sought understanding by using questions rather than statements to gather further responses (lines 24, 33-35, 41-44) and cited a credible source to support the claim that a majority of the world's "top 10 unis" have substantial athletic programs (lines 19-23). Zzzmessi1 used hedgers—"I believe," "seem," "from what I've found"—and qualifiers —e.g., "can," "almost," "more or less"—to delimit claims (lines 1, 9, 28, 36-37, 40, 45, 46) and admitted to learning new things (lines 25, 46-48). These tactics are more encouraging to co-arguers and foster a more open debate than you might find with a competitive stance.

Zzzmessi1's Δ to Ghost_of_John_Galt underscores the power of argument stances. A different respondent, whose profile has since been deleted, advanced virtually the same claim as Ghost_of_John_Galt just five minutes after Ghost_of_John_Galt but did so through a competitive stance. For instance, this person argued, among other things:

- "The culture of having parties and watching sports would exist anyway. College students just want an excuse to get drunk and have fun—if that means watching the Texans or the Cowboys instead of the Longhorns, that's what will happen.

- While I do agree that athletes are often passed through the academic system too easily in order to keep the eligible, I think you are looking at the problem the wrong way. The issue is an ethics issue with the professors and administration that getting rid of sports won't fix—as long as there is something to be eligible for, people will get shoved through."[35]

Interestingly, Zzzmessi1 ultimately conceded that the party culture would continue absent sports to Ghost_of_John_Galt but not to the person making this point explicitly. Could this be because this person used a competitive stance, evident through the certainty of claims and phrases that attacked Zzzmessi1 like "I think you are looking at the problem the wrong way" or, later in the debate, "The problem at the core of your argument . . ."?

Research about CMV supports this conclusion that the choice of stance, and the argumentation tactics within it, matter to a debate's outcome. Chenhao Tan et al. found that arguments receiving a Δ tended to be longer posts, cite credible (linked) evidence, use "calmer" language, and choose words that were different from the words in the OP's original argument.[36] These qualities represent a cooperative approach to finding the best answer and, thus, are more productive and inviting for resolving disagreement. Although this outcome best applies when all arguers are open-minded, it shows how tactics common to a cooperative approach can be more ethical and effective.

Summary

In your argumentation and debate, you will need to make choices about how to engage others, particularly concerning what ethical guidelines you will follow and what stance you will use. This chapter has offered five ethical guidelines for consideration: honesty, consistency, respect, accountability, and courage. The chapter then outlined three argumentation stances—competitive, manipulative, and cooperative—that capture the intentions and attitudes arguers might have toward others within a particular debate situation.

Awareness of these choices enables you to argue more constructively. More importantly, the Everyday Life Examples show how you can use the guidelines here to change the culture of debate in your everyday life, to make it less combative and angry, and to ensure all participants are treated like people rather than objects.

Application Exercises

Identifying Ethics & Argument Stances: Read two other CMV debates (one with a delta and one without) at https://www.reddit.com/r/-changemyview/. What ethical concerns, if any, do the debates raise? What argument stances do the OPs seem to assume? The respondents? How do you know?

Promoting Cooperative Stances: Read one of the transcripts from the 2016 presidential debates between Hillary Clinton and Donald Trump (available through the American Presidency Project, http://www.presidency.ucsb.edu/debates.php) and consider the following prompts:

- Identify where each candidate uses the various stances (competitive, manipulative, and cooperative) and determine which is most common. *Hint: The most common stance for one candidate might differ from that for the other.*

- Evaluate each candidate's choice of stance, considering the debate context, the nature of the audience, and the co-arguer's stance.

- For instances of a competitive or manipulative stance, consider how (if at all) you could revise the argumentation to be more cooperative.

Key Terms

Argumentation Ethics 47
Argumentation Stance 47

Competitive Stance 56
Manipulative Stance 57

Cooperative Stance 58

Endnotes

1. Jon Stewart, "CNN Crossfire: Jon Stewart's America," *CNN Transcripts*, October 15, 2004, http://transcripts.cnn.com/TRANSCRIPTS/0410/15/cf.01.html.

2. Bill Carter, "CNN Will Cancel 'Crossfire' and Cut Ties to Commentator," *New York Times*, January 6, 2005, http://www.nytimes.com/2005/01/06/business/media/cnn-will-cancel-crossfire-and-cut-ties-to-commentator.html.

3. Wayne Brockriede, "Arguers as Lovers," *Philosophy and Rhetoric* 5 (1972): 2.

4. Commission on Presidential Debates, "Commission on Presidential Debates Announces Format for 2016 General Election Debates," http://www.debates.org/index.php?mact=News,cntnt01,detail,0&cntnt01articleid=60&cntnt01origid=93&cntnt01detailtemplate=newspage&cntnt01returnid=80; Commission on Presidential Debates, "U.S. 2004 Debate Rules," http://www.debatesinternational.org/sites/default/files/CPD-Debate-Rules-2004.pdf.

5. Zoran Stanojević, et al., "Media Release: Debate Format and Rules," April 17, 2012, http://www.debatesinternational.org/sites/default/files/RTS-CeSID-Debate-Format-and-Rules-2012.pdf; Nigerian Elections Debates Group, "2011 Presidential Debate Format & Rules," http://www.debatesinternational.org/sites/default/files/NEDG-Presidential-Debate-Format-and-Rules-2011.pdf.

6. Argentina Debate, "Argentina Debate 2015; Segunda Vuelta: El Debate," http://www.debatesinternational.org/sites/default/files/Manual-de-Estilo-2da-vuelta-20151104-incluye-resultado-sorteo.pdf.

7. Donald J. Trump, "The President's News Conference," February 16, 2017, DCPD No. DCPD201700125, in *Daily Compilation of Presidential Documents*, p. 1.

8. Lauren Carroll, "Fact-Checking Donald Trump's Feb. 16 Press Conference," *Politifact*, February 16, 2017, http://www.politifact.com/truth-o-meter/article/2017/feb/16/fact-checking-donald-trumps-press-conference.

9. J. Vernon Jensen, "Values and Practices in Asian Argumentation," *Argumentation and Advocacy* 28 (1992): 153-167; Narahiko Inoue, "Traditions of 'Debate' in Japan," in *Bulletin of the Graduate School of Social and Cultural Studies*, Kyushu University, vol. 2 (1996), 149-161, rev. 1998, http://www.flc.kyushu-u.ac.jp/~inouen/deb-trad.html.

10. Dan Bilefsky, "Denmark is Unlikely Front in the Islam-West Culture War," *New York Times*, January 8, 2006, http://www.nytimes.com/2006/01/08/world/europe/denmark-is-unlikely-front-in-islamwest-culture-war.html.

11. George W. Bush and John Kerry, "September 30, 2004 Debate Transcript: The First Bush-Kerry Presidential Debate," *Commission on Presidential Debates*, September 30, 2004,

http://www.debates.org/index.php?page=september-30-2004-debate-transcript.

12. Angus Harrison, "The Five Stages of Getting Publicly Shamed on the Internet," *VICE*, September 6, 2017, https://www.vice.com/en_us/article/vbba43/the-five-stages-of-getting-publicly-shamed-on-the-internet.

13. Raymond Hernandez, "Stalling of Storm Aid Makes Northeast Republicans Furious," *New York Times*, January 2, 2013.

14. Chris Christie, "Governor Christie on Hurricane Sandy Federal Funding," *C-SPAN* video, January 2, 2013, http://www.c-span.org/video/?310184-1/governor-christie-hurricane-sandy-federal-funding.

15. Ashley Killough, "Rand Paul: Christie Threw a 'Tantrum,'" *CNN*, January 18, 2013, http://politicalticker.blogs.cnn.com/2013/01/18/rand-paul-christie-threw-a-tantrum; Jim Rutenberg, "Divisions in G.O.P. Are Laid Bare on First Day of Conservative Conference," *New York Times*, March 15, 2013, http://www.nytimes.com/2013/03/15/us/politics/republican-divisions-are-laid-bare-on-first-day-of-cpac.html.

16. Chris Christie, quoted in Halbfinger, "With Storm Response, Christie Earns Scorn, Praise and Much Attention."

17. Adria Richards, quoted in Jon Ronson, "'Overnight, Everything I Loved Was Gone': The Internet Shaming of Lindsey Stone," *The Guardian* (UK), February 21, 2015, https://www.theguardian.com/technology/2015/feb/21/internet-shaming-lindsey-stone-jon-ronson.

18. Adria Richards, Twitter Post, March 17, 2013, 3:32 p.m., https://twitter.com/adriarichards/status/313417655879102464/photo/1.

19. Adria Richards, Twitter Post, March 17, 2013, 3:34 p.m., https://twitter.com/adriarichards/status/313418201641922560.

20. Adria Richards, Twitter Post, March 17, 2013, 3:40 p.m., https://twitter.com/adriarichards/status/313419704226168832.

21. mr-hank, "Inappropriate Comments at Pycon 2013 Called Out," *Hacker News*, March 19, 2013, https://news.ycombinator.com/item?id=5398681.

22. Adria Richards, quoted in Ronson, "'Overnight, Everything I Loved Was Gone.'"

23. Deborah Tannen, *The Argument Culture: Moving From Debate to Dialogue* (New York: Random House, 1998), 3.

24. David Zarefsky, "Spectator Politics and the Revival of Public Argument," *Communication Monographs* 59 (1992): 412.

25. Brockriede, "Arguers as Lovers," 5.

26. Harry G. Frankfurt, *On Bullshit* (Princeton, NJ: Princeton University Press, 2005), 34.

27. Richard Williford, "Fine Print on Wheels," *Consumers' Research Magazine* 73 (September 1990): 16. For more on fine print in advertising, see: Richard H. Kolbe and Darrel D. Muehling, "A Content Analysis of the 'Fine Print' in Television Advertising," *Journal of Current Issues and Research in Advertising* 14.2 (1992): 47-61.

28. Josina Makau and Debian Marty, *Cooperative Argumentation: A Model for Deliberative Community* (Prospect Heights, IL: Waveland Press, 2001), 87.

29. Susan Zaeske, "Signatures of Citizenship: The Rhetoric of Women's Antislavery Petitions," *Quarterly Journal of Speech* 88 (2002): 147-168.

30. Brockriede, "Arguers as Lovers," 7.

31. "What is /r/changemyview?," *Change My View*, Reddit, https://www.reddit.com/r/changemyview/wiki/index.

32. "Submission Rules: Rule B," *Change My View*, Reddit, https://www.reddit.com/r/changemyview/wiki/rules#wiki_rule_b.

33. "Comment Rules," *Change My View*, Reddit, https://www.reddit.com/r/changemyview/wiki/rules#wiki_comment_rules.

34. Zzzmessi1 and Ghost_of_John_Galt, "CMV: Sports Should Not Have a Place in American Universities," *Change My View*, Reddit, May 20 2017, https://www.reddit.com/r/changemyview/comments/6ccukh/cmv_sports_should_not_have_a_place_in_american.

35. [deleted], "CMV: Sports Should Not Have a Place in American Universities," *Change My View*, Reddit, May 20 2017, https://www.reddit.com/r/changemyview/comments/6ccukh/cmv_sports_should_not_have_a_place_in_american.

36. Chenhao Tan et al., "Winning Arguments: Interaction Dynamics and Persuasion Strategies in Good-faith Online Discussions," in *WWW '16: Proceedings of the 25th International Conference on World Wide Web* (Geneva: International World Wide Web Conferences Steering Committee, 2016), 613-624, https://arxiv.org/pdf/1602.01103v2.pdf.

CONSTRUCTING
ARGUMENTS

PART II

4

UNDERSTANDING ARGUMENT STRUCTURES

In the opening scene to the pilot episode of the hit sitcom *The Big Bang Theory,* one of the main characters, Sheldon Cooper, describes to his friend Leonard Hofstadter how a photon operates when observed compared to when it is not observed. Leonard replies, "Agreed, what's your point?" To this, Sheldon comments just that it would be a good message to put on a shirt.[1]

Perhaps you can identify with Leonard in some of your everyday conversations: someone makes a statement that you incorrectly perceive as argumentative (as having a foundation with which you agree and building up to a claim, or point). Indeed, this brief exchange emphasizes the difficulty of discerning argumentation in everyday life. Leonard's perception was likely based on his prior experience in which people who explain something are trying to establish a claim. And yet, Leonard's need for clarification also reveals how people don't always argue in clear patterns or structures. Audience members are often left guessing at both the argumentative intent and content. In fact, sometimes what we perceive to be arguments may be non-argumentative.

Arguers and audience members often face the challenging task of translating content from various prose formats into understandable patterns that map onto the debate situation. Because one sign of an effective arguer is the ability to easily comprehend the stated *and* unstated messages and mentally organize the arguments and issues, this chapter provides strategies you can use to make sense of complex and messy arguments.

We will first address the distinction between formal logic and everyday argumentation to set the stage. Then, we'll turn to the role of perception in identifying arguments, particularly as it relates to when we might expect them. When faced with arguments, we will consider three strategies you can use to decode them: argument cues, supplying implied statements, and diagramming. The goal of this chapter is to give you a stronger ability to analyze arguments within a debate situation. By the end of this chapter, you should be able to distinguish formal and informal logic and be able to dissect argument structures for their stated and unstated components.

FORMAL LOGIC VS. EVERYDAY ARGUMENTATION

FORMAL LOGIC:
The study of argument forms for validity

The challenge of discerning arguments relies on an important distinction between our study of everyday argumentation and the study of formal logic. Formal logic explores argumentative claims as they relate to the form, or structure, of the supporting premises and it addresses these structures through abstract and analytical models that function independent of specific "real world" content. As such, formal logic assesses the validity rather than soundness or cogency of arguments.[2]

For example, formal logic might involve the following deductive syllogism in abstract form:

All A are B

All B are C

Therefore, all A are C

And, we could even substitute specific things for A, B, and C, like how Conan O'Brien, Stephen Colbert, and Jon Stewart did in 2008. During the presidential primaries, Colbert and O'Brien had a heated cross-program debate on their respective talk shows, both claiming credit for GOP candidate Mike Huckabee's success in the Iowa caucus. To win the debate, O'Brien advanced a syllogism on the January 18, 2008, episode of *Late Night with Conan O'Brien*: "If Colbert made Huckabee, and Conan made Colbert, then Conan made Huckabee."[3]

Colbert was stunned, claiming on *The Colbert Report* "that logic is ironclad. I mean, I live by syllogisms: For instance, God is love. Love is blind. Stevie Wonder is blind. Therefore, Stevie Wonder is God. I don't know what I'd believe in if it wasn't for that."[4] Because Colbert approached the syllogism from the vantage point of validity—a test of whether the conclusion is correct based solely on the premises—he was about to concede the claim. Stewart, however, came to the rescue, asking Colbert: "Who . . . made Conan O'Brien?"[5] Stewart, providing a VHS recording of Conan O'Brien's appearance on his MTV show, *The Jon Stewart Show*, argued: "Colbert made Huckabee. Conan made Colbert. Jon Stewart made Conan. Jon Stewart made Huckabee!"[6]

This entertaining exchange shows how the detached framework of formal logic overlooks whether the premises are "true" for the audience and context as well as considerations outside of the premises. Argument scholar Stephen Toulmin explained that because formal logic is often mathematical and/or scientific, "we must sweep away all references to thinking and rationality and the rest."[7] In this example, Stewart emphasized how formal logic did not readily offer a place to consider who made Conan O'Brien, which fundamentally changed the argument. Additionally, assessing the logic's validity overlooks whether O'Brien did, indeed, make Colbert or whether Stewart did, indeed, make O'Brien.

Beyond formal logic's impersonal nature, it is also largely impractical. That is, most people don't think in formal logic structures nor do they take the time to apply tests that determine an argument's validity. This is not to say that a focus on argument patterns is useless. Indeed, there are recurring argument models and structures that budding arguers benefit from learning, which is why later chapters are dedicated to this exploration. Rather, the study of everyday argumentation addresses how people utilize argument forms to create meaning in concrete contexts and for concrete audiences.

STRATEGIES FOR IDENTIFYING ARGUMENTS

As you read the above examples from *The Big Bang Theory* or the talk show hosts, perhaps you considered the role of perception in identifying arguments: Who decides what "counts" as an argument? How do you know if someone is advancing an argument? What gives Stewart the authority to say that Colbert's interpretation of O'Brien's argument is incomplete? This section offers some guidance in answering these questions.

Since arguments are constructed in thoughts or in spoken and written communication, an argument theoretically exists to the extent that someone *perceives* a claim advanced by support. Suppose you assert the following as a truth rather than an argument: "I'm glad I ordered the burger. It was delicious!" Even though you don't intend it to be controversial, your friend may perceive it as an argument. It even meets the minimum requirements: a claim ("I'm glad I ordered the burger") advanced by support (because "it was delicious"). Your friend might refute your argument by stating something like, "the salad was also delicious and it was a lot healthier." Despite your intentions, a debate situation may now exist based on your friend's perception of an argument.

Someone may even perceive a hypothetical argument in the absence of a claim or support by imagining both parts. For example, the TV program *Seinfeld* contributed the phrase, "not that there's anything wrong with that," because of this potential. In one episode, Jerry Seinfeld repeatedly denied being gay but added the phrase "not that there's anything wrong with that" to avoid someone perceiving his denials as advancing a claim against homosexuality.[8] To help your own perception, consider the Find Your Voice prompt.

FIND YOUR VOICE
PERCEIVING ARGUMENTS

What's the best way to respond when someone perceives you advancing an unintended argument? How *have* you responded? Here's a tip: Use a cooperative stance by considering that person's perspective and being open to the conversation. Ask a question in return or offer to support your claims. You may learn something along the way.

The above examples illustrate situations in which communication *appears* argumentative without the intent or form of an argument. To further explore the role of perception, consider whether or not you perceive the following messages as arguments:

- A president's executive order describing a new policy, such as an immigration ban.

- A memo from a company's financial officer announcing that the company is instituting layoffs to save money.

- An advertisement selling a product through visual imagery and slogans that tug at your emotions.

- A political cartoon poking fun at a politician's statement.

- A football player kneeling during a patriotic ritual.

- A chorus to a number one hit song, such as "I'm falling so I'm taking my time on my ride."[9]

Unfortunately, there's not a "correct" answer as to whether any of the above messages rightfully constitute arguments. Argument scholar Wayne Brockriede has noted that because "human activity does not usefully constitute an argument until some person perceives what is happening as an argument," argumentation is not an objective thing but rather "a frame of reference that can be related potentially to any kind of human endeavor."[10] This means we could approach each of the above scenarios from the framework of argumentation and, in so doing, we could likely find claims and/or support to engage. However, depending on the context and your own intentions, it may be more valuable to approach the scenarios as description (the executive order and the memo), persuasion (the advertisement), opinion (the political cartoon), statement (the kneel), and metaphor or allegory (the hit song) rather than as argument.

On the flip side, it's also possible for arguments to masquerade as non-argumentative. News reporting is a prime example. Let's contrast how *The New York Times* and *Washington Post* covered the numerous campus protests that occurred in late 2015 at Yale, Princeton, the University of Missouri, the University of Oklahoma, the University of Michigan, and others. On November 10, 2015, both papers published a news article—not an opinion piece or editorial—on the controversy but their first sentences offered different interpretations:

"Instances of racism and bigotry have ignited protests at colleges across the United States, and social media has amplified students' messages far beyond campus."[11]

"College campuses across the country have plunged into an intense debate that pits free-speech advocates against those who want to rein in insults, slurs and other offensive expressions."[12]

The first example, from *The New York Times*, emphasized the cause of the protests and framed them as a natural and justified response to racism and bigotry. The *Washington Post*, on the other hand, situated the protests as controversial, representing

BOX 4.1: QUESTIONS FOR IDENTIFYING ARGUMENTS

1. **Is there argumentative intent: goal and stance?** The best way to determine if something is an argument is to ask the would-be arguer. Even amateur arguers can tell you if they were intending to argue. If you are unable or unwilling to ask the arguer directly, use the message itself or the stance of the arguer to determine intent.

2. **Is there argumentative content: claim and support?** If you cannot determine intent, then consider content. Recall that both a claim and support are required, even though they don't need to be *good*—the support might just be "that's how I feel." The cues discussed in the next section can help you track down these pieces. If you can't find them, you might be dealing with something other than argument.

3. **Is there argumentative dispute: controversy?** A message may have both a claim and support but it may not be an argument if there's no dispute or disagreement. For example, the statement "when I drink too much caffeinated coffee, I get jittery" has the hallmarks of an argument but it isn't likely an argument. We expect arguments when we are dealing with disputable or uncertain claims.

4. **Is there argumentative context: spheres and audiences?** Finally, consider if the sphere or form of communication has a proclivity for argumentation. For instance, you probably expect arguments when reading an editorial or blog post but not when reading a news story. You probably expect arguments when having a class discussion about privacy rights in an online context today but not when listening to a professor's lecture about the history of the Fourth Amendment to the U.S. Constitution.

just one side of "an intense debate." These articles appear to be news reports that objectively describe the situation on college campuses but perhaps we should consider them as arguments instead.

Ultimately, those involved in the communicative exchange must decide what counts as an argument but you should be equipped to make the choice in an educated fashion that allows for productive engagement. Box 4.1 offers a set of questions that may help you distinguish arguments from other kinds of communication. This also requires you to recognize that debate situations are not in the complete control of the arguer but rather exist when others perceive an argument and respond with their own. The questions and the strategies in the remainder of this chapter are useful tools as both a communicator and audience member.

STRATEGIES FOR UNDERSTANDING ARGUMENTS

Once you determine that there is indeed an argument, you then need to make sense of it. Because this task can be equally difficult, the rest of this chapter provides strategies to facilitate your interpretation of an argument's various components.

Strategy 1: Use Argument Cues

By now, you should have a firm grasp on the two required elements for an argument to exist: a claim and support. Isolating these two components is a first step in any effort to understand an argument. However, arguments come in all shapes and sizes, differing in terms of complexity, form, and content. This diversity sometimes makes it difficult to find claims and support if you don't know what you're trying to find. One strategy is to consider the verbal and structural cues built into the argument or case.

When people communicate argumentatively, they tend to use words or phrases that indicate the relationships between claims and support. These are called **argument cues** because they should cue our brain that we're dealing with an argument and they also help signal how claims, support, warrants, or rebuttals are related to one another. Arguments and cases also tend to follow somewhat predictable patterns that we'll explore more fully in Chapters 6 and 7.

To practice, we'll use Twenty-One Pilots' hit song "Ride" alluded to earlier in the chapter. You're likely familiar with the song given that it reached number 1 on the Billboard Mainstream Top 40 chart in 2016 and it, along with "Heathens," put Twenty One Pilots in the same company as the Beatles and Elvis Presley as the only rock artists in history to have two songs simultaneously in the top 5 of the Billboard Hot 100 chart.[13] However, you may not have ever reflected on whether the song is argumentative so let's do that now. What words might cue us to an argument in the chorus:

> "Oh, I'm falling so I'm taking my time on my ride"[14]

You hopefully discerned "so" to be an argument cue that identifies the relationship between claim and support. When used argumentatively, "so" is often synonymous with "therefore" and signals that the statement prior to it is the support for the subsequent claim. The argument, then, is: <u>because</u> I'm falling (support), <u>therefore</u> I'm taking my time on my ride (claim). It also makes logical sense in this order—you would likely slow down if you were falling. However, it makes less logical sense if we reverse the order: because I'm taking my time on my ride, therefore I'm falling. This is one example of how argument cues help us make sense of an argument's progression.

To better facilitate your awareness of verbal cues, Table 4.1 identifies relationships generally indicated by various words or phrases within an argument. Being attuned to these cues can help you more easily parse argument structures.

Whereas the chorus to "Ride" has a single support for a single claim, we can also use cues to make sense of more complex arguments and cases. For instance, let's revisit part

ARGUMENT CUE: A verbal or structural indicator of the relationship between two or more statements in an argument

TABLE 4.1 ■ Common Verbal Cues of Argument Structures			
Claims	**Support**	**More Support**	**Rebuttal**
Therefore	Because	And	But
So	Since	Also	However
Consequently	As	Additionally	Conversely
Thus	For	Moreover	Although
Hence	Given that	Furthermore	Never/Nonetheless

of Zzzmessil's case against sports in U.S. colleges. As you read the excerpt, identify the cues for how the argument chain develops:

> I believe that sports in America should be similar to the club system that exists in Europe. . . . Many universities in America use sports as a way of building a brand that is based little on academics or campus life outside of sports. With the high tuition prices we have now, this level of branding, especially from public colleges, pressures students to take on large amounts of debt in order to join this sports culture.
>
> In addition, sports have diverted students' time within college to watching games and joining the parties associated with them. This can often come at the expense of academics or professional skills.[15]

Here, the proposition is "[collegiate] sports in America should be similar to the club system that exists in Europe." The excerpt includes two main sub-claims or reasons this is true: "[collegiate sport] branding, especially from public colleges, pressures students to take on large amounts of debt in order to join this sports culture" and collegiate sports culture "can often come at the expense of academics or professional skills." We know this because, structurally, each of these ideas has a separate paragraph under the proposition and, verbally, Zzzmessil uses the phrase "in addition" to transition from one point to the next. Thus, each statement offers an independent reason for the overall proposition; we could conclude collegiate sports should follow Europe's model either from the current debt system or from the distractions but both together strengthen the claim. In Chapter 2, we labeled this *convergent* support because the support functions separately but converges to bolster the claim.

Of course, true to everyday argument, this argument is more complex than just the proposition and two sub-claims given that each sub-claim has support for it as well. We'll consider in more depth the first sub-argument, on the claim that "[collegiate sport] branding, especially from public colleges, pressures students to take on large amounts of debt in order to join this sports culture." Zzzmessil provides two supporting statements for this claim: "many universities in America use sports as a way of building a brand that is based little on academics or campus life outside of sports" and "the high tuition prices we have now." We know that these are both supporting statements because Zzzmessil used the word "with" to indicate they go together. Thus, the claim here is based on *linked* supported which, you may recall from Chapter 2, means you cannot demonstrate the claim with only one of the supporting statements. The Build Your Skill feature offers additional opportunity to identify argument cues and isolate argument chains.

The three Build Your Skill arguments feature the proposition in two different locations: the middle for Gehrig and Streep and the end for Obama. We know this by attending to the verbal cues, such as the words "yet," "and," and "so," that indicate relationships as well as to the structural cues signaled by the placement of support in relation to those claims. For instance, we know the final line of Gehrig's argument is support for the middle line because it makes logical sense that he is the luckiest man on Earth *because* of the fans, not that the kindness and encouragement of the fans are *because* he is the luckiest man on Earth. Playing around with the ideas helps us make sense of the sequence of statements.

BUILD YOUR SKILL
USING ARGUMENT CUES

In each of the following examples, use the argument cues to identify the relationships between the various statements:

A. **Lou Gehrig, Farewell, July 4, 1939:** "Fans, for the past two weeks you have been reading about the bad break I got. Yet today I consider myself the luckiest man on the face of this earth. I have been in ballparks for seventeen years and have never received anything but kindness and encouragement from you fans."[16]

B. **Barack Obama, Remarks on the Situation in Syria, August 31, 2013:** "Our military has positioned assets in the region. The Chairman of the Joint Chiefs has informed me that we are prepared to strike whenever we choose. Moreover, the Chairman has indicated to me that our capacity to execute this mission is not time-sensitive; it will be effective tomorrow, or next week, or one month from now. And I'm prepared to give that order. But having made my decision as Commander-in-Chief based on what I am convinced is our national security interests, I'm also mindful that I'm the President of the world's oldest constitutional democracy. I've long believed that our power is rooted not just in our military might, but in our example as a government of the people, by the people, and for the people. And that's why I've made a second decision: I will seek authorization for the use of force from the American people's representatives in Congress."[17]

C. **Meryl Streep, Golden Globe Acceptance Speech, January 7, 2017:** "We need the principled press, to hold power to account, to call them on the carpet for every outrage. That's why our founders enshrined the press and its freedoms in our constitution. So I only asked the famously well-heeled Hollywood Foreign Press and all of us in our community to join me in supporting the Committee to Protect Journalists, because we're gonna need them going forward, and they'll need us to safeguard the truth."[18]

Nevertheless, using cues to interpret arguments is more art than science. The interpretations of Zzzmessil's post or Gehrig's speech are each just one possibility since, as noted earlier, arguments rely on perception. The interpretations were constructed through logic and inference provided by the argument cues but it's plausible that you perceive a slightly different structure.

Does this mean that anything goes when interpreting arguments? The short answer is no. There are wrong or bad perceptions of arguments so keep the following guidelines in mind as you use argument cues:

- **Take time:** Sometimes we make honest mistakes when we (mis)interpret arguments. And sometimes we are just too lazy or hasty, as evident by the cultural slang "tl;dr" (or "too long; didn't read"). Critical thinking often mandates that we pause and reflect on the content rather than quickly filtering the message through our own preexisting mental schema.

- **Check yourself:** We sometimes make assumptions and let our own biases and beliefs get in the way of our reasoned judgment. This might be why we perceive things differently than they are. For instance, someone who is self-conscious about his or her income may perceive someone else's mundane comment about an extravagant vacation to be an argumentative insult. To help prevent this, you should be conscious of your biases and filters and try to set them aside.

- **Be charitable but fair:** In our quest for critical thinking excellence, it's natural to want to "find" logical arguments. Unfortunately, people don't always make logical arguments. In fact, some people are *really bad* at arguing. In those cases, be charitable by considering the other person's perspective but do not do the heavy logical lifting for him or her. Resist the temptation to make sense of the ideas if, quite frankly, they don't make sense.

These guidelines can help you effectively use cues to interpret arguments you encounter in your everyday life. Just identifying claims and support, however, is not enough to fully understand the argument; it also requires filling in unspoken ideas.

Strategy 2: Supply Implied Statements

Identifying the claims and support of an argument is like digging up a skeleton; you've found the bare bones of the argument but are missing the vital organs that make it function as a dynamic, living object. We'll discuss two such "vital organs" here: the warrant and unstated assumptions. Most warrants and assumptions, much like human organs, go unseen despite us knowing they're there lurking beneath the surface.

An argument can't function without its warrant because, like human organs, the warrant gives an argument the necessary energy to move from support to claim. Recall from the Toulmin model of an argument discussed in Chapter 2 that the warrant is the inferential statement authorizing the claim on the basis of the provided support. Despite the importance of warrants, they are often tricky to pinpoint because we aren't used to exposing them.

Unstated assumptions comprise another vital organ of an argument. By assumptions, we mean the biases and beliefs that underlie and fuel the stated ideas of the argument. Like claims, assumptions can be about facts, values, or policies. Unstated assumptions often reveal an arguer's values and **ideology**, or set of beliefs that order the worldview of a person or group. For example, the *New York Times* article mentioned earlier promoted an ideology about the democratic value of protests that differed from the ideology promoted in the *Washington Post* article even though neither made explicit claim to these views. Thus, exposing assumptions facilitates your understanding of the content and may clue you to why others utilize the support and claims they do. In some cases, assumptions are necessary for the argument to even make sense in context. Identifying assumptions ultimately helps you better engage others' arguments.

Let's look at an example to help distinguish between warrants and assumptions. Imagine a mother says the following to her single daughter in her early thirties: "You should really find a husband soon since your biological clock is ticking." The claim is

UNSTATED ASSUMPTION: An idea or belief implied by the stated elements of an argument

IDEOLOGY: A set of beliefs that order the worldview of a person or group

"you should find a husband soon" and the support is "your biological clock is ticking." Decipher the warrant that connects the support to the claim: Why might a woman's biological clock ticking mean she should find a husband? The warrant is likely something along the lines of "women can't bear children after a certain age." Mapped onto the Toulmin model, the argument would read, "Because your biological clock is ticking, and since women can't bear children after a certain age, you should really find a husband soon." See how the warrant is implied rather than stated? You may have even mentally filled this gap yourself but stating it explicitly helps us better comprehend the argument's movement from support to claim.

We've identified the argument's warrant but now take a moment to consider the assumptions or beliefs on which the mother's argument depend. Some of the argument's assumptions are innocuous, such as supposing the daughter understands the English language. Other assumptions might be more controversial: the daughter is heterosexual and desires a male partner; the daughter is fertile and currently able to bear children (and that her eventual husband will also be fertile); the daughter is willing to get married; the daughter is willing to bear children; and that marriage should precede children. Even though the mother doesn't make any explicit claim to these assumptions and even though they are not necessary to justify the claim based on the support, they operate beneath the surface of the argument and contribute to its meaning. Put another way, these assumptions are part and parcel of the debate about whether the daughter should find a husband soon.

Implied warrants and assumptions become even more important in everyday life when people argue without clear claims and support. For instance, passive aggressive statements may disguise their argumentative intent by appearing to be an opinion or personal belief. In some cases, such statements may even be the opposite of what the person really means. You've probably interacted with people who say "whatever" or "I didn't care anyway" when they don't get what they want. Statements like these say one thing on the surface but, underneath, imply a very different claim.[19] Similarly, people might use backhanded compliments and off-color humor as forms of implied argumentation or, worse, a competitive or manipulative stance. In these cases, you should also try to supply the argumentative ideas implied by the messages and consider how best to respond based on your interpretation.

Here are some strategies for exposing these implied statements:

- **Ask "why":** You can probe an argument more fully if you keep asking why, much like an impetuous child might do. When someone makes a claim, ask why once to determine the support. When someone offers support, ask why again to determine the warrant and/or assumptions. When someone offers a warrant, ask why again to determine the backing. The more you ask and answer why, the stronger you'll understand how the stated and unstated ideas fit together.

- **Take perspectives:** Taking different people's perspectives can be especially helpful at exposing unstated assumptions. After all, many of our assumptions are based on how we understand the world. With the example above, it would be understandable if readers who are heterosexual and fertile did not immediately recognize the mother's assumptions that the daughter is both of those. However, asking yourself how a woman who is homosexual or infertile would interpret this argument, you are better able to perceive the assumptions at play.

- **Play around:** Another strategy to expose implicit statements is to test ideas. Especially for determining warrants, you might try out a few different options to see which makes the most logical sense given the stated elements of the argument. Even advanced arguers have occasional difficulty identifying warrants so you shouldn't expect to figure it out on the first try. Chapter 6 will identify some common argumentation patterns to facilitate your ability to plug and play warrants.

- **Gather information:** When all else fails, a final strategy to better understand the argument is to gather more information. Researching the topic might help you uncover assumptions. Asking an arguer his or her intentions might reveal the warrant. Considering how others have used similar arguments in the past might reveal both assumptions and warrants. The more you know, the stronger your command over an argument's meaning.

So let's use this process of identifying the warrant in our Twenty One Pilots argument: because I'm falling, therefore I'm taking my time on my ride. First, ask why: Why would someone take their time on their ride if they're falling? We might initially arrive at a statement along of lines of: "falling is dangerous." This is understandable and a true statement but, if we plug into the argument, we discover it is wrong as the warrant; the warrant must justify taking my time on my ride (claim) by connecting it to falling (support) but the warrant "falling is dangerous" doesn't have anything to do with taking one's time. So we might play with a few more ideas before arriving at the following warrant: "hastiness increases the chances of falling." When plugged into the argument, it would read as follows: "I'm falling. Since hastiness increases the chances of falling, therefore I'm taking my time on my ride." This makes more logical sense as a warrant than "falling is dangerous" (to find the argument's backing, you could ask why again: Why does hastiness increase the chances of falling?).

Now suppose you interpret the song as informal rather than formal logic and interpret the lyrics metaphorically rather than literally. What if the author isn't talking about falling in a physical sense? This thought might lead you to gather more information about the argument in the song. Chances are you don't have access to the songwriter, Tyler Joseph, to ask him what he intended. So you go to the next best option: the SongMeanings website, where people can post their interpretations of the lyrics.[20]

One common explanation on the site is that the song is about depression and possibly even suicidal thinking: because I'm descending into depression (falling), I'm choosing to savor life (taking time on my ride). This interpretation is bolstered by some of the other song lyrics, such as "Yeah, I think about the end just way too much; But it's fun to fantasize," "I'd live for you; And that's hard to do; Even harder to say; When you know it's not true," and "I've been thinking too much; Help me."[21]

BUILD YOUR SKILL
UNSTATED WARRANTS & ASSUMPTIONS

For each of the following arguments, identify the warrant and at least two unstated assumptions:

A. An assault rifle ban in the United States is unconstitutional because the Second Amendment gives us the right to own guns.

B. My success is only by the grace of God.

C. Your significant other lied to you in the past when he didn't tell you he was out partying. What makes you think he won't do it again?

What then might be the warrant here? Why would you choose to savor life if you're descending into depression? To figure out the warrant, you might need to do some perspective taking of those who experience depression. The warrant might be what user Moonbeam86, who admitted seeking help for suicidal thoughts, suggested: "the way to stay alive is to let go of that need to control—particularly that need to control the end of your life—let go of it and give control to a higher power. . . . TAKE YOUR TIME."[22] The meaning we've arrived at here is a bit different than the literal interpretation but the structure is the same: "Because I'm descending into depression, and since the way to stay alive is to let go of the need to control the end of your life, therefore I'm savoring life."

You can use the Build Your Skill feature to give you more practice with identifying implied statements. Nevertheless, as with isolating claims and support, supplying unstated warrants and assumptions is not about finding a right answer but about facilitating understanding through critical thinking and judgment. It's possible you might interpret someone's argument differently than he or she intended. This just means your interpretation becomes a part of the debate itself, enabling you to correct misinformation and provide clarity.

So far, our strategies for finding claims, support, warrants, and assumptions have worked with relatively short argumentative examples. As claims and support start to mount, however, it can become even more daunting to isolate the parts of an argument. Consequently, diagramming is a third and final strategy people can use to make sense of arguments.

Strategy 3: Diagram Arguments

ARGUMENT DIAGRAM: A graphic representation of the sequence of argumentative statements from support(s) to claim(s)

In many situations, from the classroom to the workplace to conversations with friends, we hear an argument and must comprehend it immediately in order to respond. Since the quality of our response to the argument will depend on how well we understand it, using argument cues and filling in implied statements can work fairly well in these situations. However, when we have time to digest an argument before responding, diagraming the argument facilitates understanding and helps avoid misinterpretation.

You first encountered **argument diagrams** in Chapter 2 when we used arrows and plus signs to show how support led to sub-claims which led ultimately to the proposition.

FIND YOUR VOICE
DIAGRAMMING ARGUMENTS

Consider when and why you might choose to diagram arguments. What is gained from visually representing the support-claim relationships? How does a diagram help you better participate in the controversy compared to other modes of interpreting arguments? You won't likely need to diagram every argument you encounter but doing so is helpful in some situations.

As you discovered then, diagrams visually depict relationships within complex argument structures. Basically, the diagram should take the prose format and convert it to a spatial and sequential representation of the argument chains.

The literal interpretation of the Twenty One Pilots argument is diagramed in Figure 4.1. The arrow points in the direction of the logical flow, by showing the support leading to the claim. We have signaled the warrant by adding a drop-down circle between the claim and support.

A diagram is useful for a simple argument of this sort but it becomes even more valuable when there are numerous statements that converge to form the overall case. You can signal multiple supporting statements by adding each piece of support with independent arrows leading to the claim if it is convergent support or with plus signs if it is linked support. If there is a rebuttal statement, you can indicate this with a dashed line leading to the claim or placing it next to the warrant, which you signal with a drop-down circle. You don't need to diagram unstated assumptions but you could do this with a dashed box to signal its unstated nature. Finally, issues can be diagrammed using circles on the line between claim and proposition. The single support-claim relationship can then be expanded to capture the argument chains throughout the case. Box 4.2 illustrates some of these relationships with the squares representing potential statements in an argument.

In principle, you can begin your diagram with any statement from the argument but, practically speaking, it often helps to use the following process:

1. **Listen to or read the entire case** at least once. If you're able to go through it multiple times, that's even better.

2. **Isolate the proposition**, often by using the argument cues discussed earlier. Knowing the main claim of the case will help you know the end-point of your diagram—all arrows should lead here!

FIGURE 4.1 ■ The Argument in Twenty One Pilots, "Ride"

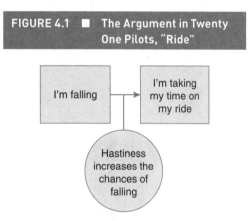

BOX 4.2: DIAGRAM MODELS

Here are some common diagram structures that you can mix and match to represent arguments you encounter in everyday life.

FIGURE 4.2 ■ Convergent Support

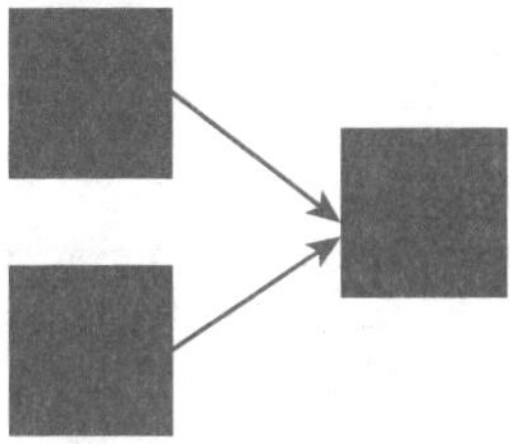

FIGURE 4.3 ■ Linked Support

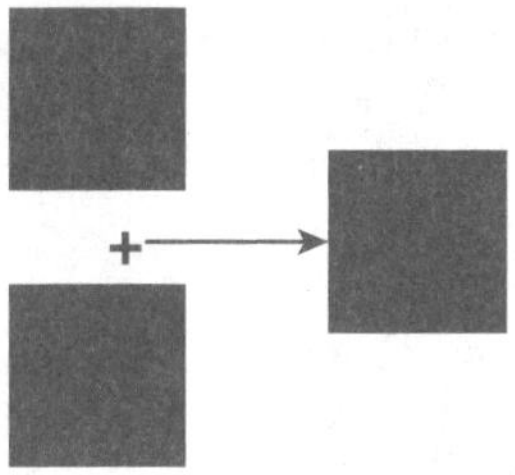

FIGURE 4.4 ■ Rebuttal Statement

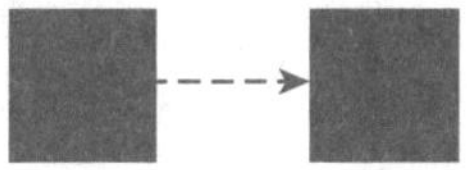

FIGURE 4.5 ■ Unstated Assumption

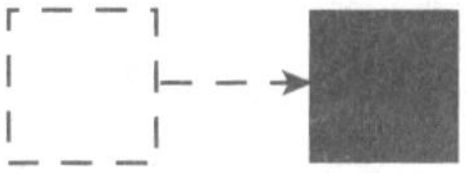

FIGURE 4.6 ■ Argument Chain

3. **Isolate the issues** for the proposition. Determining the major issues will help you determine the second-level claims (or reasons) for the proposition and provide a structure for the rest of the content. Depending on the case, this step can be difficult so be sure to use structural cues (e.g., paragraphing and section headings for written arguments; pauses and transitions for oral arguments) to guide your effort.

4. **Add in sub-claims, support, and rebuttal statements**, using plus signs and dashed lines as appropriate.

5. **Identify implied statements** such as warrants or unstated assumptions that are necessary for understanding the argument. This step is optional but can often facilitate stronger understanding of the argument.

6. **Double-check your diagram** against the original argument, making sure you haven't omitted any relevant content.

Diagramming arguments can be exciting and provide a sense of mastery, much like you feel when completing a jigsaw puzzle. But it can also be quite frustrating because, unlike a jigsaw puzzle, there's not a picture on the box that shows you how the final diagram should look. Even when following this process, it is likely that a diagram may undergo revision as you attempt to make the pieces fit and it is also likely that, on occasion, arguments may not easily lend themselves to diagrams. Box 4.3 offers some tips to help you diagram arguments. Keep in mind, though, that your perception and judgment must come into play as you find the best representation.

To provide additional application of these tools, this chapter's Everyday Life Example will consider an Instagram post on August 17, 2015, by James Harrison, linebacker for the Pittsburgh Steelers, addressing the problem of participation trophies for youth. In the wake of the post, there was a short-lived controversy about the virtue and vices of such trophies. As you read the post, you might on your own follow the process for isolating claims and support, adding in warrants and assumptions, and diagramming the argument. We'll then go through the process together.

BOX 4.3: TIPS FOR DIAGRAMMING ARGUMENTS

1. **Focus on the proposition.** The more you keep this as the focal point of your diagram and consider how the pieces converge to demonstrate it, the stronger your structure can become.

2. **Simplify and translate the prose**. You should take the prose style and strip it down to the most basic argumentative statements, eliminating non-argumentative flourishes or informational content.

3. **Test warrants as you go**. Once you identify one support-claim relationship, see if there is a viable warrant. If not, you might need to rearrange ideas in the diagram.

4. **Be true to the argument**. Your diagram should represent how the content *is* argued, not how you think it *should be*. For instance, if a support statement doesn't make logical sense to you in relation to its claim but is clearly meant as support (signaled by "because"), you should diagram it that way.

Everyday Life Example 4.1

James Harrison, Instagram Post, August 17, 2015[23]

jhharrison92

FOLLOW

13.2k likes   1d

jhharrison92 I came home to find out that
my boys received two trophies for nothing,
participation trophies! While I am very
proud of my boys for everything they do
and will encourage them till the day I die,
these trophies will be given back until they
EARN a real trophy. I'm sorry I'm not sorry
for believing that everything in life should
be earned and I'm not about to raise two
boys to be men by making them believe
that they are entitled to something just
because they tried their best...cause
sometimes your best is not enough, and
that should drive you to want to do
better...not cry and whine until somebody
gives you something to shut u up and keep
you happy. #harrisonfamilyvalues

Source: Instagram/@jhharrison92

The first step to make sense of this argument is to use argument cues to isolate the proposition, claims, and support. Reading the argument, the main point seems to be that "these trophies will be given back." Everything else in the post justifies this claim.

So how do we get there? We can break it down piece by piece. The first sentence seems largely informational rather than argumentative, telling the audience the context of his post, although it does equate "participation trophies" as "trophies for nothing." The second sentence offers the proposition alongside a rebuttal (signaled by the word "while") about his love and support. This is addressing the issue, "Does giving the trophies back mean Harrison isn't proud and supportive of his sons?" The sentence also raises the issue, "did Harrison's sons earn the trophies?" when he states that the trophies weren't earned (signaled by "until").

The next sentence is quite complex with numerous clauses. The phrase, "I'm sorry I'm not sorry," is non-argumentative and doesn't need to be included in our diagram. What matters to the argument is the statement "that everything in life should be earned," followed by his assertion that "I'm not about to raise two boys to be men by making them believe that they are entitled to something just because they tried their best." The "and" between these two statements suggests they are related ideas; the second statement helps clarify the first. There's further support for this second statement signaled by "[be]cause": "cause sometimes your best is not enough," which, in turn, "should drive you to want to do better . . . not cry and whine until somebody gives you something to shut u up and keep you happy." Each of these statements seems like it deserves a place in the overall structure of the argument. Finally, we have "#harrisonfamilyvalues," which doesn't add much to the case and could be omitted. Recognizing these various interrelations produces the complex argument diagram in Figure 4.7.

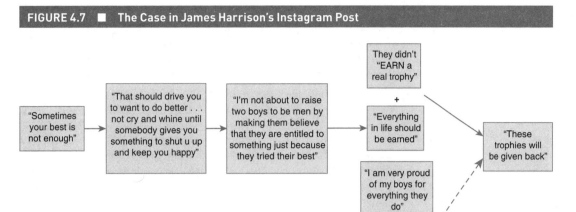

FIGURE 4.7 ■ **The Case in James Harrison's Instagram Post**

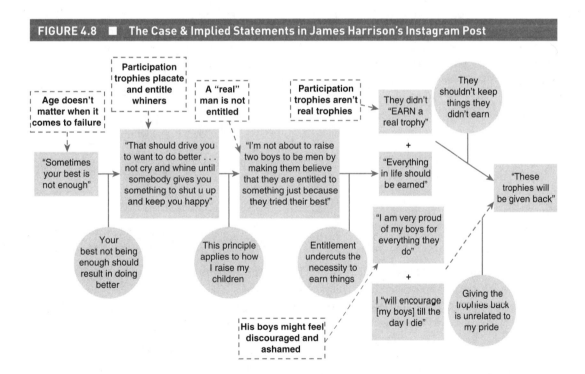

FIGURE 4.8 ■ **The Case & Implied Statements in James Harrison's Instagram Post**

Once we account for the explicit content of the argument, we can then consider the implied elements. Figure 4.8 adds warrants and assumptions. The warrants are indicated with the circles connected to each arrow in the diagram. There also are some assumptions at play, indicated by the white boxes with dashed borders. Assumptions aren't necessary to the argument's progression but they help reveal the values and ideology underlying the issues and arguments Harrison addressed. In this example, Harrison's arguments implicated beliefs concerning age (should youth be sheltered from failure?) and gender (what does it mean to be a "man"?), among others.

Identifying these assumptions also helps account for some of the controversy Harrison courted with this post. Many critiques of his proposition centered on the issue, "is there a difference between children and adults when it comes to learning lessons about entitlement?" Harrison didn't address this issue directly but his argument assumed the answer is "no," that age doesn't matter. Numerous commentators, however, argued that young children should be allowed to keep participation trophies.[24] Ultimately, then, this Everyday Life Example illustrates not only how argument cues and diagrams can help clarify complex arguments but also the importance of implied statements. Taking time to pin down the structure and fill in the gaps provides a more fulsome understanding of the case as a launching point for engagement.

Summary

Perception and interpretation play a crucial role in identifying arguments in everyday life. This chapter has provided tools to help you identify that an argument exists and make sense of its structure, recognizing that everyday argumentation (as compared to formal logic) is fluid, complex, and based on unstated ideas that have bearing on the meaning of the argument.

We've explored three possible strategies— using argument cues, supplying implied statements, and diagramming arguments—that can help you interpret argument and case structures. Cues embedded into the verbal and structural features of the argument help you isolate claims and support. Supplying implied statements such as warrants and assumptions helps you understand the deeper logic and meaning. And diagramming visualizes complex cases. The example of James Harrison's Instagram post provides a model you can use as you engage even more complex and controversial arguments in your everyday life.

Application Exercises

Identifying Warrants and Assumptions: Use a search engine to find other news articles addressing the participation trophy controversy or use the four articles on the *New York Times* "Room For Debate" discussion of this topic in October 2016: https://www.nytimes.com/roomfordebate/2016/10/06/should-every-young-athlete-get-a-trophy. For each article, identify the implied warrants and assumptions operating beneath the surface of the arguments.

Creating Argument Diagrams: Practice interpreting and diagramming arguments on the two arguments below and then check your work against diagrams in Appendix II:

A. **Susan B. Anthony, Woman's Rights to the Suffrage, 1873:** "The only question left to be settled now is: Are women persons? And I hardly believe any of our opponents will have the hardihood to say they are not. Being persons, then, women are citizens; and no State has a right to make any law, or to enforce any old law, that shall abridge their privileges or immunities. Hence, every discrimination against women in the constitutions and laws of the several States is today null and void, precisely as in every one against negroes."[25]

B. **American Psychological Association, "Violent Video Games Can Increase Aggression,"** **April 23, 2000**: "Playing violent video games like Doom, Wolfenstein 3D, or Mortal Kombat can increase a person's aggressive thoughts, feelings and behavior both in laboratory settings and in actual life, according to two studies appearing in the April issue of the American Psychological Association's *Journal of Personality and Social Psychology*. Furthermore, violent video games may be more harmful than violent television and movies because they are interactive, very engrossing and require the player to identify with the aggressor, say the researchers."[26]

Key Terms

Formal Logic 72	Convergent Support 77	Argument Diagram 82
Argument Cue 76	Unstated Assumption 79	
Linked Support 77	Ideology 79	

Endnotes

1. "Pilot Episode," Season 1, Episode 1, *The Big Bang Theory*, directed by James Burrows (2007; Burbank, CA: Warner Home Video, 2008), DVD.

2. Jeremy Barris, "The Foundation in Truth of Rhetoric and Formal Logic," *Philosophy & Rhetoric* 29 (1996): 315.

3. Conan O'Brien, "Jon Settles Colbert-Conan Feud," *The Colbert Report*, January 29, 2008, http://www.cc.com/video-clips/ncskup/the-colbert-report-jon-settles-colbert-conan-feud.

4. Stephen Colbert, "Jon Settles Colbert-Conan Feud," *The Colbert Report*, January 29, 2008, http://www.cc.com/video-clips/ncskup/the-colbert-report-jon-settles-colbert-conan-feud.

5. Jon Stewart, "Jon Settles Colbert-Conan Feud," *The Colbert Report*, January 29, 2008, http://www.cc.com/video-clips/ncskup/the-colbert-report-jon-settles-colbert-conan-feud.

6. Stewart, "Jon Settles Colbert-Conan Feud."

7. Stephen Toulmin, *The Uses of Argument*, updated ed. (New York: Cambridge University Press, 2003), 6.

8. Silpa Kovvali, "Not That There's Anything Wrong With That," *New Republic*, June 30, 2015, https://newrepublic.com/article/122211/not-theres-anything-wrong.

9. Twenty One Pilots, "Twenty One Pilots: Ride Lyrics," Lyrically: LyricWikia, http://lyrics.wikia.com/wiki/Twenty_One_Pilots:Ride. "Ride" words and music by Tyler Joseph. © 2015 Warner-Tamerlane Publishing Corp., fueled by Music and Stryker Joseph Music. All rights administered by Warner-Tamerlane Publishing Corp. All rights reserved. Used by permission of Alfred Music.

10. Wayne Brockriede, "Where Is Argument?" in *Perspectives on Argumentation*, ed. Robert

Trapp and Janice Scheutz (Prospect Heights, IL: Waveland Press, 1990), 4, 5.

11. "Racial Tensions and Protests on Campuses Across the Country," *The New York Times*, November 10, 2015, https://www.nytimes.com/2015/11/11/us/racial-tension-and-protests-on-campuses-across-the-country.html.

12. Nick Anderson and Susan Svrluga, "Can Colleges Protect Free Speech While Also Curbing Voices of Hate?" *Washington Post*, November 10, 2015, https://www.washingtonpost.com/local/education/can-colleges-protect-free-speech-while-curbing-voices-of-hate/2015/11/10/daac2b8c-87ca-11e5-be39-0034bb576eee_story.html.

13. "Twenty One Pilots Chart History, Mainstream Top 40," *Billboard*, https://www.billboard.com/music/Twenty-One-Pilots/chart-history/pop-songs.

14. RIDE Words and Music by TYLER JOSEPH © 2015 WARNER-TAMERLANE PUBLISHING CORP., FUELED BY MUSIC and STRYKER JOSEPH MUSIC All Rights Administered by WARNER-TAMERLANE PUBLISHING CORP. All Rights Reserved. Used By Permission of ALFRED MUSIC

15. Zzzmessi1, "CMV: Sports Should Not Have a Place in American Universities," *Change My View*, Reddit, May 20 2017, https://www.reddit.com/r/changemyview/comments/6ccukh/cmv_sports_should_not_have_a_place_in_american.

16. Lou Gehrig, "Farewell," *Lou Gehrig*, https://www.lougehrig.com/farewell.

17. Barack Obama, "596–Remarks on the Situation in Syria," August 31, 2013, *The American Presidency Project*. ed. John T. Woolley and Gerhard Peters, 1999-2017, http://www.presidency.ucsb.edu/ws/index.php? pid=104044. The material is in public domain.

18. Meryl Streep, quoted in Daniel Victor and Giovanni Russonello, "Meryl Streep's Golden Globes Speech," *New York Times*, January 8, 2017, https://www.nytimes.com/2017/01/08/arts/television/meryl-streep-golden-globes-speech.html.

19. Signe Whitson, "10 Things Passive-Aggressive People Say," *Psychology Today*, November 23, 2010, https://www.psychology-today.com/blog/passive-aggressive-diaries/201011/10-things-passive-aggressive-people-say.

20. "Twenty One Pilots – Ride," *SongMeanings*, http://songmeanings.com/songs/view/3530822107859506488.

21. Twenty One Pilots, "Twenty One Pilots: Ride Lyrics". "Ride" words and music by Tyler Joseph. © 2015 Warner-Tamerlane Publishing Corp., fueled by Music and Stryker Joseph Music. All rights administered by Warner-Tamerlane Publishing Corp. All rights reserved. Used by permission of Alfred Music.

22. Moonbeam86, "General Comment," "Twenty One Pilots – Ride," *SongMeanings*, http://songmeanings.com/songs/view/3530822107859506488.

23. James Harrison [@jhharrison92], Instagram post, August 17, 2015, https://web.archive.org/web/20150817160212/https://instagram.com/p/6aXCJ2JFi5.

24. Richard Greenberg, "In Defense of Participation Trophies," *Huffington Post*, August 18, 2015, http://www.huffingtonpost.com/richard-greenberg/in-defense-of-participation-trophies_b_8001758.html; Lisa Heffernan, "In Defense of Participation Trophies: Why They Really Do Teach the Right Values," *Today*, August 31, 2015, https://www.today.com/parents/defense-participation-trophies-kids-t40931; Dan Shanoff, "In Defense of Participation Trophies: Lighten

Up, James Harrison," *ESPNW*, August 18, 2015, http://www.espn.com/espnw/news-commentary/article/13464436/lighten-james-harrison; Editorial Board, "Some—Not All—Feel-Good Trophies Have Merit," *Newsday*, August 17, 2015, http://www.newsday.com/opinion/editorial/james-harrison-is-right-about-trophies-to-a-point-1.10747893; Erik Brady, "Why James Harrison Is Wrong: Participation Trophies Don't Warp Kids' Outlook," *USA Today*, August 20, 2015, https://www.usatoday.com/story/sports/2015/08/20/participation-trophies-kids-children-james-harrison/32013681.

25. Susan B. Anthony, "On Woman's Right to the Suffrage," in *The World's Famous Orations*, vol. X, ed. William Jennings Bryan (New York: Funk & Wagnalls, 1906), 60.

26. Karen E. Dill, "Violent Video Games can Increase Aggression," *American Psychological Association*, April 23, 2000, http://www.apa.org/news/press/releases/2000/04/video-games.aspx.

5

EFFECTIVELY SUPPORTING CLAIMS

The link between concussions from American football and long-term brain damage is fairly well established today. For years, however, the National Football League (NFL) used its Mild Traumatic Brain Injury (MTBI) committee to deny this connection by calling the data "speculative," "preposterous," "flawed," or "worthless."[1] For example, one 2007 study determined through NFL player surveys that playing professional football was linked to depression, but MTBI co-chair Dr. Ira Casson argued that "survey studies are the weakest type of research study." He further noted that this particular study "had no objective evaluations to determine whether or not what the people told them in the surveys was correct or not. They didn't have information from doctors confirming it, they didn't have tests, they didn't have examinations."[2] In sum, Casson argued that "anecdotes do not make scientifically valid evidence. I am a man of science. I believe in empirically determined scientifically valid data."[3]

In 2009, when additional studies confirmed the connection, Casson remained steadfast in his position. He argued that there are "gaps" in the data and that it's not "fair to jump from a couple cases that were suicides to assume that some of the others that, well, the guy was driving fast down the highway, it must have been a suicide. . . . I think there's a lot of people jumping to conclusions."[4] Dr. Bennet Omalu, one of the primary researchers in the area who discovered Chronic Traumatic Encephalopathy, or CTE, and who was profiled in the 2015 movie *Concussion*, vehemently challenged Casson's concern about the data: "Pardon me, but what is the gold standard for diagnosis? Autopsy! That is the gold standard for diagnosis. Only when you open up the body, look at the tissues, do you find proof of disease."[5]

This controversy emphasizes how the quality of support is crucial to argumentation in everyday life because it shapes the quality of the claims drawn from it. The above debate is essentially a debate over the quality of the support for the claims being made: Is there good evidence to suggest a causal connection and are there sufficient examples to represent all or most NFL players?

Knowing how to identify and evaluate support is important to your own advocacy and to understanding others'. In this chapter, then, we will first consider the distinction between "evidence" and "support," followed by best practices for gathering and evaluating research in an internet age. We'll then explore seven different kinds of support: facts, statistics, examples, testimony, definitions, principles and values, and credibility. By the end of this chapter, you should be able to gather and evaluate the supporting materials that you will learn in later chapters how to *use* in developing claims.

THE ALLURE OF "EVIDENCE" AND THE SIGNIFICANCE OF "SUPPORT"

This book uses the term "support" to refer to the content that advances an argumentative claim. In other books or contexts, you may encounter "evidence," "proof," or "data" instead. The word evidence, in particular, is attractive to us because it suggests infallibility—the root word "evident" refers to something that is obvious, conspicuous, or clear[6]—and, let's be honest, we like to be right. It's not surprising that the word became much more popular in the 1600s alongside the scientific revolution's focus on rationality and proof. The oft-cited phrase, "seeing is believing," points to the prominence of this view.

However, we know from our own experience that arguments don't always require cold, hard evidence to agree with the claims. Sometimes the claim feels right in our gut. Or, sometimes we have an inkling but not full information. Or, sometimes it aligns with other beliefs or commitments we have. Or, sometimes we simply lack a reason not to. You could probably supply examples of each of these scenarios from your own life. Despite knowing these options exist, we often labor under various myths that perpetuate the allure of support, outlined in Box 5.1.

Because the basis for an argument is often *not* evidentiary and because we shouldn't proscribe certain kinds of information that people might use to further claims, the word "support" is a better fit. The *Oxford English Dictionary* defines support as "the action or an act of helping a person or thing to hold firm or not to give way."[7] That sounds a lot like how we've discussed the foundation of an argument: It helps the claim hold firm and not give way to counter-argument.

Just because support can come in various forms, however, this doesn't mean that all support is created equal. You might recall the story of the three little pigs, in which the houses of stick and straw were susceptible to the big bad wolf's huffing and puffing but the brick house stood firm. The same is true of argumentative support. The choice of material you use to build your claims impacts the quality of the foundation, or how well the claim holds firm and doesn't give way. Thus, it's important to know how to gather, test, and use your supporting materials in the service of argumentative claims.

GATHERING AND TESTING INFORMATION

Finding quality support for claims can be challenging in our Internet age. It is true that we have a world of information at our fingertips but this breadth of content is often overwhelming rather than empowering. When a Google search for something

BOX 5.1: COMMON MYTHS ABOUT ARGUMENTATIVE SUPPORT

1. **Support must be evident.** We often position "indisputable" facts or statistics as the best kind of support because they are empirical, or evident, in the natural world. However, this kind of support doesn't necessarily make a better argument, and, in fact, some audiences may prefer support that is theoretical, abstract, or emotional rather than evident and verifiable.

2. **Support proves a claim.** Recall that claims are, by definition, debatable. Consequently, support can never prove a claim because, once proven, it is truth or fact rather than a claim. Instead of saying support *proves* a claim, we should say that it *furthers* or *advances* a claim.

3. **Some kinds of support are best avoided.** Some people may believe that some support types (e.g., the popularity of something) are always a poor foundation for a claim. This book discourages wholesale judgments about what kind of support is good or bad; it's all contextually grounded and negotiated by the participants in the debate situation. If your audience believes popularity is a good foundation for a claim, then by all means use it!

4. **Support is always logical.** Part of the appeal of the word "evidence" is that it implies logic rather than emotion. However, any type of support can be used for emotional *or* logical appeal. For example, a story—as a kind of example—might very logically demonstrate a point even though we tend to view them as emotional appeal. Conversely, a statistic— what many would view as a very logical kind of support—can generate an emotional reaction such as fear.

as concrete as "statistics about video games and violence in U.S. citizens 12-18 years old" returns more than 400,000 results, separating the proverbial wheat from the chaff becomes very challenging. As Dr. Rainbow Johnson lamented in a 2018 episode of *Black-ish*, "there's so much bad information. There used to be people we all could trust for answers. Now anyone can be an expert."[8] As a consumer of information, you are forced to distinguish fact from opinion, truth from falsity, and expertise from interest, all the while avoiding "fake news," "alternative facts," and "echo chambers." It's no surprise in today's social media age that BuzzFeed could compile a list of 50 false stories in 2016 on Facebook alone![9]

The problem isn't just that this false information is out there. The reality is that digital natives (i.e., those born since the 1990s, who grew up with the Internet) don't always use critical thinking to engage it. A 2016 study by the Stanford History Education Group tested how well students in middle, secondary, and post-secondary schools can "judge the credibility of information that floods [their] smartphones, tablets, and computers."[10] They called the findings "bleak," concluding that students at all levels "are easily duped."[11] But, distrust of all online information is just as unproductive (and mentally exhausting) as believing everything you encounter.

Luckily, there are tools to navigate this complex environment through critical think-ing combined with knowledge of what makes quality information when constructing arguments. We'll consider, first, what makes high-quality information and, second, where to find it.

How to Know if It's Quality Support

As you research arguments, you will need to assess the information you come across. You likely do this all the time. For instance, you pause on a shocking headline in your social media feed long enough to see that the source is the notorious satirical newspaper, the *Onion*, or its online subsidiary, *ClickHole*, and you chuckle before moving on. Other times you see a headline labeled "sponsored" and, recognizing that it's an advertisement, you avoid clicking the link. Still other times you see an unfamiliar source (e.g., quora. com, bustle.com, theodysseyonline.com, slate.com, or medium.com) so you first look it up on Wikipedia to make sure it's legitimate. And, other times you follow a link to cnn. com or wsj.com because you believe them to be reliable sites. In all these cases, you're making judgments about the quality of the information.

But, why would you disregard the *Onion* and sponsored sites but have no problem following links to the *Wall Street Journal*? The answer comes down to three main tests you should ask of information you gather from *any* print or digital source: Is it trust-worthy? Is it unbiased? And, is it recent?

Test #1: Is the information trustworthy? First, test the trustworthiness of the infor-mation by asking if you have reason to believe is true. After all, any information on which you base your arguments should be real and as accurate as possible. Determining the trustworthiness of information often relates to the source and the authorship of the information. By source, we mean the location (physical or digital) where the information is published. Sometimes, the source is all you need to determine trustworthiness. This is where the *Onion*, as a source, fails. The *Onion* is upfront about being a satirical site whereas the *Wall Street Journal* passes the trustworthy test because it follows rigorous journalistic standards. A book published with Harvard University Press would generally pass this test because the press is a strict gatekeeper and only publishes high quality work whereas a book published by CreateSpace might fail this test because anyone can publish a book there.

If the source doesn't tell you enough about trustworthiness, then turn to authorship. Who or what is responsible for the information? In some cases, such as an organizational report or website, the source and author are identical. In other cases, the author will be more specific than the source. For instance, a credible professor could publish a book with CreateSpace as could your younger sibling. And, in fact, your younger sibling may even be more trustworthy than a professor on some topics. Rather than writing off a source entirely, then, you'd need to consider whether the author has the expertise and experience you can trust.

You can learn whether to trust a source or author by asking people you already trust or researching them yourself. Some great places to look are the "about" page of a website, an author's biography, or reviews of websites, books, and authors. Of course, this may take some effort and time but it would be better to get the information right than to potentially mislead yourself and others.

Even if you put in the effort to evaluate the information's trustworthiness, you are rendering a judgment and, thus, it is open to debate. It's within your right to question a co-arguer's information from a source or author you find untrustworthy and you should expect that your co-arguers and audience members will do the same for your information. Being able to justify the trustworthiness of the information you gather is a first step to using high quality support.

Test #2: Is the information unbiased? A second test for information addresses its bias. Unbiased information is information that is detached from specific interests or claims relevant to the support. It may not be possible to eliminate bias completely; people always filter information based on experience, interests, etc. However, bias becomes a problem when the information is purposefully skewed to benefit the author or some cause.

As with trustworthiness, you can determine bias by considering the source and author of the information. First, reflect on who is sharing the information and why they might be doing so. For instance, when organizations such as the American Civil Liberties Union or the National Rifle Association produce reports, they tend to be biased towards claims the organizations want the audience to accept. In Chapter 3, we uncovered how something as "objective" as an opinion poll can, depending on its methodology and political leaning, be biased. The same is true in the personal and technical spheres you engage. For example, the information in workplace memos from the CEO often benefit the profit interests of the company. In cases of biased information, then, you might do additional research to see if the information is complete and reliable.

Judgments of bias are also debatable. It's theoretically possible to discount every single source as having some kind of bias, although doing so would be largely unproductive. Nevertheless, argumentation concerning the bias of the information may become a part of the debate as you and others decide whether to rely on the information.

Test #3: Is the information recent? The final test for information is recency. Recent information is information that remains accurate despite the passage of time. In general, the most recent information tends to be the best but this will depend on the content. To test for recency, you need to know when it was published and ask yourself if it still holds true. For instance, the information about the circumference of the moon may depend little on when it is published so it would equally appropriate to cite a trustworthy book from 1965 or a trustworthy website from 2015. However, recency is quite relevant to information about the average cost for a gallon of gas. Citing a statistic from 2015 on this topic would fail the test of recency because the price has changed since then.

The previous two examples are clear-cut but sometimes there is uncertainty as to what's recent, and, thus, recency is debatable. What some people think to be perfectly acceptable information may be challenged by others as outdated. For instance, is it appropriate for sports commentators to rank college teams in the preseason based on the previous year's statistics or is that information irrelevant? A general rule of thumb is to be aware of how current your supporting materials are and constantly update your knowledge so that you're not making decisions based on obsolete information.

In sum, the three tests of trustworthiness, bias, and recency require you to know and evaluate the author, source, and date of the information. If you can't find any of those three elements, then it's best to discard the information. While this may require more time researching, it will make your arguments stronger, ensure you communicate the best possible vision, and help you meet your responsibility to your audience members and co-arguers. After all, being properly informed is one way to show respect for others and avoid wasting their time. To help you meet this responsibility, the next section offers some tips to help you gather high quality information.

Where to Find Quality Support

Researching argumentative support is often an important step to making an informed decision. You no doubt know that print resources such as books, newspapers, journals, magazines, and the like are very useful for research. In many cases, these will be the primary materials you use to learn about a topic. If you're unsure how to best access them, speak with a librarian at your local library or see if they have instructional sessions on how to use research databases.

But if we're being honest, most of you won't do that. Instead, you'll do what people often do when they research a topic: go to Google or Wikipedia. And, your research might stop there. Yikes. That is not a good strategy, and, in most cases, it is a waste of time. The Internet is of course a phenomenal place to gather excellent, up-to-date information. However, people are too often a slave to the search engine. So, let's consider some tips and strategies to master online research.

Tip #1: Use free resources. Whether you know it or not, you've already paid for access to valuable electronic databases and physical materials. Taxes and student fees pay for library access to newspapers, magazines, scholarly journal articles, books, music, and movies. Why try to outsmart the *Wall Street Journal* paywall when your library may have free access to the newspaper with the click of a few buttons? Take time to learn about electronic library resources available to you because they can save you time and money.

Beyond library resources, you can access numerous free news resources. Many newspapers, including the *New York Times* and *Washington Post*, allow you to only access a few free articles per month but you can sign up for daily email briefings that send you the major headlines to keep you up to date on current events.

Tip #2: Keep track of your research. Have you ever come across an insightful webpage only to have it lost in cyberspace when you need to create a bibliography or want to access it again? To avoid this problem, you should choose a system for you that helps you keep track of important research. For example, use browser bookmarks, print digital files that you store in an elaborate folder system, create a hand-written or typed catalogue, or use citation software.

This is especially important when undertaking a more extensive argumentative project such as writing a newspaper article or public speech. In these situations, you will likely gather as much information as possible about the topic and then go back through that research for the bits that help you support your argumentative claims. Creating a file or catalog system to keep track of this information makes sure that you work smarter, not harder, when researching.

Tip #3: Use Internet Archive when pages disappear. Even if you've bookmarked a webpage, it may suddenly disappear into the digital ether. While this can be very frustrating, you may be able to go virtually back in time to see the page on an earlier date. At the Internet Archive (archive.org), use the "Way Back Machine" by typing in a URL of a webpage you want to see. Provided it's in the database, the site will show screen captures of that webpage at various points in time. Of course, keep in mind that the earlier you go, the more likely it is to fail the test of recency.

Tip #4: Conduct site specific searches. Sometimes you want to find information on a specific website but the site itself doesn't have a useful search function. For this, you can use Google by typing "site:[url]." For example, the search "unemployment rate site: bls.gov" would yield all results with the words "unemployment" and "rate" on the U.S. Federal Government's Bureau of Labor Statistics website. This can be very useful in cases where you've narrowed your search to a small selection of trustworthy and unbiased websites.

Tip #5: Domain names are largely irrelevant. Twenty years ago, the primary advice for Internet research was to consider the website's domain. The logic went that .org or .gov sites are more trustworthy than .com. The proliferation of websites across all domains has made this advice tenuous at best. In reality, many biased and untrustworthy organizations have a .org website and publish whatever they like. Additionally, many a .com (such as newspaper websites) are quite reliable. Consequently, there's not a general rule about which kind of sites to trust; you'll need to evaluate each on its merits.

Tip #6: Be aware and wary of "sponsored" content. We noted earlier that many social media and news sites will have content labeled "paid" or "sponsored." Sadly, we're not always careful about paying attention to this fine print and we might fall for clickbait, leading us into a tangled web of salacious stories and inferior information. While not all sponsored content lacks quality, a good rule of thumb is to stick to non-sponsored links. In paying for you to click on the link, the sponsored content is likely to be biased.

Tip #7: Track down primary sources. Many webpages will link to other pages, documents, or articles. In most cases, you should use these primary sources rather than relying on another webpage's summary of them (a secondary source). Be attuned to whether and how websites reference other resources so that you can ensure accuracy of the information.

Tip #8: Learn what websites and databases are trustworthy, unbiased, and recent. You should find go-to sites that you know you can trust to provide you quality information. For instance, my preferred search engine for news is Lexis-Nexis (or Nexis Uni), provided by my school library, because it is highly customizable and provides easy access to thousands of credible articles and blog posts. Other people will subscribe to and rely on a particular news site because they trust it above all else. The Find Your Voice prompt encourages you to think about your preferred sources of information. The more you learn to distinguish good from bad sources, the more easily you can gather reliable information. Of course, it's possible that we get stuck in an echo chamber in which all of our reliable sites reinforce one perspective at the expense of others. This is why you should constantly test for bias and seek out alternative perspectives.

FIND YOUR VOICE
INFORMATION SOURCES

What sources do you tend to consult for basic factual information and why are those your preferred sources? What sources do you tend to consult for current events and why are those your preferred sources? Are there sources you avoid and, if so, why? After you're aware of your existing bias for and against certain sources, you should expose yourself to different sources in order to promote a more well-rounded view.

When conducting research for debate about a public controversy, there are a few sites that tend to emerge as top contenders but not all of these are reliable. Box 5.2 rates these common sites by assigning each a smiley face (good), neutral face (neutral), or sad face (bad) based on how trustworthy, unbiased, and recent the information tends to be as well as how clearly the site references and offers access to primary sources.[12]

So, you've gathered your exceptionally high-quality research using the tests and tips above. Now what? Well, conducting research for the purposes of argumentation is rarely done independent of the issues you want to raise and claims you want to advance. Your goal isn't just to gather as much good information on the topic as possible but also to

BOX 5.2: EVALUATING COMMON DEBATE RESEARCH WEBSITES

Website	Rating	Comment
Wikipedia en.wikipedia.org		Wikipedia could be useful for background information on a topic and there are often helpful citations and external links. But, Wikipedia can also be wrong and virtually anyone can post there so only use it as a starting point.
ProCon procon.org		ProCon offers a wealth of citations for each topic, but users are better off following those links and citing the primary sources. The biggest drawback to the site is that it simplifies complex debates into two opposing sides with a list of pros and cons.
Debate.org debate.org		Debate.org provides information about the history of and "public opinion" about controversial topics in the United States but fails to cite outside material or include authorship details. You can't trust the information.
Google google.com		Google searches can be helpful, but they tend to produce a lot of junk that isn't credible and it often takes quite a bit of time to filter the millions of hits. You'd be better off using different resources or conducting site-specific Google searches.
Google Scholar scholar.google.com		Google Scholar yields only academic or scholarly results related to a topic, meaning that the information is much more reliable. Unfortunately, you may need academic databases (through a public or school library, for instance) to access the material without paying a fee.

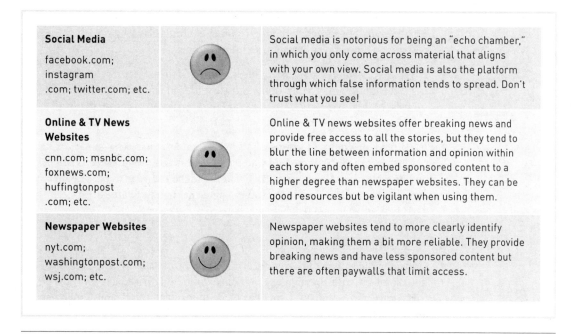

Social Media facebook.com; instagram .com; twitter.com; etc.		Social media is notorious for being an "echo chamber," in which you only come across material that aligns with your own view. Social media is also the platform through which false information tends to spread. Don't trust what you see!
Online & TV News Websites cnn.com; msnbc.com; foxnews.com; huffingtonpost .com; etc.		Online & TV news websites offer breaking news and provide free access to all the stories, but they tend to blur the line between information and opinion within each story and often embed sponsored content to a higher degree than newspaper websites. They can be good resources but be vigilant when using them.
Newspaper Websites nyt.com; washingtonpost.com; wsj.com; etc.		Newspaper websites tend to more clearly identify opinion, making them a bit more reliable. They provide breaking news and have less sponsored content but there are often paywalls that limit access.

Source: Images by GrannyEnchanted.com, 10 June 2013. Licensed under CC0 1.0.

think about how to use that information argumentatively. To begin this process, the rest of the chapter will discuss seven different options for supporting a claim.

TYPES OF SUPPORT

Facts

Facts are empirical or descriptive information that is widely accepted as true. Notice that the definition of facts requires them to be *widely accepted* as true, not 100 percent infallible now and forever. This means that facts may be subject to change or dispute, even when used as support. A frequent example of this changeability is that for years it was a "fact" that the sun revolved around the Earth before we learned it didn't. In our time, DNA testing has provided new facts about crimes, exonerating people who were deemed guilty based on earlier facts. Despite this fallibility, facts are a solid foundation for a claim when we are certain that they are reliable and the audience will accept them.

FACT: Empirical or descriptive information widely accepted as true

Why You Should Use Facts

- **Facts are tied to truth**. When people describe the "truth" about something, they often revert to facts about it. This is because, despite the ability for facts to be manipulated, we tend to equate truth with facts. By using true facts, you create a more honest and agreeable argument. This is also why the label "fake news" is so powerful at discounting information.

- **Facts are testable.** Often based in real world evidence, facts are thus testable. If a fact sounds dodgy, you can investigate it or find confirmation from other sources. In fact, you *should* do this and do it frequently to ensure that the information you gather is factually accurate.

- **Facts provide common ground.** In some situations, facts are a good starting point that provides common ground between you and the audience. They help establish what you believe to be true and invite the audience to participate in your understanding of reality. Exposing agreement and disagreement about the basic facts of your case will help you better resolve debates.

How You Should Use Facts

- **Consider the source.** The source of a fact often correlates to its quality. If you don't know or trust the source, you probably shouldn't trust facts provided by that source. Because the Internet has made it possible to find conflicting facts on any topic, use the tests for source quality earlier in the chapter.

- **Distinguish interest from expertise.** Is People for the Ethical Treatment of Animals (PETA) an expert on vegetarianism? The answer is, of course, debatable. Nevertheless, because PETA has a vested interest in the information it provides, it's probably best to avoid the organization's facts to support an argument for vegetarianism. This also applies in personal and technical spheres. Before repeating facts you've heard from friends, family members, or co-workers, consider whether the person is a credible expert on the topic and whether they might benefit from endorsing the facts.

- **Check for accuracy.** Some facts are not controversial. In other cases, however, you should check facts for accuracy. Just because something sounds right doesn't mean it is right and mistakes can be made by accepting incorrect information. However, you should test facts within the confines of the law and reason. Do not follow the example of Edgar Welch, who chose to personally investigate the "Pizzagate" conspiracy in 2016 by taking a gun into the pizza restaurant that some Internet sources falsely claimed to be running a human trafficking ring sponsored by numerous Democratic Party leaders.

- **Adapt facts to the audience.** Let me be clear: This guideline does *not* mean you should manipulate facts to satisfy the audience. Rather, use facts that your audience will accept as a starting point for an argument. For instance, some audience members might believe it a "fact" that God exists while others might not. If you support a claim by referencing God's will in front of a largely atheist audience, you'll never convince them of your claim. Recognizing that facts can create common ground, you should use facts that are shared by your audience to support your claims.

- **Be willing to be wrong.** Sometimes it seems like the "cold, hard facts" can be whatever you want them to be, provided you state them with enough conviction and repetition. This is not a good approach to the argumentative use of facts. Rather, be open to the possibility that your facts are wrong or outdated. This will produce a stronger conclusion in the end and make you a more cooperative arguer. In 2002, the *Beijing Evening News* learned this the hard way when it initially published in full and without attribution an article plagiarized from the *Onion* as a news story. When the *Los Angeles Times* revealed the Beijing paper had been duped, the newspaper initially refused to retract it, asking "How can you prove it's not correct? Is it incorrect just because you say it is?"[13] Finally, nearly a week later, the newspaper retracted the story, admitted its fault, and criticized the *Onion* for tricking people to make money.[14]

Statistics

Statistics comprise a second major category of support people use for arguments. Statistics are essentially numerical facts, or numerical representations of information. When people ask for data, they often refer to this category of information.

STATISTIC:
A numerical representation of information

The two most common types of statistics you will encounter are raw numbers and averages. *Raw numbers* are the basic figures you might use to describe something. Some examples of raw numbers might be the percentage of people who responded a particular way on an opinion poll, the total amount of your organization's budget, or the number of people who attended President Trump's inauguration. *Averages*, on the other hand, describe the distribution of the raw numbers. You likely learned how to calculate averages such as mean, median, and mode at some point. Some examples of averages might be the mean score on a test in class or the median amount of debt U.S. college graduates have upon graduation.

Why You Should Use Statistics

- **Statistics borrow the same virtues as facts.** Because statistics are facts in numerical form, they have the same benefits described earlier: They are tied to truth, are testable, and provide common ground.

- **Statistics demonstrate significance.** By quantifying information, statistics emphasize the scope and significance of something. Statistics, for instance, can tell us how widespread a problem is or how important an idea is to a group of people. A single person's statement or experience may be useful in some cases but statistics illustrate a wider scope.

- **Statistics reveal what's "typical."** Statistics emphasize what's typical or normal and what's an outlier. There are always extreme examples people can use but knowing the mean, median, and mode of a given dataset can help pinpoint normality. The power of opinion polls in U.S. society is precisely this ability to identify the range of "normal" belief to find the majority (sometimes, unfortunately, at the expense of the minority).

How You Should Use Statistics

- **Use reliable and recent sources.** Just as the source is important to facts, so too it is important to statistics. Most statistics, however, rely more on recency than facts. Outdated statistics can spread misinformation that leads to poor conclusions.

- **Identify the scales and units.** Omitting the scales and units for statistics is one common mistake beginning arguers make. For example, someone might state that the poverty rate is 22. Hearing this, you might *assume* this means that 22 percent of people in the United States live below the federally defined poverty line but the statistic itself doesn't tell you this. It's missing both the unit—what is it measuring? (in this case, people in the United States)—and the scale—22 out of what? (in this case, out of 100). Even if both of these details are provided, the statistic still may be fairly meaningless because the arguer hasn't told us what, statistically speaking, constitutes the poverty line. It's important, then, to be as explicit and concrete as possible about what the statistic represents.

- **Consider the kind of measure.** The kind of measure (mean, median, mode, correlation, etc.) can impact our claims. For instance, the mean household income in the United States in 2014 was $65,751.[15] This is the number you get if you add up the wages of all households in the United States and divide by the number of households. The median income in 2014, on the other hand, was $53,719. This is the number you get by placing half of all U.S. households on one side of it and half on the other. Both are averages but the one you cite may tell a different story about household earnings in the United States.

- **Use sparingly.** Statistics can help illustrate ideas but they can also be overwhelming for an audience, especially in quick succession. Statistics should help clarify rather than confuse ideas so only use them when they are meaningful illustrations of your claim. Effectively explaining a single high-quality statistic may be more effective argumentation than rapidly issuing three or four shoddy statistics.

- **Explain or relate to audience.** Arguers will sometimes drop statistics as though they speak for themselves but this is rarely an effective argumentation strategy. Because statistics are an impersonal type of support, arguers should be explicit about the claims they authorize and should put them into perspective. For instance, you might note that the $13,000 difference between the median and mean income in the United States is significant because it equals the price of an economy car or the cost of a year's tuition at a state university. Beyond putting statistics into perspective, supplementing statistics with additional support such as examples or testimony makes them more memorable and relatable.

Because statistics are quite common in everyday argumentation, use the Build Your Skill feature to practice evaluating their use.

BUILD YOUR SKILL
EVALUATING STATISTICS

Based on the guidelines for using statistics, evaluate the following examples as either weak or strong:

A. **MoveOn Tweet, June 1, 2018:** "It's now official U.S. policy to separate families. In the first 14 days since the new policy, 658 children have been ripped from their families. Tell congress to take action to defund ICE, CBP, and End Family Separation: 210-702-3059"[16]

B. **Donald Trump, June 1, 2018:** "A.P. has just reported that the Russian Hoax Investigation has now cost our government over $17 million, and going up fast. No Collusion, except by the Democrats!"[17]

C. **Chuck Woolery, May 15, 2018:** "Somethings fishy here at twitter. 4 weeks ago 63million impressions 28 day period. Now down to 37million, yet growing my following to 410,000. Just doesn't add up does it?"[18]

Examples

Arguers frequently use **examples**, or single instances, to illustrate a broader claim. Examples can be empirical or hypothetical. *Empirical* examples are real and based in past fact. For instance, you might justify your stance on immigration based on the experience of an immigrant you know. *Hypothetical* examples are stipulated and represent potentials. For instance, you might justify your stance on immigration based on a fictional TV show you watched or an outcome that you imagine happening to an immigrant. Empirical examples may have more persuasive power because they are grounded in reality but hypothetical examples are also useful, particularly in situations when you want to argue the possibilities of a claim.

EXAMPLE: A single instance or case used for illustration purposes

Why You Should Use Examples

- **Examples personalize ideas.** Whereas statistics offer breadth and scope, examples offer depth and specificity. When debating abstract or distant topics, examples can make the ideas more concrete and relatable. You can also use examples from your personal life to connect with your audience and co-arguers.

- **Examples widen the perspective of audiences and co-arguers.** Because you can derive examples from a variety of locations, they enable you to widen your and others' perspectives. Examples of unfamiliar people or ideas may have an educational value for you, your audience, and your co-arguers. The more diverse you make the examples, the stronger your claim can become.

- **Examples showcase both extraordinary and typical.** Examples can be extreme models we should strive for or avoid, they can be "typical" instantiations of

Lessons taught in literature, movies, television episodes, comic books, and video games all comprise a sub-set of hypothetical examples. For instance, a fable (such as "The Tortoise and the Hare") teaches a general lesson (slow and steady wins the race) on the basis of a case (what happened with the tortoise and the hare). When are these fictional examples effective support for a claim? How might you use them ethically to motivate others? When you are aware of the different kinds of examples you might use, you are a more responsible and effective arguer.

something, or they can fall anywhere in between. Consequently, examples are a very adaptable and engaging type of support. Many textbooks (this one included) rely on examples to illustrate general and abstract principles precisely because of this flexibility.

How You Should Use Examples

- **Provide texture.** When using an example as support for a claim, it often helps to develop it in depth and make it come alive for the audience rather than discussing it in a surface level manner. This guideline isn't for the sake of embellishment but rather for the sake of engaging your audience and helping them visualize your claim.

- **Use representative cases.** In most cases, the examples you choose should be representative or "typical" of the point you want to make. If you're trying to show the success of some initiative you've undertaken, for example, it might be both unethical and illogical to use the one extreme success story and omit the majority of examples that are failures.

- **Use numerous cases.** A single example, especially based on personal experience, is rarely enough to justify a claim (we'll spend more time with this in Chapter 6). Thus, you should offer a variety of examples that combine to demonstrate your claim. The more diverse they are, the stronger your claim can become.

- **Connect to audience's experience.** It can be difficult for audience members to relate to or understand even the best examples without you explicitly guiding them there. The more you connect the examples to their experience, while also recognizing their differences, the more success you'll find in using examples as support.

Testimony

TESTIMONY: Other people's words or ideas

Testimony involves using other people's words and ideas to support a claim. There are two main types of testimony worth noting: expert testimony and lay testimony. *Expert testimony* cites a person or institution that has knowledge about the topic and that the audience will trust whereas *lay testimony* uses someone who has first-hand experience with or interest in the topic but who isn't an expert. For example, when persuading your friends to eat at a particular restaurant, citing the executive chef's statement on the restaurant's website or a published review from the *New York Times'* restaurant critic are both expert testimony whereas citing Yelp reviews of average customers is lay testimony.

Why You Should Use Testimony

- **Testimony enhances trust.** Unfortunately, you are not an expert on every topic and, thus, the audience may not trust your arguments. Testimony is an effective type of support in these scenarios because it borrows credibility from other people. If the audience trusts the person whose testimony you cite, they are more likely to agree with your claim.

- **Testimony fosters identification.** Especially when using lay testimony, you can help the audience understand and appreciate other people's perspectives. Whereas examples might draw upon people's experiences, testimony can capture their motivations in their own words.

- **Testimony is efficient.** If you want to find the median household income in the United States, you could visit every U.S. household, ask what their income is, and then calculate the median yourself. Or, you could visit the U.S. Census Bureau website. This is just one (extreme) illustration of how testimony saves you time and effort by using the labor of others. Of course, you must still *cite* the source both for it to be testimony and for it to be ethical argumentation.

How You Should Use Testimony

- **Cite trustworthy and unbiased sources.** The best testimony is trustworthy and unbiased. This doesn't mean that you should always use expert testimony; lay testimony can be trustworthy when the source speaks from experience. As we discussed earlier, unbiased sources do not have a vested interest in the information such that its testimony is polluted. In newspapers, we often see "a source speaking on the condition of anonymity" or "a senior administration official" as a citation for testimony. This is not a trustworthy citation and, as a general rule, you should avoid such concealment.

- **Indicate qualifications when appropriate.** When using testimony to support a claim, you should explicitly identify why the source is qualified to authorize the claim you're advancing. This might include the source's credentials or the source's experience with the topic of the claim to help the audience better judge the worth of your testimony.

- **Identify the kind of source when possible and appropriate**. Beyond citing the source's name and qualifications, you might also indicate the kind of source. At a basic level, is it expert or lay testimony? In cases of biased testimony, you might note the bias explicitly (to build goodwill with your audience) and explain why the testimony still stands in the context of your argument. The opposite of biased testimony—what we call *reluctant testimony*—can be particularly powerful. Reluctant testimony refers to a source that states something against its own interests (e.g., a pharmaceutical representative admitting the company's drug caused dangerous side effects). Reluctant testimony goes against the audience's expectations of bias and adds legitimacy to your conclusions.

Definitions

DEFINITION:
The dictionary or cultural meaning attached to something

Definitions—the dictionary or cultural meaning attached to something—may initially seem non-argumentative but they can be when the arguer explicitly uses the assigned meaning to further a claim.

Definitions might operate in numerous ways as support for a claim. In some cases, you might advance a *formal definition*, in which you describe the meaning of something based on its primary qualities or its dictionary meaning.

A second way to use definitions as support is through *definition by association or dissociation*, in which you characterize something by its relationship (or lack thereof) to other things. Definition by association and dissociation might also be evident when people classify an object, for example claiming something is not a crime perpetrated by a criminal but rather an attack perpetrated by a terrorist (dissociating the act from crime and associating it with terrorism).

Finally, a third form of definition might be through an *exemplar*, in which you use the best example of something to reach a definition. For instance, you may not know how to formally define the qualities of the best movie sequel ever made but you might be able to identify a specific film as the exemplar that demonstrates what it means to be the best movie sequel ever made. Regardless of the definition's form, it should be support that you anticipate the audience will accept.

Why You Should Use Definitions

- **Definitions provide focus**. Defining a concept ensures that you, your co-arguers, and audience members have a communal understanding of the key terms in the debate. Definitions might also help focus the argumentative claim on the important meaning, qualities, or functions of a defined object. In Chapter 4, you encountered Harrison's definition of participation trophies as trophies for nothing. This definition focused the debate by explaining how he was later using the term "participation trophy."

- **Definitions characterize reality**. Definitions can powerfully and strategically depict reality. Rhetorical scholar David Zarefsky has noted that this power derives from the appearance of the definition as "natural and uncontroversial rather than chosen and contestable."[19] For instance, students often define grades as things that they "receive" rather than "earn." This characterization of reality reduces the student's ownership over the grade and implies that the teacher is the true agent who determines it. When this definition of grades is used as argumentative support, it can implicate the nature of the claims drawn from it.

How You Should Use Definitions

- **Define relevant terms the first time you state them.** If your case relies on important or technical terms that require definition, define each the first time you mention it. Waiting to define concepts might cause confusion and ultimately be unproductive for your argumentation goals. In Chapter 7, we'll discuss in greater depth how to define concepts as part of an argumentative case.

- **Be consistent.** One hallmark of poor argumentation is inconsistency. In the context of definitions, this might involve equivocation, or defining a word two or more different ways throughout your case. When intentional, inconsistency is unethical because it involves the willful manipulation of your audience. When unintentional, inconsistency is counterproductive because it makes your ideas harder to identify and accept. In many cases, consistency requires being attentive to the language you're using. For instance, people may use "the greenhouse effect," "climate change," and "global warming" as synonyms for the same phenomenon but each has a slightly different scientific meaning that you'd want to recognize when debating the topic.

- **Have a rationale for your definitions.** You shouldn't assume that your terms are agreeable to the audience even when used as support in an argument. Rather, be prepared to offer a rationale for your definitions. This is especially necessary if definitions further your own position in a debate but are not easily anticipated by others. The more grounded your definitions are, the stronger support they will provide.

- **Illustrate or apply definitions as appropriate.** Just stating a definition as support may be sufficient in some cases but often it helps your audience understand the idea if you illustrate or apply the definition. Essentially, this would involve providing further support for your support. Abstract verbal definitions are more palatable for your audience if you make them concrete through such illustrations.

Principles and Values

Whereas definitions describe what something is, principles and values apply worth to something as a starting point for an argument. **Principles** are truths or beliefs that guide one's conduct, often in a moral sense. You may know people who say they do things "on principle" or "for the principle of it," often meaning that they are supporting their action with a moral stand. **Values**, or things of worth to a community, are a related concept. Values such as equality, honesty, or responsibility might serve as support for a claim.

PRINCIPLE: A truth or belief that guides one's (moral) conduct

VALUES: Things of worth to a person or community

It's important to recognize how our personal and collective identity is defined, in part, by our connection to principles and values. For example, to be an "American" is not an innate feature of an individual but rather a commitment to a particular ideology of principles outlined in landmark documents such as the Declaration of Independence or Constitution and revised by advocates who continue to argue about what it means to be an American.[20] Similarly, to be a member of a club or organization often requires commitment to a mission statement, which outlines a set of principles and values. Members of scouting organizations, for example, memorize and recite the oath as a commitment to certain principles and values. Those principles and values, in turn, might be used to support argumentative claims among community members.

Why You Should Use Principles and Values

- **Principles and values engage audience's priorities.** Because principles and values are tied to identity, using them as support in an argument often speaks to deep-seated priorities within audience members. For instance, those who approach college from the value of education will have different priorities, motivations, and arguments about the education system compared to those who approach college from a different value, such as job placement rate, "finding yourself," or earning a 4.0.

- **Principles and values are motivational.** Appealing to the audience's principles and values is motivational because it gets at *why* people do things, not what they do or how they do it. This might explain why Mel Gibson's appeal to "freedom!" in *Braveheart* was so motivational in leading his fellow Scots to battle. You can likely think of times in your own experience when a value or principle motivated you in a way that facts and statistics couldn't.

- **Principles and values have looser evidentiary standards.** Because facts, statistics, and examples are all tied to empirical and verifiable information, they are beholden to standards of accuracy and recency. Principles and values, on the other hand, aren't factual in the same way, meaning that arguers can use them to support claims absent any empirical information on the topic. This provides greater flexibility when compared to other kinds of support.

How You Should Use Principles and Values

- **Be aware of principles and values in argumentation.** Insofar as principles and values are deeply ingrained in people, they may lurk beneath the surface of argumentation rather than being stated explicitly. As an audience member, you might need to uncover implied values much like we discussed identifying unstated warrants and assumptions in Chapter 4. As an arguer, you should be attentive to the principles and values you explicitly *and* implicitly advance when arguing.

- **Principles and values should relate to audience's identity.** As not any principle or value will be effective support for an argument, strive to use values that speak to the audience's identity. The more purchase the value has in the person's everyday life, the more likely they are to pursue it. For example, claiming that everything in life should be earned may not relate to, and ultimately be ineffective for, those who believe assistance programs for the needy are necessary and just.

- **Use other support types to bolster principles and values.** The looser evidentiary standards for principles and values is a double-edged sword; principles and values are easy to throw around but this may make them a weak or cheap type of support. Consequently, you might use other types alongside principles and values to strengthen the claim.

FIND YOUR VOICE
USING IDENTITY ROLES TO MOTIVATE ACTION

When motivating people to take action, we often place them in one of three common roles, each connected to a different motivation and emotion:

Hero → Pride
Victim → Fear
Villain → Guilt

For instance, you might convince a roommate to clean the bathroom because it would really help you out during a stressful week (hero), because you and your roommate might get sick and eventually die from the unseen mold (victim), or because your feelings are hurt that your roommate hasn't cleaned up his or her mess (villain). These roles, like principles and values, are connected to our sense of self. Which tend to motivate you most? Do you have a sense of which motivate your friends and family members? You should spend time reflecting on these options so you are more aware of how they operate and can use them in an honest rather than exploitative fashion.

- **Expectations should be consistent and reasonable.** Don't expect principles and values to be a magic wand that compels belief and action. Rather, think critically about what commitments are consistent with the values and principles you use as support for a claim and have reasonable expectations about how the audience might respond to your use of those principles and values.

Credibility

Finally, arguers can use personal authority or credibility to further a claim. Credibility, as a type of support, refers to the arguer's use of his or her competence and character. This definition indicates two main features. *Competence* refers to the arguer's expertise, knowledge, and preparation. You can trust arguers with competence because they know what they're talking about. Even if a speaker is competent, however, that may not be enough for credibility; used car salesmen get a bad rap precisely because they *exploit* their competence for personal gain by selling lemons. Consequently, *character*—the arguer's goodwill, honesty, and charisma—is a second important quality of credibility. You can trust arguers with character because they are unlikely to manipulate or deceive you and they have your back. Goodwill, or the idea that you are acting in the interests of your audience, is a particularly powerful aspect of credibility.

CREDIBILITY: The arguer's competence and character

Why You Should Use Credibility

- **Credibility can be very persuasive.** Because credibility is hard to gain but easy to lose, it can be a rare commodity in your argumentation. In fact, Aristotle identified *ethos* (loosely translated as appeals to the speaker's credibility) as the most powerful rhetorical proof in his time, noting that audience members are more likely to accept a claim if it comes from an arguer with strong credibility. The power of credibility is still present today. Like the cultural phrase "trust me,

I'm a doctor" suggests, using your credibility to support a claim may be a quick way to earn the audience's assent.

- **Credibility demonstrates your own investment.** Unlike other forms of support, credibility demonstrates your personal connection to a topic. We often debate topics in which we don't have strong investment or interest but using credibility puts your own skin in the game, as it were. This may make you more committed to finding the best outcome and may also generate greater interest from your audiences and co-arguers.

- **Credibility is always there.** Credibility is always available to you as a resource. Provided you have high character and competence, you might as well use these qualities in your argumentation. Credibility does, however, depend on the sphere, situation, and participants of the debate. Some audiences will assign you stronger credibility than others and you will be more competent on some topics than others.

How You Should Use Credibility

- **Be aware of (and use) your credibility.** Your competence and character, as with facts, statistics, and examples, are grounded in empirical reality. Consequently, if the projected image of yourself in your arguments doesn't match the image in the minds of your audience members and co-arguers, then this support may fail. You've probably debated with people who have asked you to trust them even though their actions have caused the opposite reaction. Thus, the image and reality should align if you are aware of your credibility.

- **Create common ground.** Supporting a claim with credibility may create common ground with audience members by showing that you understand and empathize with their experiences. You might also accomplish this common ground through sharing personal stories or anecdotes that put yourself into your arguments.

- **Undersell and overdeliver.** A final caution about credibility: You will lose credibility very quickly if you oversell and underdeliver. You may know people who present themselves as an expert on all topics and make wild claims about their knowledge and experience (oversell). These people may win short-term favor and acceptance but, over time, people find them frauds and stop trusting them (underdeliver). It's also common for people to fake goodwill by claiming to speak for the interests of the audience (oversell) and then act purely for selfish gain (underdeliver). The better approach is to undersell your credibility and overdeliver through consistent use of competence and character. This doesn't mean you should be self-deprecating but rather measured about your credibility.

To consider how arguers use support in everyday argumentation, we'll look at an infographic from 2012 created by WalletHub (formerly CardHub). Called "Credit Cards Go Social," the infographic describes the climate of credit card advertising young consumers face following Congressional enactment of the Credit Card Accountability, Responsibility, and Disclosure (CARD) Act. If you're unfamiliar with WalletHub, the website explains the company is "the first-ever website to offer free credit scores and full credit reports that are updated on a daily basis." They offer services with "three primary functions, providing: 1) customized credit-improvement advice; 2) personalized savings alerts; and 3) 24/7 wallet surveillance. Such features are supplemented by more reviews of financial products, professionals and companies than any other website offers and a diverse community of subject matter experts."[21] It is a for-profit corporation so keep this bias in mind as you engage its use of supporting materials.

The term, "infographic," does imply that the content is informative rather than argumentative but there are arguments present in the document. Consequently, read the infographic first to find the proposition. Then identify the various types of support within it and identify how well they meet the guidelines for using support outlined above. Following the infographic, we'll explore these topics.

Source: John S. Kiernan, "Credit Cards Go Social and Why You Should Care," WalletHub, July 11, 2012, https://wallethub .com/edu/credit-cards-go-social/25683

TABLE 5.1 ■ Support in Wallethub Infographic			
Support Type	Statements from Infographic	Use of Guidelines?	
Facts	– CARD Act curbed aggressive credit card companies' tactics – Under-21 consumers must have income or co-signer – Companies are ramping up social media strategies	Consider the source:	☒
		Distinguish interest from expertise:	☑
		Check for accuracy:	☑
		Adapt facts to the audience:	☑
		Be willing to be wrong:	☑
Statistics	– Delinquency decreased by 20% & charge-offs by 37% – Top credit card complaint percentages – Student interest rates and change from Q1 to Q2 – Consumers expected to add $50 billion in debt in 2012	Use reliable & recent sources:	☒
		Identify the scales & units:	☒
		Consider kind of measure:	☑
		Use sparingly:	☒
		Explain/relate to audience:	☒
Examples	– American Express, Chase, CapitalOne, Discover, and Citi strategies through social media	Provide texture and depth:	☑
		Use representative cases:	☑
		Use variety of cases:	☑
		Connect to audience's experience:	☒
Testimony	– Quotation from Beverly Harzog, credit card expert – "http://online.wsj.com/articles/sb . . ." [beneath "Social-Media Endeavors" box] – Quotation from Ed Mierzwinski, U.S. Public Interest Research Group	Cite qualified & unbiased sources:	☒
		Indicate qualifications when appropriate:	☑
		Identify kind of source if possible & appropriate:	☒
Definitions	– Delinquency and charge-offs decreased – CARD Act restricts "tangible" gifts but omits social media	Define relevant terms first time you state them:	☒
		Be consistent:	☑
		Have a rationale for your definitions:	☑
		Illustrate/apply definitions as appropriate:	☑
Principles & Values (P&V)	– Credit scores are important – Better credit means better rewards (rewards are valuable) – "Play Responsibly"	Be aware of P&V in argumentation:	☒
		P&V should relate to audience's identity:	☑
		Use other support types to bolster P&V:	☑
		Expectations should be consistent & reasonable:	☑
Credibility	– WalletHub's latest credit card debt study (competence) – "Why should you care?" (character/goodwill)	Be aware of (and use) your credibility:	☑
		Create common ground:	☑
		Undersell & overdeliver:	☒

Source: John S. Kiernan, "Credit Cards Go Social and Why You Should Care," WalletHub, July 11, 2012.

You hopefully noticed how the infographic built up to a single, debatable proposition. Put in proper format for a policy debate, it would be something like: You should use WalletHub to play responsibly with your credit. We arrive here because the information all points to the claim at the bottom: "Play Responsibly and see what's ahead, at WalletHub.com." This proposition also makes sense because WalletHub would likely produce the infographic to interest audience members in its services.

Once we recognize the proposition, we can then consider the use of support within the infographic. Each type of support appears at least once in the infographic. Table 5.1 summarizes their presence and applies the guidelines for each to evaluate how well WalletHub used it. A checkmark in the right column means the support on the whole passes that guideline while an "x" indicates that at least one use of that support type violated that guideline.

Table 5.1 demonstrates that WalletHub generally used support effectively. The examples, in particular, did a great job illustrating the "going social" element by including numerous, representative cases. The facts were largely on track, although some of them lacked source information. The principles, values, and credibility were limited but effective, although the principles and values were sometimes buried and implied rather than stated explicitly. For example, the question "why should you care?" signals goodwill but the infographic didn't directly answer the question. Similarly, the appeal for you to "play responsibly" was an explicit use of principles and values but it was not clear what constitutes *responsible* play or how you could achieve that (apart from signing up for WalletHub's services).

The most problematic area of the infographic is the use of statistics. First, there were far too many with too little context for them to be useful. Additionally, the "Top Credit Card Complaints" wheel said nothing about the scale and units of these statistics: Do they refer to the percentage of official complaints filed, to survey results of a particular group of consumers, or something else entirely? Similarly, the infographic claimed delinquency and charge-offs have decreased but didn't indicate years—between when and when? Moreover, WalletHub didn't relate these statistics to the consumer or define the terms upon first use; if you don't know what delinquency or charge-offs are, the argument is largely meaningless.

On the whole, the infographic provided helpful information for the consumer. Do you feel it did enough to justify the proposition that you should use WalletHub to play responsibly with credit? Why or why not? This example illustrates the benefits and drawbacks of the various support options available for everyday argumentation. While we've considered each support type in turn, the next section offers some general strategies for using support.

STRATEGIES FOR USING SUPPORT

To this point, we've considered the quality of supporting statements on their own. However, we also know that supporting statements can be of low or high quality in relation to the claims they advance, the spheres in which they are used, and the audiences for whom they are argued. We'll conclude the chapter, then, with some general support strategies that account for these various factors.

1. **Support should be of high quality.** This might go without saying but we'll say it anyway. Even though the quality of support is contextual and debatable, you probably have a sense of what makes for high quality support and what doesn't. Thus, don't use bad support just because it's there. Instead, take the time to find high quality support using the material in this chapter.

2. **Support should guide claims.** It's common to start argumentation with the end point—the claim—and then support it. In many cases, this is both possible and appropriate. In some cases, however, if you are unable to find *good* support for your claim, it might be tempting to manipulate or skew information to make your claim look better. We noted in Chapter 3 that this would be unethical. In such cases, you should adjust your claims accordingly. As a general rule, support should guide claims rather than claims guiding support.

3. **Support should be acceptable to your audience.** Even if support is of high quality and guides your claims, your audience may not find it acceptable. Not everyone believes scientific evidence of climate change. Not everyone trusts opinion polls. Not everyone has the same experience as you. Consequently, be aware of how your audience will react to the support you use. We'll spend more time with acceptable support and audience adaptation in Chapters 9 and 11, respectively.

4. **Support should fit the sphere and situation.** Beyond adapting support to your audience, you should also adapt it to the sphere and situation. Private sphere debates rarely have expectations for what kind of support to use but public and technical spheres often do. The debate between Casson and Omalu at the beginning of this chapter illustrates this importance; that debate addressed to what degree interviews (a kind of testimony), surveys (a kind of example or statistic), and autopsies (a kind of fact) were appropriate for the scientific, technical sphere in which the debate occurred.

5. **Support should be stacked for stronger claims.** Stacking multiple types of support enhances your argument in three ways. First, it provides more help for your claim. Citing statistics, a striking example, and expert testimony, for instance, would make for a stronger claim than each of those on its own. Second, stacking support means that if your audience doesn't accept one kind, you might convince them with another. Third, stacking support enables you to provide a variety of considerations, new alongside time-worn ones, rather than rehashing the same information everyone has already heard.

6. **Support should engage both logic and emotion.** Logic is important, and we want support that provide a reasonable foundation for our claims. At the same time, emphasizing logic alone can often be impersonal and alienate audience members rather than invite them to be a part of your vision. Consequently, you should use support that engages both logic *and* emotion. We noted earlier that arguers can use any support type to get emotional investment in addition to logical agreement.

Heeding the above guidelines can help you advance arguments grounded in strong, persuasive support. The next few chapters are dedicated to how you might use this support to authorize strong, persuasive claims.

Summary

This chapter has addressed the important role of support in argumentation. As you research topics, use tests of trustworthiness, bias, and recency to assess the quality of information and follow the strategies for gathering information. It's important in an online environment to heed the tips outlined in this chapter as well as use critical thinking when assessing the source, author, and date of the information.

Recognizing that support is more than just evidence, we also considered seven different options for supporting claims: facts, statistics, examples, testimony, definitions, principles and values, and credibility. When used properly with an eye toward the guidelines in this chapter, each type of support has unique benefits. Table 5.2 outlines the tests of support for all information you gather as well as the specific types you encounter. We'll draw upon this information in subsequent chapters as we learn how to construct and evaluate arguments.

TABLE 5.2 ■ Summary of Tests of Support	
Start Here	
All Information	Is the information trustworthy?
	Is the information unbiased?
	Is the information recent?
If you answered "yes" to all three questions above, then use the specific tests below tailored to each support type	
Facts	Is the fact from a reliable source?
	Is the fact based on expertise rather than interest?
	Is the fact checked for accuracy?
	Is the fact adapted to the audience?
	Is the fact based on a willingness to be wrong?
Statistics	Is the statistic reliable and recent?
	Is the statistic indicating clear scales and units?
	Is the statistic the best measure?
	Is the statistic used sparingly in relation to other statistics?
	Is the statistic related to the audience?

(Continued)

TABLE 5.2 ■ (Continued)	
Examples	Is the example textured and deep?
	Is the example representative?
	Is the example one of a variety of cases?
	Is the example connected to the audience's experience?
Testimony	Is the testimony from a trustworthy and unbiased source?
	Is the testimony from a source with identified qualifications?
	Is the testimony from a source whose kind is appropriately identified?
Definitions	Is the definition provided on first use of the term?
	Is the definition consistently applied when the term is used?
	Is the definition accompanied by a rationale?
	Is the definition illustrated or applied?
Principles & Values	Is the principle or value argued explicitly with awareness?
	Is the principle or value related to the audience's identity?
	Is the principle or value bolstered by other support types?
	Is the principle or value based on consistent and reasonable expectations?
Credibility	Is the credibility used with awareness?
	Is the credibility used to create common ground?
	Is the credibility used to undersell and overdeliver?

Application Exercises

Evaluating Support: Next time you see advertisements while flipping through a magazine or watching a television program, consider the kinds of support used in the advertisements by answering the following questions:

1. Are certain kinds of support more common in advertising than others? Are there similarities based on the product category? If so, why might advertisers use those kinds of support rather than others?

2. For each advertisement, how well does the advertiser heed the guidelines for that type of support? To what degree is the support used in an effective and ethical manner?

3. As appropriate, what is one change to the support that would make it more effective at achieving the advertiser's goals? As appropriate, what is one change to the support that would make it more ethical?

Defending Against Sponsored & Opinion Content: You can more easily expose sponsored and opinion content by recognizing patterns of appearance. To assist with this, consider the below questions in relation to the landing page of one or more of the following online news and commentary websites: *CNN, FOX News, The Huffington Post, The Hill, Politico, The Blaze,* and *BuzzFeed*.

1. For each site, can you determine what content is site-created and what content is sponsored or paid? If so, based on what features?

2. For each site, can you determine what site-created content is news and what content is opinion? If so, based on what features?

3. In general, is the landing page mostly site-created or sponsored? Mostly news or opinion?

Key Terms

Fact 101
Statistic 103
Example 105

Testimony 106
Definition 108
Principle 109

Value 109
Credibility 111

Endnotes

1. Jeanne Marie Laskas, "Bennet Omalu, Concussions, and the NFL: How One Doctor Changed Football Forever," *GQ*, September 14, 2009, http://www.gq.com/story/nfl-players-brain-dementia-study-memory-concussions; Alan Schwarz, "Concussions Tied to Depression in Ex-N.F.L. Player," *New York Times*, May 31, 2007, http://www.nytimes.com/2007/05/31/sports/football/1concussions.html.

2. Ira Casson, quoted in Schwarz, "Concussions Tied to Depression in Ex-N.F.L. Player."

3. Ira Casson, quoted in Lauren Ezell, "Timeline: The NFL's Concussion Crisis; June 2007: NFL Hosts Concussion Summit," *FRONTLINE*, PBS, October 8, 2013, www.pbs.org/wgbh/pages/frontline/sports/league-of-denial/timeline-the-nfls-concussion-crisis.

4. Ira Casson, quoted in Laskas, "Bennet Omalu, Concussions, and the NFL: How One Doctor Changed Football Forever."

5. Bennet Omalu, quoted in Laskas, "Bennet Omalu, Concussions, and the NFL: How One Doctor Changed Football Forever."

6. *Oxford English Dictionary*, 3rd edition, s.v. "evidence," I.1.a.

7. *Oxford English Dictionary*, 3rd edition, s.v. "support," I.1.a.

8. "Bow Knows," Season 4, Episode 12, *Black-ish*, directed by Rob Sweeney, ABC, January 16, 2018.

9. Craig Silverman, "Here Are 50 Of The Biggest Fake News Hits On Facebook From 2016," *BuzzFeed News*, December 30, 2016, https://www.buzzfeed.com/craigsilverman/top-fake-news-of-2016.

10. "Evaluating Information: The Cornerstone of Civic Online Reasoning," Stanford History Education Group, November 21, 2016, 3, https://sheg.stanford.edu/upload/V3LessonPlans/Executive%20Summary%2011.21.16.pdf.

11. "Evaluating Information," 4.

12. Websites may change so these ratings are as of June 2018.

13. Henry Chu, "Reeled In by a Spoof, Chinese Daily Shrugs Off Its Capitol Error," *Los Angeles Times*, June 7, 2002, http://articles.latimes.com/2002/jun/07/world/fg-whoops7. In the next chapter, you'll learn this response is an argument ad ignorantiam.

14. Henry Chu, "Beijing Newspaper Retreats, Apologizes for Capital Gaffe," *Los Angeles Times*, June 13, 2002, http://articles.latimes.com/2002/jun/13/world/fg-whoops13.

15. Matthew Frankel, "Here's the Average American Household Income: How Do You Compare?" *USA Today*, November 24, 2016, https://www.usatoday.com/story/money/personalfinance/2016/11/24/average-american-household-income/93002252.

16. MoveOn, Twitter Post, June 1, 2018, 4:50 p.m., https://twitter.com/MoveOn/status/1002698815835602945.

17. Donald Trump, Twitter Post, June 1, 2018, 4:05 a.m., https://twitter.com/realDonaldTrump/status/1002506360351846400.

18. Chuck Woolery, Twitter Post, May 15, 2018, 10:53 p.m., https://twitter.com/chuckwoolery/status/996629658727800832.

19. David Zarefsky, "Presidential Rhetoric and the Power of Definition," *Presidential Studies Quarterly* 34 (2004): 612.

20. Benedict Anderson, *Imagined Communities: Reflections on the Origin and Spread of Nationalism*, rev. edition (New York: Verso, 1991); Michael Calvin McGee, "In Search of 'The People': A Rhetorical Alternative," *Quarterly Journal of Speech*, 61 (1975): 235-249.

21. "About WalletHub," *WalletHub*, 2017, https://wallethub.com/about.

22. John S. Kiernan, "Credit Cards Go Social and Why You Should Care," *WalletHub*, July 11, 2012, https://wallethub.com/edu/credit-cards-go-social/25683/.

6

COMMON ARGUMENT
TYPES

In August 2017, protests in Charlottesville, Virginia, reinvigorated the controversy about Confederate monuments in the United States and U.S. race relations more generally. Members of the "alt-right," including white nationalists and neo-Nazis, clashed with anti-fascist protestors, culminating in the murder of one person after a white supremacist drove his vehicle into a group of counter-protestors. President Trump did not denounce the white supremacists and observed instead that "many sides" shared the blame, sparking even more controversy about Trump's allegiances and role in emboldening the white supremacists in Charlottesville. Newspapers and citizens across the country tried to make sense of the situation: Who or what is to blame for the violence?

Statements of blame are argumentative claims. In many cases, we can't know for certain why one thing caused another and so we rely on inferential reasoning. The Editorial Board of the *Wall Street Journal* recognized this difficulty in their editorial response to those who blamed Trump for normalizing white supremacy. They called the focus on Trump a "cop-out" because "it lets everyone duck the deeper and growing problem of identity politics on the right and left." Later, the article more finely indicated Trump's role: "Mr. Trump didn't create this identity obsession even if as a candidate he did try to exploit it. He is more symptom than cause, though as President he now has a particular obligation to renounce it."[1]

We should reflect on the *Journal's* argument not to endorse it but to recognize the importance of argument types in everyday life. Essentially, the article critiqued others who argued Trump was a cause rather than sign of the problem, two different kinds of arguments you'll learn by the end of this chapter. In this case, the distinction between these two argument types mattered to understanding the relationship between presidential (campaign) rhetoric and action. Moreover, viewing Trump as cause rather than as sign will influence what actions people believe are necessary to address the problem. In other words, argument types have consequences.

When we talk about "argument types," we mean the recognizable and unique patterns of support-claim relationships that people frequently employ when arguing. This chapter builds on the previous one by exploring how arguers *use* support in the service of claims. We'll survey in depth six common types of arguments: classification, generalization, cause, sign, analogy, and authority. We'll then more briefly consider four additional argument types—*ad populum*, *ad ignorantiam*, *a fortiori*, and disjunctive—that often surface in everyday life.

Please note that this chapter is dedicated to *defining* the argument types and offering diverse examples that help you generate and identify them. In Chapter 10, we'll return to these argument types to discuss tools for *evaluating* and *refuting* them. The goal is to provide a repertoire of argumentative options from which to choose when interpreting others' arguments and building your own. It will also help facilitate your understanding of arguments that we discussed in Chapter 4. By the end of this chapter, you should be able to identify and construct ten different argument types.

APPLYING THE TYPES OF ARGUMENT TO EVERYDAY LIFE

We will label each type of argument as we encounter it throughout the chapter. This might give you a strong feeling of mastery as we explore them one at a time but keep in mind that recognizing argument types is not as easy in everyday life as it may initially appear because people don't label their arguments. Not only are warrants often unstated but the same kind of support (facts, examples, etc.) can authorize claims conforming to numerous argument types.

Identifying argument types in others' argumentation should start with the same process we've used all along—first isolate the proposition, claims, and support. Chapters 4 and 5 give you tools to do just that. Knowing each support-claim relationship should be enough information to determine the argument type but it does require you to add the warrant. As you'll discover, arguments of the same type have the same basic warrant pattern. This means you need to engage in detective work by using the available content to reach a reasoned judgment.

Using argument types in your own argumentation requires going in the other direction to some degree, considering what kind of support and warrant is appropriate for the claim you want to advance. Here, you should first determine your claim and then determine the support based on the appropriate kind of argument. As we've learned, the more support for a claim, the stronger the overall case tends to become. It's beneficial, then, to support a single claim with multiple argument types. At the same time, you should limit your claims or support to only those warrants for which you can provide backing. If not, it's best to shift the argument entirely. Ultimately, the content that follows is designed as a framework to assist your use of argument patterns in everyday life.

ARGUMENT FROM CLASSIFICATION

You are playing a game with friends and think one of them has broken the rules so you explain the rule and how your friend has violated it. You want an organization to pursue a course of action so you argue that it will satisfy the mission statement of that organization. You mull over potential definitions of love to decide if you love your significant other. All of these examples illustrate argument from classification, in which the argument begins with a general statement or idea and applies it to a specific instance.

More concretely, the *support* in an **argument from classification** comprises a general definition, principle, value, rule, guideline, law, etc. Using the material from the previous chapter, we can isolate <u>definitions</u>, <u>principles</u>, and <u>values</u> as frequent support types for argument from classification. The *claim* involves the application of that general statement to an object or instance that falls under the jurisdiction of the general statement. As the label "classification" suggests, this kind of argument frequently categorizes (or classifies) objects to facilitate the application.

> **ARGUMENT FROM CLASSIFICATION:** An argument claiming that a general statement of definition, rule, or principle applies to one or a few instances under that general statement's jurisdiction

---

Everyday Life Examples 6.1

Arguments from Classification

1 "Prudence . . . will dictate that Governments long established should not be changed for light and transient
2 causes; and accordingly all experience hath shewn, that mankind are more disposed to suffer, while evils
3 are sufferable, than to right themselves by abolishing the forms to which they are accustomed. But when a
4 long train of abuses and usurpations, pursuing invariably the same Object evinces a design to reduce them
5 under absolute Despotism, it is their right, it is their duty, to throw off such Government, and to provide
6 new Guards for their future security. — Such has been the patient sufferance of these Colonies; and such is
7 now the necessity which constrains them to alter their former Systems of Government. The history of the
8 present King of Great Britain is a history of repeated injuries and usurpations, all having in direct object the
9 establishment of an absolute Tyranny over these States. . . . We, therefore, the Representatives of the united
10 States of America, in General Congress, Assembled, appealing to the Supreme Judge of the world for the
11 rectitude of our intentions, do, in the Name, and by Authority of the good People of these Colonies, solemnly
12 publish and declare, That these United Colonies are, and of Right ought to be Free and Independent States"

13 **—The United States Declaration of Independence, July 4, 1776**[2]

14 "We could not just stand by and see those injustices of the terrorists denying our rights, ruthlessly
15 killing people, and misusing the name of Islam. We decided to raise our voice and tell them: Have you
16 not learnt, have you not learnt that in the Holy Quran Allah says: if you kill one person it is as if you kill
17 the whole humanity?

18 Do you not know that Mohammad, peace be upon him, the prophet of mercy, he says, do not harm
19 yourself or others.

20 And do you not know that the very first word of the Holy Quran is the word 'Iqra,' which means 'read'?"

21 **—Malala Yousafzai, Nobel Lecture, December 10, 2014**[3]

22 "Because we care about our planet, this 85% post-consumer fiber cup sleeve uses 34% less paper than
23 our original."

24 **—Starbucks Hot Beverage Cup Sleeve, 2015**

To explore the form of argument from classification in greater depth, we'll look at three empirical examples from different contexts. As you read the Everyday Life Examples 6.1, isolate the general statement comprising the support and the application comprising the claim for each.

Hopefully, you recognized the commonalities between the examples. Each offered a general statement or principle as support: People have the right and duty to "throw off" a despotic government (lines 1-6); Islam and the Quran promote peace and education (lines 16-20); Starbucks cares about the planet (line 22). Then, each applied that general idea to a specific topic or object: the colonies have a right to declare independence from the British government (lines 9-12); the terrorists are misusing the name of Islam by their actions (lines 14-15); Starbucks makes this cup sleeve with 34 percent less paper than the original (lines 22-23).

Although we've identified the claim and support, we know from earlier chapters that the warrant is essential to the argument's meaning. The *warrant* in an argument from classification, then, explains how the specific instance falls under the jurisdiction of the general principle. When the pieces are put together, the general model of an argument from classification is depicted in Figure 6.1.

The argument pattern holds up for each of the above examples (and others you might encounter). For instance, Yousafzai noted that the terrorists were "denying [education] rights" and "ruthlessly killing" people (lines 14-15), which enables the connection between Islam's teaching and the terrorists' perversion of it. The Declaration of Independence more explicitly models this warrant. How do we get from the people having a right and duty to throw off a despotic government to declaring independence? The argument tells us that the current King of Great Britain has been despotic toward the colonies (lines 6-9). This is depicted in Figure 6.2 and the Starbucks argument is depicted in Figure 6.3. As audience members, we must fill in the warrant (and backing,

FIGURE 6.1   ■   Model of Argument from Classification

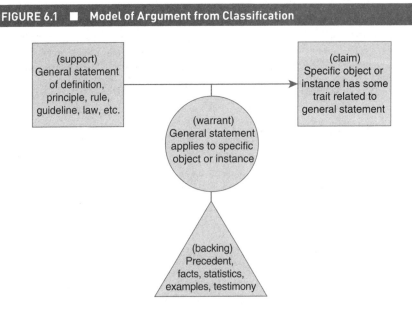

FIGURE 6.2 ■ Argument from Classification in the Declaration of Independence

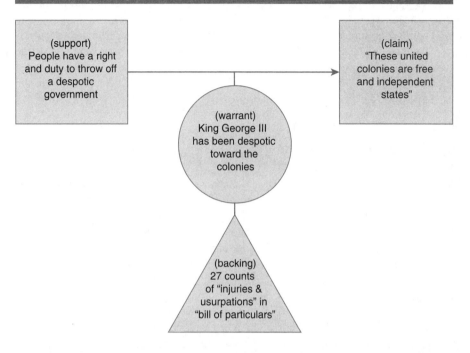

FIGURE 6.3 ■ Argument from Classification on the Starbucks Sleeve

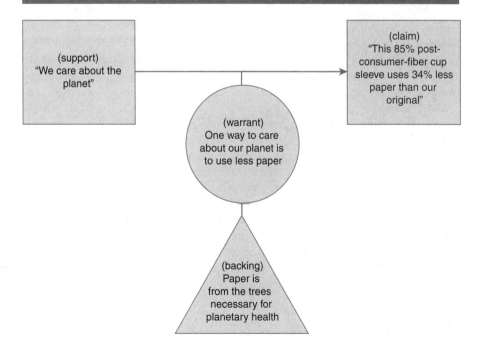

on occasion) to understand the argument's logic. Similarly, we should be aware of the logic by which arguments from classification operate when we construct our own arguments of this type.

The three arguments above also illustrate different uses of argument from classification: to justify a policy action in the case of the Declaration of Independence, to define the reality of something in the case of Yousafzai, and to promote goodwill through shared values in the case of Starbucks. These are some of the ways that classification arguments might help you further your argumentative goals.

ARGUMENT FROM GENERALIZATION

ARGUMENT FROM GENERALIZATION: An argument claiming that what is true of the sample is likely true of the category

SAMPLE: The group of examples from which the support is derived

CATEGORY: The entire category or group represented by the sample

You try to read all books by a specific author because you've read a few and really liked them. You talk to a few friends about an outfit choice and change your outfit when they say it isn't flattering. You form a stereotype about a group of people based on your experience with a few members of that group. These scenarios all rely on **argument from generalization,** which uses what is true of one or a few specific examples within a category to reach a general definition, principle, or rule about that category.

The *support* in a generalization argument relies primarily on examples (which, in turn, yield statistics) as the relevant category of supporting materials. We call the group of examples used as support the **sample.** You may have heard this term used in the context of opinion polls to talk about the group of people who were surveyed. Based on the qualities we know about the sample, the *claim* then generalizes those specific examples to all relevant instances, or what we call the **category.**

A generalization serves as an argument because the claim is about all related *unknown* cases. For instance, you don't know if you'll like the author's books you've not yet read but you can form an argumentative guess using your knowledge of that author's previous writing (perhaps a sample of two books). The idea of *related* cases is also important. Continuing with the book example, if you believe authorship is a relevant quality for your liking a book, you might conclude based on those two books that you will like all books by that author. If, on the other hand, you believe authorship and genre are both important, then perhaps you might conclude more narrowly that you will like all books of the same genre by that author. For instance, you might be more willing to read a new fiction novel by Stephen King than you would a new cookbook from him. As this example illustrates, generalization arguments use categories like classification arguments but argue in the opposite direction: from specific to general rather than from general to specific.

As you consider the Everyday Life Examples 6.2, look for what's known about the sample as the support and what's then extended to the category as the claim.

Each argument started with a sample and arrived at a general conclusion based on that sample. Roosevelt's sample included Hawaii, Malaya, Hong Kong, Guam, the Philippine Islands, Wake Island, and Midway Island (lines 2-8) to conclude—signaled by the term "therefore"—that Japan's attacks have extended "throughout the Pacific area" (line 9). Cox's sample included the experiences of herself, Islan Nettles, and Amanda Milan (lines 11-18) to reach a general principle that all trans women's lives are at risk (line 19). Finally, Strada-Gallup used a sample of more than 32,000 U.S. college students (line 21) to conclude what all U.S. college students believe (lines 22-26).

Everyday Life Examples 6.2

Arguments from Generalization

1   "Yesterday, December 7, 1941—a date which will live in infamy—the United States of America was
2   suddenly and deliberately attacked by naval and air forces of the Empire of Japan. . . . Yesterday the
3   Japanese Government also launched an attack against Malaya.

4   Last night Japanese forces attacked Hong Kong.

5   Last night Japanese forces attacked Guam.

6   Last night Japanese forces attacked the Philippine Islands.

7   Last night the Japanese attacked Wake Island.

8   This morning the Japanese attacked Midway Island.

9   Japan has, therefore, undertaken a surprise offensive extending throughout the Pacific area."

10   *—President Franklin Roosevelt, War Message, December 8, 1941*[4]

11   "Street harassment started first because these men found me attractive, because I'm a woman. Then
12   they realized that I was trans, and it became something else. It turned into something else. So many
13   trans women have to experience this.

14   Just last month in New York City, a young girl named Islan Nettles was walking down the street in
15   Harlem with her friend and she was catcalled by a few guys. They realized that she was trans, and
16   then they beat her to death.

17   In 2001, a trans woman named Amanda Milan, who I knew but not very well, something similar
18   happened to her in the Times Square area, and she was stabbed to death.

19   Our lives are often in danger, simply for being who we are, when we are trans women."

20   *—Laverne Cox, Speech at We Are Family Spirit Day rally, October 17, 2013*[5]

21   "Representing the views of more than 32,000 students at 43 randomly selected four-year institutions,
22   this [Strada-Gallup 2017 College Student] survey reveals a crisis of confidence among most students
23   regarding their readiness to launch careers:

24   Only a third of students believe they will graduate with the skills and knowledge to be successful in
25   the job market (34%) and in the workplace (36%).

26   Just half (53%) believe their major will lead to a good job."

27   *—Strada-Gallup 2017 College Student Survey Results, 2017*[6]

What allows each of the above arguments to move from one or a few examples to an entire category? The *warrant* in a generalization argument is that the sample is representative of the category in relevant qualities. To be representative means that the breakdown of relevant qualities of the sample matches the breakdown of those same qualities in the category. Figure 6.4 offers a model of a generalization argument including this warrant.

This model applies to all three arguments above. Roosevelt implied that the locales he listed are representative of "the Pacific area" category. Cox implied that her and two others' experiences are representative of all trans women. And, Strada-Gallup explicitly provided this warrant in its report, explaining that "the survey . . . is *representative* of

FIGURE 6.4   ■   Model of Argument from Generalization

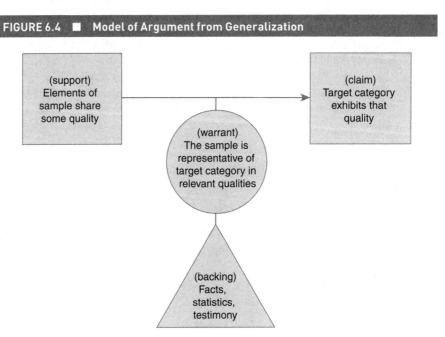

four-year, degree-granting U.S. institutions in terms of control (public vs. private institutions) and enrollment size."[7] Gallup further noted that "the margin of sampling error is ±0.8 percentage points at the 95% confidence level."[8] Adding the warrant and backing, we could diagram this argument in Figure 6.5.

Indeed, the sample's representativeness matters more than its size to a generalization argument. Gallup has assured us that their sample is representative but, to determine this, we would need to consult the raw numbers from their survey related to relevant qualities that influence how someone determines their preparation for the job market and workforce. Gallup believed control and enrollment size were important (that is, a college's status as private or public and a college's number of students both influence how prepared students feel for the job market and workforce), evident when it accounted for these qualities in selecting the sample. It might also be the case that the student's sex, race, and major matter to the results. Geographic region in the United States or political party affiliation, on the other hand, are not likely to be relevant qualities to how prepared U.S. college students feel for the job market or workforce.

Once you determine the relevant qualities, you then need to ensure the breakdown of those qualities in the 32,585 U.S. college students who are polled match the breakdown of students in the entire country. If Gallup were to poll 25,000 women and 7,585 men, the sample would not be representative because it doesn't match the distribution in all U.S. college students (provided the student's sex is a relevant quality to the claim). If sex was more representative but 90 percent of those polled were in STEM fields, we'd still have an unrepresentative sample (if the student's major is a relevant quality to the claim) because fewer than 90 percent of all U.S. college students major in STEM fields.

Consequently, a poll of 3,000 U.S. college students with a representative breakdown of relevant qualities would comprise a stronger sample for what all U.S. college students think than a non-representative poll of 30,000.

The above examples also illustrate different functions for a generalization argument: to add emphasis to a claim in the example from Roosevelt, to reach a general statement or principle in the example from Cox, and to speak for an entire group in the example of Strada-Gallup. Being attentive to the samples you and others select for generalization arguments and understanding how they function argumentatively can help you become a better arguer and audience member.

FIGURE 6.5 ■ **Argument from Generalization for Strada-Gallup Poll Results**

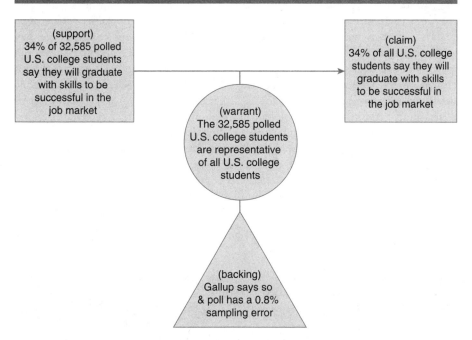

FIND YOUR VOICE
REPRESENTATIVE EXPERIENCE

We often reason based on our own experience and the experiences of those close to us, as the case of Cox illustrates. But when is your experience representative of others? Under what circumstances can you generalize from your own experience? Good arguers rarely presume that everyone has the same interpretation or experience as him- or herself. Cox illustrated this when she included additional examples to compound her own.

ARGUMENT FROM CAUSE AND CONSEQUENCE

ARGUMENT FROM CAUSE: An argument claiming that one or more elements are an influencing factor for another

You criticize a group member who is unfocused because he is preventing successful completion of the task at hand. Your computer crashes, and you try to determine if there's a virus responsible. You follow a superstitious habit to make sure your sports team wins when you watch the big game. Each of these examples rely on an **argument from cause**, proposing that one or more elements (the cause) are an influencing factor or reason for another (the effect). In some cases, we may argue from *cause to effect*, by using a cause to conclude some effect exists, while in others we may argue from *effect to cause*, using the effect to deduce the existence of some cause. The *support* in a cause argument relies primarily on facts, statistics, or testimony to establish the cause or effect. If the support identifies a cause, then the *claim* asserts an effect. If the support identifies an effect, then the claim asserts a cause.

CORRELATION: A relationship or association between two things.

It is important to distinguish causation from **correlation**. Things are correlated when they are associated with each other. Correlations are quite common and may or may not mean two objects are related, let alone that one caused the other. In fact, Tyler Vigen created a website and now has a book called *Spurious Correlations* dedicated to showing bizarre relationships between two objects.[9] Did you know the divorce rate in Maine correlates almost perfectly with per capita consumption of margarine in the United States? However, just because two things go together, that doesn't mean one of them caused the other. Causation requires stronger evidence to show that the cause precedes and produces the effect. The *Wall Street Journal* example to open this chapter addressed this very distinction, arguing that Trump's rhetoric is a symptom that *correlates with* but did not *cause* the violence in Charlottesville, Virginia.

Below, the Everyday Life Examples 6.3 include three arguments that do posit causation rather than correlation. As you read each, try to determine if the argument is from cause to effect or effect to cause by isolating the claim and support.

Everyday Life Examples 6.3

Arguments From Cause

1 "These United States are confronted with an economic affliction of great proportions. . . . For decades
2 we have piled deficit upon deficit, mortgaging our future and our children's future for the temporary
3 convenience of the present. To continue this long trend is to guarantee tremendous social, cultural,
4 political, and economic upheavals. . . . In this present crisis, government is not the solution to our
5 problem; government is the problem."

6 —*President Ronald Reagan, Inaugural Address, January 20, 1981*[10]

7 "WARNING: Tobacco smoke can harm your children."

8 —*Surgeon General Warning, Cigarette Packages, 2012-Present*[11]

9 "Education is transformative. It literally changes lives. . . . Education, more than any other force, can
10 help to erase arbitrary divisions of race and class, arbitrary divisions of culture, and to unlock every
11 person's God-given potential."

12 —*Condolezza Rice, Commencement Speech at High Point University, May 7, 2016*[12]

All three Everyday Life Examples demonstrate a causal relationship. Reagan argued from effect to cause: the economic crisis (line 1) is an effect of government deficits being a problem (lines 1-4). The cigarette warning and Rice argued from cause to effect: tobacco smoke causes harm to your children (line 7) and education causes the erasure of race and class divisions and the unlocking of everyone's potential (lines 10-11).

Causal arguments rely on a *warrant* that makes the causal connection explicit. A general statement of this warrant is that the cause likely results in the effect. Figure 6.6 offers a model of this argument pattern. Each causal argument, however, would have a variation of the warrant based on the specific cause and effect identified in the argument and the strength and direction of the causal relationship being advocated.

Indeed, when we say one thing "causes" another, we might mean one of four different causal relationships with differing degrees of strength:

- A cause is a *sufficient cause* for an effect when it is enough on its own to produce the effect. A sufficient cause might exist even if there are other ways that the effect could come about. For example, texting while driving is a sufficient cause for a car accident; it is enough on its own to produce the effect but car accidents can, of course, still occur absent texting.

- A cause is a *necessary cause* for an effect when it is required to produce the effect. Put another way, the effect cannot be reached without a necessary cause. When we say that watering flowers causes them to grow, we are isolating a necessary cause. Water is required for the effect to occur but it's not sufficient; flowers also need light and oxygen, for instance.

FIGURE 6.6 ■ Model of Argument from Cause

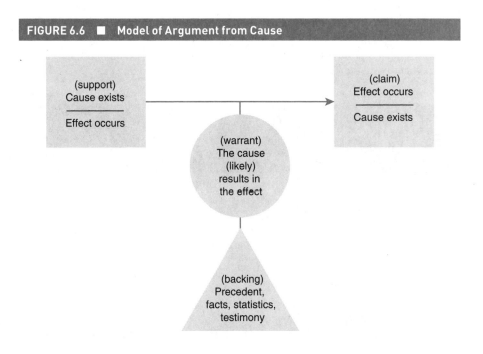

- A cause is a *necessary and sufficient cause* for an effect when the cause and only the cause produces the effect. A classic example of this relationship is to say that having four sides causes something to be a rectangle. Conversely, having four sides is a necessary cause for a square but not sufficient because we would need to add a second necessary requirement that the sides are of equal length. As this example illustrates, a necessary and sufficient cause is the strongest causal relationship and often requires substantial support.

- A cause is a *contributory cause* for an effect when it is one of many causes that combine to produce the effect. We mean this type of cause when the factors are not sufficient on their own and require other intervening ones. For instance, the argument that walking causes you to lose weight uses this meaning: Walking is a contributory cause that, combined with other factors such as diet, nutrition, and genetics, can produce the effect. Consequently, a contributory cause is the weakest causal relationship, requiring less stringent support.

Arguers rarely specify the kind of cause they mean despite its importance to the argument. As an audience member, you should try to identify the strength of the warrant *implied* by the argument and use that to guide your understanding. Similarly, as an arguer, you should be aware of the cause options and, when possible and appropriate, be explicit about how you intend the term "cause."

Considering our examples above, Reagan and Rice seem to argue sufficient causes, that government deficit piling or education are enough to produce the economic crisis and cultural transformation, respectively, but they are not necessary causes (other things could bring about those effects). Rice even noted that there are other causes but that education brings about the effect "more than any other force" (line 9). The health warning suggests a contributory cause when it states that exposure to smoke "can harm" children, implying that exposure to smoke is not necessary or sufficient for harm but one of the factors that might contribute to it. We could indicate this difference through the warrant in our diagrams, as demonstrated in Figures 6.7 and 6.8. Use the Build Your Skill box to practice identifying the kind of cause meant in each example argument.

BUILD YOUR SKILL
KINDS OF CAUSE

Identify the most likely type of cause for each argument:

A. Studying causes you to get an "A" on the test.

B. Providing the correct answer to all questions causes you to get an "A" on the test.

C. Showing up to class on test day causes you to get an "A" on the test.

D. Being a female causes you to be a sister.

E. Being a female sibling causes you to be a sister.

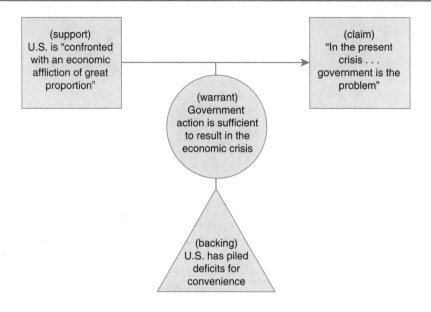

FIGURE 6.7 ■ **Argument from Cause in Reagan's Inaugural Address**

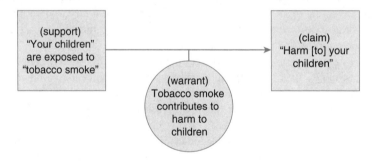

FIGURE 6.8 ■ **Argument from Cause in Cigarette Health Warning**

The above examples all centered on factual claims about existing causes or effects. Sometimes, however, arguments stipulate *anticipated* effects from *hypothetical* causes, what we call an **argument from consequence**. These arguments establish causal chains in an if-then format (if we do *x* action, then *y* will occur). It will become apparent in Chapter 7 that argument from consequence is quite common when we debate policy propositions.

One famous example of an argument from consequence appeared in the movie *Field of Dreams*: "If you build it, he will come." Figure 6.9 demonstrates that it uses the same warrant pattern as causal arguments.

ARGUMENT FROM CONSEQUENCE: An argument claiming that a hypothetical cause will produce an anticipated effect

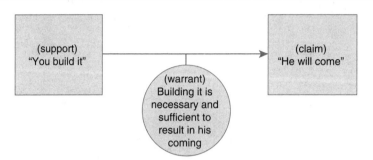

FIGURE 6.9 ■ Argument from Consequence in *Field of Dreams*

Despite the similarities, we distinguish arguments from cause and arguments from consequence to recognize that they function in two different tenses (the present and future, respectively). Nevertheless, we are concerned in both cases with the likelihood that the cause results in the effect. These arguments are useful when we are considering the value of a future action, trying to isolate why a problem or benefit exists, and discouraging or encouraging certain behaviors.

ARGUMENT FROM SIGN

ARGUMENT FROM SIGN: An argument claiming that observable signs indicate the existence of some condition or state of affairs

You consider your symptoms to diagnose an illness. You look at statistics to predict the winner of a sporting event or political election. You serve on a jury to determine someone's guilt or innocence. Each of these conclusions rely on **argument from sign** by using observable symptoms or signs to conclude the existence of some condition or state of affairs. The *support* in a sign argument can be of almost any variety, including facts, statistics, testimony, examples, principles, values, and credibility. Based on those signs, the *claim* then concludes that some condition exists or will exist.

Consider how the Everyday Life Examples 6.4 use observable signs or indicators to identify a condition.

Each example argues from observable indicators to reach the conclusion. Obama considered signs about the economy, education, health care, national confidence, energy, etc. (lines 1-6; 7-8) to conclude that the nation was in crisis (line 1). The College Board used SAT scores (lines 11-17) to conclude whether someone is ready for college and career (line 10). The CDC used various health symptoms to conclude whether you have "a cold or flu."

So how does this argument pattern work? The *warrant* connecting the support to the claim must establish that the signs are symptomatic or indicative of the condition. Figure 6.10 depicts the argument model in general terms. The logic of the three examples is identified if we follow the warrant pattern. The CDC identified symptoms that signal either a cold or flu. The College Board has created the SAT test that it believes is an indicator of college preparedness. And, Obama has identified factors that he believed are signs of crisis. In fact, Obama stated the warrant explicitly, noting "these are the indicators of crisis, subject to data and statistics" (lines 6-7). Figure 6.11 diagrams Obama's argument.

Everyday Life Examples 6.4

Arguments from Sign

1 "That we are in the midst of crisis is now well understood. Our Nation is at war against a far-reaching
2 network of violence and hatred. Our economy is badly weakened, a consequence of greed and
3 irresponsibility on the part of some, but also our collective failure to make hard choices and prepare
4 the Nation for a new age. Homes have been lost, jobs shed, businesses shuttered. Our health care is
5 too costly. Our schools fail too many. And each day brings further evidence that the ways we use energy
6 strengthen our adversaries and threaten our planet. These are the indicators of crisis, subject to data
7 and statistics. Less measurable but no less profound is a sapping of confidence across our land, a
8 nagging fear that America's decline is inevitable, that the next generation must lower its sights."

9 *—President Barack Obama, Inaugural Address, January 20, 2009*[13]

10   **SAT College and Career Readiness Benchmarks**

11   Evidence-Based Reading and Writing: **480**

12   Math: **530**

13   **SAT Section Score Ranges**

14   200–800 Point Scale

15

	Red	Yellow	Green
Evidence-BasedReading and Writing	200–450	460–470	480–800
Math	200–500	510–520	530–800

18   *—College Board, Readiness Benchmarks, 2017*[14]

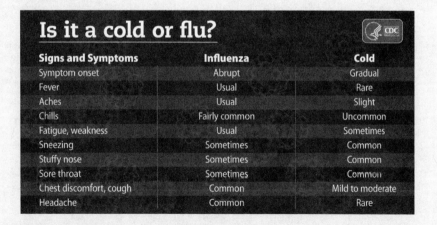

Is it a cold or flu?

Signs and Symptoms	Influenza	Cold
Symptom onset	Abrupt	Gradual
Fever	Usual	Rare
Aches	Usual	Slight
Chills	Fairly common	Uncommon
Fatigue, weakness	Usual	Sometimes
Sneezing	Sometimes	Common
Stuffy nose	Sometimes	Common
Sore throat	Sometimes	Common
Chest discomfort, cough	Common	Mild to moderate
Headache	Common	Rare

19   *—U.S. Centers for Disease Control, "Cold Versus Flu," January 30, 2018*[15]

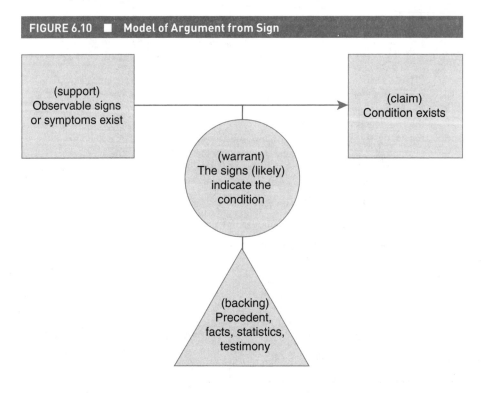

FIGURE 6.10   ■   Model of Argument from Sign

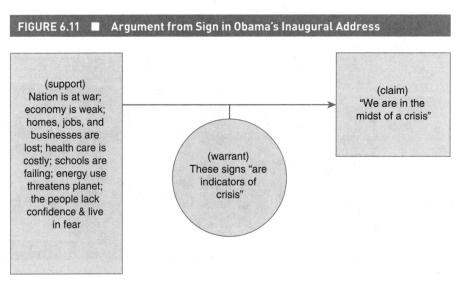

FIGURE 6.11   ■   Argument from Sign in Obama's Inaugural Address

It is easy to confuse sign arguments with cause arguments because warrants often go unstated and because the two types look so similar. Yet, notice the difference between Reagan's cause argument and Obama's sign argument, both concluding a crisis. Reagan identified the cause of (or reason for) the crisis—government deficits—to claim that government is the problem. Obama, on the other hand, identified the symptoms or signs of crisis; he argued not that the factors he listed caused the crisis but that they indicate its existence.

Ultimately, sign arguments use what we can see in our environment to conclude a specific state of affairs. These are particularly useful, the above examples illustrate, to identify the existence of problems, to reveal and predict correlations, and to classify objects based on their observable features.

ARGUMENT FROM ANALOGY

You decide not to see a movie sequel because the first movie was really bad. You want to improve morale in your workplace so you see what programs other, similar workplaces have implemented. You use a metaphor to explain a complex process. These are examples of **argument from analogy**, a comparative argument that uses what is known in one case to conclude something about another, unknown case. The *support* in an analogy uses examples, facts, statistics, and/or testimony to establish the known case and emphasize a quality of it. The *claim* then extends or rejects that quality in relation to the unknown case.

ARGUMENT FROM ANALOGY: An argument extending what is true of a known case to an unknown case

Consider how the Everyday Life Examples 6.5 use a known case (support) to reach a conclusion about an unknown case (claim).

Everyday Life Examples 6.5
Arguments From Analogy

1   "You have a row of dominoes set up, you knock over the first one, and what will
2   happen to the last one is the certainty that it will go over very quickly. So you
3   could have a beginning of a disintegration that would have the most profound
4   influences. . . . Asia, after all, has already lost some 450 million of its peoples to
5   the Communist dictatorship, and we simply can't afford greater losses. But when
6   we come to the possible sequence of events, the loss of Indochina, of Burma, of
7   Thailand, of the Peninsula, and Indonesia following, now you begin to talk about
8   areas that not only multiply the disadvantages that you would suffer through loss
9   of materials, sources of materials, but now you are talking really about millions
10   and millions and millions of people."

11   —*President Dwight Eisenhower, News Conference, April 7, 1954*[16]

12   "Life is a box of chocolates, Forrest. You never know what you're gonna' get."

13   —*Mrs. Gump, played by Sally Field, Forrest Gump, 1994*[17]

14   "I think in some way I may be connected to Trump. . . . sort of like Harry Potter and
15   Voldemort. Because I feel like I came out of nowhere and people were like, 'who?'
16   And then this thing also came out and they were like, 'it can't happen.' And now it's
17   happening. I think I may need to die to save America. To save you all."

18   —*Comedian Trevor Noah, The Late Show, September 14, 2016*[18]

Each example begins with a familiar case: one falling domino in a row causes them all to fall (lines 1-4), a box of chocolates is unpredictable (line 12), and Harry Potter and Voldemort were connected in good vs. evil opposition (lines 14-15). This quality is extended to an unknown or undecided case: one nation falling to communism would cause all surrounding nations to fall (lines 4-10), life is unpredictable (line 12), and Noah may need to die to save America from Trump (line 17). Essentially, the comparison borrows the quality of the known case and applies it to the unknown case.

The *warrant* for an analogy argument, then, requires that the similarities between the two cases outweigh the differences. This pattern is represented in Figure 6.12 and also helps explain each of the three examples. The domino theory of international relations makes sense if nations behave like dominos. Similarly, Mrs. Gump's argument relies on life being more similar to than different from a box of chocolates. And, Noah's argument hinged on the similarity between his connection to Trump and Harry Potter's connection to Voldemort. In fact, Noah explicitly provided backing for this warrant by describing how the comparison makes sense (lines 15-16).

In some situations, people may use analogies to establish a difference rather than similarity between the two cases. These arguments use a similar pattern to Figure 6.12 but the claim of the argument is that the quality of the known case does *not* apply to the unknown case and the warrant, then, is that the two cases are more different than similar. For instance, in the early 1990s, some people were skeptical of the Persian Gulf War because of the lingering scars of the Vietnam War. President George H. W. Bush

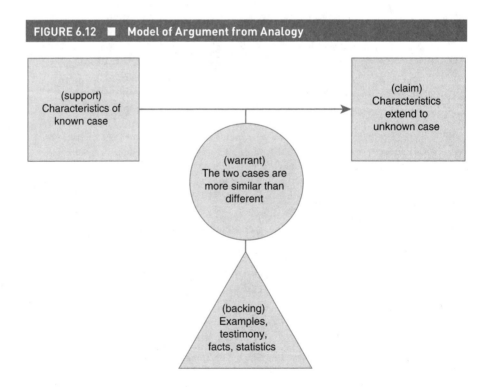

FIGURE 6.12 ■ Model of Argument from Analogy

FIGURE 6.13 ■ Argument from Analogy in Bush's Press Conference

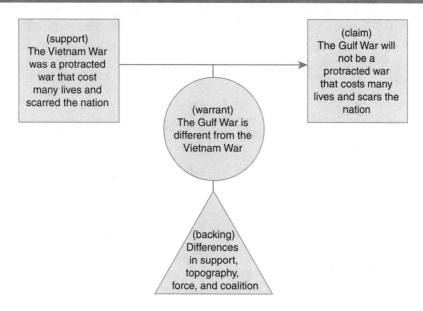

responded to such concerns by adamantly arguing that the two wars would not be the same, telling reporters for instance (diagrammed in Figure 6.13):

> I have looked into it enough and talked to enough of the planners and those responsible, not only in our country but leaders around the world, to be totally confident and tell the American people we are not looking at another Vietnam. The analogy is totally different in who is supporting you, what the topography is, what the force is, what the determination of the military is—the whole array—the coalition. All of these things come together and argue very forcefully this is not another Vietnam.[19]

The quality of each analogy will boil down in large part to the fundamental similarity or difference between the two cases. Analogies can helpfully offer perspective on a situation, encourage directed conduct, or differentiate competing ideas.

ARGUMENT FROM AUTHORITY

You give your friend directions after getting lost, commenting "trust me, I've made this same mistake before." You cite a credible expert who establishes the main point you want to argue in a paper you write for class. You agree to take the medication your doctor prescribes. These cases all illustrate reasoning from authority. **Arguments from authority** conclude something because an authority said so. The *support* in an authority argument is almost always <u>testimony</u> or <u>credibility</u>, although it may on occasion be <u>definitions</u> (such as when a theory or a law is named after those who generated it). The *claim* then affirms the ideas stated in the support.

ARGUMENT FROM AUTHORITY: An argument concluding that something is true based on the expertise of the source

Arguments From Authority

1   "I've received a lot of letters in these last terrible days. One stood out because it came from a young
2   widow and a mother of three whose own husband was murdered with over 200 other Americans when
3   Pan Am 103 was shot down. Here is what that woman said I should say to you today: 'The anger you feel
4   is valid, but you must not allow yourselves to be consumed by it. The hurt you feel must not be allowed
5   to turn into hate, but instead into the search for justice. The loss you feel must not paralyze your own
6   lives. Instead, you must try to pay tribute to your loved ones by continuing to do all the things they left
7   undone, thus ensuring they did not die in vain.' Wise words from one who also knows. You have lost too
8   much, but you have not lost everything."

9   *—President William Clinton, Oklahoma City Bombing Memorial, April 23, 1995*[20]

10   "Jesus loves me—this I know,

11   For the Bible tells me so"

12   *—Anna Bartlett Warner, Say and Seal, 1860*[21]

13   "You will do this because I said so."

14   *—Every mother, speaking to her children, any time and place*

Consider the Everyday Life Examples 6.6 for how they base a claim on an authority. The above examples are all authority arguments insofar as they use testimony to support a conclusion. Clinton used "wise words" from the widow (lines 3-7) to encourage those suffering following the Oklahoma City bombing to heed her message of hope (lines 7-8). The poem (and later song) by Warner cites the Bible (line 11) as a reason Jesus loves you (line 10). And, mothers invoke their own authority as a parent when they tell you to do something because they said so (line 13). You'll notice that an argument from authority requires the arguer to *explicitly* appeal to or cite the authority as the support for the argument. A teacher giving a lecture or a president delivering a speech aren't arguing from authority unless they state directly that you should believe them because of their knowledge or expertise.

How, then, do we move from someone's saying something to us believing it? The *warrant* in an authority argument is that the source is a credible authority on the topic. The argument model is depicted in Figure 6.14. This warrant holds up in the three examples. Clinton noted explicitly that the message came from "one who also knows" how it feels to lose someone you love in a terrorist attack. Warner's argument relies on the Bible as an authority about Jesus's love. And, your mom implies that she's an authority on what you should do and when you should do it.

This warrant is crucial to distinguishing argument from authority from argument from generalization. Recall that generalizations might also use one or a few people's opinions to reach a general conclusion but the difference comes down to the warrant. Argument from generalization considers the people to be representative of others in the category and doesn't require any expertise or knowledge on the topic. Argument from authority, however, depends on the expertise or authority of the source. Cox,

FIGURE 6.14 ■   Model of Argument from Authority

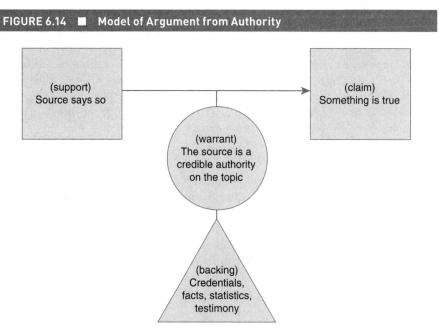

for instance, reached her conclusion about violence not on the basis of her expertise but on the basis of her (representative) experience. The difference is slight but it changes the nature of the warrant that moves the audience from Cox's example to the conclusion.

In sum, authority arguments conclude something is true because an authority said so. They are useful when you want to enhance or use credibility when arguing, to rely on the work others have already done, and to have the audience take someone else's (more believable) word for your claim.

ADDITIONAL ARGUMENT TYPES

Although the previous six arguments are perhaps the most common ones, there are many additional types that you may encounter in everyday argumentation. The ability to discuss all of these would be impossible but the remainder of the chapter will consider four additional argument types: argument from popularity, from ignorance, from the stronger, and from disjunct. Each of these is worth knowing because they are common in everyday life and are often poor forms of reasoning, failing the standards for argument evaluation we'll explore in later chapters.

Argument From Popularity (*ad populum*)

In democratic societies such as the United States, *ad populum* **arguments**, or arguments from popularity, can be quite common because they are rooted in what the people believe and want. The *support* for arguments from popularity comprise public or popular

ARGUMENT
AD POPULUM:
An argument
concluding
something is good,
bad, right, wrong,
true, false, etc.
based on what is
popular

opinion about something, usually <u>facts</u>, <u>statistics</u>, or <u>testimony</u>. The *claim* then accepts what is popular as right. The *warrant* justifying the use of this support is often that the audience should heed what is popular.

For example, a company's president might argue that the company should enact a policy because a majority of stakeholders believe it is a good policy. Or, you might justify going to a particular restaurant with a group of friends because it is always packed with people. Or, a lobbyist might advocate a policy to Congress because the American people want it. Each of these is an example of argument from popularity.

Argument From Ignorance (*ad ignorantiam*)

ARGUMENT *AD IGNORANTIAM*:
An argument concluding something is true or false based on the lack of support for or against it

Arguments from ignorance support a conclusion based on the lack of counter-knowledge or evidence. There are two variations of this. In one variation, the *support* indicates that a <u>fact</u> or <u>statistic</u> has not been proven, and the *claim* then takes the lack of proof as evidence for its falsity. The *warrant* implies that the inability to prove something (ignorance) means it is false. In the second variation, the *support* indicates that a <u>fact</u> or <u>statistic</u> has not been disproven and the *claim* then concludes the fact or statistic must be true. The *warrant* here is that the inability to disprove something means it is true.

For example, people may argue aliens don't exist because scientists can't prove they do. Or, someone may support a superstition because no one has proven it won't achieve its goal (whether or not they have evidence that it will). It is also common to find arguments from ignorance when people respond to another person's arguments. You might see a debate, for example, where one arguer claims that their plan will work because we don't have evidence to the contrary. The co-arguer then might respond by claiming the lack of evidence about the plan's feasibility means it *won't* work. In all cases, the support boils down to ignorance, or a lack of knowledge.

Argument From the Stronger (*a fortiori*)

ARGUMENT *A FORTIORI*:
An argument concluding something based on a weaker or stronger version of that thing.

Translated as argument "from the stronger," *a fortiori* **arguments** are rooted in a stronger case to justify a weaker case or a weaker case to justify a stronger. The *support* for *a fortiori* arguments is usually a <u>fact</u>, <u>statistic</u>, or <u>example</u> of some sort. The *claim* then concludes a weaker (or stronger) version of that fact, statistic, or example. The *warrant* observes that more (or less) is required for the support than for the claim.

You may come across *a fortiori* arguments in a variety of contexts. For example, you might use the fact that you can run a mile in 10 minutes to conclude you can run it in 12 minutes (a variation would be to conclude you can't run a mile in 8 minutes because you haven't run it in 9 minutes). Your boss might argue that if even hourly employees support a wage decrease for the benefit of the company, then other employees should also support it. Or, a religion might argue that if a deity can love prostitutes and murderers, that deity can surely love you as well. In each case, the argument uses the stronger or weaker version of a case to conclude something.

Argument from Disjunct (either-or)

ARGUMENT FROM DISJUNCT:
An argument concluding that one option is the right choice based on the undesirability of the others

Disjunctive arguments pick an option based on a dilemma or choice between two or more options. The *support* for this kind of argument involves offering two or more options, usually stated as an undisputable <u>fact</u>. The *claim* then chooses one of them.

The *warrant* is that the other options are worse or unacceptable. Often, a disjunctive argument will explicitly state the warrant to reject one or more options before settling on the claim.

Politicians often use disjunctive arguments, often in some variation of "either you are with us or you are against us." Here, the implied claim is that you should be with rather than against them. You might have used this kind of argument with your parents to get them to let you do or buy something (e.g., "either you let me go to the party willingly, or I'll sneak out"). Organizations also frequently use disjunctive reasoning when considering the path forward. In each case, the argument first posits a dilemma and then selects either explicitly or implicitly the "right" choice.

FIND YOUR VOICE
WHEN IS IT APPROPRIATE?

People often discount the above four argument types as "bad" arguments because the support offers a poor foundation. There are, however, some circumstances when they are quite appropriate and effective. For instance, it's appropriate for an elected official to use an *ad populum* argument in debating a law but inappropriate for you to use it when convincing your parents to buy you something. For each of the four, consider scenarios when that type would be appropriate and when it would be inappropriate.

Summary

This chapter has explored 10 argument types that represent unique warrant patterns connecting claims and support. Arguments from classification argue that a general principle, rule, definition, or guideline applies to a specific instance. Arguments from generalization argue what's true of a representative sample is also true of an entire category. Arguments from cause argue that one thing precedes and is the reason for another. Arguments from sign argue that one or more signs indicate the existence of a condition. Arguments from analogy argue that what's true of a known case is also true of a similar, unknown case. And, arguments from authority argue that the audience should accept the claims of a relevant expert.

Beyond the major six, we also considered four additional types: Arguments *ad populum* argue that the audience should accept what's popular or supported by public opinion. Arguments *ad ignorantiam* argue that something is true if it can't be disproven or something is not true if can't be proven. Arguments *a fortiori* argue that a stronger case justifies a weaker case and vice-versa. And, arguments from disjunct argue that one choice is the right one given a decision between two or more. By learning these patterns of argumentation, you are better equipped to understand and generate arguments in everyday life.

Application Exercises

Identifying Argument Types: Now that you have more advanced skills in understanding arguments and warrant patterns, return to the Everyday Life Examples from previous chapters: The *Scary Mommy* post in Chapter 1, Roosevelt's "War Message" in Chapter 2, Zzzmessi1's original *Change My View* post in Chapter 3, and James Harrison's Instagram post in Chapter 4. For these argumentative cases, identify the various argument types and determine the warrant for each.

Creating Argument Types: For the following claims, consider how you could support the claim with each of the six major argument types (classification, generalization, cause, sign, analogy, authority), using the example below as a model of what this might look like. Also, determine the warrant for each argument based on the patterns described in the chapter. Keep in mind that some claims may work more naturally with some argument types and less so with others. Thus, also consider which kinds of arguments are best for each of the claims and why that might be the case.

1. Social media is beneficial to society.

2. The education system in the United States is broken.

3. Climate change is occurring.

4. Everyone should use their passport.

Example: Claim: People should take time to enjoy life because. . .

Classification: . . . to live is to be in the present rather than fret about the future (support). [warrant: enjoying life is classified under or a part of living in the present]

Generalization: . . . my friends and I always feel better when we enjoy life (support). [warrant: my friends and I are representative of all people]

Cause/Consequence: . . . the world will be a more pleasant place (support). [warrant: people enjoying life likely results in a more pleasant world]

Sign: . . . . life is fragile and you could die at any moment without warning (support). [warrant: the fragility of life likely indicates people should enjoy life]

Analogy: . . . people don't want to live in a prison (support). [warrant: not enjoying life and prison are more similar than different]

Authority: . . . Twenty One Pilots said so in "Ride" (support). [warrant: Twenty One Pilots is a credible authority on living]

Key Terms

Endnotes

1. Editorial Board, "The Poison of Identity Politics," *Wall Street Journal*, August 13, 2017, https://www.wsj.com/articles/the-poison-of-identity-politics-1502661521.

2. "Declaration of Independence: A Transcription," *America's Founding Documents*, National Archives, https://www.archives.gov/founding-docs/declaration-transcript.

3. Malala Yousafzai, "Malala Yousafzai—Nobel Lecture," *Nobelprize.org: The Official Website of the Nobel Prize*, https://www.nobelprize.org/nobel_prizes/peace/laureates/2014/yousafzai-lecture_en.html.

4. Franklin D. Roosevelt, "138–Address to Congress Requesting a Declaration of War with Japan," December 8, 1941, *The American Presidency Project*. ed. John T. Woolley and Gerhard Peters, 1999-2017, http://www.presidency.ucsb.edu/ws/index.php?pid=16053.

5. Laverne Cox, "Laverne Cox on Bullying and Being a Trans Woman of Color," Keppler Speakers, YouTube video, 6:49, December 19, 2013, https://youtu.be/7zwy5PEEa6U.

6. Gallup, Inc., "Strada-Gallup 2017 College Student Survey," *Gallup*, 2017, http://news.gallup.com/reports/225161/2017-strada-gallup-college-student-survey.aspx.

7. Emphasis added. Gallup, Inc., *2017 College Student Survey: A Nationally Representative Survey of Currently Enrolled Students*, 2017, 1, http://news.gallup.com/file/reports/225161/Strada-Gallup%20January%202018%20Student%20Survey%20Report.pdf.

8. Gallup, Inc., *2017 College Student Survey*, 28.

9. Tyler Vigen, *Spurious Correlations* (New York: Hachette Books, 2015).

10. Ronald Reagan, "Inaugural Address," January 20, 1981, *The American Presidency Project*. ed. John T. Woolley and Gerhard Peters, 1999-2017, http://www.presidency.ucsb.edu/ws/index.php?pid=43130.

11. Food and Drug Administration, Department of Health and Human Services, "Required Warnings for Cigarette Packages and Advertisements," *Federal Register* 76, no. 120, pt. II (June 22, 2011), 36628, https://www.gpo.gov/fdsys/pkg/FR-2011-06-22/pdf/2011-15337.pdf.

12. Condoleezza Rice, "Condoleezza Rice to Grads: 'Don't Let Anyone Else Define Your Passion,'" *TIME*, May 10, 2016, http://time.com/4323641/condoleezza-rice-high-point-university-commencement-speech.

13. Barack Obama, "Inaugural Address," January 20, 2009, *The American Presidency Project*. ed. John T. Woolley and Gerhard Peters, 1999-2017, http://www.presidency.ucsb.edu/ws/index.php?pid=44.

14. College Board, "Benchmarks: SAT College and Career Readiness Benchmarks," 2017, https://collegereadiness.collegeboard.org/about/scores/benchmarks.

15. Centers for Disease Control, "Cold Versus Flu," January 30, 2018, https://www.cdc.gov/flu/about/qa/coldflu.htm.

16. Dwight D. Eisenhower, "73–The President's News Conference," April 7, 1954, *The American Presidency Project*. ed. John T. Woolley and Gerhard Peters, 1999-2017, http://www.presidency.ucsb.edu/ws/index.php?pid=10202.

17. *Forrest Gump*, directed by Robert Zemeckis (1994; Hollywood, CA: Paramount, 2001), DVD.

18. Trevor Noah, "Don't Put Trevor Noah in a Basket," *The Late Show with Stephen Colbert*, YouTube video, 4:54, September 15, 2016, https://youtu.be/UbPbCGnUj5g.

19. George Bush, "The President's News Conference With Regional Reporters," December 18, 1990, *The American Presidency Project*. ed. John T. Woolley and Gerhard Peters, 1999-2017, http://www.presidency.ucsb.edu/ws/index.php?pid=19166.

20. William J. Clinton, "Remarks at a Memorial Service for the Bombing Victims in Oklahoma City, Oklahoma," April 23, 1995, *The American Presidency Project*. ed. John T. Woolley and Gerhard Peters, 1999-2017, http://www.presidency.ucsb.edu/ws/index.php?pid=51265.

21. Susan Warner and Anna Bartlett Warner, *Say and Seal*, vol. II (1860; Philadelphia, PA: J. B. Lippincott & Co., 1888), 115.

7

BUILDING EFFECTIVE CASES

It's highly probable that you own a smartphone. If you do, you should thank Nokia for its design. If you didn't live through much of the 1990s and early 2000s, it may surprise you that Nokia manufactured more than one third of the world's phones in 2001 and that its sales outpaced "those of its three closest rivals combined."[1] Nokia achieved this success in large part by emphasizing form alongside function, transforming mobile phones into customizable fashion accessories.[2] One of Nokia's engineers, Erik Anderson, explained that this transformation occurred because of a bar in Salo, Finland.[3] The engineers would gather there and put their phones on the table. At the end of the night, they couldn't tell them apart so they decided to paint them different colors. As Anderson noted, "It isn't so glamorous, but that's where the route to color and fashion phones begins."[4]

Of course, the outcome was not as simple as one person dreaming it up and Nokia producing it. In this case, there was conflict between the engineers and designers at Nokia. Phone designers wanted to eliminate the unsightly external antennas that were industry standard at the time by placing it inside the phone but engineers and the general public were resistant to this idea.[5] Consequently, the designers used argumentation skills to convince the engineers that they could find a solution. Using terms introduced in Chapter 1, designers had a high burden of proof because presumption favored the *status quo*. Nokia ultimately succeeded by placing the antenna alongside the battery pack in the wider and thicker top portion of the Nokia 3210, the first phone of its kind. Even though the redesign solved the problem of all phones looking alike, it would not have survived without various stakeholders advancing argumentative cases and resolving controversial issues related to the decision.

The Nokia story is just one illustration of how people use argumentation to find solutions to vexing problems and to persuade others to accept a proposition. In this chapter, we will consider the process of and structure for building effective cases on propositions of fact, value, and policy. The material in this chapter serves as your *offense* in a debate because it involves strong arguments that demonstrate your stance. We'll consider how to refute other's arguments—your *defense* in a debate—in later chapters.

Although the content in this chapter may feel like it's designed for more formal debate situations, it is also useful for advocacy in everyday life. Perhaps think of this material like a cookbook that gives you structural "recipes" to generate your own cases. The recipes can be used in virtually any context to effectively organize your ideas, but, much like real cooking, you need to be creative in adapting the argumentative ingredients to specific tastes and topics relevant to the debate situation. By the end of this chapter, you should be able to effectively construct and dissect cases on propositions of fact, value, and policy.

DEBATING FACT PROPOSITIONS

We debate fact propositions when we want to determine whether a statement is true or false. These debates are common in all spheres of life, such as debating what an unknown food is, diagnosing an illness based on symptoms, discussing a causal relationship between two things, judging the guilt or innocence of an accused individual, or considering the meaning of an abstract concept.

While fact debates are important on their own, they are also often a starting point in a larger controversy that involves debates about propositions of value or policy. As we saw in Chapter 1, for instance, the debate about whether vaccines cause autism (a fact debate) was fundamental to the debate about whether parents should vaccinate children (a policy debate). In this section, we'll discuss two facets of fact debates: how to resolve them and how to argue them.

Resolving Fact Debates

When you've debated fact propositions such as those mentioned earlier, how do you tend to reach a decision? The stakes differ but the process was likely the same: you weighed the support (related to various issues relevant to the proposition) and determined which side was stronger. The label we use for this decision-rule is **preponderance of evidence**. That is, we tend to side with the proposition when there is superior support or stronger reasons to agree with it than to disagree with it.

PREPONDERANCE OF EVIDENCE: Resolving a fact debate by weighing the superiority of support for and against the proposition

Recall that debates are organized around issues, those neutral yes/no questions that capture the specific argumentative disagreements. In a fact debate, the disagreements address various reasons the proposition is true or false. Deciding the debate, then, requires lining up those reasons to determine which are more important. Once you have the answers to the issues, you're ready to weigh the support and determine which side is correct. Of course, as new support emerges, you may be forced to revisit the claims on the issues and revise them accordingly. And, the burden of proof will differ depending on presumption in the debate.

How do we know if the support is of high quality? We spent some time with this in Chapter 5, but the decision usually comes down to the following criteria:

- *Credibility*: How reliable is the support? How much is it based in expertise?

- *Recency*: How current is the support?

- *Relevance*: How strong are the warrants connecting the support to the claim(s)?

Resolving fact debates, then, involves determining the importance of issues and weighing the arguments about those issues. The next section explores how to structure cases in such debates.

Affirming and Opposing Fact Propositions

Knowing that fact debates are decided on the quality of the reasons for and against the proposition, it should be no surprise that argumentative cases tend to explicitly argue these reasons. In many cases, however, a fact debate may require the arguer first to define relevant words in the proposition as they impact the eventual reasons. This is evident in Supreme Court opinions, for instance, which first define concepts using precedent and then argue how those concepts apply to the current case.

We'll discuss both steps—defining terms and arguing reasons—in relation to the following fact proposition: "Adolescents who play violent video games are more likely to engage in violent behavior." Chances are you played video games as an adolescent or had friends who did, making it a relevant proposition to your own experience. Moreover, it is a controversial claim that many scholars, politicians, parents, and gamers have deliberated, providing a good example for our consideration. Before reading further, take a moment to consider your presumption: Are you disposed to agree or disagree with it?

Defining Terms

Defining terms in a fact debate ensures all participants agree to the very meaning of the proposition before tackling the substantive arguments concerning its truth. Defining terms in many cases is a minor part of the debate and sometimes may not need to happen if the proposition is self-evident (e.g., "I have the flu"). In other cases, though, defining terms may be crucial to resolving the debate.

For our example proposition ("adolescents who play violent video games are more likely to engage in violent behavior"), defining terms is likely important. What words or phrases might you to define to ensure others have the same meaning as you? It depends on the audience, but the following terms are potential candidates: "adolescents," "play," "violent video games," "more likely to engage in," and "violent behavior."

FIND YOUR VOICE
DEFINING TERMS

Consider how you would define these terms. What does each mean to you? If you wanted to see how experts studying this topic have defined them, where would you go? Library reference materials tailored to the controversy are usually a better starting point than Google or dictionary.com.

Once you select the words or phrases requiring definition, you should follow three guidelines for defining them:

1. Definitions should be *reasonable*. Because everything is technically debatable, you could use obscure or tricky definitions to give you the upper hand. From a competitive or manipulative stance, this might be wise. If, however, you're working toward cooperative argumentation, you want definitions that your audience would readily accept. In many cases, you should find these definitions through research or use official definitions of the appropriate sphere when possible.

    For our example, we might turn to the American Psychological Association (APA) to define "violent behavior." The APA resolution on violent video games in 2015 observed that violence constitutes "an extreme form of aggression or the intentional use of physical force or power that either results in or has a high likelihood of resulting in harm." The APA further explained that "all violence, including lethal violence, is aggression, but not all aggression is violence."[6] The definition of "violent behavior" is reasonable because it is grounded in research but it is also still debatable; co-arguers could propose an equally plausible alternative.

2. Definitions should *provide clarity*. Defining terms should make the proposition's meaning more rather than less comprehensible. If you use definitions that themselves need definition, you've probably failed at this task. For instance, defining "violent video games" as "games that involve killing" may clarify some boundaries but would still leave substantial ambiguity (e.g., Is *Super Mario Bros.* a violent video game since Mario "kills" Goombas by stomping on them?). Instead, you might be more specific about "violent video games" by identifying a genre, rating level, markers of violence such as blood splatters, or perhaps all of the above.

    One way to ensure clarity of your definitions is to substitute the word in the proposition with the definition. For "Adolescents who play violent video games are more likely to engage in violent behavior," the defined proposition might read "People aged 12 to 17 who spend more than 5 hours a week with games rated M that involve the main character using guns as a weapon are more likely to engage in the intentional use of physical force or power, that either results in or has a high likelihood of resulting in harm." As you can see, the defined version more clearly reveals the meaning of the proposition. However, doing this for yourself doesn't settle the definitional debate; co-arguers can still challenge your definitions by proposing better alternatives.

3. Definitions should *indicate argumentative burdens* (but not arguments). Once defined, it should be evident what someone would need to demonstrate to affirm or oppose the proposition. To clarify, the definitions do not advance arguments for or against the proposition but rather indicate the appropriate scope and range of those eventual arguments.

    For example, we could define "more likely to engage in" as a statement of causation rather than correlation (you can review this distinction in Chapter 6). This would mean that the arguments need a higher burden of proof, so it would not be sufficient to merely establish that playing violent video games correlates with violent behavior.

Once arguers establish the meaning of the proposition, they turn to the substantive arguments about it.

Arguing Reasons

As noted earlier, the core of a fact debate revolves around the reasons the proposition is true, using support to bolster claims on relevant issues. When arguing fact propositions, an organized structure is important to help audiences and co-arguers understand your major arguments. Box 7.1 outlines what a case might look like, whether written or spoken and whether formal or informal.

Debating our example proposition would require generating issues and arguments concerning why it is or is not true. There are numerous relevant issues you might consider: Have rates of violent behavior increased at the same pace as sales of violent video games? Do scientific studies support a connection between violent video games and violent behavior? Do people who commit mass atrocities also play violent video games? Do violent video games produce a cathartic effect? Do violent video games desensitize players to violence? Do results differ based on short- vs. long-term play? Do other factors beyond violent video games contribute to or account for violent behavior? These are just some of the relevant issues that people have explored in trying to resolve this proposition.

There are strong arguments for both sides. The APA has published the most thorough support that violent video games desensitize people to violence, producing increased aggression. The APA Task Force on Violent Media published in 2015 an extensive review of existing research about violent video games. The summary of the study stated explicitly that, "on the basis of our review of the literature directly addressing violent video game use, we concluded that violent video game use has an effect on aggression."[7]

BOX 7.1: CASE STRUCTURE FOR FACT DEBATES

I. **Introduction and Thesis**

  A. Gain interest in controversy and its significance

  B. State your thesis/stance on the proposition

  C. Preview your reasons for that stance

II. **Definitions**

  A. Define term #1

    1. Justify the definition

    2. Explain why preferable to co-arguer's definition [as appropriate]

  B. Define term #2

    1. Justify the definition

    2. Explain why preferable to co-arguer's definition [as appropriate]

  C. [continue as needed]

III. **Arguments**

  A. Claim 1 for/against the proposition

    1. Support for claim

    2. Warrant/backing [as appropriate]

  B. Claim 2 for/against the proposition

    1. Support for claim

    2. Warrant/backing [as appropriate]

  C. [continue as needed]

IV. **Conclusion**

  A. Summarize arguments

  B. Conclude with impact (quotation, motivational statement, story, etc.)

Although not all aggression is violence, we can extrapolate from this research that some aggression gets channeled into violent behavior. Indeed, beyond scientific research suggesting a connection, advocates also cite the mass shootings in Columbine and Aurora, Colorado; Newtown, Connecticut; and the Washington Navy Yard. The perpetrators in all of these cases played violent video games.[8] More than mere coincidence, this likely suggests that violence and violent video games go hand-in-hand. That is, not all people who play violent video games turn violent but those who do turn violent tend to have played violent video games.

Those opposing this proposition also have strong reasons. For instance, more than 200 professors wrote an open letter in response to the Task Force on Violent Media where they critiqued the APA's reliance on meta-analysis and "controversial laboratory measures" as inadequate tools for real-world application.[9] In the debate on this resolution, the quality of the support itself became an issue.

A further oppositional case comes from the Entertainment Software Association (ESA), the video game industry's primary trade association. We'll consider their webpage, "Essential Facts about Games and Violence," designed to combat the fact proposition linking video games and violence as an Everyday Life Example in this chapter. In reading the case, identify the issues and arguments the ESA addressed and consider how well the case structure maps onto Box 7.1. Then, refer to Table 7.1 for an outline of the case.

Everyday Life Example 7.1

The ESA, "Essential Facts about Games and Violence," 2017[10]

1   **Essential Facts about Games and Violence**

2   Facts, common sense and numerous studies all refute the claim that there is a link between video
3   games and violence. Blaming video games for violence in the real world is no more productive than
4   blaming the news media for bringing violent crimes into our homes night after night. Numerous
5   authorities have examined the scientific record and found that it does not establish any causal link
6   between media content and real-life violence.

7   Credible real-world evidence demonstrates the fallacy of linking games and violence:

8   Violent crime, particularly among the young, has decreased dramatically since the early 1990s.
9   During the same period of time, video games have steadily increased in popularity and use, exactly
10   the opposite of what one would expect if there were a causal link.

11   Many games with violent content sold in the U.S. – and some with far more violence – are also sold
12   in foreign markets. However, the level of violent crime in these foreign markets is considerably
13   lower than that in the U.S., suggesting that influences such as the background of the individual, the
14   availability of guns and other factors are more relevant to understanding the cause of any particular
15   crime. In fact, an analysis by The Washington Post of the 10 largest video game markets across the
16   globe found no statistical correlation between video game consumption and gun-related deaths.

17   Numerous authorities, including the U.S. Supreme Court, U.S. Surgeon General, Federal Trade
18   Commission and Federal Communications Commission have examined the scientific record and
19   found that it does not establish any causal link between violent programming and violent behavior.
20   The truth is, there is no scientific research that validates a link between computer and video games
21   and violence, despite lots of overheated rhetoric from the industry's detractors. Instead, a host of
22   respected researchers has concluded that there is no link between media violence and violent crime.

23   Read our Essential Facts About Video Games and Violence to learn more about what the science says.

Source: The Entertainment Software Association, "Essential Facts About Games and Violence," 2017, http://www.theesa.com/article/essential-facts-about-games-and-violence

The ESA's case is succinct but offers no fewer than three reasons to reject the proposition that "adolescents who play violent video games are more likely to engage in violent behavior." To help you organize the content, Table 7.1 maps the content from the ESA case onto the case structure from Box 7.1 while identifying the issues in the right column.

Table 7.1 shows how the ESA's case was appropriately structured for a fact debate. Although the ESA chose to not define any terms, the case included an introduction and conclusion and offered three arguments against the proposition. Notice, too, that the ESA's case relied not on its own authority but on testimony from credible sources. This was a wise decision because the ESA is biased and we would expect it to defend the video game industry. Relying on authority arguments provided a stronger justification. This is just one example of how advocates in fact debates use available resources to build a preponderance of evidence for their stance on the proposition.

TABLE 7.1 ■ The ESA's Case against the Proposition*	
I. Introduction and Thesis	**[Addressed Issue]**
A. "Facts, common sense and numerous studies all refute the claim that there is a link between video games and violence." [2-3]	
II. Arguments	
A. Rates of violence do not correlate with sales of video games [10]	Have rates of violent behavior increased at the same pace as sales of violent video games?
1. Violent crime has decreased since the 1990s [8]	
2. During that time, sales of video games have steadily increased [9-10]	
B. "The background of the individual, the availability of guns and other factors are more relevant than video games to understanding the cause of any particular crime" [13-15]	Do other factors beyond violent video games contribute to or account for violent behavior?
1. Violent crime in foreign markets is less than in the United States even though the same games are available [11-13]	
2. There is no statistical correlation between violent video game use and gun-related deaths [16]	
a. According to a *Washington Post* analysis of 10 markets [15]	
C. Scientific research does not support a causal link between observing violent content and violent behavior [20-21]	Do scientific studies support a connection between violent video games and violent behavior?
1. The U.S. Supreme Court, U.S. Surgeon General, Federal Trade Commission, and Federal Communications Commission all said so after examining the scientific record [17-19]	
2. "A host of respected researchers concluded that there is no link between media violence and violent crime" [21-22]	
3. Contrary claims are "overheated rhetoric from the industry's detractors" [21]	
IV. Conclusion	
A. Read the more extensive factsheet "to learn more about what the science says." [23]	

The bracketed numbers refer to the lines in the case where you can find the sentence or idea.

Source: The Entertainment Software Association, "Essential Facts About Games and Violence," 2017.

DEBATING VALUE PROPOSITIONS

We debate value propositions when we want to evaluate something. As with fact debates, value debates pervade all aspects of life. This includes debates about the best/worst book, song, or TV show of all time; about whether a particular food such as a banana is healthy; about the intentions and attitudes of other people; or about whether a law is moral or just. All are examples of value debates because the proposition involves a judgment about or evaluation of something. As with fact propositions, value debates may be significant on their own accord or may feed into other debates. Our exploration of value debates will first address how to resolve them before considering a typical case structure.

Resolving Value Debates

VALUE CRITERION:
Resolving a value debate by weighing the application of the criteria defining the value for and against the proposition

When you debate value propositions, such as those noted earlier, how do you tend to reach a decision? In most cases, you have likely defined what it means to be best, important, moral, healthy, etc. and then considered how well that meaning applied to the specific case. If the *value* is healthy, we call the meaning behind that value—i.e., how we are to understand healthy—the *criterion* (or criteria, if there are multiple parts to it). The label for this decision-rule is the **value-criterion** (VC) standard, which means we tend to side with a value proposition when the best criterion for understanding the value applies to the specific topic being evaluated in the proposition.

Nevertheless, value debates in everyday life are often more complicated than simply identifying and applying criteria. There are often divergent criteria for a single value. For instance, rhetorical scholars John Louis Lucaites and Celeste Michelle Condit analyzed how Martin Luther King Jr. and Malcolm X meant different things when arguing for "equality"; King viewed equality as "a formal and identical sameness between two entities," and Malcolm X saw a "relationship of equivalence between two or more clearly separate entities."[11]

Other times, there can be competing values that are both desirable. In fact, Perelman and Lucie Olbrechts-Tyteca contend that value hierarchies are often "more important to the structure of an argument than the actual values" because the hierarchies reveal the priorities of those involved in the debate.[12] In theory, we can all agree that equality or justice or liberty are important. The challenge becomes defining each value in practice and resolving value trade-offs.

When faced with divergent criteria in a debate, you often need to resolve the criteria before considering the criteria's application. Let's return to our example that a banana is healthy. I might argue that healthy food is low in carbohydrates and fat while you might define healthy food as natural rather than processed. We would first need to resolve which of these (or perhaps both) criteria constitute healthy food before even considering bananas. This matters to the debate because, in this case, bananas meet the naturalness criterion but fail the carbohydrates criterion.

To assess the VC, value debates often utilize the following standards:

- *Significance*: How important is the value and/or criteria to the value hierarchy?

- *Resonance*: How strongly do the value and/or criteria echo the interests, goals, and experiences of audience members?

- *Relevance*: How relevant is the criteria to the value? How relevant is the value to the specific topic being evaluated?

Significance and resonance may seem two sides of the same coin but significance is more focused on consequence and impact whereas resonance is more focused on feeling and affinity. For instance, privacy has strong resonance for U.S. citizens (it matters a lot to their feeling of autonomy and individualism) but security has strong significance for those same citizens (it matters a lot to their well-being and survival). In these cases of conflict, you need to determine which value should matter most in the hierarchy by using the three VC standards. The next section explores the argumentative structure for establishing and applying the VC.

Affirming and Opposing Value Propositions

Advocates who participate in value debates often must first resolve the criteria by which we are to understand the value in the proposition and then consider the concrete application of it. We'll discuss these two steps—establishing criteria and applying it—in relation to the following value proposition: "The *Godfather Part II* is the best movie sequel ever made." This debate may seem trite but debates like it are common in everyday life and it usefully illustrates the importance of criteria to resolving value debates.

Establishing Criteria

Value debates require the arguers to define the criteria for understanding the value in the proposition. This step is about ensuring all participants agree to the meaning of the value before addressing the arguments concerning its application. Depending on the nature of the proposition, its sphere, and the participants in the debate, establishing criteria may be a minor task or a vital requirement to resolving the debate.

Establishing criteria may be done explicitly or implicitly. Advocates will overtly establish the criteria in some debates but often the criteria are implicit, based on how people *use* the value in context. This requires you, as an audience member or co-arguer, to interpret the criteria behind the value being applied. Because the implicit nature of criteria is often evident in debates about the best movie sequel, take a second to reflect on the Find Your Voice questions.

Establishing criteria in value debates should follow the same three guidelines for defining terms in fact debates:

1. The criteria should be *reasonable*. Criteria should be relevant to the sphere and audience of the debate, perhaps using official value guidelines as possible. For instance, colleges and universities as well as corporations have a mission statement or statement of values that guide them. Often, the evaluation of policies and ideas will be filtered through those criteria: A good policy is one that supports particular pillars of the organization's mission. In personal spheres, we tend to focus on criteria related to personal happiness and financial well-being.

   For our example of best movie sequel ever made, there are numerous ways to establish the meaning of "sequel" but some are less reasonable. For instance, some define sequel as only the second movie chronologically produced in a series. This is reasonable but others might open it up to any movie after the first one produced in a series (e.g., *Fast and the Furious 16* would count once it's made). Is this reasonable? If so, does this include reboots (e.g., *Batman Begins* rebooted the Michael Keaton/Val Kilmer/George Clooney Batman series)? Still others might define a sequel as any movie in a series in which the *action* occurs chronologically after the first one. This would mean *Star Wars Episode IV: A New Hope* (1977) counts as a sequel even though it was produced first. This is probably the most unreasonable criterion for "sequel."

2. The criteria should *provide clarity*. Once established, the audience should know exactly how to apply the value to the specific situation. Because we're dealing with the meaning of values, the definition of that value as found in a dictionary rarely provides such clarity. For instance, defining "best" as "of the highest excellence; surpassing all others in quality"[13] may be a literal definition of the term but would not help us resolve the debate because it doesn't indicate *why* it is of the highest excellence or what features of "quality" it has. You would want to be more precise about what is intended: a movie sequel is best if it increases box office revenue, or if it promotes the brand, or if it wins the most awards. Or, perhaps a sequel must achieve *all* of these to be best.

   As with fact debates, you can check the clarity of your criteria by plugging it into the proposition. Instead of "*The Godfather Part II* is the best movie sequel ever made," the proposition with the established criteria for the value might read "*The Godfather Part II* effectively propelled the original story and won more awards than any other sequel." The second version more clearly indicates how we're to understand the meaning of "best." Keep in mind, though, that criteria are debatable; your co-arguers could challenge yours and propose alternatives.

3. Finally, the criteria should *indicate argumentative burdens* (but not arguments). After the criteria are established, we should know exactly how we are to implement the criteria in assessing the value. The criteria don't demonstrate *which* movie sequel is the best, just that we should use the criteria of propelling the original and winning awards to determine the best movie sequel.

   The criteria ultimately function to limit the scope of the debate to the specific factors we should employ as benchmarks for understanding the value. If we agree that box office success compared to the original is the criterion for best movie sequel, then any arguments about cinematic quality, character development, or awards are irrelevant to the debate. Once the criteria are established, cases on propositions of value then apply them to the specific topic.

Applying Criteria

The application of criteria should flow logically from the criteria itself, using support to develop the claims. As with fact propositions, cases on value propositions should provide a systematic structure. Box 7.2 outlines a typical case structure.

To see this application process in action, Everyday Life Example 7.2 catalogues how various movie- and ranking-based websites define the VC for "the best movie sequel ever made" and apply it to the existing sequels. Although these don't conform to the case structure in Box 7.2, this example better illustrates the *debate* on this proposition. As you peruse the table, be advised that the publication date may exclude some sequels simply because they hadn't yet been made.

FIND YOUR VOICE
ESTABLISHING CRITERIA

What criteria do you use when determining the "best movie sequel ever made"? If you generated more than one criterion, how would your rank order them in terms of resonance, significance, and relevance? What are two other ways you could define this value? Brainstorming criteria helps you generate your own and prepares you for others' interpretations.

As you can see, the VC are crucial to determining the best movie sequel of all time. The differing criterion produced five different applications. Those that focused on award winning (*Entertainment Weekly* and *Ranker Film*) easily arrived at *The Godfather Part II*, as did ScreenRant but for different criteria. You may have noticed that all but two of the sources (*Empire* and *Rotten Tomatoes*) used the criterion that a sequel must be the second film in a series. Despite this, *Empire* still chose a second movie—*Aliens*—as the best sequel. They noted "it beat *The Godfather Part II* . . . [b]ecause that doesn't have a single acid-veined xenomorph in it."[14] *Rotten Tomatoes* was the only one to exclude spinoffs and prequels explicitly and to use reviews, leading to *Toy Story 2* as the best movie sequel. If, however, we define the criterion for "best" as box office sales as a percentage of the original (Wikipedia), we'd conclude that *Boondock Saints II: All Saints Day* is the best sequel since it earned 33,000% more than the original *Boondock Saints*.[15] And yet, this criterion for "best" seems unsatisfying (likely on standards of significance and resonance) given that all the other lists of "best movie sequels"—whether of 10, 25, or 50 movies—omitted this box office gem entirely.

BOX 7.2: CASE STRUCTURE FOR VALUE DEBATES

I. Introduction and Thesis

   A. Gain interest in controversy and its significance

   B. State your thesis/stance on the proposition

   C. Preview your criteria and application for that stance

II. Criteria

   A. Explain criterion #1 for value

     1. Justify the criterion

     2. Explain why preferable to co-arguer's criteria [as appropriate]

   B. [continue as needed]

III. Arguments

   A. Claim 1 for/against the proposition

     1. Application of criteria

     2. Warrant/backing [as appropriate]

   B. Claim 2 for/against the proposition

     1 Application of criteria

     2. Warrant/backing [as appropriate]

   C. [continue as needed]

IV. Conclusion

   A. Summarize arguments

   B. Conclude with impact (quotation, motivational statement, story, etc.)

Everyday Life Example 7.2		
Conflicting Criteria for Best/Greatest Movie Sequel Ever Made		
Source & Year	*Criteria*	*Application*
Entertainment Weekly, 2006[16]	Only the second movie in a series (implicit) Epic nature (implicit) Award winning (implicit)	*The Godfather Part II*
Empire (UK magazine), 2017[17]	Any movie in a series after the first one (explicit) "We have disregarded films that are really all of a piece, like *Lord Of The Rings* and *Kill Bill*, and also series that share elements but restart each time, like *Carry On* or *Three Colours*." (explicit) "There's also no Bond since, with 23 examples to choose from, that franchise could easily run to a best-sequels list of its own." (explicit) How it "stack[s] up to the original" (explicit) Whether it has "a single acid-veined xenomorph in it" (implicit)	*Aliens*
Rotten Tomatoes, 2012[18]	"We've used a weighted formula that takes the Tomatometer, the number of reviews, and the year of release into account." (explicit) "In addition, a film needs at least 20 reviews to qualify." (explicit) "We've also excluded spinoffs and prequels." (explicit)	*Toy Story 2*
ScreenRant, 2016[19]	"enrich the first film without completely rehashing the story or character beats" (explicit) "a direct sequel, meaning it was produced as the second film" (explicit) "more compelling than the original" (implicit)	*The Godfather Part II*
Ranker Film & public vote, no date[20]	"film number two in a series" (explicit) Award winning (Ranker Film's explicit criterion) Most votes (public vote's implicit criterion)	*The Godfather Part II* (Ranker Film pick) *Star Wars Episode V: The Empire Strikes Back* (public pick)
Wikipedia, First Sequels by Box-Office Improvement, updated 2018[21]	"first sequel" [i.e. second movie in series] (explicit) Percent box office improvement over original (explicit)	*The Boondock Saints II: All Saints Day*

Of course, knowing that "best" refers to the *single* greatest, it's impossible for all five of these movies to be the "best" sequel. Thus, we could only resolve the debate about whether *Aliens, Boondock Saints II, The Empire Strikes Back, The Godfather: Part II,* or *Toy Story 2* is the best movie sequel by explicitly debating the criteria each list used to determine the value of "best" in this context. Interestingly, none of the sources justified their criteria; each just asserted (explicitly or implicitly) the criteria as the most appropriate.

This debate over the best movie sequel demonstrates how value debates should engage both the criteria for determining values as well as their applicability to the specific topic. Resolving this debate requires considering the three standards noted earlier—significance, resonance, and relevance—insofar as selecting the criteria within the value hierarchy is a matter of significance and resonance while applying the criteria is a matter of relevance. Being aware of these argumentative requirements will help you better engage value debates in everyday life.

DEBATING POLICY PROPOSITIONS

We debate policy propositions when we want to interrogate a call for change and determine the best course of action. We noted in Chapter 2 that most debates you have in your daily life center on policy propositions (although they involve sub-debates about facts and values), such as whether to buy a new computer or phone, whether to ask someone out on a date, or our example from Chapter 2 of whether to attend college. Unlike fact and value propositions, however, the sides in a policy debate have different argumentative requirements to meet their burden of proof. To understand these different burdens, we will first discuss how people often decide whether to pursue a policy proposition and then explore how arguers develop cases to facilitate that decision.

Resolving Policy Debates

When you make policy decisions like those mentioned earlier, the stakes differ but the process for making them tends to be the same: Will taking the action bring about more advantages than disadvantages? Sometimes, you may even create a pro/con list to help you decide. Occasionally, you may weigh two possible actions: *which* computer to buy, *which* person to ask on a date, *which* college to attend. When weighing multiple options, the decision boils down to a similar but slightly different question: Which course of action from the available options brings about the most advantages while avoiding the most disadvantages? The label we often use for this decision mechanism is **net benefits** (or NB), the idea that we should support the proposition only if the potential advantages/benefits of the policy are greater than the potential disadvantages.

NET BENEFITS: Resolving a policy debate by weighing advantages vs. disadvantages of the proposition

Of course, NB is not just about counting up the number of pros versus cons. If that were the case, people would avoid taking any risky behavior, such as binge drinking, because the potential disadvantages to the action are more numerous than the potential advantages. Rather, people weigh the advantages and disadvantages, often in relation to three primary criteria:

- *Probability:* How likely is the advantage/disadvantage to occur?

- *Significance:* How strong and impactful is the consequence of the advantage/disadvantage if it does occur?

- *Timing:* How soon is the consequence of the advantage/disadvantage likely to occur?

Because policy debates are decided through weighing these factors, effective arguers should explicitly address them when advancing their own arguments and refuting others'. Doing so may help their points resonate with members of their audience and account for the concerns of those who ultimately decide the course of action. The next section, then, describes how to effectively advocate a case for policy change.

Affirming Policy Propositions

STOCK ISSUES:
The primary issues arguers must address to justify a policy proposition

The issues guiding arguments for a policy proposition tend to follow what we call a **stock issues** structure. The phrase "stock issues" refers to the typical questions an advocate must address to satisfy the burden of proof in supporting change.

There are five primary stock issues, indicated in Table 7.2, and often abbreviated to significant harm, inherency, plan, solvency, and advantages. If you can successfully convince the audience that the answer to *all* stock issues is "yes," you are well on your way to advocating your policy. So, let's take a look at what goes into each.

Significant Harm

SIGNIFICANT HARM: The harm, problem, or defect in the *status quo* motivating policy change

Policy advocates often begin with a reason for change, arguing that there is a **significant harm** or substantial defect in the *status quo* that demands the audience's attention. For example, the harm of personal hunger may lead you to argue that you and your friends should go to a restaurant for dinner. The potential harm of your company downsizing leads you to argue that your company should reduce spending in a particular area. The harm of societal gun violence leads you to argue for gun control at the federal level.

Since issues represent multiple sides in a debate, the significant harm must be *argued* and it is open to refutation. We'll consider a running example in this section concerning production of the U.S. penny. As for the harm, we might point out that it costs more to produce a penny in the United States than the penny is worth. In 2016, it cost 1.5¢ to create and distribute a coin with the face value is 1¢ (1.31¢ to create the penny, 0.19¢ to sell and distribute it).[22] Is this a significant harm? Now, consider that the U.S. Treasury in 2016 produced 9.1 billion—yes billion—pennies.[23] If the federal government loses half a cent on each, that's more than $45 million in waste. Has this information changed your thinking on whether this is a significant harm?

TABLE 7.2 ■ Stock Issues for Cases Affirming Policy Propositions	
Label	**Issue**
Significant Harm	Is there a significant harm, problem, or flaw in the *status quo*?
Inherency	Is the significant harm inherent to the system such that it won't go away on its own?
Plan	Is there a solution that is feasible, fundable, and enforceable?
Solvency	Is the solution likely to solve the harm or remove the inherency?
Advantages	Is there likely to be additional benefit(s) to the plan?

Now, consider that the federal budget in 2016 was $3.9 trillion—yes trillion.[24] Consequently, the $45 million in waste is approximately .00001% of the total federal operating budget. Is producing the penny a significant harm? Should citizens dedicate energy to addressing this problem? How could you convince your friends to be concerned about this waste? This example illustrates that advocates who want policy change must meet their burden to demonstrate that a significant harm currently exists.

Inherency

Beyond arguing the harm exists, policy advocates should also address the inherent nature of that harm. Something is "inherent" if it is intrinsic or built into the systems and structures. **Inherency**, then, addresses how the harm is built into the present system and won't go away on its own (or, ideally, won't go away but for the policy solution you're advocating). Another way to think of inherency is the blame for the significant harm: What enables the harm to exist and thrive? Most forms of inherency are either structural— for example, having or not having a law, procedure, or regulation in place— or attitudinal—for example, people's biases and ideologies. Both kinds, however, capture the barriers that prevent solving the harm.

INHERENCY: The structures and/or attitudes in the present system that (help) produce and perpetuate the significant harm

Inherency is important to a case for policy change for two main reasons. First, if a harm is temporary or already being addressed, then there is no reason to act. Recall that audience presumption often favors the *status quo*, or no change, unless audience members are convinced otherwise. Demonstrating that there is a significant harm and that the harm is inherent to the system better primes the audience to accept and recognize the need for a solution.

Second, pinpointing the inherency may help generate an effective solution to the harm. If the solution doesn't address the inherency, then it may be a bandage over a much deeper wound. For example, if workplace and housing discrimination exist because of attitudinal inherency (i.e., racism, sexism, ableism), then advocating a law banning such forms of discrimination may be ineffective for not targeting the root blame.

Suppose we agree that the $45 million wasted annually to produce pennies is a significant harm. Consider the Find Your Voice box to reflect on the inherency before reading further. In determining inherency, we might follow precedent and consider the cost of materials to make pennies. The rising cost of copper in the 1970s led the Treasury in 1982 to change the penny's composition from 95 percent copper and 5 percent zinc to 97.6 percent zinc and 2.4 percent copper.[25] While this made sense in 1982 when zinc cost approximately $745 per metric ton (in 1982 dollars; closer to $1,900 when adjusted for 2016 dollars), zinc prices in 2016 exceeded $2,600 per metric ton, their highest point since 2007.[26]

FIND YOUR VOICE
INHERENCY

If the penny is so wasteful, why does the U.S. Mint still produce it in its current form? What barriers might exist to prevent change? How could you discover the systemic blame rather than the symptoms or indicators of the harm? In many cases, the inherency is much more complex than a single factor but you could likely identify a few things that contribute to its existence.

If the rising cost of zinc represents the inherency in this situation—the barrier that prevents reducing the cost of pennies—then we have a stronger rationale for change. It helps rule out other costs (such as worker wages at the U.S. Mint or distributing pennies to banks) that might be to blame, and it helps strengthen the policy solution. If the price of zinc is projected to fall in the future, then the harm may be temporary and not require (drastic) action. If, on the other hand, projections indicate that zinc prices will rise or remain stable, then policy action is more strongly justified. As you can see, inherency is as debatable as the significant harm and, thus, arguers need to have strong support for their claims to inherency. Establishing clear inherency leads directly into the proposed policy action.

Plan

PLAN: The proposition and any provisions relevant to enacting it

If the significant harm and inherency successfully fuel an audience's appetite for action, the **plan** satisfies that craving. The term "plan" includes the proposition (*agent* should *action*) as well as provisions about what it would require to enact it. Two important provisions are funding and enforcement but there are others, such as timing or scope, that may matter to your case.

The importance of the plan can be evident by considering even the most mundane (yet properly worded) policy proposition: We should go to the new steak restaurant for dinner tonight. We could debate this proposition in theory, but the debate would be more productive if we have a plan that specifies the time we are leaving, how we will get there, who will pay for dinner, and any other facets that need to be defined to enact the proposition in real practice. These details will impact the advantages and disadvantages of the proposition. For instance, going to the restaurant at 8 p.m. would yield different consequences than going at 4 p.m. Taking an Uber would yield different consequences than driving one of our own cars (or even taking a Lyft or a cab). Anytime you've experienced awkwardness about who gets stuck with the bill at the end of the meal, it means you didn't generate an effective plan.

Let's return to our penny problem. If we know that the cost to make the penny exceeds the value of the penny and this is most likely because the materials in the penny have risen in price without any indication they will fall, then two practical solutions seem apparent: The U.S. Treasury should construct the penny from a less expensive substance or the U.S. Treasury should abolish the penny entirely.

The plan for each of these propositions would require careful thought. On your own, you can likely generate some of these important considerations for a viable plan. If we advocate the first option, what substance is durable yet impressionable and inexpensive? When would the U.S. Treasury change to the new substance? Can the current presses accommodate it? If we advocate abolition, there are likely as many if not more provisions: Would production of pennies be phased out or stopped immediately? Would consumers be able to continue using them or would they need to convert them to larger denominations? What would happen to the existing pennies?

For either solution, the plan would offer a proposition and explain for the audience what it would take to implement it. So, let's advocate that the U.S. Treasury should abolish the penny. A plan might sound something like this: Abolishing the penny would involve a phased withdrawal in which the penny will still serve as legal tender for all consumers but, starting next fiscal year, the U.S. Treasury will stop production of pennies, banks will stop distribution, and retailers will no longer give pennies as change. The mint will buy pennies back at face value and eventually melt down the collected pennies for sale or use in other coin production. Retailers who accept cash payments will be required to round up or down to the nearest 5 cents (e.g., a purchase for $4.92 would round down to $4.90 while a purchase for $4.93 would round up to $4.95).

Does this sound like a reasonable plan? Are there other provisions that would need to be addressed? The plan is itself debatable and open to amendment. Nevertheless, it is a good starting point for thinking about the consequences of this policy. After establishing that a solution exists, the final two stock issues—solvency and advantages—explain the benefits of that solution.

Solvency

The fourth stock issue, **solvency**, argues how the plan will bring about the desired outcome motivating the plan. Solvency imagines a hypothetical world in which the plan goes into effect and explains why we have reason to believe it would eliminate the harm.

SOLVENCY: How the plan solves the harm (and/or inherency)

We can't, of course, predict the future with 100 percent certainty—hence why it's an argument—so solvency often relies on argument from consequence as described in Chapter 6.

Solvency is important because anyone can come up with creative solutions but not all solutions are created equally. Some are more likely to succeed in solving the harm than others. Some are more likely to bring about greater benefits than others. And, some may effectively solve the harm but do so at high cost or disadvantage.

Given the earlier plan to abolish the penny, how might we know if this will help address the harm of wasted money? Well, the plan was modeled on Canada, which used this exact procedure to abolish its penny in 2012. According to the Canadian Department of Finance, the decision saved taxpayers $11 million a year.[27] Canadians don't appear to regret this decision or desire to reinstate the penny so the plan ostensibly found success. The actions of Canada, a country similar to the United States in many respects, suggests that the United States could benefit from abolishing its penny. Indeed, ceasing production would guarantee that we stop the $45 million in waste every year. And while there might be a few years of extra costs in phasing out the penny and melting down the ones that are collected, the long-term savings would certainly outweigh the costs. The solvency seems to be there. Is this $45 million in savings enough to justify the U.S. Treasury cease production of pennies? If not, the final stock issue offers further advantages to the plan.

Advantages

The fifth and final stock issue an advocate should address is the **advantages** to implementing the policy. The primary concern of any plan is solving the harm. However, addressing advantages, or additional benefits, furthers the case for action by advancing numerous positive outcomes to a single policy action. The more advantages you can effectively demonstrate, the stronger your case becomes and the better you meet your burden as an advocate.

ADVANTAGES: Positive consequences of enacting the plan in addition to solving the harm

One additional benefit to eliminating the penny is to increase efficiency in the checkout line. Research suggests that transactions involving pennies take 2 to 2.5 seconds longer than transactions without them.[28] That time adds up over the span of days, weeks, and years to cost billions of dollars in lost efficiency.

Beyond improved efficiency, abolishing pennies would help reduce environmental harms. *Smithsonian Magazine* reported that the production of pennies involves severe environmental impact at multiple steps in the process.[29] The mining of zinc and copper and the punching process consume power and release pollutants into the atmosphere. Once minted, many pennies are discarded as useless currency and wind up in landfills or the bottom of fountains rather than being recycled. Abolishing the penny would eliminate these negative impacts for an entire coin category.

LINK: A statement explaining how the plan connects to the advantage or disadvantage

IMPACT: A statement explaining the ultimate consequence of the advantage or disadvantage

To effectively demonstrate solvency and advantages (and disadvantages, as we'll discuss later), you should include at least two parts to the argument: a **link** and an **impact**. The link explains how your plan links, or connects, to the advantage/solvency. Usually, the link takes the form of a conditional, if-then statement: "if the U.S. Treasury abolishes the penny, then it will substantially reduce zinc mining." The impact says why this is a good or bad thing. So what if we cease zinc mining? The impact would state what this ultimately means for your case: "Ceasing zinc mining will prevent further pillaging of natural resources from the environment and reduce the number of pollutants that hasten climate change."

By developing these arguments through a systematic structure bolstered by research, you can effectively argue policy change. When it is all put together, you have a case for action. Table 7.3 outlines our case for abolishing the penny.

The cost savings to taxpayers and businesses combined with the environmental benefit to abolishing the penny make it a no brainer, right? If you're on board, then I've effectively established a case for the policy proposition. The Build Your Skill activity offers a second example that tests your ability to identify and apply the stock issues.

TABLE 7.3 ■ Stock Issues Advocating the U.S. Treasury Should Abolish the Penny	
Issue Label	**Argument Summary**
Significant Harm	The U.S. Government wastes $45 million annually by producing the penny because the production costs exceed the coin's value.
Inherency	The costs of zinc, which comprise nearly 98 percent of each penny, have continued to rise since the early 1990s.
Plan	The U.S. Treasury should stage a phased withdrawal of the penny. It will still be legal tender for all consumers but, starting next fiscal year, the U.S. Treasury will stop production of pennies, banks will stop distribution, and retailers will no longer give pennies as change. The mint will buy pennies back at face value and eventually melt down the collected pennies for sale or use in other coin production. Retailers who accept cash payments will be required to round up or down to the nearest 5 cents.
Solvency	Abolishing the U.S. penny will likely save the U.S. government substantial money in the long run. Canada, which is similar to the United States, saw positive results when it abolished the penny in 2012.
Advantages	Abolishing the U.S. penny will likely increase efficiency in retail stores because it reduces the length of transactions. Also, abolishing the U.S. penny will likely reduce environmental degradation because it eliminates the mining, production, energy, and waste of an entire coin category.

BUILD YOUR SKILL
ASSESSING STOCK ISSUES

Greg Mankiw, Professor of Economics at Harvard University, wrote a blog post in 2006 outlining a case to abolish the penny.[30] Identify the stock issues in the post and then evaluate the quality of the case: Which arguments on the stock issues are strong and weak? How would you improve the case?

Get Rid of the Penny!

1   Today's New York Times reports: "it costs the mint well more than a cent to make a penny."
2   The solution, in my view, is to get rid of the penny.
3   Indeed, I would advocate this even if the penny were free to manufacture, as I argued earlier
4   this year in the Wall Street Journal. The purpose of the monetary system is to facilitate
5   exchange. The penny no longer serves that purpose. When people start leaving a monetary
6   unit at the cash register for the next customer, the unit is too small to be useful. It is just
7   wasting peoples' time—the economy's most valuable resource. The fact that the penny is
8   costly to make only adds force to the argument.
9   Maybe we should get rid of the nickel, too. We can then round all prices to one decimal
10 rather than two.

Source: Greg Mankiw, "Get Rid of the Penny!" Greg Mankiw's Blog: Random Observations for Students of Economics (blog), April 22, 2006, http://gregmankiw.blogspot.com/2006/04/get-rid-of-penny.html.

Mankiw's case illustrates how everyday arguers advocate policy change without drawing explicit attention to the argumentative moves they're making and without following a rote stock issues pattern. That is, the stock issues are designed not as a formulaic approach with explicit identification like "The significant harm is. . ." but rather as a tried and true framework you can use to meet your burden in advocating a course of action.

Opposing Policy Propositions

Even the strongest stock issues case is susceptible to counter-arguments. This section will discuss two categories of arguments advocates use to oppose policy propositions: disadvantages and counterplans.

Disadvantages

Disadvantages are your main line of offense in opposing a policy proposition. Because policy debates are decided by weighing pros vs. cons, disadvantages represent the "con" side or the drawbacks to the plan.

It's tempting to oppose change by merely arguing that the plan may not make a substantial difference and beginning advocates often oppose policies by arguing that the plan *doesn't make the world better.* This is not enough for a disadvantage, though, which

DISADVANTAGES:
Negative consequences of enacting the plan

FIND YOUR VOICE
DISADVANTAGES

We've considered the benefits to the U.S. Treasury abolishing the penny. Can you generate some disadvantages? How might the plan to eliminate the penny make things *worse*? What kind of research might you gather to explore these points? Even if you agreed with my case that the U.S. Treasury should abolish the penny, considering the other side makes you more knowledgeable.

should argue that the plan *makes the world worse*. For instance, you could respond to our penny plan by arguing that $45 million is not a lot of money in the total GDP. If this was the extent of your response, you've failed to offer a reason *not* to act. I would likely respond by arguing, "Saving $45 million is better than nothing and there's no harm in at least trying." Until you show drawbacks to enacting the proposition, you've not met your oppositional burden of proof.

An oppositional response, then, would argue that the plan brings about negative consequences or involves substantial costs, material or otherwise. To fully develop a disadvantage, an advocate would need to provide a *link* and *impact* just as you would to demonstrate solvency and advantages: how does the plan connect to the disadvantage (link) and why is the disadvantage a bad thing (impact)?

To effectively determine whether the U.S. Treasury should abolish the penny, we would need to weigh disadvantages to that plan against the proposed advantages. Use the Find Your Voice exercise before continuing.

Advocates against the abolition of pennies might advance numerous disadvantages but we'll discuss two. First, eliminating the penny would disproportionately harm the poor in society. This *links* to the plan in two ways: First, poorer people tend to use cash rather than credit for retail transactions, meaning they will be most impacted by the rounding provision of the plan and have to pay more for items, especially since most prices end in 9.[31] Second, pennies are frequently used as a source of charitable donations, such as the Salvation Army's red kettles during December.[32] Abolishing pennies may result in fewer charitable donations. The *impact* to this disadvantage is that those who are poor will have a more difficult time breaking out of the cycle of poverty.

The second disadvantage is that the plan would eliminate a cultural and national icon. "A penny saved is a penny earned." "A penny for your thoughts." "My two cents." These cultural phrases all rely on the existence of the penny. Take the penny away, and these phrases become meaningless. Plus, "my two nickels" and "a nickel for your thoughts" just don't sound right. Moreover, the penny has national significance, commemorating President Abraham Lincoln. Abolishing the penny would take Lincoln with it, especially since the plan doesn't offer a provision to place Lincoln's image on any of the remaining coins. The plan to abolish the penny would have a negative effect on national culture and disregard Lincoln's legacy.

These disadvantages demonstrate that abolishing the penny is not as beneficial as it initially appeared. If getting rid of the penny brings some negative consequences and if keeping the penny is wasteful, perhaps there's an alternative solution that might be better. A counterplan, then, is the second kind of argument you might advocate against a proposition.

Counterplan

Recall that the default advocacy for opposing policy propositions is to support the *status quo*—to advocate that the agent should *not* take the specified action. However, if you agree there's a significant harm but disagree with the plan, a **counterplan** is a valuable tool for opposing policy change. Advocates propose a counterplan as a better solution that solves the significant harm while avoiding one or more disadvantages to the plan.

Chances are you have advocated a counterplan at some point in your life: A friend suggests you watch one movie but you propose watching a different one; a colleague asks for a meeting at a certain time and you suggest a more convenient one; a parent or guardian creates a rule and you request an exception. In each of these cases, you were motivated by reducing the negative consequences of the original plan and promoting the positive consequences of the counterplan.

Counterplans require the same thoughtful development as a plan. Counterplans should be robust because, argumentatively speaking, they assume the same burden of proof as the plan in advocating policy change. This also means that the debate then becomes determining which plan produces greater net benefits.

Returning to our penny example, we might propose a counterplan that starting next fiscal year, the U.S. Treasury will use steel in place of zinc while still coating the penny in copper (to prevent rust and keep the current color). Whereas zinc in 2016 cost $2,600 per metric ton, steel cost under $550 per metric ton that same year.[33] Thus, this counterplan would solve the harm by decreasing the penny's production value below its face value.

COUNTERPLAN: An alternative plan to the proposition that solves the harm and avoids one or more of the disadvantages

TABLE 7.4 ■ Weighing Plan & Counterplan in Penny Debate			
Advantage/Disadvantage	**Probability** (High/Med./Low)	**Significance** (High/Med./Low)	**Timing** (Immed./ Soon/Long Term)
Save Money			
Plan	High	Med.	Soon
Counterplan	High	Low	Soon
Increase Purchasing Efficiency			
Plan	High	Low	Immediate
Counterplan	Low	Low	Immediate
Reduce Environmental Destruction			
Plan	High	Med.	Long-term
Counterplan	Low	Med.	Long-term
Harm Poor People			
Plan	Med.	High	Soon
Counterplan	Low	High	Soon
Eliminate Cultural Icon			
Plan	Med.	Med.	Immediate
Counterplan	Low	Med.	Immediate

There's precedent here as well; the U.S. Treasury briefly used steel in the 1940s when the availability of copper was low during wartime.[34] This counterplan would both solve the harm associated with producing the penny and avoid the disadvantages of hurting the poor and extinguishing a cultural icon.

Once both cases are laid on the table, resolving this debate between the plan and the counterplan would require the audience to return to the criteria of probability, significance, and timing to weigh the advantages and disadvantages alongside one another. Table 7.4 organizes these considerations for easy reference but this is just one possible interpretation of how to rate the arguments; these ratings become part of the debate itself as arguers address the consequences of action.

Table 7.4 reveals that there is not a clear answer to which is the better policy. For instance, how do we weigh the strong likelihood of eliminating a cultural icon against the environmental impact of penny production? Does the medium risk, high significance of harming poor people, mean we should avoid it at all costs or that it is an unlikely scenario? These are some of the questions that arguers must consider when figuring out whether and how to bring about change to the penny. This scenario provides one example of the complex considerations that must be argued and weighed to select the best solutions to problems we face in everyday life.

Summary

This chapter has outlined argumentative cases on propositions of fact, value, and policy. Fact debates are resolved through a preponderance of evidence, requiring cases that offer relevant reasons for the proposition grounded in strong support and definitions of terms. Value debates are resolved through value-criterion, requiring cases that establish criteria for the value and then apply the criteria to the topic. Finally, policy debates are resolved through net benefits, requiring cases that weigh the hypothetical advantages and disadvantages of the proposition. Understanding these burdens better enables arguers to tailor their ideas to the audience, sphere, and proposition.

Application Exercises

Understanding Musical Cases: Locate the lyrics to the following political songs from the 21st century in the United States and, for each, identify the proposition being advocated, outline or diagram how the song builds the case for that proposition (using tools from Chapter 4), and evaluate how well it meets the burden of proof for that case type.

A. Green Day, "21 Guns"

B. John Mayer, "Waiting on the World to Change"

C. Against Me, "White People for Peace"

D. Darryl Worley, "Have You Forgotten?"

E. Kendrick Lamar, "Alright"

F. J. Cole, "Be Free"

Generating Case Structures: For the following propositions, identify the kind of proposition (fact, value, or policy) and then generate appropriate main points for a case that affirms that proposition (definitions & reasons, criteria & application, or stock issues).

A. The pen is mightier than the sword.

B. Ignorance is the root of all evil.

C. Don't judge a book by its cover.

D. A bird in the hand is worth two in the bush.

E. Better safe than sorry.

F. Look before you leap.

G. Don't count your chickens before they hatch.

H. Two heads are better than one.

Key Terms

Preponderance of Evidence 148

Value-Criterion 154

Net Benefits 159

Stock Issues 160

Significant Harm 160

Inherency 161

Plan 162

Solvency 163

Advantages 163

Link 164

Impact 164

Disadvantages 165

Counterplan 167

Endnotes

1. Michael Specter, "The Phone Guy: How Nokia Designed What May Be the Best-Selling Cellular Products on Earth," *The New Yorker*, November 26, 2001, LexisNexis Academic.

2. John A. Daly, *Advocacy: Championing Ideas and Influencing Others* (New Haven, CT: Yale University Press, 2011), 56.

3. Specter, "The Phone Guy."

4. Specter, "The Phone Guy."

5. Will Oremus, "When Cellphones Became Cool: How the Nokia 3210 Started the Mobile Revolution," *Slate*, September 20, 2016, http://www.slate.com/articles/technology/the_next_20/2016/09/the_development_of_the_nokia_3210_the_cellphone_that_started_the_mobile.html.

6. American Psychological Association, "Proposition on Violent Video Games," August 2015, 2, http://www.apa.org/news/press/releases/2015/08/violent-video-games.pdf.

7. APA Task Force on Violent Media, *Technical Report on the Review of the Violent Video Game Literature*, 2015, 16, http://www.apa.org/pi/families/review-video-games.pdf.

8. Erik Kain, "Do Games Like 'Grand Theft Auto V' Cause Real-World Violence?" *Forbes*, September 18, 2013, https://www.forbes.com/sites/erikkain/2013/09/18/do-games-like-grand-theft-auto-v-cause-real-world-violence/#1413d5243241; John Dickerson, "Grand Theft Auto V Sales Set Record—Why Are We Surprised When Virtual Violence Becomes Reality?" *Fox News*, September 19, 2013, http://www.foxnews.com/opinion/2013/09/19/grand-theft-auto-v-sales-set-record-why-are-surprised-when-virtual-violence.html.

9. "Scholars' Open Statement to the APA Task Force on Violent Media," September 2013, 1-2, http://www.christopherjferguson.com/APA%20Task%20Force%20Comment1.pdf.

10. The Entertainment Software Association, "Essential Facts about Games and Violence," 2017, http://www.theesa.com/article/essential-facts-about-games-and-violence.

11. John Louis Lucaites and Celeste Michelle Condit, "Reconstructing <Equality>: Culturetypal and Counter-Cultural Rhetorics in the Martyred Black Vision," *Communication Monographs* 57 (1990): 6-7.

12. Chaim Perelman and Lucie Olbrechts-Tyteca, *The New Rhetoric: A Treatise on Argumentation*, trans. John Wilkinson and Purcell Weaver (Notre Dame, IN: University of Notre Dame Press, 1969), 81.

13. *Oxford English Dictionary*, 3rd edition, s.v. "best," A.1.a.

14. Team Empire, "The Greatest Movie Sequels," *Empire Online*, March 6, 2017, https://www.empireonline.com/movies/features/50greatestsequels.

15. Shane Snow, "The Paradox of Sequels," *Shane Snow: Unconventional Explorations of Humanity, Data, and the Future* (blog), April 17, 2016, https://blog.shanesnow.com/the-paradox-of-sequels-aad538eba747.

16. Chris Nashawaty, "The 10 Best Movie Sequels," *Entertainment Weekly*, March 3, 2006, http://ew.com/article/2006/03/03/10-best-movie-sequels.

17. Team Empire, "The Greatest Movie Sequels."

18. "Best Sequels," *Rotten Tomatoes*, 2012, https://www.rottentomatoes.com/guides/best_sequels_2012.

19. Joseph Allen, "25 Best Movie Sequels Ever Made," *ScreenRant*, September 2, 2016, https://screenrant.com/best-movie-sequels-ever-made.

20. Ranker Film, "The Best Movie Sequels Ever Made," *Ranker*, n.d., https://www.ranker.com/list/best-movie-sequels/ranker-film.

21. "List of Film Sequels by Box-Office Improvement," *Wikipedia*, n.d., https://en.wikipedia.org/wiki/List_of_film_sequels_by_box-office_improvement.

22. United States Mint, *2016 Annual Report*, 2016, 7, https://www.usmint.gov/wordpress/wp-content/uploads/2017/02/2016Annual Report.pdf.

23. United States Mint, *2016 Annual Report*.

24. Leigh Angres and Maureen Costantino, "The Federal Budget in 2016: An Infographic," Congressional Budget Office, February 2017, https://www.cbo.gov/sites/default/files/115th-congress-2017-2018/graphic/52408-budgetoverall.pdf.

25. "History of the Lincoln Cent," U.S. Department of Treasury, January 2011, https://www.treasury.gov/about/education/Pages/lincoln-cent.aspx.

26. Luzi-Ann Javier and Mark Burton, "Zinc Rises to Highest Since 2007 as Metals Rally on China Demand," *Bloomberg*, November 28, 2016, https://www.bloomberg.com/news/articles/2016-11-28/zinc-explodes-with-lead-in-surge-to-highest-level-in-nine-years; "Primary Commodity Prices: Zinc," International Monetary Fund Data, February 2017, http://data.imf.org.

27. Department of Finance, *Jobs, Growth, and Long-Term Prosperity: Economic Action Plan 2012* (Ottawa, CA: Public Works and Government Services Canada, 2012), 265, http://www.budget.gc.ca/2012/plan/pdf/Plan2012-eng.pdf.

28. Sebastian Mallaby, "The Penny Stops Here," *Washington Post*, September 25, 2006, http://www.washingtonpost.com/wp-dyn/content/article/2006/09/24/AR2006092400946.html.

29. Michelle Z. Donahue, "How Much Does it Really Cost (the Planet) to Make a Penny?" *Smithsonian Magazine*, May 18, 2016, http://www.smithsonianmag.com/science-nature/penny-environmental-disaster-180959032.

30. Greg Mankiw, "Get Rid of the Penny!" *Greg Mankiw's Blog: Random Observations for Students of Economics* (blog), April 22, 2006, http://gregmankiw.blogspot.com/2006/04/get-rid-of-penny.html.

31. Mark W. Weller, "America Needs the Penny," *USA Today*, July 27, 2006, http://usatoday30.usatoday.com/news/opinion/editorials/2006-07-27-opposingview-penny_x.htm.

32. Here's one example: Sandra T. Molina, "Woman Donates a Year's Worth of Pennies to Whittier Salvation Army," *San Gabriel Valley Tribune*, December 23, 2009, http://www.sgvtribune.com/article/zz/20091223/NEWS/912239772.

33. Chloe Pfeiffer, "The Steel Rally Is Going to 'Fizzle Out' Soon," *Business Insider*, July 21, 2016, http://www.businessinsider.com/steel-price-rally-ending-2016-7.

34. Natalie Wolchover, "How to Make the Penny Worth 1 Cent Again," *Live Science*, February 16, 2012, https://www.livescience.com/18528-penny-worth-1-cent.html.

CONTESTING ARGUMENTS

PART III

GENERATING PRODUCTIVE CLASH

Steve Jobs, former CEO of Apple, shared in his "Lost Interview" from 1996 the following parable about the value of teamwork and engaging others' ideas:

> I've always felt that a team of people doing something they really believe in is like when I was a young kid there was a widowed man that lived up the street. . . . And one day he said to me, "come on into my garage I want to show you something." And he pulled out this dusty old rock tumbler. It was a motor and a coffee can and a little band between them. And he said, "come on with me." We went out into the back and we got just some rocks. Some regular old ugly rocks. And we put them in the can with a little bit of liquid and little bit of grit powder, and we closed the can up and he turned this motor on and he said, "come back tomorrow." And this can was making a racket as the stones went around.
>
> And I came back the next day, and we opened the can. And we took out these amazingly beautiful polished rocks. The same common stones that had gone in, through rubbing against each other like this, creating a little bit of friction, creating a little bit of noise, had come out these beautiful polished rocks.
>
> And that's always been in my mind my metaphor for a team working really hard on something they're passionate about. Is that it's through the team, through that group of incredibly talented people bumping up against each other, having arguments, having fights sometimes, making some noise, and working together they polish each other and they polish the ideas, and what comes out are these really beautiful stones.[1]

Source: Steve Jobs *The Lost Interview*, directed by Paul Sen (1995; Los Angeles, CA: Magnolia Pictures, 2012), DVD. Reprinted with permission from John Gau, John Gau Productions.

Jobs's metaphor of polished stones illuminates the value of clash in everyday argumentation. It is only through creating **clash**—multiple sides of a debate colliding and creating friction by arguing the same issues as one another—that argumentation can refine ideas and

CLASH: Arguing the same issues as your co-arguer(s) in a debate

help the outcome surpass the materials that originally entered the debate situation. If there's not enough clash, the metaphoric stones remain the ugly old stones they have always been. Of course, clash can also be destructive rather than productive. If there's too much clash, the metaphoric stones will whittle away to dust. The trick is to provide a right balance.

This chapter is designed to give you tools for generating valuable clash. In Chapter 7, we looked at how to develop your offensive case on a proposition. If the argumentation were to stop there, with each side just offering its own arguments, we would have a few statements standing on their own but no debate. For debate, we must have an *exchange* of arguments that involves you responding to the case your co-arguer has presented and your co-arguer responding to the case you've presented. Nevertheless, some responses are of better quality than others.

Thus, we'll first consider an ideal posture for clash. Then, we'll explore strategies for generating clash in chronological order: anticipation prior to a debate, refutation during a debate, and weighing sides at the end or resolution of a debate. In everyday life, we may not have time to prepare for clash so learning the options now will give you tools you can use in the future. By the end of this chapter, you should be able to use a productive posture for clash that helps resolve debates through anticipating, refuting, and weighing arguments.

A PRODUCTIVE POSTURE FOR CLASH

Based on prior debates you've had in everyday life, you might be tempted to view clash negatively. In fact, people spend a lot of energy every day trying to avoid debate with others. Embracing the mantra, "why can't we all just get along?!" some recognize clash as one step on the path to shouting matches, verbal insults, and the like. If you have ever felt this concern, I don't blame you and you're not alone. It is very common for people to equate debate with fighting and, thus, something to be eliminated in our lives (consider, for instance, Michelle Brody's self-help book, *Stop the Fight! How to Break Free from the 12 Most Common Arguments and Build a Relationship That Lasts*).[2]

But, it's equally true that productive clash can have an opposite effect: It deepens respect and identification between arguers, allows people to refine ideas, generates creative and effective solutions, and fosters individual growth. A world without clash would be a fairly stagnant and uninteresting place. Use the questions in the Find Your Voice box to reflect on your own experience of clash. Then, compare that experience to the following guidelines for productive clash:

1. **Embrace rather than avoid clash.** Some people—perhaps even you—avoid conflict or are passive aggressive rather than direct in confrontation. As we noted earlier, people who behave this way often fear what clash will bring. However, because clash is often necessary to resolve debates and controversies, you should embrace rather than avoid it when appropriate and encourage others to do the same. Sometimes you may need to prompt a debate when others are unwilling to address lingering issues. But, not all situations should become debate situations so be wise about it by considering the stakes of argumentation.

FIND YOUR VOICE
PRODUCTIVE CLASH

Think about a debate or two you've had that you felt was really productive. What about the exchange of arguments made it productive? What behaviors, stances, or attitudes enabled the debate to accomplish its goals? Now, think about a debate or two you've had that was unproductive. Why? What about the content or conduct of arguers made it unproductive? The more you can isolate patterns that generate productive clash, the stronger your argumentation can become.

2. **Keep the proposition as your focal point.** We sometimes get caught up in the back-and-forth sparring of debate that we lose sight of our overall purpose. All arguments in a debate should lead back to the proposition. In everyday life, keep your focus on the purpose of the debate even if your co-arguer distracts you with irrelevant points. This will help avoid personalizing the arguments and make your arguments more productive.

3. **Use the ethical guidelines and a cooperative stance**. Ethical clash is productive clash. As we discussed in Chapter 3, you could choose to win a debate through force or manipulation, but it would be a hollow victory and likely accomplish little of value. Alternatively, heeding the ethical guidelines may involve risk to yourself through honest clash, but it would produce a stronger outcome and help your co-arguers better understand your perspective.

4. **Recognize the limits of your interpretation.** We often enter debates assuming our co-arguer is wrong or to blame. Especially in personal sphere debates, we may start debates with statements focused on our co-arguer's behavior ("you didn't clean the dishes"; "why do you always do such and such things that annoy me?") or use an accusatory tone that leads to unproductive clash. Instead, you should recognize the limits of your own interpretation and be willing to be wrong. For instance, you might say something like, "I was frustrated that the dirty dishes were still in the sink. Is there a reason you didn't have a chance to get to them?"

5. **Don't ignore support for claims.** When we hear arguments, we often fixate on and counter the claims. This can sometimes be valuable. But, if you want to dismantle a structure, you should start at its base or foundation. In the case of an argument, that base is the support. Consequently, overlooking the support leaves some ideas untested and gives your co-arguer's arguments a stronger foundation.

6. **Remember that you concede argumentative points you don't address.** In a formal debate setting, not addressing a co-arguer's point at first opportunity

is equivalent to conceding it. While our training is not for formal debate, the lesson is true in everyday life. For instance, if someone offers three examples as support and you only address one, they would probably point out the other two examples still stand. Thus, clash requires strong engagement with all of your co-arguer's major ideas (later in the chapter we'll discuss when conceding points may at times be useful).

Heeding these guidelines will help you to more fully clash with your co-arguers and, ultimately, produce a stronger outcome. In what follows, we'll look at strategies you can pursue to enhance clash and make sure that you're not surprised by how it develops.

ANTICIPATION

ANTICIPATION:
Examining the
proposition from
your co-arguers'
perspectives

Anticipation, the first step for productive clash in a debate, occurs before you even say anything. To anticipate something means you expect and are prepared for it. Thus, in a debate, anticipation refers to your expectation of certain arguments and your preparation for them. Basically, anticipation involves considering how your co-arguers might interpret and argue the proposition.

The definition of anticipation includes co-arguers because your co-arguers determine, to some degree, the issues and arguments you might anticipate. When you share some of your brilliant ideas for how to increase efficiency at work, for instance, you can anticipate different counter-arguments from your boss than your co-workers. Thus, you'd prepare differently for a debate with those different co-arguers. Beyond the individual interests, the sphere also matters. You'd anticipate different issues in a public sphere debate and a technical sphere debate even if both are debating the same proposition.

Anticipation is valuable in many facets of life but it requires practice. For example, athletes who have been playing their game for many years are able to anticipate plays based on formations or certain tells in others' body language. Students who take practice tests can more easily anticipate the kinds of questions that may be on the real test and improve performance. And, job candidates who have a lot of experience tend to fare better in interviews than those starting out; the more interviews you have, the more you are able to anticipate potential questions. In each case, anticipation skills are honed through experience and practice, better preparing you each step of the way. With debate, experience enables you to more easily anticipate and prepare for your co-arguer's arguments and audience's concerns.

Chances are you've anticipated in a debate setting before. If you've ever written a lengthy argumentative email and revised the wording because you thought it might offend the other party, that's anticipation. If you've ever planned your case to your parents about why they should let you go to some event based on concerns you think they'll have, that's anticipation. If you've ever considered possible questions someone might ask you after a class presentation and how you would answer them, that's anticipation.

The above examples illustrate how anticipation involves two major facets: evaluating your own arguments and generating responses to likely counter-arguments. First, you should test your own arguments for weakness. Chapters 9 and 10 will give you tools to do this so we won't spend much time on that here. Second, you should consider counter-arguments to your stance on the proposition. Once you generate those arguments, then use the material in the next section to prepare refutations to them. In this regard, anticipation is like playing chess: You want to think a few moves ahead, mentally prepared for how the debate will evolve.

One primary strategy for anticipation is to create **argument briefs**. A brief is a written outline or list of your research findings organized around claims (and issues) relevant to the proposition.[3] A brief differs from a case. Recall from Chapters 2 and 7 that a case comprises the arguments you plan to communicate on a proposition. A brief, on the other hand, should include additional information and research that you may need to use as the debate unfolds. You often see this in political candidate debates. The candidates will have "briefing books" that include their opening statements (i.e., their case) as well as talking points and information about other topics that might arise (i.e., briefs on the economy, immigration, nuclear weapons, drug policy, etc.). Especially for significant or formal argumentative occasions, you should create multiple briefs each dedicated to a separate issue in the debate. Box 8.1 offers some tips for creating argument briefs.

ARGUMENT BRIEF: An easy to reference document, often organized around a particular issue, including the major arguments you may need to advance

Based on the discussion of anticipation thus far, you hopefully recognize that anticipation brings many benefits:

1. **Stronger arguments.** Anticipation helps you better tailor your arguments to your audiences and co-arguers. Experiment with anticipation next time you write an argumentative email to someone: as you're about to send it, stop first to think about how that person may refute your arguments (using the strategies outlined in the next section). Doing so may lead you to refine the arguments before sending it.

BOX 8.1: BRIEFING TIPS

1. **Be organized**. The best briefs are easy to find and reference. If you have them physically on paper, you might organize them in a folder with tabs and clearly structure them with bullet points or visual cues to identify claims, support, warrants, etc. If you have them digitally, you might use bookmarks or outline format to make them easy to navigate.

2. **Be focused**. The best briefs are to the point and not overly verbose, focused around clear claims that you may need to demonstrate. If you have too much irrelevant content on a single page or if you muddle the issues in a single brief, they become difficult to reference in the moment.

3. **Be ethical**. The best briefs include ethical citations of your research. You should indicate where you learned the information you're sharing and if someone questions the quality of your authors and sources, be prepared to defend them.

4. **Be thorough**. The best briefs have more content than you could ever hope to use in a single debate. In fact, effective debaters intentionally overprepare argumentative content because debates are so unpredictable. It may seem like wasted effort if you don't use everything you've prepared but you'll feel better having done so.

2. **Better clash.** In addition to improving your own arguments, anticipation helps you better clash with others' arguments because you are prepared. You can experiment with this as well by brainstorming the major arguments for your co-arguer's stance and generating answers to them. Then, if your co-arguer raises that point, you are ready to produce effective clash.

3. **Increased confidence.** Finally, anticipation boosts your confidence in a debate. Anytime you are prepared for something, you tend to feel more at ease and confident. This applies to argumentation because the more prepared you are for a debate through anticipation, the more confident you'll be participating in it.

While anticipation is the first step, it does little on its own to produce clash unless you bring your anticipated responses into the debate. This is where refutation becomes a second step toward productive clash.

REFUTATION

REFUTATION:
The process of articulating flaws in the logic of your co-arguer's arguments

In a debate, the primary means of clash is **refutation** of arguments. To refute an argument is to articulate its weaknesses. Refutation is necessary for clash because it represents your direct engagement with the content raised by your co-arguers and ensures that you and your co-arguer don't talk past one another; it provides the necessary friction to polish the stones. Even if you haven't anticipated and briefed arguments, you can still refute them.

Refutation, like all facets of argumentation, involves choice. Depending on the format and sphere of your debate, it's unlikely for you to respond to every statement your co-arguer has made even though you know that ignoring statements may concede them. Consequently, effective refutation involves strategically assessing what you can and should respond to as well as how you should respond. Box 8.2 outlines some of the factors you might consider when focusing your refutation and the Find Your Voice prompt encourages you to consider clash on moral disagreements.

FIND YOUR VOICE
MORAL DISAGREEMENTS

Disagreements of a moral nature—over what is right or wrong—provide some of the most challenging moments for clash. The most intractable controversies, from abortion and the death penalty to immigration and healthcare, persist largely because moral standards differ from person to person despite each person's morality being a significant, often non-negotiable aspect of his or her identity. How have you handled moral disagreements in the past? What has worked and what hasn't worked? Some scholars have suggested we set aside moral disagreements and focus on other issues while others have argued that we confront them head on, offering everyone an opportunity to defend their moral position.[4] Which do you think is the better approach to moral clash and why?

BOX 8.2: REFUTATION CONSIDERATIONS

1. **Audience Disposition**: You may be tempted to focus your refutation around your co-arguer's structure, but, when the co-arguer differs from the audience, the audience should be your focus. You should only address points that resonate with the audience; if something is not persuasive to the audience, don't waste your time on it.

2. **Argument Strength**: We'll explore what makes strong arguments in Chapter 9. Knowing this, you'll want to refute stronger rather than weaker arguments. Weak arguments are low hanging fruit—easy to grab onto but not likely to get into the thick of it. Instead, focus your efforts on the arguments that make a difference.

3. **Refutation Strength**: In some cases, you may not have a strong response to a strong argument. If so, you probably shouldn't focus your effort there. Instead, you'll want to address arguments for which you have a strong response. Hopefully, these aren't the weak arguments from the original case. Again, the goal is productive clash so you want to balance the strength of the original argument with the strength of the response.

4. **Issue Importance**: Finally, you should consider the importance of the issues. You should refute arguments related to issues of significance rather than irrelevant or insignificant issues. We sometimes waste our time addressing trivial points in the broader debate that we don't make much progress or end up just spinning our wheels. Choose significant issues to ensure your refutation makes a difference.

Beyond the choice of *which* arguments to refute, you also have the choice of *how* to refute them. The four major ways you might refute an argument are to reject, mitigate, turn, or transcend it. We'll discuss each below before seeing them in action through an Everyday Life Example.

Refutation by Rejection

As the name suggests, **refutation by rejection** involves rejecting or denying a co-arguer's claim or support outright. People often use this strategy when they disagree about the facts or the conclusions drawn from those facts. Anytime in a debate you've said, "that's just not true," you've used this strategy.

    However, just rejecting a claim is not enough to convince the audience. Rather than asserting a counter-claim on its own, you should support that claim and explain why your support is preferable to your co-arguers'. Without this crucial step, the debate devolves into a "they say, I say" debate and your audience is left to decide based on what seems most intuitive to them rather than on the best information.

REFUTATION BY REJECTION: Refuting an argument by denying the claim

Refutation by Mitigation

A second strategy is **refutation by mitigation**. The definition of mitigate is to moderate or reduce the severity of something. Mitigating arguments, then, is about moderating the force of a claim. This is often done by pinpointing flaws in the logic of the argument. To do so, you need to understand the relationship between the support and the claim (using tools from Chapters 4-6) and assess to what degree the claim is authorized based on that support (using tools from Chapters 9-10).

REFUTATION BY MITIGATION: Refuting an argument by weakening the support's relationship to the claim

Imagine your co-arguer's case as a piece of fabric. Offering a refutation by mitigation is the equivalent of poking a hole through the fabric. Of course, one hole on its own won't do much damage. However, if you poke five or 10 holes of this nature, the entire piece of fabric rips much more easily. This strategy, then, is about testing the strength of your co-arguer's case.

Refutation by Turning

REFUTATION BY TURNING: Refuting an argument by flipping the valence of the claim

Whereas mitigation is largely a defensive strategy, **refutation by turning** is a more assertive strategy that flips the valence, or emotional value, of the claim by arguing that what your co-arguer says is good is actually bad or vice-versa. Put another way, you agree with part of the argument but then dispute another part. Imagine a scenario where your friend argues that you shouldn't go to a particular restaurant because it's crowded. You might turn this argument and claim that being crowded is a good thing because it has a lively atmosphere and suggests the food is delicious. This helps turn the claim, justifying why you *should* go to the restaurant.

As the example illustrates, turning someone's argument is one of the most powerful refutation strategies because it converts the argument from your co-arguer's stance to your own. As with the previous strategies, however, you require strong support to demonstrate the turn. Not all arguments will be susceptible to turns so you should think carefully about when it is an appropriate strategy and the implications of using it.

Refutation by Transcendence

REFUTATION BY TRANSCENDENCE: Refuting an argument by surpassing the argument's content

A final strategy is **refutation by transcendence.** Whereas the previous three strategies largely addressed the content of the argument as stated by your co-arguer, transcendence goes beyond (or transcends) the argument's content to critique its focus and scope. There are many options for transcendent refutation but we'll explore four:

- **Provide additional content**. One common refutation by transcendence strategy is to provide additional content. This strategy challenges the limited scope of your co-arguer's claim by adding content or considerations that generate a more accurate or complete picture. Sometimes this could mean supplying an argument's unstated assumptions or adding facts that contradict the claim. Keep in mind that this is still a form of *refutation*, or of disputing an argument. This is a useful strategy if you want to provide a more complex and complete understanding of a particular issue.

REDUCTIO AD ABSURDUM: Exploring the absurd and extreme consequences of a claim

- ***Reductio ad absurdum***. *Reductio ad absurdum* is a Latin term that translates as reduction to the absurd. This strategy transcends the scope of your co-arguer's claim by playing it out to the extreme and exploring the consequences of accepting it. When someone asks you, "if your friends jumped off a cliff/bridge, would you, too?" they are using *reductio ad absurdum* (i.e., showing the absurd consequence of your stance) to refute your acquiescence to peer pressure. In legal argumentation, judges often raise hypothetical scenarios to consider the end result of a particular legal interpretation. *Reductio ad absurdum* can be useful if you want the audience to consider the implications of accepting your co-arguer's claims.

- **Identify contradictions and inconsistencies**. If your co-arguer happens to advance arguments that contradict or are inconsistent with one another, one strong refutation strategy is to expose this. Identifying contradictions is a strategy of transcendence because it involves a big picture view of your co-arguer's entire case rather than a response to a single argument. Although it is often difficult for beginning arguers to identify such inconsistencies and contradictions, doing so moves the debate forward by forcing your co-arguer to reconsider his or her assumptions and arguments. Nevertheless, simply identifying contradictions may not be a very effective strategy; you should also resolve the dilemma by arguing which of the contradictory or inconsistent ideas is more accurate and proceed from that starting point.

- **Critique the argumentative performance**. A final type of transcendent refutation involves critiquing the performance of the argument. You would use this strategy to address breaches concerning *how* others argue rather than *what* they argue. For instance, you might identify violations of an ethical guideline such as interrupting you, you might correct discriminatory and exclusionary language, or you might address your co-arguer's competitive stance. In these scenarios and others, the stated arguments fuel the refutation but the response transcends the arguments by addressing their enactment rather than content.

Use the Build Your Skill feature to practice generating refutations.

Two Other Response Options: Preemption and Strategic Concession

The discussion of refutation thus far has focused on strategies that meet two conditions: (1) they respond to another person's argument and (2) they disagree with the argument. However, not all responses meet these qualities. Two possible alternatives are **preemption**,

PREEMPTION: Raising and refuting an anticipated argument

BUILD YOUR SKILL
GENERATING REFUTATION

If you were to refute the following arguments, could you use all four types (rejection, mitigation, turning, transcendence)? For the refutations you are able to generate, which are strongest and why?

A. You are at risk of pregnancy because you are having unprotected sex.

B. It's obvious that Santa Claus is a dangerous capitalist conspiracy. Just consider the way companies exploit Christmas for profit.

C. "I'm falling. So I'm taking my time on my ride"

STRATEGIC CONCESSION: Intentionally granting a co-arguer's claim

in which an arguer introduces and responds (using the previous strategies) to a *potential* rather than *stated* argument, and **strategic concession**, in which an arguer purposefully agrees with a co-arguer's claim, usually for some broader tactical aim.

Both preemption and strategic concession should be used sparingly, but for different reasons. Preemption may initially seem like a good strategy because it lets you debate counter-arguments on your own terms and shows how prepared you are. However, this is generally counter-productive for the debate. One common objection to preemption is that it may give your opponent and audience ideas to doubt your stance. This is certainly true but, if you're genuinely interested in finding the best solution to the proposition, doing so would be beneficial for enabling the participants to consider all important issues in the debate. The bigger concern is that if you preempt all the arguments your co-arguer might advance, you may deter your co-arguer from objecting at all. By stealing his or her argumentative thunder, you might lessen the quality and productivity of the debate. Beyond that, preemption gives more time for your co-arguer's stance and less time for yours. A debate should offer balance for all sides so, in general, your focus should be on developing arguments for your own case.

So, when might preemption be a good strategy? There are two basic conditions that, if met, might justify preempting arguments. First, only preempt an argument if you are confident (or as confident as you can be) that your co-arguer will raise it. This will ensure that you're enabling strong clash on the relevant issues rather than offering a distraction for your audience. Second, only preempt an argument if doing so is necessary to move the debate forward. Perhaps your audience's presumption favors your co-arguer and they aren't giving your arguments a fair shake. In such a scenario, you might preempt this counter-argument or presumption explicitly to get into the substance of the arguments. The decision to preempt arguments should be contextual, requiring your reasoned judgment about whether it would produce a more productive and engaging debate.

Strategic concession is also generally counter-productive. Arguers commonly use this response strategy by conceding a small point that leads into a turn or offensive argument. However, if your focus is on strategically conceding something to gain an upper hand, strategic concession may hamper rather than enhance quality argumentation. This could happen in a couple ways. First, strategic concessions may promote winning or

BOX 8.3: PREEMPTION AND STRATEGIC CONCESSION

As a general rule, only preempt arguments if:

1. You are confident your co-arguer will raise the argument, and

2. Your preemption is necessary to enhance clash in the debate

As a general rule, only concede arguments if:

1. You are confident your audience will understand your purpose, and

2. Your concession is necessary to enhance clash in the debate

gamesmanship at the expense of learning. Additionally, concession may be a strategic way to shut down a debate and eliminate clash altogether. You've likely been in situations where you have agreed with someone's argument simply because you were tired of debating. While we've all been there, you likely recognize that this is not a good strategy for productive clash and resolving conflict.

So, why might strategic concession be a good strategy? You might decide to concede an argument if two conditions are met: First, only concede an argument if the audience understands what is at stake and why you're doing it. Explaining that you're conceding the point might generate goodwill while arguing that concession's relationship to the proposition will produce stronger clash. Second, only concede an argument if doing so moves the debate forward. Like preemption, concession should be about productive debate. If you and your co-arguer reach agreement on a particular issue, then say so, set that issue aside, and move on to other issues. In general, concede an argument because you agree with it, not because it fits some grand strategy to win or end the debate.

Table 8.1 summarizes the major response options outlined above. The purpose of exploring these strategies is not for you memorize and perform them in a rote fashion but rather to understand the options you have for responding to any given argument. Beginning arguers often view rejection—arguing "no" to every "yes" claim or "yes" to every "no" claim—as the best or primary mode of refutation. If this was the extent of refutation, there wouldn't be much movement because we'd be stuck disputing the mere truth of claims rather than their value, support, or focus and scope. Instead, refutation should be adapted to the content, context, and audience of the argument.

To consider how arguers might employ these strategies, we'll turn to President Trump's argumentation on Twitter. Specifically, the Everyday Life Example includes five tweets in chronological order, each refuting arguments about the investigation into the Trump campaign's ties to Russia. As you read the examples, try to determine the refutation strategies (noting that the examples don't involve preemption or concession, especially since Trump is not one to concede someone else's claim).

Trump's refutation strategies are outlined in Table 8.2 with an assessment of their quality. His mitigation (lines 8-13) and turn (lines 3-5) are generally productive because they address the substantive issues and offer considerations that help the audience more fully understand the context and meaning of the issues in the debate.

TABLE 8.1 ■ Summary of Refutation Strategies	
Reject	Counters the **truth** of the support or claim
Mitigate	Counters the **relationship** between support and claim
Turn	Counters the **valence** of the support or claim
Transcend	Counters the **focus and scope** of the support or claim
Preemption	Counters an anticipated claim (using the above strategies)
Concession	Concedes rather than counters the claim

Everyday Life Example 8.1

Donald J. Trump (@realDonaldTrump), Tweets about Russia Investigation, 2017–2018

1   "The Democrats had to come up with a story as to why they lost the election, and so badly (306), so they
2   made up a story - RUSSIA. Fake news!"[5]

3   "When will all the haters and fools out there realize that having a good relationship with Russia is a good
4   thing, not a bad thing. There [sic] always playing politics - bad for our country. I want to solve North
5   Korea, Syria, Ukraine, terrorism, and Russia can greatly help!"[6]

6   "Great jobs numbers and finally, after many years, rising wages- and nobody even talks about them. Only
7   Russia, Russia, Russia, despite the fact that, after a year of looking, there is No Collusion!"[7]

8   "The Failing New York Times purposely wrote a false story stating that I am unhappy with my legal team
9   on the Russia case and am going to add another lawyer to help out. Wrong. I am VERY happy with my
10 lawyers, John Dowd, Ty Cobb and Jay Sekulow. They are doing a great job and . . . ."[8] ". . . have shown
11 conclusively that there was no Collusion with Russia.just excuse for losing. The only Collusion was
12 that done by the DNC, the Democrats and Crooked Hillary. The writer of the story, Maggie Haberman, a
13 Hillary flunky, knows nothing about me and is not given access."[9]

14 "Why doesn't Fake News talk about Podesta ties to Russia as covered by @FoxNews or money from
15 Russia to Clinton - sale of Uranium?"[10]

Source: Twitter/@realDonaldTrump

TABLE 8.2 ■ Refutation Strategies in Trump's Tweets		
Strategy	**Location**	**Quality of Response**
Reject	**Lines 1-2**: Trump denies that there is collusion with Russia, declaring it "fake news."	**Low**: Response doesn't provide any reason to believe him instead of the original claim of collusion.
Mitigate	**Lines 8-13**: Trump mitigates the strength of the *NYT*'s claim that he is unhappy with his legal team noting that he is happy with them and that the author (Haberman) is not in a position to know this.	**Moderate**: Response effectively weakens *NYT*'s claim but the audience might not be swayed to Trump's side given the aggressiveness of the tweet.
Turn	**Lines 3-5**: Trump agrees that he is trying to improve ties with Russia and argues that this is beneficial for national security rather than proof of collusion.	**High**: Response flips audience's anxiety on its head and considers how close ties with Russia would benefit U.S. citizens.
Transcend	**Lines 6-7**: Trump discusses his role in improving the economy as reasons for the media to stop reporting on the Russia investigation. **Lines 14-15**: Trump points fingers at the Clinton campaign's ties to Russia.	**Low**: Responses shift focus to things that don't help resolve the debate. Trump's "whataboutism" in Lines 18-19 is particularly toothless; even if the Clinton campaign had ties with Russia, it doesn't mean Trump didn't as well.

However, Trump's rejection and transcendence are lacking. Of most concern is Trump's response in lines 14-15, which transcends the claim for collusion by discussing the Clinton campaign's ties to Russia. Trump's attack is unproductive because it takes the debate into a personal and largely irrelevant direction. This is an instructive example because some of us may be very Trumpian in our debating, prone toward escalating debates and pointing fingers when our strong emotional investment gets the best of us. But responding in this manner, as you can see here, does little to resolve the controversy.

Trump's rejection in lines 1-2 is also weak because it doesn't include adequate support for the refutation. This pits Trump's word against others' and provides little guidance for the audience to resolve the dilemma. This is true to everyday argumentation, in which people frequently assert counter-claims but fail to provide adequate support for the rejection. You may have noticed how Trump's assertion of "fake news" did not address the issues at the heart of the debate. Ultimately, then, Trump's tweets are instructive for how the choice of content, process, and scope shape the quality of your refutation. In the next section, we'll explore the process of communicating refutation to enable meaningful responses to your co-arguers.

Communicating Refutation

As illustrated above, debates may turn unproductive when refutations aren't developed enough to emphasize their significance for the audience. Machine gun style refutation, in which arguers throw out a lot of shots and hope something sticks, is not a very effective method compared to a more trained marksman style that emphasizes quality engagement with the target.

To get the most bang for your refutation buck, then, you should communicate your refutation following a tried and true four-step process. First, briefly *summarize the argument* you're going to refute. This is important because it cues the audience and it also double-checks your own interpretation of the argument. Recall that some of the excitement of debate comes down to competing perceptions. If you summarize the argument differently from how your co-arguer intended it, he or she can correct your understanding before your refutation proceeds.

Second, *state your response*. Concisely explain why the argument is flawed by offering your rejection, mitigation, turn, transcendence, or concession. Because a refutation is itself an argument, think of this as your claim; it's the ultimate conclusion you want your audience to accept about your co-arguer's argument. Unfortunately, a lot of refutation stops here, resulting in the "they say, I say" debate mentioned earlier. But, you know by now that just asserting a claim on its own isn't enough for effective argumentation.

BOX 8.4: COMMUNICATING REFUTATION

1. Summarize the argument
2. State your response
3. Support your response
4. Conclude with impact

Third, *support your response.* If you assert there's a contradiction or a rule violation, quote or paraphrase your co-arguer's statements to demonstrate it. If you reject or mitigate your co-arguer's claim, provide support and warrants to assist your own claim and explain why your support is better than your co-arguer's. Basically, find some way to justify your refutation using reasoning and research.

It's possible for you to refute an argument by offering multiple responses and multiple supports. When you do, stack them by explaining each in turn after summarizing the argument. Ideally you would be organized about this effort, perhaps even enumerating your responses for the audience to follow along (e.g., "there are two flaws with the claim that I colluded with Russia. First. . . Second. . ."). Just as stacked support produces a more meaningful argument, stacked responses produce a more meaningful refutation.

Identifying flaws in an argument is nice and all but it has little effect on the overall debate unless you explicitly tell the audience what to do with the refutation in deciding on the proposition. Thus, fourth, you should *conclude with impact* about what your refutation means for the debate as a whole. Why should we care if your co-arguer's claims are exaggerated? Why should we care if your co-arguer used discriminatory language? Why should we care if your co-arguer contradicts him- or herself? You must tell the audience why these are significant errors and how, concretely, they should change the audience's judgment on the proposition. Concluding with impact is the most challenging but also the most crucial step because it's where the debate gets decided in the minds of the audience members.

When all four steps are put together, it forms a single complete refutation. To see this process in action, let's spend more time with Trump's mitigation since that was his most fulsome refutation and consider how we might revise it to be a more impactful response. As a reminder, here was Trump's original two-part tweet with the refutation steps indicated in brackets:

> "The Failing New York Times purposely wrote a false story stating that I am unhappy with my legal team on the Russia case and am going to add another lawyer to help out [**summarize the argument**]. Wrong. I am VERY happy with my lawyers, John Dowd, Ty Cobb and Jay Sekulow. [**state first response**] They are doing a great job and. . .."[11] ". . .have shown conclusively that there was no Collusion with Russia.just excuse for losing. [**support first response**] The only Collusion was that done by the DNC, the Democrats and Crooked Hillary. The writer of the story, Maggie Haberman, a Hillary flunky, knows nothing about me and is not given access [**state second response**]."[12]

The refutation included two and a half of the four steps: It summarized the original argument, stated two responses, and supported one of them but didn't provide much of the supporting materials discussed in Chapter 5. It also didn't impact the refutation for the overall debate. Even if Trump's audience agreed with him that the *New York Times* article was flawed, what does this mean for the claim that he is "going to add another lawyer to help out" or for the broader debate on his alleged collusion with Russia? All arguments and refutation should lead back to the proposition, something Trump failed to do here.

Now, imagine that Trump was debating this in person with Haberman, giving her a chance to respond to Trump's refutations. What do you think that might look like? In general, responding to refutations follows the same procedure as refutation itself, using the strategies outlined above. This middle stage of a debate is the most crucial time for arguers to interrogate the ideas and for those ideas to marinate with the audience. Rather than just repeating the ideas outlined in your original case, you should work to provide additional considerations, offer new reasoning and analysis, and use tools of refutation when responding to the responses of others. Through such exchanges, the goal is to deepen consideration of the issues and move the audience toward resolution of the controversy.

But, this middle stage can't go on forever. Debate must come to an end, if for no other reason than you need to go to the bathroom or get some sleep. The final element of productive clash, then, is to effectively conclude the debate.

ENDING PRODUCTIVELY

You could exchange and refute arguments to your heart's content and still accomplish very little. Chances are you've participated in debates where you and your co-arguers rehash the same ideas over and over and get nowhere. Most debates require you to capitalize on the clash by effectively concluding the debate for yourself, your co-arguer, and the audience. Use the Find Your Voice prompt to reflect on how this normally happens in your everyday life before reading the below strategies for productively ending debates.

Let's first consider why a debate ends. Ideally, it ends because people settle on the best course of action and there's no longer disagreement. In these cases, "concluding the debate" is the same thing as "resolving the controversy." Unfortunately, everyday argumentation rarely conforms to this ideal and debates often end for other reasons. Sometimes the participants decide the debate is over, they run out of things to say, or they run out of time to say them. In other cases, a formal mechanism such as rebuttal speeches or closing statements may function to end the debate. In other cases, the debate might end once all participants have shared their ideas and all options are on the table. These cases illustrate that debates frequently end while controversies linger.

The focus here concerns how to conclude a debate as productively as possible in order to best achieve your goals. Even though we know that no two debates will proceed exactly the same, there are several general strategies that can help participants end on good terms

FIND YOUR VOICE
CONCLUDING DEBATES

In your everyday life, why and how do most of your debates end? Who tends to decide when it's over and what are some of the typical outcomes? If you've had a debate that you think ended really well, why? What about the situation, the argumentation, the participants, etc. made it productive? The more you are aware of what allows for a valuable conclusion, the more you can implement those strategies in your everyday debates.

rather than in frustration, anger, or apathy. The strategies below are largely chronological, addressing steps you can take prior to the debate through your final sentence and beyond.

Determine What Goals Are Acceptable

Because you should begin a debate with a sense of what you hope to accomplish, determining acceptable goals is a first strategy to effectively concluding it. We noted earlier that refutation can make a debate complex and messy, causing you to lose sight of the bigger picture. However, if you keep your goal in mind, you are less likely to get distracted by the minutiae and more likely to pursue that main motivation for the debate.

Some debates (especially personal sphere ones) are motivated not by an argumentative outcome but rather by relational goals to make people feel included, listened to, or respected. That is, debates with friends or family members may occur not because you care a whole lot about the proposition but because the process of debating is one way to experience your relationship; debate is the equivalent of playing a game or seeing a movie together. At work, debates might be about ensuring everyone has a stake in the process and gets to share their perspectives, not because there is a pressing decision that needs to be made. In these debates, it's often pretty easy to decide in the moment how to end.

In most cases, however, your goal is related to the proposition: to find the best solution or to convince someone of your stance. Even still, you should think more carefully about what outcomes would satisfy you: Do you want your audience to agree with you wholeheartedly? To consider your stance in making a more informed decision? To "agree to disagree" with your stance and respect you for having it? Each of these outcomes might be appropriate in particular contexts so having a clear sense of your goals can guide your effort of when and how to resolve the debate.

Knowing your goal also helps you construct final appeals to your audience. In concluding the debate, perhaps be up front with your audience members by emphasizing directly what you want them to take away from it. For instance, if you are just seeking a fair shake in the debate, you might close by saying something like, "I don't care if you agree with me completely, but hopefully you better understand my stance and how it relates to your preexisting beliefs." This honesty helps focus both you and the audience on the important stakes of the debate.

Establish an Ending Mechanism

A second strategy for effectively concluding a debate is to establish a mechanism for ending it. The most common method is to set a time limit but there are other means, such as establishing a specific number of statements or enabling audience members to call a vote. The method itself may depend on the context and sphere of the debate (technical sphere debates, for instance, tend to have existing mechanisms while public sphere debates tend to be more open-ended and based on the participants' judgment of when it's over). And, in fact, the ending mechanism may itself be debatable!

Regardless of what mechanism you choose, it's best to establish it early in the debate. This will ensure all participants know and agree to the parameters of the debate and aren't caught by surprise. Perhaps you've been in a debate where you wanted to say something but time ran out. You likely were frustrated. Now, imagine if you didn't know there was a time limit and you were excluded because time ran out. Your frustration would likely turn to anger. This is why it is crucial for arguers and audiences to know in advance how the debate will play its course.

Weigh the Important Issues and Arguments

Whereas the first two strategies were related to the procedure for concluding a debate, this strategy addresses the content. Earlier we noted that the conclusion of a debate should consider the "big picture." This is another way of saying that you should weigh the issues and arguments in the debate for the audience. We'll consider three factors that go into weighing the content in a debate.

First, weighing the issues and arguments requires you to clash with your co-arguer's arguments. In your mind, it's probably obvious why your side is right, but you must at least consider and address the reasons against your stance. If you stay in your own silo and just repeat your points over and over without accounting for your co-arguer's arguments, then your audience is not likely to understand how to resolve the disagreements.

Second, weighing issues and arguments requires that you engage *issues*—those neutral questions that help organize arguments with respect to the proposition—as well as *arguments*. Emphasize the most important issues to help the audience makes sense of the arguments' significance to the debate. If you convince the audience that the questions you're answering are crucial to resolving the debate, then you can more clearly indicate the significance of their decision.

Third, weighing issues and arguments requires you to put these issues in conversation with one another. This idea of weighing sides is evident when we visualize debate as a scale. You place the arguments side by side and see which one comes out on top based on the relative importance of the issues and strength of the arguments. To do this, though, you must explain which issues are most important and how they should be resolved in the debate. Part of this involves recognizing and applying the particular standard we discussed in Chapter 7 that is appropriate for the type of proposition (preponderance of evidence for fact propositions, value-criterion for value propositions, and net benefits for policy propositions). Your conclusion should explain why your evidence is stronger than your co-arguers, why your value-criterion is more applicable, or why your stance is net beneficial.

Keep in mind, though, that it also requires you to compare your arguments to your co-arguer's. When we plan to wrap up a debate, we may be tempted to focus our conclusion on our own arguments because we're comfortable with the content; we know it best and are committed to it. When you just restate ideas rather than explain how they all interrelate, you don't provide a full analysis of the debate. Rather than leave the audience's judgment up to chance, you should tell them exactly how to resolve the issues. This brings us to the final strategy for concluding a debate.

Empower Audience Members

The final strategy to effectively conclude a debate is to be audience-centered by putting the power in its hands to make a difference on the proposition. This strategy may differ depending on the nature of the controversy and your audience. If your co-arguer is also your audience, you should return to why you're having the debate in the first place (go back to your goal) and address it explicitly with him or her. Explaining how your arguments have accomplished the goal of the debate is one way to begin this process but you should ensure that your co-arguers also feel the debate accomplished what they desired.

If your co-arguer differs from your audience, then you and your co-arguer are both trying to secure the audience's assent. In this scenario, you should explain why aligning with you is the better choice and what members of the audience stand to gain from doing so. Empowering audience members involves helping them see themselves as part of the action or belief going forward. If there's no payoff from the debate, then it might just be wasted time.

These strategies for concluding a debate—establishing clear goals and an ending mechanism, weighing the content, and empowering the audience—are related to the broader blueprint for effective clash because they require explicit consideration of the purpose and procedure of the debate, addressing what we learned and what ideas were weak or strong.

Summary

This chapter has explored how to generate productive clash, or argumentation on the same issues in a debate. Clash begins with a positive posture that uses ethical guidelines and embraces the opportunity to learn and grow through engaging the arguments of others. Clash also involves a set of argumentative strategies—anticipation and briefing, refutation, and concluding the debate—that enable you, your audience members, and co-arguers to get the most out of the arguments in a debate. Trump's tweets show how clash is at the heart of all debate even though some everyday argumentation lacks openness and impact to make it meaningful and productive. By honing your own clash skills, you can be a more cooperative and constructive participant in any debate.

Application Exercises

Practicing Anticipation: Read the major headlines on the opinion page of a newspaper or news website. For each headline, answer the following questions and then test your answers:

1. What proposition do you anticipate the article will advocate?

2. What arguments for that proposition do you anticipate?

3. Knowing the source of publication, what arguments against that proposition do you expect to surface in the comments section?

Evaluating Refutation Strategies: Search online for the lyrics to "Cabinet Battle #1" and "Cabinet Battle #2" from *Hamilton: An American Musical.* Then, analyze Alexander Hamilton's refutation strategies for refuting Thomas Jefferson's cases:

1. Identify the kinds of refutation in Hamilton's responses to Jefferson's arguments.

2. Evaluate the strength of each refutation, particularly in relation to the four-step process.

3. Rewrite each refutation (in prose or lyrical format) to make it more effective in using one of the refutation strategies and following the correct four-step process.

Extra Credit: Consider how well the participants concluded the debate, using the guidelines above.

Key Terms

Clash 175

Anticipation 178

Argument Brief 179

Refutation 180

Refutation by Rejection 181

Refutation by Mitigation 181

Refutation by Turning 182

Refutation by
   Transcendence 182

Reductio ad Absurdum 182

Preemption 183

Strategic Concession 184

Endnotes

1. *Steve Jobs: The Lost Interview*, directed by Paul Sen (1995; Los Angeles, CA: Magnolia Pictures, 2012), DVD. Reprinted with permission from John Gau, John Gau Productions.

2. Michelle Brody, *Stop the Fight! How to Break Free from the 12 Most Common Arguments and Build a Relationship That Lasts* (New York: The Experiment, LLC, 2015).

3. You may have heard of a legal brief before, which refers to the written case that the lawyer submits to the court prior to oral arguments. An argument brief follows the same idea but is not as formal.

4. Bruce Ackerman, "Why Dialogue?" *Journal of Philosophy* 86 (1989): 5–22; Chantal Mouffe, "Deliberative Democracy or Agonistic Pluralism?" *Social Research* 66 (1999): 745–758.

5. Donald J. Trump (@realDonaldTrump), Twitter Post, February 16, 2017, 6:39 a.m., https://twitter.com/realDonaldTrump/status/832238070460186625.

6. Donald J. Trump (@realDonaldTrump), Twitter Post, November 11, 2017, 4:18 p.m., https://twitter.com/realDonaldTrump/status/929503641014112256.

7. Donald J. Trump (@realDonaldTrump), Twitter Post, February 3, 2018, 4:26 p.m., https://twitter.com/realDonaldTrump/status/959946200488271872.

8. Donald J. Trump (@realDonaldTrump), Twitter Post, March 11, 2018, 6:41 a.m., https://twitter.com/realDonaldTrump/status/972829763067883523.

9. Donald J. Trump (@realDonaldTrump), Twitter Post, March 11, 2018, 6:50 a.m., https://twitter.com/realDonaldTrump/status/972832210222043137.

10. Donald J. Trump (@realDonaldTrump), Twitter Post, March 28, 2018, 3:41 p.m., https://twitter.com/realDonaldTrump/status/846854703183020032.

11. Trump, Twitter Post, March 11, 2018, 6:41 a.m.

12. Trump, Twitter Post, March 11, 2018, 6:50 a.m.

9

EVALUATING
ARGUMENTS & CASES

M any inspirational movies about the law—from *To Kill a Mockingbird, 12 Angry Men,* and *Amistad* to *Legally Blonde, Erin Brockovich,* and *My Cousin Vinny*— emphasize the power of good arguments to change minds and bring about justice. For instance, Elle Woods won her first big case in *Legally Blonde* by using known facts about hair perms to discredit the main witness in the case. According to these movies, good arguments are necessary to protect people's lives and livelihoods. But how do we know Woods made a "good argument"? That is, how do we know that her claim was authorized on the basis of the support she provided?

This chapter is dedicated to answering that question through an adaptable set of tools for evaluating arguments. Specifically, there are three questions you can ask about any argument to effectively interrogate its quality. The best part about these questions is that you can answer them without having knowledge of the topic, although having such knowledge will only make your evaluation stronger. The ideas in this chapter build on the previous chapter's discussion of clash to improve your argument construction and refutation skills. Additionally, the lessons in this chapter are important because you are constantly bombarded by arguments—in class, at your job, from your friends, through the mass media. One of the most valuable critical thinking skills you can cultivate is to quickly make sense of and evaluate those arguments in everyday life.

Before turning to the three questions (or conditions) for evaluating arguments, we should consider what exactly we're evaluating arguments *for*. If you ponder this question, you may come up with numerous answers. Perhaps a good argument is logical: It has quality support for the conclusion. This makes sense until you realize that your dentist has given you an airtight, logical argument about why flossing twice daily will do wonders for your teeth, and yet, I would venture you and many of your friends and family members fail to do so. Clearly, logic is not enough. So, maybe you think of an argument that is appropriately tailored to persuade the audience. Effectiveness is certainly important but do we really want to conclude that this is the best criterion? If so, then any argument that wins (including those through competitive and manipulative stances) would be a "good" argument. So, this might bring ethics into the conversation; perhaps "good" arguments use claims and support honestly.

The previous paragraph reveals how logic, persuasiveness, and ethics may conflict with one another and often depend on the specific debate situation. For instance, an advertisement may play on our emotions, persuading us to buy a product even though we find it to be illogical or unethical. Similarly, sometimes what some audiences find to be logical support—such as the use of opinion polls—just doesn't work for other audiences. In these cases, you would likely resist labeling them "good" arguments. But, why is this? And how would you articulate the flaws with either example?

COGENT:
Rationally
persuasive

To answer these questions, we will rely on **cogency** as the most complete criterion for evaluating arguments. A cogent argument is an argument that is "rationally persuasive." That is, a cogent argument is logical, persuasive, and ethical. For instance, the dentist will offer a cogent argument for flossing if it is logical (i.e., the support justifies the claim), persuasive (i.e., it speaks to the audience's interests and motivations), and ethical (i.e., it avoids manipulation, force, faulty information, etc.). It should be evident, then, that cogency is a comprehensive judgment that considers numerous elements.

So, what are these elements? An argument is cogent if, and only if, the *support* in the argument is:

- **A**cceptable to the audience,
- **R**elevant to the claim, and
- **G**rounds sufficient for the claim

We will call these three elements the ARG conditions. This should be easy to remember because A-R-G are also the first three letters of the word argument. The ARG conditions fit well into the Toulmin model of an argument we explored in Chapter 5. As noted in Figure 9.1, each ARG condition evaluates a different element within the model. Given this coverage of the support, warrant, and rebuttal, it's not surprising that the ARG conditions enable a far-reaching evaluation of an argument.

The remainder of this chapter will explain these standards or conditions in turn. As we discuss each ARG condition, we'll illustrate its application by evaluating James Harrison's Instagram post about participation trophies that we first encountered in Chapter 4. After we've defined all three ARG conditions, we'll then turn to a more extensive consideration of how you can use the ARG conditions to assess entire argumentative cases and controversies, culminating in an Everyday Life Example. You should note at the outset that the ARG conditions in this chapter apply to any claim and support relationship, but, in the next chapter, we will refine this tool by considering what it means for different argument types to be cogent; this chapter provides the general framework whereas the next one offers more concrete direction related to recurring patterns. By the end of this chapter, you should be able to critically evaluate any argument for cogency by assessing the support's acceptability, relevance, and grounds.

FIGURE 9.1 ■ The Toulmin Model and the ARG Conditions

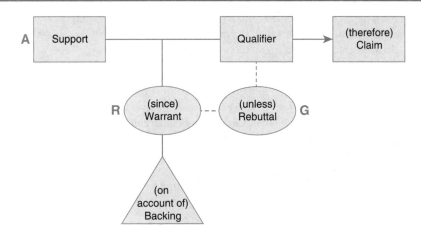

THE *A* CONDITION: ACCEPTABILITY

The first criterion for a cogent argument is **acceptability**. Acceptability focuses exclusively on the support for the claim because support is the starting point for an argument. To be acceptable, then, your audience must deem the support to be reasonably permissible in the debate. However, an audience member might find support permissible in a debate even if that person does not *accept* it; we sometimes take support with a grain of salt or allow it "for argument's sake." On the flipside, unacceptable support tends to be information that is incorrect, biased, unethical, or not agreeable to the audience. Honesty is especially important insofar as false information (or even manipulation of true information, such as skewed statistics) would be unacceptable support for a claim. The Find Your Voice prompt encourages you to consider the acceptability of disinformation in contemporary society.

ACCEPTABILITY: The degree to which the audience finds the support reasonably permissible in a debate

FIND YOUR VOICE
ACCEPTABILITY AND DISINFORMATION

Online contexts in the past few years have been plagued by disinformation, or what people commonly call "fake news." In these situations, audience members find the information acceptable even if it is not (entirely) true. Does acceptability require truthfulness? Under what circumstances is it appropriate to evaluate support as unacceptable despite the audience accepting it? The more you establish your own standards of acceptability, the more aware you can be of how arguers manipulate information to authorize claims.

Support can be reasonably permissible in one of two ways:

1. First, an arguer could offer further support or backing for it. This would create an argument chain, in which the claim of one argument becomes support for the subsequent one. In many cases, co-arguers will address acceptability by demanding further information.

2. Adding further support could go on *ad infinitum*, in which someone demands support for or asks "why" of every statement that is provided. This is not how real debates work. So, a second way support is acceptable is if the audience finds it reasonable without requiring further information or further defense. At some point for productive debate, your co-arguers and audience members should find your support acceptable. One way to decide acceptability would be to apply the guidelines from Chapter 5 for that type of support.

There are three qualities of acceptability worth noting:

1. **Acceptability is an *external measure*,** tied to the audience and situation. Support that is acceptable for one context or for one audience may not be for another. A judge may not deem hearsay evidence acceptable for determining someone's guilt but you might be willing to permit hearsay evidence from a co-worker when concluding who stole your Coke from the work fridge. The Bible illustrates the contextual nature of acceptability; citing the Bible is perfectly acceptable to support a claim for some audiences and situations (such as a pastor preaching to a congregation) but not for others (such as a U.S. Attorney General advocating a policy to a national audience). Determining acceptability, then, requires you to consider the perspective of the argument's audience members.

2. **Acceptability resides in *each* piece of support**. If there are two pieces of support for a claim, it's possible that one is acceptable while the other is not. For instance, in reaching a claim about someone's guilt, a judge might not accept hearsay evidence but might permit a video of the accused committing the crime. The more pieces of support that are acceptable, the more cogent the argument becomes (although don't forget that acceptability is only one of three conditions for cogency).

3. **Acceptability is a *matter of debate*.** There is no handbook or magic wand to make support acceptable. Rather, it's established through trial and error and contestation in real debate. You might use support that no one questions in one context but then gets skewered in another. As an audience member, you may critique a particular arguer's support more than another's based on factors such as credibility or use of citations. Keep in mind, though, that an acceptability challenge does not automatically mean a non-cogent argument. Rather, it provides one chance to question the quality of an argumentative claim.

To explore the nature of acceptability, let's return to a portion of James Harrison's case about participation trophies from Chapter 4. This is a useful example because you are ostensibly an audience member for this public Instagram post and because we can dissect the argument's component parts. The first part of the argument we'll analyze is diagramed in Figure 9.2. The circles in the diagram indicate the two supporting statements that you would need to individually appraise for acceptability as a first step to determining the cogency of his case for returning the trophies.

To judge the acceptability of this argument, you should ask yourself if you find *each* support acceptable. First, is the statement that Harrison's sons didn't earn the participation trophies permissible in this debate? Not having been at the event itself, you can't know for sure why the sons received the trophies, but, barring a reason to doubt Harrison's characterization, this statement would likely satisfy the *A* condition as an acceptable starting point. This may explain why Harrison didn't feel the need to provide further support for this statement.

Do you find the statement that everything in life should be earned acceptable on its own? This support is more debatable. Some audience members might find it acceptable but others might not. Perhaps anticipating this, Harrison provided support for the support, as diagramed in Figure 9.3.

The circles in Figure 9.3 represent the new tests of acceptability needed to fully evaluate whether Harrison's support is acceptable. If you were initially skeptical that everything in life should be earned, are the other three statements permissible in the debate? Maybe, maybe not, depending on your perspective.

This example illustrates how there is not a "right" answer with acceptability; each audience member must reach a judgment based on his or her interpretation of and interaction with the argument. Acceptability provides one way to articulate possible flaws in an argument and interrogate its quality. It's one choice of refutation you have at your disposal. You could, of course, always ask for more information for the support in an argument, but, in the spirit of productive debate, you should consider when such information is necessary rather than desirable.

FIGURE 9.2 ■ Acceptability in James Harrison's Abridged Post

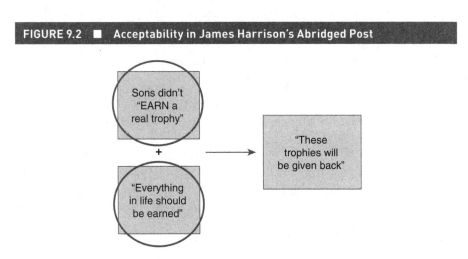

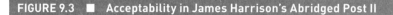

FIGURE 9.3   ■   Acceptability in James Harrison's Abridged Post II

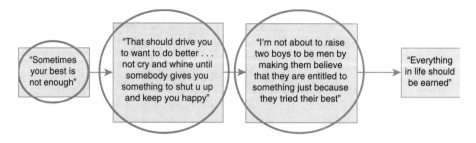

"Sometimes your best is not enough"

"That should drive you to want to do better . . . not cry and whine until somebody gives you something to shut u up and keep you happy"

"I'm not about to raise two boys to be men by making them believe that they are entitled to something just because they tried their best"

"Everything in life should be earned"

THE *R* CONDITION: RELEVANCE

RELEVANCE: The degree to which the support has bearing on the claim

A second condition required for cogency is **relevance**. Whereas acceptability considers support on its own, relevance addresses the relationship between support and its subsequent claim. Specifically, an argument passes the *R* condition if the support has bearing on the claim, insofar as there is a reasonable warrant to justify that support in relation to the claim. Because warrants often go unstated, arguers tend to assume relevance and build it into the chain of reasoning rather than stating it explicitly.

Even if we determine support to be *acceptable* in a debate, the question of *relevance* is entirely separate; support might be acceptable but irrelevant or, conversely, unacceptable but relevant. This difference is evident in an exchange from an episode of the ABC sitcom, *The Goldbergs*, in which the eldest son, Barry, is given an opportunity to throw out the first pitch at a Phillies game. Beverly, Barry's mother, expressed concerned to Murray, his father, that it was not a good idea because Barry crumbles under pressure. Murray responded with an argument: "I played baseball in high school [support]. Barry's got this [claim]." While the support that Murray played baseball in high school is certainly acceptable, Beverly immediately recognized its irrelevance, exclaiming: "That makes no sense! One thing has nothing to do with the other."[1] Relevance, as Beverly recognized, requires that support has something to do with the claim.

There are three important qualities of the *R* condition:

1. **Relevance is an *internal measure*** that tests the relationship between claim and support. Unlike acceptability, relevance is largely (but perhaps not entirely) independent of the context or audience. Judgments of relevance should ostensibly be the same whether the argument is spoken in a presidential speech, written in an organization's tweet, or yelled by your friend in a heated exchange.

2. **Relevance is a *qualitative judgment* of the relationship between *each convergent support* and the claim**. That is, it considers to what degree each support justifies its subsequent conclusion. In cases of linked support, you would assess the support in combination as it justifies the claim. In a diagram, you essentially evaluate the strength of each arrow.

3. **Relevance is *a matter of debate*.** As with acceptability, there's not a right or wrong answer, and the quality of the support's relevance needs to be hashed

BUILD YOUR SKILL
CONSIDERING STATISTICAL RELEVANCE

If you want to claim that your town suffers from poverty, you could choose many supporting materials but it might be wise to use statistics. Which of the following statistics is more relevant to the claim that your town suffers from poverty?

1. Sixty-four percent of children in communities of similar geographic and population size as yours live in food deserts and have reduced or free lunch in schools.

2. The average income for a household of four in your town is $20,000 ($800 below the 2018 federally established poverty guideline for that category[2]).

out through actual contestation. Because statements of relevance are often implied rather than established overtly, they are ripe for questioning. While some standards of relevance depend on the kind of argument being advanced (see Chapter 10), even they don't offer a strict formula for cogency.

To practice assessing relevance, use the Build Your Skill feature and also consider Harrison's case for returning the trophies on the basis. For Harrison's case, we'd need to determine and then evaluate the warrant. Luckily, we already identified it in Chapter 4. Figure 9.4 depicts the argument with a circle indicating what we would assess for relevance. Does the fact that Harrison's sons didn't earn the trophies have bearing on

FIGURE 9.4 ■ Relevance in James Harrison's Abridged Post

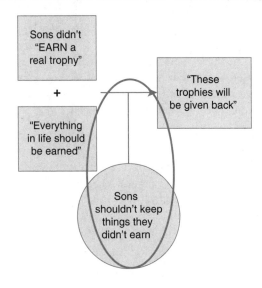

(or warrant) giving them back? Put another way, is it true that people shouldn't keep things they didn't earn? In all likelihood, this argument would meet the relevance condition but this is nevertheless a debatable warrant. Were you to challenge it, the Toulmin model indicates that Harrison might then provide backing to demonstrate the warrant's suitability. Again, there's not always a right answer but relevance provides one site of dispute that you could raise in evaluating Harrison's argument.

THE *G* CONDITION: SUFFICIENT GROUNDS

GROUNDS: The degree to which the support is sufficient to justify the claim

The third and final condition required for cogency is sufficient **grounds**. Grounds asks whether all the support, taken together, provides enough justification for the claim. The *G* condition relates to the rebuttal of an argument, because, unlike relevance, grounds requires the person evaluating the argument to raise considerations not included in the argument and generate conditions under which the warrant for the argument would not apply. Put another way, relevance assesses what *is* there to authorize the claim while grounds assesses what *is not* there but needs to be to authorize the claim. Grounds are established when the provided support is immune to possible rebuttals and the magnitude and range of support is adequate for the claim.

The judgment of grounds is independent from the judgment of acceptability and relevance. Support may be acceptable and relevant to the claim, but it may not be enough to justify the claim. Here are the three important qualities of the *G* condition:

1. **Grounds is an *internal measure*** that tests the relationship between claim and support. Like relevance, grounds can be determined largely independent of the context or audience. Particular argumentative forms have particular expectations when it comes to grounds.

2. **Grounds is a *quantitative judgment*** **of the relationship between *all the support*** **and the claim**. Grounds considers if all of the support for a claim is of enough scope and variety to justify the conclusion. Returning to the poverty example discussed under relevance, you would have a more cogent argument (on the basis of grounds) if you used both statistics rather than just one of them. At the same time, you would consider whether statistics alone are enough of an indicator of poverty. For instance, would testimony from people in the community be required for sufficient grounds? This is just one illustration of how grounds might be contested in that argument.

3. **Grounds is *a matter of debate***. Like acceptability and relevance, there are not firm guidelines for grounds to immunize an argument from criticism. This is especially the case since grounds incorporates ideas not provided for in the argument. As with relevance, the type of argument might offer clues as to what counts as sufficient grounds, but these are debatable and depend on critical judgment and interpretation. Use the Find Your Voice feature to consider the requirement for sufficient grounds in social media arguments.

FIND YOUR VOICE

SUFFICIENT GROUNDS ON SOCIAL MEDIA?

Can you make a cogent argument in 280 characters or less? As arguments become more compact in our culture of social media, soundbites, and short attention spans, is the demand for sufficient grounds now unrealistic? For instance, if you revisit Trump's tweets from Chapter 8, should they need to satisfy the grounds condition and would they? You should consider what the ARG conditions mean for the quality of your own argumentative engagement on social media.

FIGURE 9.5 ■ Grounds in James Harrison's Abridged Post

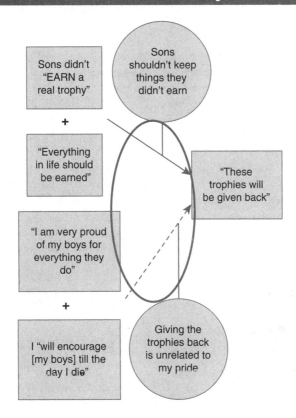

Let's return to Harrison's argument. The grounds assessment is indicated by the circle in Figure 9.5. So, even if we agree that everything in life should be earned and Harrison's sons didn't earn the trophies and even if we agree that this has bearing on whether or not Harrison should return the trophies, we would still need to ask ourselves if this is *enough* to justify the claim, especially in light of Harrison's own rebuttal argument that he is proud of his boys and will encourage them. Would we require different or additional kinds of support? Are there conditions under which the sons should keep things they didn't earn? These are just some of the questions that help evaluate this argument's grounds.

The grounds in Harrison's argument is the weakest of the three requirements for a cogent argument. Not only does Harrison provide the audience a potential refutation (if he loved his sons, he'd let them keep the trophies) but his proposition relies almost exclusively on the principle that everything in life should be earned. There are numerous ways a co-arguer could mitigate this argument through refutation. You may recall from Chapter 4 that one common refutation of Harrison's argument was that his sons are just children. Their age provides a rebuttal that limits the strength of his claim on the basis of grounds. Put another way, his sons shouldn't keep things they didn't earn *unless* they are young children. Of course, it wouldn't be in Harrison's interest to raise this rebuttal himself. This is why it is the responsibility of audiences and co-arguers to generate rebuttals to the warrant and consider factors beyond the scope of the original argument's content when evaluating an argument for grounds.

Once we've considered Harrison's argument from each of the ARG conditions, we can render a judgment on its cogency. Recall that an argument must pass all three ARG conditions to be cogent. In this case, Harrison's argument passed the *A* and *R* conditions and had one rebuttal for the *G* condition. Do you find this rebuttal about the age of his sons acceptable, and, if so, is it enough to sink Harrison's claim? Because Harrison's argument largely passes muster when it comes to the three ARG conditions, we would likely deem it cogent.

The three ARG conditions combined provide a complete test of any given argument. Box 9.2 offers a quick reference of the major questions you should ask. The question format is intentional because it emphasizes the ARG conditions as potential *issues* that organize disagreements in a debate. Challenging the acceptability, relevance, and/or grounds of an argument makes it an issue in the debate. Having now explored all three ARG conditions for cogency, we should consider how to put them into practice through refutation.

BOX 9.2: ARG CONDITIONS QUICK REFERENCE

An argument is cogent if you can answer "yes" to **all** of the following questions:

- Will the audience find the support permissible in the debate? (A)

- Is the support accurate and unmanipulated? (A)

- Does the support have bearing on the claim? (R)

- Is the support immune to possible rebuttals? (G)

- Is the magnitude and range of support adequate for the claim? (G)

APPLYING THE ARG CONDITIONS THROUGH REFUTATION

The ARG conditions provide a comprehensive set of questions that consider both the content *and* context when evaluating an argument for cogency. As we've seen, the ARG conditions can empower you to critique an argument based on the audience for and structure of it, without requiring any research or knowledge on the topic.

The ARG conditions, then, become a primary tool for refutation by mitigation as described in Chapter 8. They function best by raising critical questions about the quality of the presented arguments, and they invite you, your co-arguer, and audience to ensure that numerous considerations have been interrogated before agreeing to any claim or proposition. The ARG conditions fit nicely into the four-step refutation process described in Chapter 8; the second step would involve identifying the weakness based on the ARG conditions, and the third step would explain your assessment.

For instance, using the ARG conditions might produce the following refutation of Harrison's argument for returning his sons' trophies:

> "Harrison argues that he is returning the trophies because everything in life should be earned and his sons didn't earn the trophies [**summarize the argument**]. This principle is true for adults but it doesn't apply to children and, thus, is not enough to justify returning his sons' trophies [**state response—fails *G* condition**]. This is because children of his sons' age are often denied the choice between "earning" and "receiving" something and they should be encouraged through positive rein-forcement rather than taught to live life with a chip on their shoulder [**explain response**]. The age difference in this case undermines the applicability of the prin-ciple that everything in life should be earned, meaning there's no real reason to return the trophies [**conclude with impact for the proposition**]."

This is one possible refutation of Harrison's argument that targets the grounds. We know this is a grounds challenge because it generates a rebuttal to the argument's war-rant. There are, however, other refutations that you could advance using any of the ARG conditions. And, the refutation is not the final say that concludes debate on the propo-sition. Rather, it is one way to explore the quality of the argument. Harrison (or others) might respond with further justification of the principle in relation to children, deepen-ing the debate on this issue.

While anyone can learn to use the ARG conditions, they do require critical thinking and judgment instead of a prescribed or cookie-cutter approach to argumentation. Part of the excitement of debate arises when arguers engage each other's arguments through critical thinking and analysis. This can't happen if you expect the ARG conditions to be a check-list. Instead, use them as a springboard to facilitate clash. To help you practice, use the Build Your Skill exercise. Beyond evaluating other's arguments, you can strengthen your own advocacy by considering how well your arguments stand up to the rigorous test for cogency. Before considering a few additional applications of the ARG conditions, we'll briefly address how the ARG conditions relate to fallacies, a common concept in argumentation.

BUILD YOUR SKILL
EVALUATING COGENCY

For the following arguments and responses, identify which response targets acceptability, which targets relevance, and which targets grounds.

1. "Because the sky is blue; It makes me cry" (The Beatles, "Because")

   A. You're crying for some other reason.

   B. The sky is violet, not blue.[3]

   C. Colors can't make you cry.

2. "If I was gay, I would think hip-hop hates me; Have you read the YouTube comments lately?" (Macklemore feat. Ryan Lewis, "Same Love")

   A. A few comments on YouTube can't tell us about the entire hip-hop world.

   B. There are plenty of YouTube comments that celebrate rather than hate on gay people.

   C. YouTube comments are anonymous, biased, and unreliable.

ARGUMENT FALLACIES & THE ARG CONDITIONS

FALLACY: A logical error

Many argument textbooks and websites offer **argument fallacies** to evaluate and refute arguments. In traditional argument theory, a fallacy is a logical impossibility or error in which the conclusion does not follow from the premises (or support). In more common usage, people tend to label any bad, or non-cogent, argument a fallacy. As such, our approach to fallacies is that they are shortcuts one can use for identifying flaws that a full ARG assessment would reveal. In fact, fallacies can be classified in categories reminiscent of the ARG conditions: relevance, grounds, and language (acceptability).

RELEVANCE FALLACY: An error when the argument lacks a satisfactory warrant

A **relevance fallacy** exists when the argument lacks a satisfactory warrant. False analogies, hasty generalizations, and false dilemmas are all examples of relevance fallacies because the support they provide, while potentially acceptable in a debate, does not justify or warrant the conclusion. We'll consider numerous relevance fallacies in Chapter 10.

GROUNDS FALLACY: An error when the support is an insufficient basis for the claim

A **grounds fallacy** exists when the argument lacks sufficient support or grounds for the claim. Personal attacks and appeals to fear, popularity, and tradition are potential examples of grounds fallacies because they are poor support or distract co-arguers and audiences from ideas and issues that matter. They count as grounds rather than acceptability fallacies because the focus is on the relationship between the support and the claim, not the support on its own. For instance, an accurate statement about something's popularity is likely acceptable in a debate but it doesn't justify you buying or doing that thing.

A **language fallacy** exists when arguers (intentionally or unintentionally) manipulate language. Euphemisms and equivocation are two common examples of language fallacies. They fit best as violations of acceptability, especially given the *A* condition's emphasis on honesty and audience adaptation. However, language fallacies may transcend the specific argumentative content to implicate the very rules and performance of a debate.

The study of common fallacies can be helpful but you should not use fallacies as "gotcha" weapons hurled at co-arguers to shut down debate. Instead, use them with a broader understanding of their purpose within a debate and be able to explain *why* a particular fallacy means the argument lacks cogency. In the end, fallacies should service the broader evaluation of an argument that ultimately promotes the best outcome. To further explore this potential, we'll look at the use of ARG conditions to evaluate cases and controversies, not just single arguments.

LANGUAGE FALLACY: An error when the argument manipulates language

EVALUATING CASES AND CONTROVERSIES WITH THE ARG CONDITIONS

Our exploration of the ARG conditions earlier in the chapter considered how to evaluate a single argument but you can also use the ARG conditions to refute an entire argumentative case or to enter into a debate on a broader controversy. The Everyday Life Example in this chapter engages one such situation. In 2017 and 2018, the cryptocurrency Bitcoin saw a huge increase in value, peaking in December 2017 at nearly $20,000 USD for 1 Bitcoin.[4] This led to a flurry of investment interest in Bitcoin, so much so that a major British bank outfit, Lloyds, banned customers from buying Bitcoin with bank-issued credit cards for fear of being in debt when the Bitcoin bubble burst.[5]

Renowned personal finance blogger, Mr. Money Mustache (MMM), participated in the broader controversy by posting an argumentative case to his blog (and later published in the UK newspaper, *The Guardian*[6]). Entitled "Why Bitcoin Is Stupid," the post addressed various reasons not to invest in Bitcoin and refuted other people's arguments for doing so. The excerpt below includes MMM's refutation of two arguments for investing in Bitcoin. As you read it, identify the arguments he is refuting and determine the ARG conditions that motivate his responses. Then, consider how well he impacts each refutation for the overall controversy.

This excerpt of MMM's post illustrates the ARG conditions in action, although he probably didn't realize he was using them. His section headings indicate that he was addressing two major issues (rephrased into "yes/no" questions):

1. Is Bitcoin a valuable alternative to government-issued currencies? (lines 12-36)

2. Will Bitcoin become a world currency? (lines 37-75)

MMM's refutation of the first argument is closer than the second to how we've discussed using the ARG conditions through the four-step refutation process. Here is that content abridged and annotated as we did with the refutation of Harrison's argument earlier in the chapter:

". . .the assumption that giving national governments the ability to monitor flows of money in the financial system and use it as a form of law enforcement is *wrong*. . .

Everyday Life Example 9.1

Mr. Money Mustache, "Why Bitcoin is Stupid," *Mr. Money Mustache* (blog), January 2, 2018.[7]

1 Well, shit. I've been watching this situation for a few years, and assuming it would just blow over so
2 we wouldn't have to talk about it here in this place where we are supposed to be busy improving our
3 lives.

4 But a collective insanity has sprouted around the new field of 'cryptocurrencies', causing a totally
5 irrational worldwide gold rush. It has reached the point that a big percentage of stories in the
6 financial news and questions in Mr. Money Mustache's email inbox are about whether or not we
7 should all 'invest' in BitCoin.

8 We'll start with the answer: **No, you should not invest in Bitcoin.** The reason is that it's not an
9 investment. Just like gold, tulip bulbs, Beanie Babies, 1999 dotcoms without any hope of a product
10 plan, "pre-construction pricing" Toronto condominiums you have no intent to occupy or rent out, and
11 rare baseball cards are not investments. . . .

12 **Why was Bitcoin Even Invented?**

13 Understanding the motivation is a big part of understanding Bitcoin. As the legend goes, an
14 anonymous developer published this whitepaper [link: https://bitcoin.org/bitcoin.pdf] in 2008
15 under the fake name Satoshi Nakamoto. It's well written and pretty obviously by a real software
16 and math person. But it also has some ideology built in – the **assumption that giving national**
17 **governments the ability to monitor flows of money in the financial system and use it as a form of**
18 **law enforcement is wrong**.

19 This financial libertarian streak is at the core of Bitcoin, and you'll hear echoes of that sentiment in
20 all the pro-crypto blogs and podcasts. The sensible-sounding ones will say, "Sure the G20 nations
21 all have stable financial systems, but Bitcoin is a lifesaver in places like Venezuela where the
22 government can vaporize your wealth when you sleep."

23 The harder-core pundits say "Even the US Federal Reserve is a bunch 'a' CROOKS, stealing your
24 money via INFLATION, and that nasty Fiat Currency they issue is nothing but TOILET PAPER!!"

25 It's all the same stuff that people say about Gold, which is also a totally irrational waste [link: http://
26 www.minyanville.com/trading-and-investing/commodities/articles/Warren-Buffett-brka-gold-
27 investing-investing/10/3/2012/id/44617] of human investment energy.

28 Government-issued currencies have value because they represent **human trust and cooperation.**
29 There is no wealth and no trade without these two things, so you might as well go all-in and trust
30 people. There are no financial instruments that will protect you from a world where we no longer
31 trust each other.

32 So, Bitcoin is a protocol invented to solve a money problem that simply does not exist in the rich
33 countries, which is where most of the money is. Sure, an anonymous way to exchange money and
34 escape the eyes of a corrupt government is a good thing for human rights. But at least 98% of MMM
35 readers do not live in countries where this is an issue.

36 So just relax, lean into it, and grow rich with me.

37 **OK, But What if Bitcoin Becomes the World Currency?**

38 The other argument for Bitcoin's "value" is that there will only ever be 21 million of them, and they will
39 eventually replace all other world currencies, or at least become the "new gold", so the fundamental
40 value is either the entire world's GDP or at least the total value of all gold, divided by 21
41 million.

42 People then go on to say, "If there's even a ONE PERCENT CHANCE that this happens, Bitcoins are
43 severely undervalued and they should really be worth, like, at least a quadrillion dollars each!!"

44   This is not going to happen. After all, you could make the same argument about Mr. Money
45   Mustache's fingernail clippings: they may have no intrinsic value, but at least they are in limited
46   supply **so let's use them as the new world currency!**

47   Why not somebody else's fingernail clippings? Why not one of the other 1500 cryptocurrencies? Shut
48   up, just send me $100 via PayPal and I'll send you a bag of my fingernail clippings.

49   Let's get this straight: in order for Bitcoin to be a real currency, it needs several things:

50   **easy and frictionless trading between people**

51   **to be widely accepted as legal tender for all debts, public and private**

52   **a stable value that does not fluctuate (otherwise it's impossible to set prices)**

53   Bitcoin has none [link: https://www.reuters.com/article/uk-markets-bitcoin-risks-insight/bitcoin-
54   fever-exposes-crypto-market-frailties-idUSKBN1E724X] of these things, and even safely storing
55   it is difficult (see Mt. Gox [link: https://en.wikipedia.org/wiki/Mt._Gox], Bitfinex [link: https://
56   en.wikipedia.org/wiki/Bitfinex], and the various wallets and exchanges [link: https://arstechnica
57   .com/tech-policy/2017/12/a-brief-history-of-bitcoin-hacks-and-frauds] that have been hacked)

58   The second point is also critical: Bitcoin is only valuable if it truly becomes a critical world currency.
59   In other words, if you truly need it to buy stuff, and thus you need to buy coins from some other
60   person in order to conduct important bits of world commerce that you can't do any other way.
61   Right now, the only people driving up the price are **other speculators**. The bitcoin price isn't rising
62   because people are buying the coins to conduct real business. It's rising because people are buying
63   it up, hoping someone else will buy it at an even higher price later. It's only valuable when you cash
64   it out to a real currency again, like the US dollar, and use it to buy something useful like a nice house
65   or a business. When the supply of foolish speculators dries up, the value evaporates – often very
66   quickly.

67   Also, a currency **should not** be artificially sparse. It needs to expand with the supply of goods and
68   services in the world, otherwise we end up with deflation and hoarding. It also helps to have wise,
69   centralized humans (the Federal Reserve system and other central banks) guiding the system.
70   In a world of human trust, putting the wisest and most respected people in a position of Adult
71   Supervision is a useful tactic.

72   Finally, nothing becomes a good investment just because "it's been going up in price lately."

73   If you disagree with me on that point, **the price of my fingernails has just increased by 70,000% and**
74   **they are now $70,000 per bag**. Quick, get me that money on PayPal before you miss out on any more
75   of this incredible "performance!"

Source: Mr. Money Mustache, "Why Bitcoin Is Stupid," *Mr. Money Mustache* (blog), January 2, 2018.

is at the core of Bitcoin, and you'll hear echoes of that sentiment in all the pro-crypto blogs and podcasts [**summarize the argument**]. . . . Government-issued currencies have value because they represent human trust and cooperation. There is no wealth and no trade without these two things, so you might as well go all-in and trust people [**state response—unacceptable for those in "rich countries" who trust their government**]. There are no financial instruments that will protect you from a world where we no longer trust each other. So, Bitcoin is a protocol invented to solve a money problem that simply does not exist in the rich countries, which is where most of the money is. Sure, an anonymous way to exchange money and escape the eyes of a corrupt government is a good thing for human rights. But at least 98% of MMM readers do not live in countries where this is an issue [**support response—MMM's audience and most of those investing in Bitcoin live in "rich countries"**]. So just relax, lean into it, and grow rich with me [**conclude with impact**].

Almost a textbook refutation! True to most everyday argumentation, MMM didn't explicitly state the condition of acceptability but his refutation identified that flaw. Why was this a matter of acceptability rather than relevance or grounds? The claim to the argument, as MMM articulated it, is that Bitcoin is a valuable alternative to government-issued currency and the support is that government-issued currency is wrong (lines 16-24). Acceptability evaluates the support independent of the claim but in relation to the context and audience. In this case, MMM perceived the support to be impermissible in the debate because government-issued currency does have value, which he supported in relation to his blog's audience (lines 28-35). Before we even consider whether Bitcoin is a valuable alternative, he critiqued the need for an alternative in the first place; Bitcoin is designed, in his words, "to solve a money problem that simply does not exist in the rich countries" (lines 32-33). He concluded his refutation by encouraging the audience to ignore the Bitcoin craze and "grow rich with [him]" (line 36).

MMM's refutation of the world currency argument, while not as organized, also used the ARG conditions. Here, MMM considered the relationship between claim and support when he targeted the causal warrant that Bitcoin's limited supply will result in it becoming a world currency of value. Specifically, his refutation addressed relevance rather than sufficient grounds by arguing that the support—limited supply of Bitcoin—does not have bearing on the claim—becoming a world currency (line 44). He supports his response by comparing Bitcoin to his fingernail clippings (lines 44-48) and by showing how Bitcoin fails the three requirements for a "real currency" (lines 49-60). He further supports the argument by noting that the reason for its increase in price is that people are buying it, not because it has intrinsic value as an investment (lines 60-71), and arguing that something going up in price is not a sufficient indicator of a good investment, as evident with the fingernail clipping analogy (lines 72-75).

You should note five important features of MMM's responses as they relate to employing the ARG conditions:

1. **Using the ARG conditions is a choice**. As with our Harrison refutation, MMM's refutation is only one possible option, addressing just two arguments for investing in Bitcoin. Were you to write a blog post supporting the proposition that "you should not invest in Bitcoin," you would likely generate a different case targeting different issues (adding, again, to the excitement of debate). The value of the ARG conditions is that they give you options when engaging the arguments of others and these options are what make each debate unique.

2. **Using the ARG conditions is realistic.** MMM's response raises sensible objections to the case for investing in Bitcoin through the ARG conditions but it avoids jargon and technical argumentation. People don't argue in the real world by saying things like, "your claim lacks sufficient grounds" or "your argument fails the *A* condition." However, people do argue what these statements *mean* in the context of concrete arguments.

3. **Using the ARG conditions deepens debate**. The ARG conditions provide numerous options advocates can use to fully interrogate arguments. For instance, MMM's refutation of the world currency argument is approximately quadruple the length of the original argument he summarized. It also included numerous supporting ideas rather than a single response, productively expanding consideration of the proposition.

4. **Using the ARG conditions is refutative.** Notice that MMM's responses—that Bitcoin doesn't solve a problem his readers have and that Bitcoin will not become a world currency—are entirely defensive refutation that mitigated the arguments raised by co-arguers. The ARG conditions, then, are a tool not for developing your own case on a proposition (those tools are available in Chapter 7) but for critically engaging the arguments of others. MMM's offensive argumentation occurred in other parts of his post (excluded from the earlier excerpt) where he raised disadvantages to the proposition that you should invest in Bitcoin: Bitcoin is speculation that costs "time and life energy" for the investor and Bitcoin mining using money and energy that could instead be used to "change the course of the entire human race" rather than going toward "valueless bits of computer data."

5. **Using the ARG conditions can be improvised.** MMM's response is well-rounded and well-reasoned despite having little research. Debate in real time can't wait for you to research a topic, so the ARG conditions offer a straightforward method to spontaneously respond to someone else's argument. Sometimes it's as simple as comparing cryptocurrency to your fingernail clippings! Of course, preparation is still important and knowledge on the topic will only make for a stronger response (you'd have to know, for instance, the criteria for a "real currency"), but the ARG conditions give you some flexibility to address arguments you didn't anticipate.

Mr. Money Mustache's blog post shows how standards of acceptability, relevance, and sufficient grounds undergird refutations of others' arguments. Although he might have better focused his refutation efforts, it offers a model for the kind of refutative skills you can build. The more you practice with the ARG conditions and the more you acquaint yourself with argument forms, the more useful the ARG conditions will become as a tool for effective and impromptu refutation.

Summary

This chapter has advocated that we should evaluate arguments for cogency, or the degree to which they are rationally persuasive. This criterion is the most comprehensive one, accounting for context, content, and ethics. You can evaluate an argument for cogency by applying the ARG conditions. Acceptability, the *A* condition, evaluates the support for how permissible it is for the audience in the debate. Relevance, the *R* condition, evaluates the support for how much bearing it has on the claim. And grounds, the *G* condition, evaluates the support for how sufficient it is to establishing the claim.

Whereas argument fallacies helpfully pinpoint logical flaws, the ARG conditions enable you to understand why the argument is flawed and how it could be improved to be more cogent. In the chapter, we explored applications of the ARG conditions to a single argument (Harrison's argument for returning participation trophies) and to a controversy at large (Mr. Money Mustache's response to the Bitcoin boom). These applications reveal how the ARG conditions are both practical and adaptable to argumentation in everyday life.

Application Exercises

Applying ARG Conditions to Social Media: Go to the Twitter or Facebook profiles of people or organizations you follow and locate some argumentative posts. Do the posts include cogent arguments? Why or why not? When you take the time to critically think about the arguments, which ARG conditions are met and which are not? Then, revisit the Find Your Voice features earlier to consider challenging questions related to acceptability and sufficient grounds.

Assessing Your Own Arguments: Choose an argumentative paper or email you recently wrote and assess the quality of your arguments with the following steps:

1. Can you identify the proposition clearly? Do you make your ultimate claim explicit?

2. Can you identify the major issues? Do you offer organized arguments for the proposition?

3. Do your arguments pass the ARG conditions for cogency? If an argument is non-cogent, how could you revise it to better meet the ARG conditions? *HINT: You'll want to take the perspective of your audience when performing this task.*

Key Terms

Cogency 196
Acceptability 197
Relevance 200

(Sufficient) Grounds 202
Fallacy 206
Relevance Fallacy 206

Grounds Fallacy 206
Language Fallacy 207

Endnotes

1. "The Opportunity of a Lifetime," Season 5, Episode 20, *The Goldbergs*, directed by Anton Cropper, ABC, May 2, 2018.

2. U.S. Department of Health & Human Services, "Poverty Guidelines," January 13, 2018, https://aspe.hhs.gov/poverty-guidelines.

3. Brian Koberlein, "Earth's Skies Are Violet, We Just See Them as Blue," *Forbes*, January 11, 2017, https://www.forbes.com/sites/briankoberlein/2017/01/11/earths-skies-are-violet-we-just-see-them-as-blue/#6ad24525735f.

4. "Bitcoin Charts," *CoinMarketCap*, 2018, https://coinmarketcap.com/currencies/bitcoin/#charts.

5. Press Association, "Lloyds Bank Bans Customers from Buying Bitcoins Using Credit Cards," *The Guardian*, UK edition, February 5, 2018, https://www.theguardian.com/business/2018/feb/05/lloyds-bank-bans-buying-bitcoins-credit-cards.

6. Mr. Money Mustache, "So You're Thinking About Investing in Bitcoin? Don't," *The Guardian* (UK), January 15, 2018, https://www.theguardian.com/technology/2018/jan/15/should-i-invest-bitcoin-dont-mr-money-moustache.

7. Mr. Money Mustache, "Why Bitcoin Is Stupid," *Mr. Money Mustache* (blog), January 2, 2018, http://www.mrmoneymustache.com/2018/01/02/why-bitcoin-is-stupid.

10

EVALUATING ARGUMENT TYPES

During the 2016 presidential campaign, President Trump's son, Donald Jr., tweeted an image of a bowl of Skittles with text that asked: if "just three would kill you. Would you take a handful?" The punchline then stated: "That's our Syrian refugee problem."[1] The tweet went viral and became quite controversial for its seeming insensitivity to the plight of refugees. But many responses to Trump's tweet involved more than knee-jerk shock or dismissal. For instance, Denise Young, VP of Corporate Affairs for Wrigley, Skittles' parent company, told Seth Abramovitch, a writer for the *Hollywood Reporter*, that "Skittles are candy. Refugees are people. We don't feel it's an appropriate analogy."[2] Melissa Fleming, a spokesperson for the United Nations High Commissioner for Refugees, called the tweet "dehumanizing, demeaning and dangerous," explaining that "Syrian refugees are fellow human beings who have left their country to escape war and terrorism."[3]

And, the *Washington Post* published an entire article determined "to figure out what the analogy is," concluding that Trump Jr. inaccurately scaled the argument upward. Using the statistical chance of being killed by a refugee, the article concluded "we're talking about one-and-a-half Olympic swimming pools of Skittles. . . . And in that pool: Three poison Skittles."[4] If you could eat a handful of Skittles every minute, you "would hit a poisoned Skittle, on average, every 130 years." The article further bristled at "depicting refugees fleeing war as inanimate candies."[5]

The above responses to Trump Jr.'s argument all recognized the argument as an analogy, one of the common argument types we explored in Chapter 6. Moreover, they all understood how the warrant in an analogy relies on the comparison between the two cases and used that to judge the argument's cogency. The comparison didn't hold up because Syrian refugees immigrating to the United States are not like a bowl of Skittles. As we'll learn in this chapter, this refutation is equivalent to a failure of relevance, or the *R* condition, for an analogy.

This example illustrates that the ARG conditions apply to the major types of arguments discussed in Chapter 6: classification, generalization, cause, sign, analogy, and authority. While you can use the general conditions from the previous chapter to evaluate any argument, knowing the different argument types enables you to more productively tailor your evaluation. Ultimately, this chapter explores what it *means* for the different argument types to be cogent by addressing and applying concrete questions you should ask when evaluating them.

For each, we'll briefly revisit the form of the argument and then consider its requirements for cogency before applying it to one of the example arguments we first encountered in Chapter 6. In some cases, we'll also identify common fallacies related to violations of the relevance condition. This material will help you not only think more critically about the arguments you encounter in your everyday life but also adapt the ARG conditions to the contours of those arguments. By the end of this chapter, you should be able to assess all six argument types for cogency through the applicable ARG conditions.

EVALUATING ARGUMENT FROM CLASSIFICATION

An argument from classification, you may recall, starts with a general definition, principle, value, rule, guideline, law, etc. and claims that the general statement applies to a specific instance. The logic of this argument, found in the warrant, is that the specific instance is under the jurisdiction of the general statement. Figure 10.1 depicts the structure and ARG conditions for an argument from classification.

Acceptability evaluates the support independent of the claim but in relation to the context and audience. Applied to an argumentation from classification, support is acceptable if the audience finds the general statement of principle, definition, etc. a permissible starting point for debate. The general test of relevance is a test of the warrant,

FIGURE 10.1 ■ Argument from Classification & The ARG Conditions

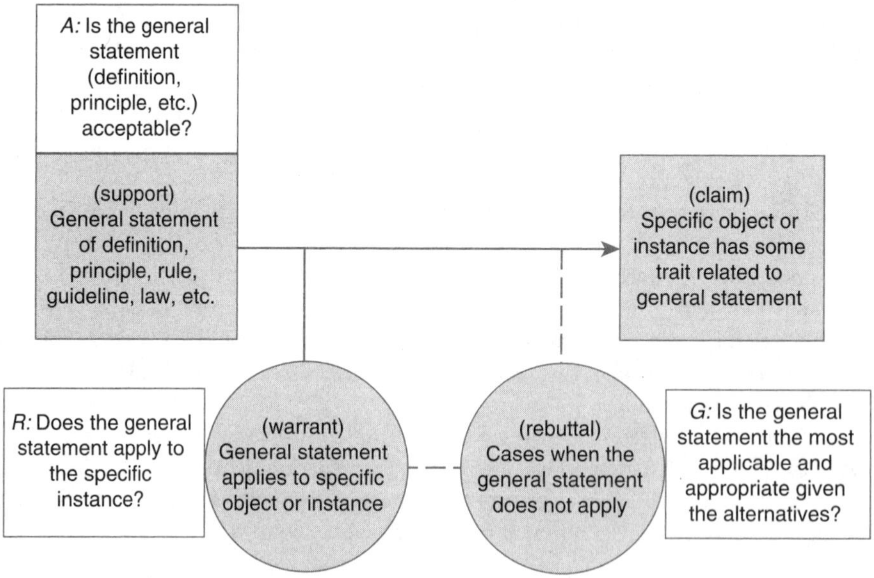

A: Is the general statement (definition, principle, etc.) acceptable?

(support) General statement of definition, principle, rule, guideline, law, etc.

(claim) Specific object or instance has some trait related to general statement

R: Does the general statement apply to the specific instance?

(warrant) General statement applies to specific object or instance

(rebuttal) Cases when the general statement does not apply

G: Is the general statement the most applicable and appropriate given the alternatives?

which states in an argument from classification that the general statement applies to the specific case. The *R* condition, then, questions as a possible point of refutation whether the statement does apply to the instance. And, grounds considers the rebuttal by going beyond the argument itself to raise additional considerations. In this case, does the general statement hold up in light of alternative statements or applications?

Let's return to the Declaration of Independence argument from Chapter 6 to see these ARG conditions in action. The Declaration argued that because people having a right and duty to throw off a despotic government, and, since the current King of Great Britain has been despotic toward the colonies, the colonies are declaring independence. To evaluate the cogency of the Declaration of Independence's argument, you would answer the following questions:

A: Is the principle that people have a right and duty to throw off a despotic government acceptable for the audience? Knowing that the Declaration was designed not just for the colonists but also a world audience, you would consider to what degree those various constituents would find the principle permissible in a debate. Given the general political philosophy at the time, this was likely an acceptable principle.

R: Does the principle that people have a right and duty to throw of a despotic government apply to the British colonies? To assess this warrant, you'd need to account for more than 20 grievances with King George III that the Declaration provided as backing. In general, there was probably enough backing to authorize this application, but you could debate to what degree the grievances illustrate despotism.

G: Is the principle that people have a right and duty to throw off a despotic government the most applicable and appropriate given alternative principles? To assess this condition, you should generate possible rebuttals to the warrant and raise considerations outside the scope of the argument. Some opposed to revolution, for instance, felt that the situation required compromise rather than independence. Ultimately, the *G* condition ensures the principle provides enough support to justify the radical step of declaring independence.

As we noted in the previous chapter, arguments must pass all three ARG conditions for them to be cogent. And, of course, the above conditions are all debatable and certainly were in the Declaration's time. Using the specific ARG conditions for an argument from classification deepens understanding of how the argument functions by recognizing that it requires an acceptable general statement and a relevant and sufficient application of that statement to the specific case.

EVALUATING ARGUMENT FROM GENERALIZATION

Generalizations start with what is known about a sample and, on the presumption that it is a representative sample, concludes something about an entire category. Figure 10.2 indicates the focus of the ARG conditions for argument from generalization. Acceptability evaluates the quality of the sample to ensure it's permissible in the debate. If the

FIGURE 10.2 ■ Argument from Generalization & the ARG Conditions

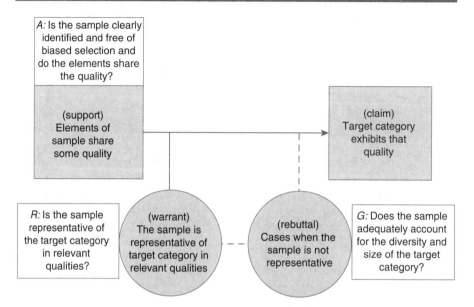

sample is mischaracterized (e.g., the quality ascribed to it isn't accurate) or if the sample is biased (e.g., chosen to obviously prove the point), then it would fail the *A* condition. The *R* condition ensures there's a good warrant—that the sample is indeed representative of the category in relevant qualities—while the *G* condition raises any missing components to the sample that are necessary for it to be sufficient.

Let's evaluate the Gallup poll results as a familiar generalization argument. Gallup based the argument on a survey of 32,585 U.S. college students to determine how prepared all U.S. college students feel for the job market and workforce. Here's how you would evaluate this argument for cogency:

A: Is the survey's sample clearly identified and free of biased selection? We know that the sample is 32,585 U.S. college students who completed web surveys between March 21 and May 8, 2017.[6] Is this enough information for you to permit the sample or would you, as part of the audience for this argument, require more information about it? In all likelihood, the support is likely acceptable but the lack of details may cause problems for relevance and grounds.

R: Are the 32,585 surveyed people representative of all U.S. college students? Unfortunately, we don't have any demographic breakdowns (of race, gender, class, age, religion, hair color, etc.) so it is hard to be certain that the sample is representative in relevant qualities. Recall, however, that Gallup asserted it was representative based on public vs. private institutions and enrollment size with a 0.8

percent margin of error. Thus, your likelihood of critiquing the sample's relevance comes down to how much you trust Gallup's claim. If you trust it, then you'll give a pass on the *R* condition. If you don't trust it, you'd likely raise an objection on account of relevance.

G: Do the 32,585 surveyed people account for the diversity and size of all U.S. college students? Here, again, your judgment would likely come down to your level of trust in Gallup's assertion that the sample is representative. Surveying more than 32,000 people is certainly a substantial sample size, but we'd likely need more information before we'd fully accept the poll results as a representation of what all U.S. college students think.

As this ARG assessment illustrates, it is difficult to produce cogent generalization arguments. Detecting counter-examples can often weaken generalizations that rely on a small sample. Generalizations with a larger sample require more information about the degree to which the individual parts are representative of the category in relevant qualities. Generalizations, then, are prone to a common fallacy, often called a **hasty generalization**. This weakness in relevance occurs when someone reaches a claim too quickly, based on a small or unrepresentative sample.

> **HASTY GENERALIZATION:** A non-cogent argument that reaches a claim from a small or unrepresentative sample

In sum, generalization arguments are cogent when the sample is clearly and accurately defined, lacks bias, and is representative of the category. As you engage generalizations in your everyday life, you should use these tests to evaluate their cogency.

EVALUATING ARGUMENT FROM CAUSE AND CONSEQUENCE

Arguments from cause posit that one thing, a cause, is the reason for another, an effect. The warrant in a causal argument states that the cause is likely to result in the effect. As a reminder, causal arguments can argue from cause to effect or effect to cause. They can also stipulate anticipated effects, what we labeled an argument from consequence. Causal arguments are quite common in our everyday argumentation as we seek to understand phenomena and justify future action so it's important to consider what makes them cogent. Figure 10.3 outlines the ARG conditions for an argument from cause, the same conditions you would ask of an argument from consequence.

For acceptability, your evaluation would focus on the degree to which the cause or effect is identified, defined, and acceptable. If you are the audience, can you identify what the cause or effect *is* and do you agree with the arguer's characterization of it? Tests of relevance ask if the support and/or backing substantiate a causal connection. To what degree does the cause have bearing on the effect? Finally, even if the cause does have bearing on the effect, our grounds assessment questions if there's enough support in the argument to agree with the specific causal relationship being advocated (sufficient cause, necessary cause, necessary and sufficient cause, or contributory cause). Grounds is best tested by considering alternative explanations beyond cause-effect that might explain the relationship between the two factors.

FIGURE 10.3 ■ Argument from Cause & the ARG Conditions

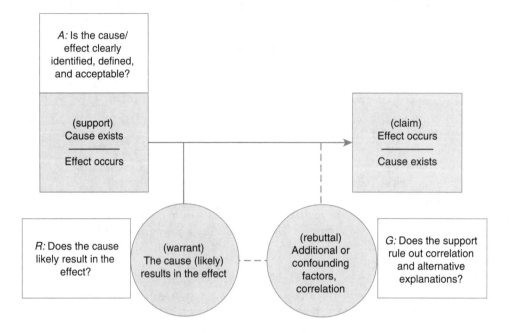

Applying the conditions to the Surgeon General warning on cigarette packages will illustrate how to use them. The argument stated that exposure to tobacco smoke can harm children. We would assess this argument by asking the following questions:

A: Is the cause of exposure to tobacco smoke clearly identified, defined, and acceptable for the audience? The Surgeon General identifies the cause as "tobacco smoke" but doesn't specify how frequently or how much smoke. Do you find this acceptable for the debate or would you demand a more precise cause?

R: Is exposure to tobacco smoke likely to result in harm to your children? The argument just asserts this warrant without backing, but it is also qualified as a contributory cause with the use of the word "can" rather than, say, "will." Would you accept that the cause of tobacco smoke has bearing on the claimed effect of "harm" or would you request backing for the warrant? Most of you probably recognize the relevance is there.

G: Does exposure to tobacco smoke rule out correlation and alternative explanations? It's likely that the support rules out correlation but are there alternative explanations or factors that may weaken the warrant? If so, then the argument might lack sufficient grounds. You might also critique the vague nature of "harm" in the claim on the basis of grounds insofar as there's not enough information to conclude that "harm" occurs from exposure to smoke.

Cogent cause arguments are difficult to generate because they require accounting for various factors that might contribute to any given effect. As such, cause arguments are susceptible to numerous fallacies that represent failures of relevance:

Post hoc, ergo propter hoc (often shortened to *post hoc*): Translated as "after the fact, therefore because of the fact," this classic fallacy identifies a false cause based on the sequence of events. In earlier chapters, we examined the link between violent video games and mass shootings. Some arguers claimed this was a *post hoc* fallacy; just because playing violent video games happened before the mass shooting, we don't know that the video games caused it.

Single Cause: In cases where contributory causes are at play, a single cause fallacy attributes the effect of a complex situation to a single, sufficient cause. The Surgeon General argument would exhibit this flaw were it to claim that exposure to tobacco smoke *will* harm your children. Many people who credit a president for economic growth or high gas prices are advancing a single cause fallacy; the president alone is not responsible for the fluctuations in the economy or prices of things.

Slippery Slope: You may have heard of this fallacy before. This describes an argument that claims an inevitable chain reaction from a single cause. This is often a non-cogent argument because there can be any number of intervening factors at each step of the process to prevent the effect from occurring.

Fundamental Attribution Error: The Fundamental Attribution Error (FAE) concept comes from psychology and refers to an error we might make when interpreting another's behavior. Whether you realize it or not, determining someone's motive is, in effect, a causal argument. The FAE states that we often erroneously attribute such behavior to the person's internal disposition rather than external or situational factors. For example, if someone comes late to a meeting, we might say the person arrived late because he or she is irresponsible (an internal quality) rather than looking for a situational factor, such as a bus delay or personal crisis, that caused tardiness. This is only sometimes an error—there are feckless people who show up to meetings late because they can't be bothered—but it would be unfair to attribute internal disposition as the cause in every situation.[7]

> **POST HOC:** A non-cogent argument that erroneously claims an effect after some cause is because of that cause
>
> **SINGLE CAUSE:** A non-cogent argument that erroneously claims an effect of a complex situation is the result of a single cause
>
> **SLIPPERY SLOPE:** A non-cogent argument that erroneously claims a single cause will produce an inevitable series of events leading to an extreme effect
>
> **FUNDAMENTAL ATTRIBUTION ERROR:** A potentially non-cogent argument that claims a person's internal factors (character, personality, attitudes, etc.) are the cause for that person's behavior

FIND YOUR VOICE
CAUSES VS. REASONS FOR BEHAVIOR

How can you know what caused someone's behavior? You probably answer this question more frequently than you are aware. Argumentatively speaking, a person could use any type of argument as a reason for their behavior: I did it out of principle (classification), because God told me to (authority), because I saw someone else do it (analogy), etc. The cause, on the other hand, ostensibly would be beyond the control of the actor given that effects follow from causes.[8] The distinction may encourage you to look beneath the surface of causal statements and help you better understand arguments related to human behavior.

The ARG conditions for causal arguments ultimately prompt careful consideration of the degree to which the cause results in the effect rather than the cause being some corresponding or related factor. The numerous fallacies of relevance indicate the propensity for non-cogent causal arguments in everyday life.

EVALUATING ARGUMENT FROM SIGN

Arguments from sign conclude some condition exists on the basis of observable symptoms or signs. The warrant, you may recall, connects the two by stating that the signs likely point to the condition. Evaluating a sign argument, then, requires answering the ARG conditions identified in Figure 10.4.

Acceptability assesses the signs on their own to ensure they are clearly identified, defined, and acceptable. If someone identifies a sign that isn't observable, potentially fabricated, or vague, we might challenge the argument on the basis of acceptability. Relevance and grounds assess the connection between the signs and the condition. Relevance asks if the signs do, indeed, indicate the condition whereas grounds considers rebuttals to the argument by raising alternative conditions or signs for which the argument must account.

To put these ARG conditions into practice, we'll assess the sign argument from the College Board about the SAT test, which concludes the condition of college and career readiness on the basis of a single sign (the test). Here's how you can determine its cogency:

FIGURE 10.4 ■ Argument from Sign & the ARG Conditions

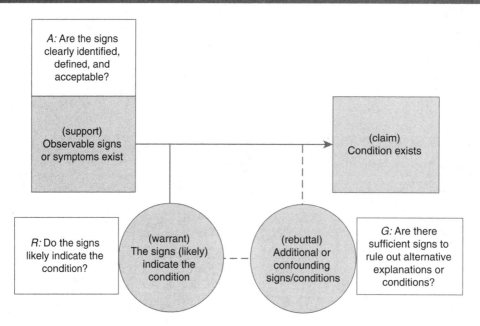

A: Are the test score signs clearly identified, defined, and acceptable for the audience? The argument indicates benchmarks for college readiness (480 in reading and writing; 530 in math), as well as red, yellow, and green ranges for the scores. Do you find these signs permissible in the debate? Do you require more information? In general, the signs would likely pass the *A* condition.

R: Does the SAT score indicate college readiness? The heart of the argument is that a student's performance on the SAT test indicates that student's college and career readiness. Do you agree that performance on the SAT has bearing on whether or not someone is ready to attend college? You might answer "yes" here—the test does indicate readiness for most students—but might challenge the argument more fully on grounds.

G: Grounds is where the argument probably falls short. While the test score may be an indicator of college readiness, you must consider if there are outside factors that cast doubt on the test as sufficient (on its own) to point to college readiness. That is, SAT scores may be an indicator of college readiness *unless* there are other signs, such as a stellar high school GPA or social and study skills, that indicate a different condition. In fact, standardized tests are a controversial form of support, with some arguing that they are biased based on socioeconomic status, race, and sex.

The College Board's argument is particularly useful for distinguishing the difference between relevance and grounds when it comes to a sign argument. Just because a sign points to a condition, that doesn't mean we should accept the claim if there are also alternative conditions we could conclude based on those or additional signs. For cogency, then, sign arguments must use acceptable signs that are sufficient and relevant indicators of the condition.

EVALUATING ARGUMENT FROM ANALOGY

Arguments from analogy compare two things to conclude that what is true of a known case is also true of an unknown case. Donald Trump Jr.'s argument about Skittles to start the chapter is an example of an analogy argument. As we saw there, the cogency of an analogy relies in part on the quality of the comparison between the two cases. The full ARG conditions for an analogy argument are outlined in Figure 10.5.

Acceptability considers only the known case to ensure that the characterization of it is acceptable. If an arguer misrepresents or is unclear about the known case, then the argument may lack cogency. Relevance and grounds evaluate the comparison. Relevance determines if there are appropriate similarities to support the claim about the unknown case while grounds tests the differences between the cases. No analogy argument is going to identify its own failings so audience members must generate these differences themselves.

Let's apply the ARG conditions to Mrs. Gump's famous argument that life is unpredictable because a box of chocolates is unpredictable. This is certainly an oft-repeated statement but is it cogent?

FIGURE 10.5 ■ Argument from Analogy & the ARG Conditions

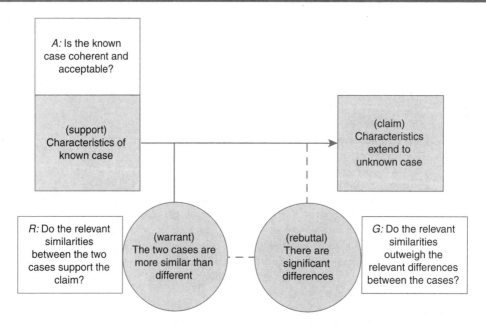

A: Is the explanation of the unpredictability of a box of chocolates acceptable for the audience? If you've ever had a box of chocolates that lacked a guide, you wouldn't dispute the acceptability of how Mrs. Gump characterized it. While you could argue that some boxes of chocolate are predictable, you might also recognize that we often don't know what we will get when we choose a chocolate at random from an unmarked box of chocolates.

R: Do the similarities between a box of chocolates and life support the claim? This question is a bit more challenging to answer. It does seem plausible that life is like a box of chocolates but the argument provides no backing for this warrant. What's your judgment: Are there relevant similarities between the two?

G: Do the relevant similarities between a box of chocolates and life outweigh the relevant differences? This is arguably the weakest condition. She presumed the similarity, but, as a critical thinking audience member, you must go outside the stated argument to generate the differences before deeming it cogent. Some of these relevant differences—for example, life is more complex than a box of chocolates, life has non-sweet outcomes as well as sweet outcomes—may weaken the comparison.

FALSE ANALOGY: A non-cogent argument that reaches a claim by comparing two fundamentally dissimilar cases

Mrs. Gump's argument shows the impediments to reaching a decisive evaluation of analogies that rely on a stipulated comparison. This draws attention to **false analogy** as a common fallacy. A false analogy is an analogy argument that compares two things that are fundamentally dissimilar. For an analogy to be cogent, then, the argument must offer an acceptable characterization of the known case and that case must be more similar to than different from the unknown case about which the arguer is advancing a claim.

EVALUATING ARGUMENT FROM AUTHORITY

Argument from authority is the final argument type we'll consider from the vantage point of the ARG conditions. Authority arguments claim something is true because some source says so. The warrant is that the source is an authority or expert on the topic. Figure 10.6 indicates the ARG conditions you would use to evaluate an authority argument

As you can see, the cogency of an authority argument relies on the authority being clearly identified, free of bias, and a credible authority on the topic. The *A* condition focuses on the citation of the source to ensure that the authority is identified, unbiased, and accurately portrayed. An authority argument fails acceptability if the source didn't say what the arguer claimed, is taken out of context, or is biased toward the claim in a way that pollutes the source's testimony. If the source is acceptable, relevance ensures that the source is an expert or authority on the topic. Finally, grounds solicits conditions in which the source is not an expert on the topic, including the possibility that other authorities have contradicted the source.

We can use these conditions to evaluate an example that may hit close to home: A parent or guardian saying you will do something because he or she said so. Here, the parent is flexing his or her muscle as an authority over you. Is this a good argument? Let's see:

A: Is the parent clearly identified and free of bias and did he or she say the alleged demand? In this scenario, you know your parent is the clear source of the demand but the question of bias persists. As *the* audience member for the argument, the judgment of acceptability is under your control. If you believe your parent is a biased source,

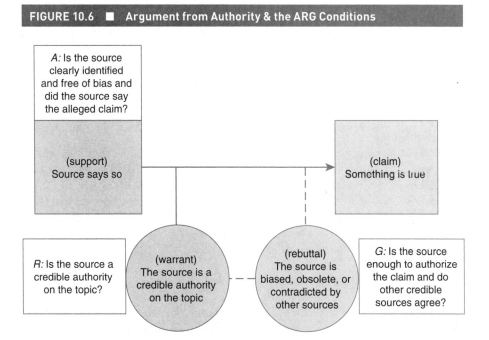

FIGURE 10.6 ■ Argument from Authority & the ARG Conditions

BUILD YOUR SKILL
ARG CONDITIONS & ARGUMENT TYPES

The example arguments from the application exercise at the end of Chapter 6 are posted below in random order without labeling the types. First, determine the type of argument and then evaluate it for cogency using the ARG conditions, pinpointing the weakest of the three conditions for each.

A. People should take time to enjoy life because the world will be a more pleasant place.

B. People should take time to enjoy life because Twenty One Pilots said so in "Ride."

C. People should take time to enjoy life because to live is to be in the present rather than fret about the future.

D. People should take time to enjoy life because my friends and I always feel better when we enjoy life.

E. People should take time to enjoy life because life is fragile and you could die at any moment without warning.

F. People should take time to enjoy life because people don't want to live in a prison.

you might respond by noting that the argument lacks cogency because the support is unacceptable; the source's bias prevents him or her from offering an objective judgment in the situation. Or, you can just stay quiet and do what is demanded of you.

R: Is your parent a credible authority on what you should do and when? This likely depends on your situation. If you're under 18 or if your parent pays for your housing, tuition, etc., it may be hard to dispute the relevance. However, when faced with a situation like this, a common refutation is to claim, "but I'm an adult." This response is a shorthand way of saying that the argument fails the *R* condition because your parent is not the source that dictates your conduct. Next time you are faced with this scenario, perhaps try this more fulsome response and see how it goes.

G: Is your parent's authority enough to authorize the claim that you should do what he or she says? Do other sources agree with your parent's claim? How many times have children played parents off one another (e.g., "but Dad said I didn't have to do this"). Such responses challenge the grounds of the argument; you admit that your parent is an authority (granting relevance) but you invoke another authority that contradicts him or her (challenging sufficient grounds). As with relevance, grounds is a judgment call based on the degree to which you might generate rebuttals to the warrant.

The example of your parent's argument, while somewhat trite, shows how the ARG conditions are quite common in everyday responses to authority arguments. For a cogent argument from authority, the source of the claim must be known, unbiased, and a credible expert on the topic. If any of those are lacking, you may have a reason to refute the argument.

Having explored the ARG conditions for all six argument types, it should be clear that tailoring your ARG evaluation to the specific requirements of each type helps your critical thought about and engagement with them. Use the Build Your Skill prompt for more practice applying these tailored ARG conditions. As we've discussed, there's not a right or wrong answer provided you support your judgment with cogent analysis of your own.

UNCOVERING THE ARG CONDITIONS IN EVERYDAY ARGUMENTATION

We've addressed thus far how you can employ the ARG conditions to evaluate and refute arguments, but you should also learn to recognize when others use them. If you don't correctly understand the relationship between argument types and the responses others advance to your arguments, you can't effectively respond to those refutations. Imagine a scenario in which someone perceives you making a cause argument and challenges its relevance (e.g., claiming the cause does not likely result in the effect) but you meant the argument as a sign argument (e.g., that the signs indicate the condition). In this scenario, you must recognize the misunderstanding to generate productive clash and address the same issue as your co-arguer.

Despite the importance of correctly interpreting ARG complaints, decoding them in everyday argumentation can be challenging. Just as people don't develop their arguments and cases in an explicit or transparent fashion, so too people don't invoke the ARG conditions explicitly. This is even more challenging when we consider that most arguers don't have knowledge of the ARG conditions to effectively articulate the flaws they perceive in others' arguments. This section, then, first offers tips to help you uncover how others implicitly use the ARG conditions and then this chapter's Everyday Life Example provides an opportunity for you to decipher in real world argumentation the ARG conditions for the six argument types.

While there's no guaranteed way to effectively understand your co-arguer's refutation, keep in mind the following guidelines insofar as they might assist your efforts:

1. **Determine for yourself the type of argument.** Because the type of argument helps you determine the conditions for cogency, first ensure that you understand its type. Once you take this step, you can then map the response to the argument onto those specific ARG conditions.

2. **Pay attention to verbal cues.** Because most arguers don't use the words "(un) acceptable," "(ir)relevant," and "(in)sufficient" when responding to arguments, use verbal cues to determine the focus of the refutation. For instance, a response that claims something is "beside the point" is usually a challenge to relevance. Assertions that "you're wrong" or "not true" tend to be acceptability challenges. A response that offers a "counter-example" indicates a grounds challenge to a generalization while a statement that "this isn't how it happens" is likely addressing the relevance of a causal argument.

3. **The response's condition matters less than its content.** Although we've spent quite a bit of time so far distinguishing the three ARG conditions, figuring out which condition it addresses is not as important as understanding what the

refutation *means* for the argument. You should focus on the ideas in the debate rather than the technical jargon, although understanding the technicalities make your involvement in the debate more productive.

4. **Ask for clarification as appropriate**. Not all arguers are as skilled as you so some of their responses may not be very clear, productive, or useful. Chances are you've argued with people who ineffectively respond to another's argument, raising irrelevant refutations or taking the debate on tangents. If you're able, first ask for clarification. If that doesn't help, perhaps push back on the response (e.g., "I interpret your response to be about such and such a concern rather than my argument. How is this response legitimate?"). Productive debate relies on the give-and-take between co-arguers so make sure you understand the nature of the refutations before addressing them.

Everyday Life Example 10.1

Selected Comments to Mr. Money Mustache, "Why Bitcoin Is Stupid," *Mr. Money Mustache* **(blog), January 2018.**[9]

1	**Tawcan (Jan. 2, 2018 5:37pm):** Agree, the valuation of these cryptocurrencies are out of whack. . . .
2	Putting evaluation aside, what boggles my mind is how much electricity is being wasted on bitcoin
3	every single day.
4	**Vijay (Jan. 3, 2018 6:53am):** Power consumption from bitcoin mining would only amount to a fraction
5	of 1 percent of global demand even in 2020. Please don't fall for Hype, generally fed by the Banks
6	and their Media!
7	https://www.cnbc.com/2017/12/21/no-bitcoin-is-likely-not-going-to-consume-all-the-worlds-
8	energy-in-2020.html
9	**Tawcan (Jan. 3, 2018 3:00pm):** From the article:
10	"According to the index, the amount of energy consumed by mining bitcoin surged about 26 percent
11	in November alone and now totals nearly 36 terawatt hours, enough energy to power about 3.3
12	million homes. Digiconomist notes this would make bitcoin the 59th biggest energy consumer if it
13	were a country."
14	That's a lot of electricity that can be used to power 3.3 million homes wasted. Given that China has a
15	lot of bitcoin mines and electricity is produced by coal in China mostly. . . that's a lot of unnecessary
16	CO2 that just got bumped in the atmosphere.
17	**Vijay (Jan. 3, 2018 3:11pm):** We will move it to renewables then.
18	**Jacob (Jan. 3, 2018 10:14pm):** Not likely, bitcoin mining farms are in China because of the cheaper
19	energy costs. You can't "vote with your wallet" in this situation, so you have no control over what
20	practices the miners use. . . .
21	**Andreas (Jan. 4, 2018 6:11am):** We? The ones who own the farms you mean?
22	Sorry for commenting again but the farms will not give you money or distribute it to those who
23	cannot afford.
24	36 terawatt is not something taken easily from renewables at current rates.
25	**Vijay (Jan. 4, 2018 6:45am):** Have you done this due diligence for all Fiat Currencies printed and
26	circulated every where? Let me know which one consumes more energy overall?
27	**Mark (Jan. 4, 2018 10:21am):** I have done this, and Bitcoin has a carbon footprint which is about
28	500–30,000 times larger than the US dollar.

29   **Vijay (Jan. 5, 2018 1:55pm):** And so my joker friend, how many Fiat currencies exist on this planet,
30   have you even counted? Bitcoin is a universal currency and is not here to just replace your USD
31   alone! Also, what is the source of that study?

32   **TomTX (Jan. 6, 2018 8:22pm):** Your question was answered. Your turn to supply real numbers.

33   **Vijay (Jan. 8, 2018 5:51am):** TomTX, nothing was answered. Mark states he has done this study with
34   no references to any data as to how he arrived at such a conclusion. Also, USD is not the only fiat in
35   this world, although many Americans cannot see anything beyond that in their puny little shells that
36   they develop and stay in such as yourself!

37   **Thaitum (Jan. 2, 2018 5:48pm):** Looks like I made a big mistake then. In one of my IRA's I bought
38   some AAPl in 2009 for $28k. It grew to $240k. Then in November I sold it and bought GBTC, which is
39   a OTC fund holding bitcoins. The account is now worth over $500k, but the high was closer to $700k.
40   Should I just get out now? No doubt it will crash but I think it still has room to go. It's cut a few years
41   from our projected FIRE date.

42   **Ben (Jan. 2, 2018 10:12pm):** Congratulations, it sounds like you gambled and won. Not a repeatable
43   strategy though, I'm sure. Get out while you can.

44   You are probably right that it has some more room to grow, but speculating on the perfect exit point
45   is no more an investment strategy than a trip to Vegas is.

46   **Lily (Jan. 2, 2018 5:53pm):** It's absolutely astounding how the general (pretty darn) intelligent public
47   can't tell the difference between an real asset vs an investment. My friend who has a Master's
48   in Computer Science inquired with me about investing in Bitcoin before Christmas and I told her
49   essentially what I thought as mania.

50   Bitcoin CANNOT shelter you, pay dividends nor feed you. It's a speculation, pretty much like buying
51   gold. It's diversification. . . . at best. It's a huge money maker if you can bet that you're not the bigger
52   fool.

53   My mother in law collected beanie babies and I had the pleasure of looking up their worth this
54   Christmas back home. . .they're about $5 each and I will owe eBay 10% + shipping. Darn things didn't
55   even pace with inflation. At least they're cute and the grand kids like them! I don't think Bitcoin will
56   be very snuggly.

57   **Justin C. (Jan. 4, 2018 5:47am):** Gold is not necessarily a "speculation". It is a commodity. Buying it
58   is not necessarily speculative.

59   That would be like saying corn is a speculation or coffee is a speculation. What if you want it for
60   yourself, or have customers or distributors that do?

61   To call gold a "non-productive asset" misses the point entirely. It is not an investment. It is a "good".
62   Do you fault coffee or corn or wheat for being "non-productive", or do you appreciate them as goods,
63   at an appropriate price?

64   There are literally centuries worth of data on the gold price and it is remarkably stable against all
65   other commodities (and paper assets) over long stretches of time because of math and physics.

66   Assuming you can know the exact price of a commodity on a given day is speculative, yes.

67   But observing long term norms of valuation and noticing when they are out of whack is not called
68   being "speculative". It is called "being informed about reality."

69   At the present time, stock index funds are priced more irrationally and speculatively high than gold
70   is. Here is one interesting chart among many that shows exactly that:

71   http://pricingold.com/charts/SP500-1880.pdf

72   Even things that can be good investments can be in a bubble. Stocks and bonds and real estate can
73   all enter into bubbles. It doesn't mean they are in bubbles at any price. It just means that some price
74   levels are reasonable, and some are not.

Source: Mr. Money Mustache, "Why Bitcoin Is Stupid," *Mr. Money Mustache* (blog), January 2, 2018.

This chapter's Everyday Life Example will help you put these tools into practice. In Chapter 9, we used the blog post from Mr. Money Mustache (MMM) about Bitcoin as an example of how people use the general ARG conditions. In this chapter, we'll use some comments responding to MMM's post to uncover how arguers apply the ARG conditions to the different argument types. This debate between real people arguing in a non-formal manner through an online discussion forum is representative of the kinds of debates people have in contemporary society. It also bridges personal, technical, and public spheres and addresses numerous argument types.

The comments are just a (non-representative) selection from the more than 600 comments to MMM's post. Nevertheless, the included comments are reproduced verbatim from the site with the same paragraphing, without correcting spelling and grammar errors, and in the same chronological order. As you read the comments, identify the issues, the types of arguments, and the specific ARG conditions that are being debated. Then, consider the overall quality of this thread for determining whether or not you should invest in Bitcoin.

There are three comment threads—lines 1-36, 37-45, 46-74—involving a variety of argument types. We'll break down each thread in turn but you can also reference Table 10.1 for a summary of the clash in the debate.

Tawcan provided the first comment, asserting that Bitcoin's energy use is concerning but offering no support (lines 2-3). Vijay responded as if it were an argument from authority, arguing that "the Banks and their Media" are not authorities on Bitcoin's energy use (the R condition, lines 5-6) and don't have agreement from other authorities, such as the CNBC article (the G condition, lines 7-8). In response, Tawcan cited the CNBC article and advanced a causal argument—Bitcoin mining results in a lot of unnecessary carbon dioxide emissions (lines 14-16)—that Vijay rebutted: Bitcoin mining has a lot of emissions unless "we . . . move it to renewables" (the G condition, line 17). Both Jacob and Andreas disputed Vijay's causal argument about renewables by offering reasons why Bitcoin farming is unlikely to move in that direction (the R condition, lines 18-24).

Losing the renewable energy issue, Vijay shifted the debate to argue that "Fiat Currencies" (e.g., the U.S. dollar) consume more energy worldwide. This shifting technique is quite common when arguers try to get an upper hand in a debate. Mark, Vijay, and TomTX addressed this issue by demanding credible authority arguments (e.g., asking for "the source of the study," line 31, or "real numbers," line 32, address the A condition of the support of whether producing the U.S. dollar consumes less energy than Bitcoin). In this sub-thread alone, the arguers exchanged evaluations of cause and authority arguments.

In lines 37-41, Thaitum supported Bitcoin investment with a different approach than Vijay. There, Thaitum used personal experience to generalize, sarcastically, that investing in Bitcoin is "a big mistake." Ben, correctly perceiving this as a generalization argument, refuted it by noting that Thaitum's experience was not representative of all cases or, in his words, "not a repeatable strategy" (the R condition, lines 42-43). Ben then compared buying Bitcoin to gambling in Las Vegas. This sub-thread engaged generalization and analogy arguments.

Finally, Lily defined Bitcoin as speculation rather than investment and supported this claim with analogies to buying gold and Beanie Babies (lines 50-56). Justin C. challenged Lily's support—that gold is a speculation—by defining it as a "commodity" instead (the A condition, line 57)—similar to corn, coffee, and wheat (lines 61-63)—and by referencing the "centuries worth" of data showing that gold is not a speculative

Commenter's Case	First Response	Subsequent Responses to Responses					
		Tawcan	**Vijay**	**Jacob** / **Andreas**	**Vijay**	**Mark**	**Vijay**
Tawcan a. Bitcoin wastes energy	**Vijay** a. Bitcoin mining is a fraction of 1% of global demand 1. Don't fall for hype from banks and media 2. CNBC article	a. A lot of CO$_2$ going into atmosphere 1. Bitcoin mining electricity could power 3.3 million homes 2. Bitcoin mining in China uses coal	a. We will move to renewables	a. Not likely 1. Cheap energy costs drive mining **Andreas** b. Farms won't give money 1. Current energy rates not meet 36 TW demand for mining	a. Do all fiat currencies in world use less energy than Bitcoin?	a. Bitcoin footprint is 500-30,000 times more than U.S. Dollar	a. What about rest of world? 1. Bitcoin is universal currency, not just U.S. b. What is your source?
Thaitum a. Bitcoin investing was (not a) mistake 1. $28,000 investment has grown to over $500,000	**Ben** a. Get out now 1. You gambled and won 2. Not a repeatable strategy						
Lily a. Bitcoin is speculation not an asset 1. Like gold & mother-in-law's Beanie Babies collection	**Justin C.** a. Gold is not speculation, but a commodity 1. Like corn, coffee, or wheat 2. Gold prices are stable over centuries 3. Stock index funds are currently more speculative than gold						

*Responses are lined up with the original argument to which they respond. For space reasons, some arguments are truncated.

Source: Mr. Money Mustache. "Why Bitcoin is Stupid." *Mr. Money Mustache* [blog]. January 2, 2018.

investment (lines 64-65). Hopefully, you noticed how Justin's responses took the debate in a direction that relates little, if at all, to the original proposition of MMM's article that "you should not invest in Bitcoin." Recalling that refutation is a choice, Justin might have better focused his response on whether gold is like Bitcoin rather than on whether gold is a speculation. A poor choice often happens in everyday argumentation when we fixate on argumentative ideas that we vehemently oppose or can easily refute even though they aren't relevant to the overall debate.

These comments show how the ARG conditions often motivate people's responses to the different types of argument in the real world. The ideas were there even if the execution was haphazard and unimpactful. Now imagine if the commenters were aware of how to effectively employ the ARG conditions. This would produce a more meaningful and organized debate and provide greater force to each refutation. This exchange reinforces four important lessons about refutation and clash:

1. **Clash is often messy and complex**. In this case, the responses to MMM's article jumped around quite a bit, taking the debate in different directions and addressing issues such as energy use that weren't even part of the original article. This complexity is even more pronounced when you consider that the reproduced debate in this book excluded other threads in response to MMM's article as well as additional comments from these threads that weren't relevant for our purposes. Tracking the flow of a debate can be challenging and often requires concentration and critical thinking.

2. **The ARG conditions can explain virtually all legitimate refutations,** excluding those that misunderstand or don't engage the logic of the original argument. The MMM debate disputed no fewer than five argument types—authority, cause, analogy, generalization, and classification—with arguers invoking ARG conditions appropriate to each kind. Although they weren't raised explicitly by name, the analysis illustrates how they fueled the arguers' refutations.

3. **Most debates come to an end but aren't resolved**. The threads each ended but it's incorrect to say that the arguers wrapped up the debate or resolved the issues; they just stopped responding to one another. This example likely rings true to many debates in everyday life that fizzle out despite lingering issues. In this case, the arguers raised some thoughtful concerns but failed to settle the main issues in MMM's article that sparked the debate: Should you invest in Bitcoin?

4. **Debate can be about more than deciding on propositions.** Even though propositions motivate debate, we have also discussed how debate can empower people. Especially with a personal topic such as financial investing, commenting gave people a forum to share their experiences and express their feelings. In some cases, arguing might have helped people vent or communicate their vision rather than actually deciding whether or not to invest in Bitcoin. Thus, although the quality of the refutation is important, you should remain focused on your goals for participating in the first place and recognize when others' goals in a debate don't align with yours. The Find Your Voice box encourages you to consider such motivations for online discussion forums.

FIND YOUR VOICE
DEBATING THROUGH ONLINE FORUMS

It's one thing to debate in a private sphere with friends and family or to post arguments behind privacy filters on Facebook, Instagram, Snapchat, and Twitter. It's quite another to engage in sustained argumentation through a publicly accessible forum, especially if your comments are not anonymous. Have you ever debated in a public online discussion board or comment section? What has or would motivate you to argue in such a public space? What is at stake (both good and bad) in doing so? Reflecting on the purpose and value of debating through online forums can help you be a more productive arguer. We'll spend more time with this in Chapter 12.

Summary

Building on the previous chapter's explanation of the ARG conditions, this chapter has explored what it means for the six major types of argument to be cogent. Box 10.1 offers a quick reference summary of the general ARG conditions as well as those for each type. Ultimately, the examples throughout the chapter, including the Everyday Life Example, illustrate how understanding the requirements for cogent argumentation can empower you to tackle challenging topics in everyday life and to generate productive clash that engages the reasoning of others.

BOX 10.1: ARG CONDITIONS QUICK REFERENCE

An argument is cogent if you answer "yes" to all ARG questions for that type.

General ARG conditions (for any argument)

A: Will the audience find the support permissible in the debate? Is the support accurate and unmanipulated?

R: Does the support have bearing on the claim?

G: Is the support immune to possible rebuttals? Is the magnitude and range of support adequate for the claim?

Argument from Classification ARG conditions

A: Is the general statement of principle, definition, etc. acceptable?

R: Does the general statement apply to the specific instance?

G: Is the general statement the most applicable and appropriate given the alternatives?

Argument from Generalization ARG conditions

A: Is the sample clearly identified and free of biased selection and do the elements share the quality?

R: Is the sample representative of the category in relevant characteristics?

G: Does the sample adequately account for the diversity and size of the category?

Argument from Cause ARG conditions

A: Is the cause/effect clearly identified, defined, and acceptable?

R: Does the cause likely result in the effect?

(Continued)

(Continued)

G: Does the support rule out correlation and alternative explanations?

Argument from Sign ARG conditions

A: Are the signs clearly identified, defined, and acceptable?

R: Do the signs likely indicate of the condition?

G: Are there sufficient signs to rule out alternative explanations or conditions?

Argument from Analogy ARG conditions

A: Is the known case coherent and acceptable?

R: Do the relevant similarities between the two cases support the claim?

G: Do the relevant similarities outweigh the relevant differences between the cases?

Argument from Authority ARG conditions

A: Is the source clearly identified and free of bias and did the source say the alleged claim?

R: Is the source a credible authority on the topic?

G: Is the source enough to authorize the claim and do other credible sources agree?

Application Exercises

Applying ARG Conditions to Argument Types: In this chapter, we evaluated one of the three arguments included in the Everyday Life Examples from Chapter 6. For the two arguments we didn't evaluate, use the appropriate ARG conditions to assess their cogency. For each non-cogent argument, consider if and how you could revise the argument to be more rationally persuasive.

Finding ARG Conditions in Everyday Argumentation: Choose a debate transcript, such as comment threads in an online forum or a presidential debate, and follow the process we used for the Everyday Life Example to identify the ARG conditions:

1. Read the transcript and isolate the various issues (points of disagreement), creating a

diagram of the debate situation if that helps you organize the content.

2. Isolate points in the transcript where one arguer explicitly responds to the co-arguer's argument.

3. As possible, determine the kind of argument being refuted.

4. Assess the refutation: Which of the ARG conditions did the arguer use to refute the argument? Did that choice match the appropriate ARG conditions for that type? Is it an effective response to the argument? Why or why not?

5. Consider if and how the arguer might have advanced a stronger refutation.

Key Terms

Hasty Generalization 217
*Post Hoc, Ergo Propter
Hoc* 219

Single Cause 219
Slippery Slope 219

Fundamental Attribution
Error 219
False Analogy 222

Endnotes

1. Donald Trump Jr. (@DonaldJTrumpJr), Twitter Post, September 19, 2016, 4:41 p.m., https://web.archive.org/web/20160920003332/https://twitter.com/DonaldJTrumpJr/status/778016283342307328.

2. Denise Young, quoted in Seth Abramovitch, Twitter Post, September 19, 2016, 9:41 p.m., https://twitter.com/SethAbramovitch/status/778091768793407488.

3. Melissa Fleming, quoted in Christine Hauser, "Donald Trump Jr. Compares Syrian Refugees to Skittles That 'Would Kill You,'" *New York Times*, September 20, 2016, https://www.nytimes.com/2016/09/21/us/politics/donald-trump-jr-faces-backlash-after-comparing-syrian-refugees-to-skittles-that-can-kill.html.

4. Philip Bump, "Donald Trump Jr. Inadvertently Encourages America to Scoop Up Refugees By the Handful,'" *Washington Post*, September 20, 2016, https://www.washingtonpost.com/news/the-fix/wp/2016/09/19/donald-trump-jr-inadvertantly-encourages-america-to-scoop-up-refugees-by-the-handful.

5. Bump, "Donald Trump Jr. Inadvertently Encourages America to Scoop Up Refugees By the Handful.'"

6. Gallup, Inc., *2017 College Student Survey: A Nationally Representative Survey of Currently Enrolled Students*, 2017, 28, http://news.gallup.com/file/reports/225161/Strada-Gallup%20January%202018%20Student%20Survey%20Report.pdf.

7. John H. Harvey, Jerri P. Town, and Kerry L. Yarkin, "How Fundamental is 'The Fundamental Attribution Error'?" *Journal of Personality and Social Psychology* 40 (1981): 346-349.

8. See, for example, Don Locke and Donald Pennington, "Reasons and Other Causes: Their Role in Attribution Processes," *Journal of Personality and Social Pscyhology* 42 (1982): 212-223; R. G. Collingwood, "On the So-Called Idea of Causation," *Proceedings of the Aristotelean Society* 38 (1937): 85-112.

9. Mr. Money Mustache, "Why Bitcoin Is Stupid: Comments," *Mr. Money Mustache* (blog), January 2, 2018, http://www.mrmoneymustache.com/2018/01/02/why-bitcoin-is-stupid#comments.

APPLIED ARGUMENTATION AND DEBATE

PART IV

11

CRAFTING VERBAL AND ORAL ARGUMENTS

Taylor Mali, a slam poet and former teacher, has dedicated much of his life's work to educating and inspiring others. One of his poems, "Totally Like Whatever, You Know?" addresses the culture of conviction in contemporary society and implores his audience members to change their argumentation habits. To fully capture Mali's meaning, search for and watch his oral performance of the poem on YouTube and consider the lesson for your own argumentation:

> In case you hadn't noticed,
> it has somehow become uncool
> to sound like you know what you're talking about?
> Or believe strongly in what you're saying?
> Invisible question marks and parenthetical (you know?)'s
> have been attaching themselves to the ends of our sentences?
> Even when those sentences aren't, like, questions? You know?
>
> Declarative sentences—so-called
> because they used to, like, DECLARE things to be true, okay,
> as opposed to other things are, like, totally, you know, not—
> have been infected by a totally hip
> and tragically cool interrogative tone? You know?
> Like, don't think I'm uncool just because I've noticed this;
> this is just like the word on the street, you know?
> It's like what I've heard?
> I have nothing personally invested in my own opinions, okay?
> I'm just inviting you to join me in my uncertainty?
>
> What has happened to our conviction?
> Where are the limbs out on which we once walked?
> Have they been, like, chopped down

with the rest of the rain forest?
Or do we have, like, nothing to say?
Has society become so, like, totally . . .
I mean absolutely . . . You know?
That we've just gotten to the point where it's just, like . . .
whatever!

And so actually our disarticulation . . . ness
is just a clever sort of . . . thing
to disguise the fact that we've become
the most aggressively inarticulate generation
to come along since . . .
you know, a long, long time ago!

I entreat you, I implore you,
I exhort you, I challenge you: To speak with conviction.
To say what you believe in a manner that bespeaks
the determination with which you believe it.
Because contrary to the wisdom of the bumper sticker,
it is not enough these days to simply QUESTION AUTHORITY.
You have to speak with it, too.[1]

Source: Taylor Mali, "Totally Like Whatever, You Know?" *Taylor Mali*, 2002, https://taylormali.com/poems/totally-like-whatever-you-know

Mali's poem emphasizes factors that produce strong argumentation: speak with authority, avoid a questioning tone, be personally invested, and don't feign being too "hip" and "cool" for conviction. That is, the force of everyday argumentation relies on the quality of its style and delivery in addition to the quality of its content.

Although our journey so far has focused almost exclusively on the structure and content of argumentation, this chapter supplements our study of cogent arguments with three other factors: audience analysis and adaptation, style and word choice, and oral delivery. Even the most cogent argument may flop because the arguer fails to adapt it to the audience, uses poor word choice, or suffers from a choppy and unengaging delivery. We'll explore each topic in turn, considering examples of everyday argumentation along the way. By the end of this chapter, you should be able to effectively craft oral and written arguments attentive to audience, style, and delivery.

AUDIENCE ANALYSIS AND ADAPTATION

Many previous chapters have emphasized the importance of an argument's audience. For instance, determining the audience's presumption is crucial to understanding a debate situation. Assessments of acceptability require you to consider whether the audience would deem the support permissible in the debate. And, productive clash requires you to address not just the arguments you and your co-arguers find important but also those that matter to the audience. Because you rarely argue independent of an intended receiver, our exploration of each of these topics has emphasized awareness of and adaptation to the audience.

We'll build on this prior consideration of audience by exploring audience analysis and adaptation here. **Audience analysis,** which usually occurs prior to argumentation, refers to the deliberate consideration of the audience's composition, beliefs, and interests in relation to the debate situation. The goal of audience analysis is to craft arguments that will be relevant and persuasive for your audience. This crafting element is **audience adaptation,** or adjusting your argumentation to the audience in order to achieve your goal.

Audience analysis and adaptation are important for many reasons:

1. **Captures and maintains interest**. Tailoring argumentation increases the likelihood that your audiences will engage your arguments. This is why Facebook's algorithm for its News Feed reinforces information and ideas already of interest to you.[2] Facebook adapts the feed to your "likes," inviting you to click on a link and, before you know it, you've just spent 45 minutes looking at cat videos. Argumentation can work the same way: When effectively adapted to audience members, they have a greater likelihood of extended engagement with the content.

2. **Fosters identification**. A second benefit to tailoring your argumentation is that it fosters identification. You identify with someone when you have an affinity for and empathy with them. Adaptation enables identification by recognizing what matters to your audience members, forging a stronger connection between you and them. Identification is valuable in itself by forming community as well as instrumentally by paving the way for persuasion.

3. **Enhances your credibility**. Third, adapting to your audience can improve your credibility. Understanding the audience's interests and motivations is one way to demonstrate the kind of character discussed in Chapter 5 that partially informs judgments of credibility. The opposite is also true: An easy way to lose credibility is to be self- rather than other-interested in your argumentation or to show that you haven't taken the time to understand the audience.

4. **Improves cogency of arguments**. Finally, it's less likely that an audience will dispute your arguments if you adapt them. Recall that support that is agreeable to your audience is a crucial starting point for any argument so you should think carefully about the support you select.

Despite the importance of accounting for your audience and despite the fact that it may seem like common sense to do so, people are surprisingly disinclined toward being audience-centered in everyday argumentation. Reflect on your own argumentation as you go through your day and you'll likely discover that much of it focuses on you and what you desire, not your audience members and what they desire. Scholars have found that even public sphere debates that should focus on the common good frequently involve "egocentric arguments" prioritizing self-interest.[3] To help you avoid this tendency Box 11.1 offers four questions as a starting point for determining and adapting to your audience and co-arguers.

AUDIENCE ANALYSIS: Deliberate consideration of the audience's composition, beliefs, and interests in relation to the debate situation

AUDIENCE ADAPTATION: Adjusting argumentation to the audience to achieve the arguer's goal

BOX 11.1: AUDIENCE CONSIDERATIONS

1. **What is your purpose or goal for arguing?** Determining what you hope to accomplish will focus your argumentation efforts. Recall you should avoid treating your audience as a means to an end by approaching argumentation with goals relevant to a cooperative stance.

2. **Who is the appropriate audience?** Each goal you have for arguing corresponds to one or more *appropriate* audience, or those who are necessary to achieve that goal. Be careful to not misallocate your time and energy by arguing to audiences who have no control over the outcome of the debate.

3. **What is the appropriate mode and manner of argumentation for the appropriate audience?** Once you know the appropriate audience, then you should consider how to best reach that audience through your arguments, using material from earlier chapters.

4. **Who are my co-arguers and how do they relate to my arguments?** You should also account for your co-arguers. If you ignore other perspectives, you prevent fulsome debate because you essentially fail to *exchange* arguments on a topic.

Once you determine your appropriate audience, then you should employ some tools and strategies for being audience-centered.

Audience Analysis

Anytime you are able to construct your argumentation in advance—whether writing a text message, social media post, paper, email, article, or oral presentation—you should consider factors of your audience members that might influence how they engage with and respond to the debate situation. Chances are you already do this on some occasions, considering how your parents or guardians might respond to a particular request or preparing for the worst when breaking bad news to a friend. Here we will consider systematic processes for such analysis.

Demographics and psychographics are two general categories of information about your audience that can help. **Demographics**, translated as measure of the people, entail the composition of your audience as based on various (mainly physical) characteristics. Anytime you classify an audience by race, age, sex, gender, religion, nationality, socioeconomic status, or occupation, you've engaged in demographic analysis. Demographics may help you understand the kinds of concerns your audience members have. For instance, students under the age of 18 have a different stake in education reform than the parents of those students, which also differs from that of adults without children. As an arguer, you would want to consider those stakes when preparing to argue to help you better understand what motivates members of the audience to participate in the debate and what stances they might have.

Psychographics are also useful to audience analysis. Psychographics refer to your audience's psychological make-up, based on mental characteristics such as attitudes, hopes, fears, values, and interests. Just as you can classify audiences based on demographics, you can also classify them based on psychographics. For instance, it would be helpful to know if most of your audience members share a particular fear or strive for a particular value.

DEMOGRAPHICS: The audience's composition based on its various qualities

PSYCHO-GRAPHICS: The audience's composition based on its mental characteristics

FIND YOUR VOICE
ARE YOU YOUR ZIP CODE?

Marketers commonly use ZIP (postal) codes—a demographic quality (geography) as a sign or indicator of a psychographic quality (lifestyle)—to understand and segment their audiences. Claritas "MyBestSegments" and Esri's "Tapestries" are two online services that do this.[4] If you live in the United States, look up your ZIP code on one or both of the sites and see how well it reflects you and your lifestyle. How useful are ZIP codes to understanding your audience, particularly relative to other demographic factors (e.g., age, race, sex, religion)? The more aware you are of the factors that might influence an audience's lifestyle, the more targeted your argumentation can become.

Presumption is another psychographic indicator because it designates the audience's initial attitude toward the proposition. The Find Your Voice feature on this page encourages you to consider to what degree postal codes are a useful tool for understanding audiences.

Finally, **situational factors** may be relevant to understanding the audience's relationship to your argumentation. Situational factors refer to characteristics of the audience unique to the specific context of the debate situation. Aspects such as time of day, location, medium of communication, and format for the argumentation may all influence how your audience engages it. If you present an argumentative case in a class, for instance, the audience members who are tired, hungry, or feel they are captive may not be listening openly and honestly. If you reply anonymously to an online article, your audience may not trust your arguments compared to a non-anonymous reply. If you speak arguments through video, your audience will likely interact with those argument differently than if you put those very same arguments in writing.

SITUATIONAL FACTORS: The audience's characteristics based on the debate situation

Your own case's relationship to co-arguers is also an important situational factor. We've discussed how argumentative cases don't occur in a vacuum, independent of other communication about the controversy or the people who make the arguments. It matters if you're the first or last arguer or wedged in between others. It matters if you have more or less power than your co-arguers and audience members. And, it matters if you are arguing unopposed or participating in a debate with clear respondents. These are just a few examples of how situational factors—some that are beyond the control of the participants—are important elements to analyze in advance of your argumentation.

You may not be able to engage in audience analysis for all debates, especially those that occur with little or no advance warning. Nevertheless, analyzing demographics, psychographics, and situational factors provides the opportunity to better adapt your arguments.

Audience Adaptation

Audience adaptation involves catering your arguments to the perspective of your recipients. Even if you don't have a chance to fully analyze your audience in advance of arguing, adaptation is possible in any debate situation. We'll discuss five principles that help ensure effective audience adaptation.

1. **Account for demographics, psychographics, and situational factors**. Audience analysis of the above features enables you to craft arguments that address your audience's concerns and interests.

2. **Consider audience's knowledge**. You should also adapt your arguments to the audience's level of knowledge about the controversy. Chances are you've experienced argumentation that did this improperly, either assuming you knew more than you did or speaking down to you as though you are an idiot. You should be more careful in your own argumentation by adapting appropriately.

3. **Avoid pandering**. There is a fine line between adapting to an audience and pandering to it, in which an arguer tells audience members what they want to hear. Politicians are often accused of pandering but it can occur in everyday argumentation as well (e.g., when you compliment a parent before asking for something, when you agree with a friend's argument simply to avoid a fight, or when you say what you think the teacher wants to hear when writing a paper). Unlike pandering, audience adaptation enables you to be honest while still considering the topic from your audience's perspective. One way to achieve this is to advance your own claims but tailor the support to the audience.

4. **Avoid stereotyping**. As with pandering, there is a fine line between adapting to an audience and stereotyping it, when you assume that someone has some quality because he or she belongs to a particular group or has a particular identity characteristic. Some stereotypes may be based on fair assumptions about the general attitude of *most* audience members but you might alienate members who do not fit the stereotype. You should think critically about when these kinds of assumptions about your audience constitute appropriate adaptation.

5. **Be flexible**. The final principle for audience adaptation is flexibility. If you expect a debate to go according to a planned script, you'll inevitably find frustration and disappointment. Instead, address things as they develop in the debate. If your co-arguer raises an issue you hadn't previously considered, don't ignore it but rather adapt and respond directly. If members of your audience look bored or confused, address those perceived concerns rather than taking it personally. If you make a mistake or violate an ethical guideline (it sometimes happens), acknowledge your error and correct it rather than being stubborn. These are some illustrations of what it means to be flexible in a debate.

To consider audience analysis and adaptation in action, this chapter's Everyday Life Example is an argumentative case that Zach Wahls delivered to the Iowa House Judiciary Committee during public hearings about an amendment to the state constitution banning same-sex marriage. Wahls, a then 19-year-old college student and the son of a lesbian couple, used his own experience to oppose the amendment. It's a great example of how ordinary people arguing about topics of personal importance can make a difference in local communities, even if Wahls's speech did benefit from his training as a member of

Everyday Life Example 11.1

Zach Wahls, "Zach Wahls Speaks about Family," Feb. 1, 2011[6]

1	Good evening Mr. Chairman, my name is Zach Wahls. I'm a sixth-generation Iowan and an
2	engineering student at the University of Iowa, and I was raised by two women. My biological mom
3	Terry told her grandparents that she was pregnant, that the artificial insemination had worked, and
4	they wouldn't even acknowledge it. It actually wasn't until I was born and they succumbed to my
5	infantile cuteness that they broke down and told her that they were thrilled to have another grandson.
6	Unfortunately, neither of them lived to see her marry her partner Jackie of fifteen years when
7	they wed in 2009. My younger sister and only sibling was born in 1994. We actually have the same
8	anonymous donor, so we're full siblings, which is really cool for me. You know, and I guess the point is
9	that our family really isn't so different from any other Iowa family. You know, when I'm home, we go to
10	church together, we eat dinner, we go on vacations. But, you know, we have our hard times too; we get
11	in fights. Actually, my mom, Terry, was diagnosed with multiple sclerosis in 2000. It is a devastating
12	disease that put her in a wheelchair, so we've had our struggles. But, you know, we're Iowans. We
13	don't expect anyone to solve our problems for us. We'll fight our own battles. We just hope for equal
14	and fair treatment from our government.
15	Being a student at the University of Iowa, the topic of same sex marriage comes up quite frequently
16	in classroom discussions. You know, and the question always comes down to, well, "Can gays even
17	raise kids?" And the conversation gets quiet for a moment, because most people don't really have an
18	answer. And then I raise my hand and say, "Actually, I was raised by a gay couple, and I'm doing pretty
19	well." I score in the 99th percentile on the ACT. I'm actually an Eagle Scout. I own and operate my own
20	small business. If I was your son, Mr. Chairman, I believe I'd make you very proud. I'm not really so
21	different from any of your children. My family really isn't so different from yours. After all, your family
22	doesn't derive its sense of worth from being told by the state, "You're married, congratulations!" No,
23	the sense of family comes the commitment we make to each other to work through the hard times so
24	we can enjoy the good ones. It comes from the love that binds us. That's what makes a family.
25	So what you're voting here isn't to change us. It's not to change our families; it's to change how the
26	law views us, how the law treats us. You are voting for the first time in the history of our state to
27	codify discrimination into our constitution, a constitution that but for the proposed amendment is the
28	least amended constitution in the United States of America. You are telling Iowans that "Some among
29	you are second-class citizens who do not have the right to marry the person you love." So will this
30	vote affect my family? Would it affect yours? Over the next two hours, I'm sure we're going to hear
31	plenty of testimony about how damaging having gay parents is on kids. But in my 19 years not once
32	have I ever been confronted by an individual who realized independently that I was raised by a gay
33	couple. And you know why? Because the sexual orientation of my parents has had zero effect on the
34	content of my character. Thank you very much.

Source: Zach Wahls, "Zach Wahls Speaks About Family," Iowa House Democrats, YouTube video, 3:00, February 1, 2011, https://youtu .be/ FSQQK2Vuf9Q.

his high school debate team.[5] As you read the case, identify who Wahls is addressing *as* his audience and then identify and evaluate how well he adapted his case to it.

Choosing the appropriate audience is often an important first step to argumentation. Despite there being a public audience in the room, Wahls wisely targeted the legislators who would be voting on the amendment as his audience. He then adapted to this audience explicitly in the speech. Table 11.1 identifies some examples of audience adaptation.

TABLE 11.1 ■ Audience Adaptation in Wahls's Speech	
Lines	**Adaptation**
8-9	Describes his family as "typical" Iowa family to foster identification
12-14	"We're Iowans" emphasizes common values of perseverance and equality
20-24	Encourages Chairperson and other audience members to recognize Wahls as similar to their own children
25-27, 28-29	Emphasizes the active nature of the committee's vote, indicating it has consequences
27-28	Appeals to Iowan pride for having the least amended constitution among all states
29-30	Asks audience members to consider if and how vote would affect their family
30-34	Recognizes situational factor of the hearing to preempt argument about the damaging nature of having same sex parents

Source: Zach Wahls, "Zach Wahls Speaks About Family," *Iowa House Democrats*, YouTube video, 3:00, February 1, 2011, https://youtu.be/FSQQK2Vuf9Q.

Half of the examples in the table relate to Iowa or being an Iowan. This is a particularly valuable illustration of how Wahls appealed to common ground by using a quality that all members of the audience share. Consider if he had instead focused on what it means to be an American. This would also have applied to all audience members but it would have lacked the specificity and connection that the narrower identity of Iowan carried.

Wahls emphasis on himself and his family as "typical" challenged the anticipated testimony that same sex parents are detrimental to child development. Was it appropriate for Wahls to assume that proponents of the amendment held this concern or did he engage in potentially unethical stereotyping of his audience and co-arguers? Knowing that this was his only opportunity to speak, do you agree with his decision to preempt this argument?

Beyond these examples, there are likely places that Wahls could have more fully adapted the arguments to the audience rather than focusing on his own experience or interests. Particularly at the start of the speech, he provided helpful information about himself but might have more fully related his arguments to the audience. Doing so might have avoided some people's perception that Wahls was making a bad generalization "without offering a shred of evidence beyond a single cherry-picked case (his own) to prove that children of gay parents sometimes turn out just fine."[7]

Nevertheless, there is much to commend about how Wahls accounted for various demographic, psychographic, and situational factors, appropriately adjusted his speech to the audience's knowledge of the topic, and avoided pandering. Although his speech was ultimately ineffective at preventing the Iowa House from passing the amendment (which would later die in the Iowa Senate), the viral nature of the video attests to how his arguments created common ground with a wide audience and reinforced shared values.

STYLE

Style, like audience adaptation, helps you craft effective arguments. Style refers to how the arguer uses word choice and figures of speech to communicate a message. Style focuses on *how* you say something rather than *what* you say. That is, an arguer could make the same general point numerous ways: explicitly and verbatim, with a metaphor, quoting someone else, employing a euphemism, etc. Even though the claim is the same, the style choice will convey a slightly different message. Thus, while an argument's content certainly matters—we'd have wasted 10 chapters to this point if it didn't—style is also a significant factor that can impact how audience members and co-arguers engage your argumentation. This section will first explore the importance of style to argumentation followed by three principles of effective style: clarity, connection, and creativity.

STYLE: The arguer's use of figures of speech and word choice

To help you avoid thinking of style as merely ornamental or supplemental to the message, consider the following benefits of effective style:

1. **Captures and maintains interest**. Using style, speaking with eloquence, and communicating a vision makes the argumentation more interesting for your audience. When you use effective style, the speech is memorable in a good way. Of course, using bad style can also make a speech memorable, but that's not the kind of interest you want to capture.

2. **Prompts an emotional reaction from the audience**. Beyond capturing the audience's interest, effective style can also elicit an emotional response. Chances are the messages that have truly inspired you did so in large part to the style and word choice the arguer used alongside the arguments. For instance, style helps explain why Martin Luther King's "I Have a Dream" speech is widely regarded as one of the best speeches of all time. As Albus Dumbledore noted in *Harry Potter & the Deathly Hallows*, words are "our most inexhaustible source of magic, capable of both inflicting injury and remedying it."[8]

3. **Communicates your personality**. Style is also a way to communicate your identity and personality. One of the main motivations for arguing is to convey your beliefs, something that involves self-investment. Using effective style lets you put a personal touch on the arguments because it makes those arguments distinct from other arguers who might make the same points.

4. **Improves precision of arguments**. Finally, intentional use of style ensures that your arguments are as precise as they should be. The more conscious you are of how words communicate meaning (a topic you'll encounter below), the more deliberately you can choose the right words for your intended meaning and avoid the miscommunication that often occurs when we aren't as careful as we should be. Moreover, in situations that have limited time or space to argue, style helps you get the most bang for your buck.

Because style is so important to the meaning of your argumentation, we'll consider clarity, connection, and creativity as three principles that can help you productively use style.

Clarity

Clarity, the first principle, means that your style communicates your intended message to the audience. One means of clarity is directness, by stating what you mean. Directness can be useful in some argumentative situations, such as sending an email or text message, or in some spheres, such as generating a technical guide, where the message takes priority. Nevertheless, there are indirect ways to communicate a message with clarity. The use of metaphor or a narrative—e.g., the fables you may have read as a child—can powerfully convey the meaning of an idea to some audiences even if it does not involve a direct statement of the claim.

Mali's poem to open the chapter addressed the importance of assertive word choice. While effective arguments tend to avoid clutter and be forceful, this doesn't mean that every claim must be asserted with certainty. Rather, you should learn to distinguish *hedges*, which detract from clarity, and *qualifiers*, which add to it. Qualifiers, as we learned in Chapter 2, indicate the scope and force of the claim on the basis of the support. They help clarity because they inform audience members how certain we are of the claims we ask them to accept. **Verbal hedges**, on the other hand, are words or phrases that circumscribe the claim on the basis of other factors besides the support. For instance, saying "I believe that everything in life should be earned" does not enhance clarity in the same way that saying "probably everything in life should be earned." Phrasing arguments as questions, saying "I believe" or "I think," and similar hedges can get in the way of stylistically rich and forceful argumentation and contribute to the culture of "meh" that Mali identified. Beyond avoiding hedges, you should use active verbs and fresh adjectives to speak to your audience.

Clarity also requires understanding how words convey meaning. Two rhetorical scholars, C. K. Ogden and I. A. Richards, generated a helpful model called the **semantic triangle** to explain this process.[9] Depicted in Figure 11.1, the triangle's points represent three elements illustrating how words connect abstract thoughts and concrete things.

The **referent** is the thing about which you want to communicate. It is the object, emotion, idea, etc. in the "real world." This doesn't mean it's always physical—you can communicate about the thing we call love even though you can't point to love. So, suppose you laughed at someone's text message and want to communicate that. The referent would be the fact that you laughed. A **symbol** is what you use to represent the referent in communication. The word "symbol" refers to anything that stands for or represents something else. In most arguments, words are the primary symbols we use. However, symbols can also be non-verbal, such as sounds or images. If you want a symbol to communicate the referent that you laughed at your friend's text message, you could type "I laughed," "that's funny," or "LOL." Alternatively, you could insert an emoticon such as XD or:-D. Or, most likely, you could use an emoji: 😊 Each is a symbol that stands for or communicates the referent of you laughing although some might be clearer than others. How does this work? Those symbols connect to the general **reference** of laughing, the third part of the triangle. In your head, you have a general idea of what it means to laugh—that you have a smile, that your eyes are closed, that you may shed tears, etc.—which the emoticons and emojis symbolize. And, we distinguish laughing from smiling or crying based on particular qualities of the referent: there's usually sound (the OL or "out loud" part of LOL), there's usually a facial expression of enjoyment or amusement, it's usually spontaneous. Because our general concept of what it means to laugh refers to a physical referent, we can communicate about it with symbols that others understand.

The example of laughing is pretty mundane but the triangle can also explain more consequential word choices. One controversial example arose in 2005 following Hurricane

VERBAL HEDGE: A word or phrase that restricts a claim through factors other than the support

SEMANTIC TRIANGLE: Visual representation of how words communicate meaning

REFERENT: A thing about which we want to communicate

SYMBOL: The communicated thing that stands for or represents the referent

REFERENCE: The general concept of the symbol and referent

FIGURE 11.1 ■ The Semantic Triangle*

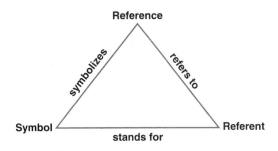

Source: *Adapted from C. K. Ogden and I. A. Richards, *The Meaning of Meaning: A Study of the Influence of Language upon Thought and of the Science of Symbolism* (New York: Harcourt Brace, 1923), 11.

Katrina's destruction in New Orleans. Agence France Press published an image of two white people in chest deep water with food and soda captioned "Two residents wade through chest-deep water after finding bread and soda from a local grocery store after Hurricane Katrina came through the area in New Orleans, Louisiana."[10] The same day, the Associated Press published an image of a black man in chest deep water with food and soda captioned: "A young man walks through chest deep flood water after looting a grocery store in New Orleans on Tuesday, Aug. 30, 2005."[11] Although both referents seemed similar—people in chest deep water using available resources to survive the flood—many audience members recognized how the symbols argued different meanings: "residents" who "find" food and soda are lucky people who have a stake in the area while people who "loot" for food and soda are criminals who may or may not be from the area. Thus, despite the apparent similarity of the referents, the meaning hinged on the conceptual difference between "finding" and "looting." Add in the element of race and it might suggest implicit prejudice, that only black people commit the crime of looting. Whether intentional or not, the word choice led Van Jones to conclude that these photos represent "the kind of shameful bias that keeps the country divided, even during awful tragedies like this."[12]

The above examples illustrate how your choice of symbols (especially words) are themselves argumentative and a potent means of shaping the audience's understanding of reality based on the concept behind those words. This is why it's important to be as concrete as possible about the intended meaning. For example, to claim that something is "great," "bad," or "interesting" doesn't tell the audience a whole lot about the thing. To say that something is a "problem" doesn't help the audience understand why it is or how it connects to them. To say in a job interview that you bring "value" to a company doesn't indicate your concrete contributions. Using precise words that convey your intended meaning makes your argumentation clearer for your audiences and co-arguers.

Connection

Beyond clarity, style should connect arguer and audience. Words, to borrow from scholar Kenneth Burke, serve as "a symbolic means of inducing cooperation in beings that by nature respond to symbols."[13] Our natural response to symbols as audience members is often tied to our ability to identify with the speaker's message; if we see in it a reflection of ourselves, we are more likely to "cooperate."

Identification requires audience adaptation to select the words and ideas that will speak to them. Even if you're prone to a particular style, you shouldn't count on that to carry your argumentation if the audience won't have it. For instance, you should probably avoid using sarcasm in an argumentative email you send to your boss because, even if you're known as a sarcastic person, meaning can often get lost in the disembodied nature of email. Chances are you've hurt someone's feelings or had your feelings hurt based on digital miscommunication.

In addition to adapting your style to the audience and situation, finding common ground and using inclusive pronouns are two tried and true means of fostering connection. Common ground involves isolating ideas, principles, values, beliefs, or opinions that you and your audience members share. Wahls illustrated that with his focus on what it means to be an Iowan. You should also consider using inclusive pronouns—"we," "us," and "our"—as appropriate to connect with your audience members. Especially when urging action, you should verbally demonstrate that you are part of the solution.

Finally, connection requires awareness of how style reinforces or challenges elements of identity and culture. The distinction between "finding" and "looting," for instance, triggered concerns about racial profiling as the word "looting" alienated rather than connected some audience members to the argument. The symbolism of laughing, while perhaps less obvious, also reinforces identity and belonging because your choice of LOL, an emoticon, or an emoji may signal something about your own identity at the same time that it requires the receiver to understand the symbolic reference; those who aren't "down with the lingo" might be outsiders who feel alienated by your choice of symbol. Style, then, can function to unite or divide people based on how well it fosters connection.

Creativity

Creativity is the third principle of effective style. In this context, creativity refers to how you make the argument stand out from clutter and reflect your personality. You want to use style that will appeal to your audience but you also want to use style that is natural to you. If you think poignant quotations or narratives are powerful and you can spin a good yarn, use them as appropriate. If you're witty or good at satire, use them as appropriate. If you think metaphor and repetition add perspective and emphasis, use them as appropriate. We'll survey two main creative strategies: thematization and figures of speech.

One useful strategy is to generate memorable themes and labels that help communicate your vision. Especially in today's soundbite culture and especially because you now know how words convey meaning, having a colorful label for something becomes an implicit argument about it. This is why President Obama eventually embraced the label "Obamacare" as a shorthand reference to the Affordable Care Act; even though the Republicans created the label as a pejorative term, Obama campaigned for reelection by using the label and claimed "I do care! You should care, too."[14] While Obamacare illustrates an instance where a co-arguer created the label an arguer later coopted, it is often better to set the terms of the debate and exert more control over the audience's perception of your ideas by establishing labels and themes yourself.

FIGURE OF SPEECH: A word or phrase used for eloquence or rhetorical effect

A second way to creatively use style is through **figures of speech** that add rhythm and momentum to arguments or provide imagery and emphasis. Table 11.2 lists figures of speech that often appear in argumentation. As you read over them, you can likely think of examples from your own experience where these have been compelling.

TABLE 11.2 ■ Common Figures of Speech in Argumentation

Figure	Description
Alliteration	Repetition of the same sound in successive or nearby words. It adds rhythm and momentum to the argument.
Amphiboly	Using ambiguous grammatical structure or language (e.g., if someone wrote in a letter of recommendation, "you'd be lucky to get this person to work for you," is it good or bad?). Amphiboly is unethical due to its intentional manipulation of language.
Antithesis	A juxtaposition of two contrasting ideas. Common in political speech and often helps provide emphasis to your claim.
Euphemism	Words or phrases that obscure more unpleasant meanings (e.g., you were "downsized" rather than fired). Common in political speech to diminish the disadvantages of a policy and often dishonest.
Hyperbole	A really awesome use of exaggeration to make the greatest point ever. While used often to rile up an audience and provide emphasis, it may be a distraction technique that limits the argument's cogency.
Innuendo	Implying or hinting at something rather than stating it outright, often as a negative (e.g., the talk of "hand size" in the 2016 Republican primary debates). Innuendo may plant seeds in the minds of the audience but it can also lead to confusion or misunderstanding.
Metaphor/ Simile	Comparing two things by saying one thing *is* the other (metaphor) or that one is *like/as* the other (simile). Unlike an analogy, simile and metaphor assert rather than argue the comparison for rhetorical effect and imagery.
Paralipsis	Emphasizing something by claiming not to mention it (e.g., "Far be it from me to question your ethics but you did receive slush fund money."). Often meant to provide an "out" for the arguer to deny that he or she intended harm by the statement.
Parallelism	Using the same structure or format for successive statements. Can develop momentum in an argument and build up to your point.
Repetition	Using the same word or phrase in successive or nearby statements. Like parallelism, repetition fosters rhythm and emphasis.
Rhetorical Question	Asking a question to make a point rather than receive an answer. Helps the audience to pause and think but can be unproductive for argumentation if answer is not obvious.
Satire	Ridiculing a subject, often through various other devices (e.g., hyperbole). Satire can powerfully uncover the absurdity of something or emphasize a point but it can also be excessive, backfiring if unbelievable or nasty.

BUILD YOUR SKILL
IDENTIFYING STYLE

Identify at least three different figures of speech in the opening of Mary Fisher's famous argumentative speech from 1992, "A Whisper of AIDS":

"Less than three months ago, at platform hearings in Salt Lake City, I asked the Republican Party to lift the shroud of silence which has been draped over the issue of HIV and AIDS. I have come tonight to bring our silence to an end. I bear a message of challenge, not self-congratulation. I want your attention, not your applause."[15]

FIND YOUR VOICE
STYLE

You may recall our penny debate from Chapter 7, where we noted that the penny cost 1.5¢ in 2016 to create and distribute. With 9.1 billion pennies minted, that is more than $45 million in waste. Generate a single paragraph that argues this significant harm to an audience of friends your age. This paragraph should practice style through the following three components:

1. Convey this information with *clarity* so that the audience doesn't get confused by the statistics. Consider in particular how you could help them understand the magnitude of the significant harm.

2. Convey this information with *connectivity* to your audience of peers. Consider what values, interests, motivations, etc. might make them care about this significant harm.

3. Convey this information with *creativity* to showcase your personality and encourage the audience to feel something. Incorporate at least two figures of speech from Table 11.2 and generate a creative label for the significant harm.

Learning the above figures of speech should not be about haphazardly peppering them throughout your argumentation but thinking about how you can argue ethically and with power. Figures of speech are choices arguers make when deciding when, what, and how to communicate their ideas.

Understanding figures of speech also help you better understand others' arguments as an audience member. If you're aware of how insidious paralipsis can be, it might not wield as much power over you in the future. If you're aware of how parallelism can inspire, you might guard against an emotional reaction that limits your critical thinking. While style can make an argument come alive for the audience, style should not override the consideration of cogency—we still want arguments to be *rationally* persuasive rather than just persuasive.

The above principles—clarity, connection, and creativity—provide some guidelines for using style effectively but you should avoid using style to manipulate your audience. A dishonest label, for instance, is counterproductive to the value of clarity. An overstated claim without an appropriate qualifier can lead to bad decisions even if a qualifier detracts from your argument's force. And, toilet humor has an appropriate time and place even if you are a toilet humor virtuoso. Use the Find Your Voice feature to help you consider and use style before turning to our final topic in this chapter: oral delivery.

ORAL DELIVERY

Oral delivery refers to the spoken communication of an argument. Unlike audience adaptation and style that apply to all arguments, only some arguments use oral delivery. Nevertheless, oral delivery is important to the meaning and effectiveness of your argumentation. People in the United States indicate public speaking as one of their greatest personal phobias, with more than one in five survey respondents saying that they are afraid or very afraid of public speaking.[16] Even in interpersonal face-to-face conversation, people have anxiety about being unprepared or feeling pressure to say the "right thing."[17]

Thus, effective delivery and management of this anxiety can benefit your argumentation in numerous ways:

1. **Captures and maintains interest**. As with audience adaptation and style, delivery can capture and maintain interest when done effectively. But, delivery can often backfire more than style and audience adaptation. Whereas a perfunctory style and weak audience adaptation may not *lose* your audience's interest, poor delivery (e.g., insufficient eye contact, monotone voice, lackluster gestures and movement) can distract from and undermine your argument no matter how cogent it is.

2. **Fosters emotional reaction**. Oral argumentation can have an energy and presence to it, making it motivational for yourself and your audience. This is why watching an argumentative speech is often much more impactful than just reading the transcript of it. Research also suggests that orally arguing with a co-arguer fosters a substantially stronger emotional reaction than arguing through non-face-to-face means.[18] Even when this is a negative emotion, such as anger, it attests to the powerful effect that oral communication can have on the audience.

3. **Enhances the arguer's credibility**. Effective delivery is part and parcel of credibility. When a speaker is prepared and delivers a forceful, clear argument, you are more likely to trust what he or she says. Alternatively, poor delivery can weaken the audience's trust in the arguer. Studies also reveal that, when compared to online communication, real time face-to-face communication of arguments fosters a greater feeling of social presence among the arguers and greater comfort for others to communicate their arguments.[19]

Just as oral delivery is powerful, so too is it fleeting. This transitory nature means that arguers should use separate verbal strategies for oral and written arguments. Box 11.2 identifies some key differences. To explore oral delivery in greater depth, this section will

BOX 11.2: ORAL VS. WRITTEN ARGUMENTATION

The main message of oral and written argumentation can be the same but the two modes should use different formats and structure:

Feature	Oral Argumentation	Written Argumentation
Sentence Length	Short with few clauses	Longer with numerous clauses
Argument Format	Start with claims and then provide support	Start with claims followed by support or start with support and build up to claims
Presentational Elements	Verbal, visual, and audio	Verbal and visual
Research Citations	Provide author, source, and date orally	Reference using the proper citation format for that sphere
Feedback & Response	Immediate and spontaneous	Delayed based on turn-taking

first discuss four methods of delivery, each representing a different way of using notes, followed by the nonverbal elements that comprise it: eye contact, vocal quality, movement and gestures.

Methods of Delivery

When you deliver your arguments orally, you have a choice of how to prepare your remarks. In general, the four choices are: impromptu, manuscript, memorized, and extemporaneous.

In an ideal world, you'd have the ability to craft each of your arguments in advance to ensure that it is adapted to the audience, stylistically rich, and presentationally sound. Unfortunately, we don't live in that world. Instead, most of our daily debates are spur of the moment, in which you make an argument on the spot and someone immediately responds or vice versa. These debates involve **impromptu** delivery, or delivery characterized by limited to no preparation and the use of few if any notes. You experience impromptu debates across all three spheres of argumentation and across all mediums (face-to-face conversation, social media, text messaging, email, etc.). In fact, *most* of your debates are probably impromptu and unexpected.

IMPROMPTU: Oral delivery from short preparation time and limited notes

Use the following strategies for effective impromptu argumentation:

1. **Learn patterns of argument**. Learning to identify hidden warrants based on argument patterns enables you to more quickly generate arguments and respond to others'. Learning the common argument types from Chapter 6

and the ARG conditions for those types from Chapter 10 will improve your impromptu debating.

2. **Practice.** It may seem a bit odd to say that you should practice impromptu debating but the reality is that your skill will only be improved if you continually use it. Trying different strategies (and occasionally failing) helps you figure out what resonates with particular audiences and helps you find your own voice. It also builds confidence, which will ultimately improve your delivery and connection with the audience.

3. **Learn from your mistakes**. Related to the previous point, you should also debrief your argumentative experiences to diagnose errors and learn from your mistakes. You'll sometimes stumble or say things you regret, but you can always vow to do better next time and apologize to those you may hurt. The sooner you recognize there's no such thing as "the right thing to say" but rather a range of options, the more you'll get yourself into the argumentative arena.

4. **Remember the Rule of Three.** Finally, a more practical tip is to use the Rule of Three, a writing principle that things are more memorable and impactful if they come in threes. Because communicating three things generates rhythm and suggests a pattern, it can build momentum for your claims.

We've spent quite a bit of time with impromptu delivery because of its prevalence but not every argument you deliver will be impromptu. When you have more time to develop your case and prepare for your presentation, you then must choose how to use notes.

One option is to deliver the content through a **manuscript** delivery, in which everything is written out word-for-word in front of you. When used effectively, manuscripts allow the arguer to communicate the message exactly as written while still engaging the audience. You have likely used manuscript delivery at some point, perhaps in a presentation at school, work, or church. Especially for those who don't have a lot of experience with oral delivery, the temptation to speak from a manuscript can be very strong so you should be careful not to make the manuscript a crutch that limits effective communication.

MANUSCRIPT: Oral delivery from a fully prepared script

A third method of delivery—**memorized** delivery—offers one way to avoid this reliance on notes. As the name suggests, memorized delivery involves the arguer memorizing the content and reciting it. As with manuscript delivery, memorized delivery is used when the specific words are important to the overall message. But, memorized delivery liberates the arguer from the need for notes, so it can be useful when an arguer delivers the same or similar arguments multiple times. A motivational speaker, a politician on the campaign trail, and a preacher are just some of the people who might use this method. You may also have used this method in the past, for instance when preparing answers to anticipated questions during a job interview or preparing an apology for hurting someone. In these cases, you can't refer to your notes but you also want to have a carefully crafted message. Of course, the risk of your mind going blank is quite strong so be careful about using this method for longer arguments.

MEMORIZED: Oral delivery from recall of a fully prepared script committed to memory

The final method of delivery, **extemporaneous delivery**, involves a middle way of sorts between impromptu and manuscript delivery. You use this method when you have prepared arguments you want to advance or main ideas you want to communicate but

EXTEMPORANEOUS: Oral delivery from prepared outline of ideas (rather than complete script) that may use key words or bullet points

you don't have a scripted explanation of them. Your notes would comprise bullet points of information that you can reference as needed but you come up with the specific style of communicating the argument on the spot. Most teachers use extemporaneous delivery when teaching a lesson; they have a point they want to communicate but they don't script out the entire lesson word for word. You have probably used this method in presentations at school, work, or an organizational meeting.

Extemporaneous delivery is the preferred method for most debate situations involving advance preparation because it brings advantages that are much harder to achieve using the previous three methods. First, since the focus is on the message rather than the wording, delivery tends to be more natural and conversational with strong eye contact. People talk through rather than perform the content and are better able to showcase their personality through vocal quality, better able to connect with the audience, and better able to appear confident and in control. Extemporaneous delivery is also more flexible than manuscript or memorized, which both are limited by the prepared content. Despite this, extemporaneous delivery tends to be the least stylistically rich method because the specific wording is decided in a largely impromptu manner. To help with this, you should still practice extemporaneous argumentation when you have the opportunity to do so.

The above methods—impromptu, manuscript, memorized, and extemporaneous— represent the options arguers have when orally presenting their ideas. In some cases, there may be no choice at all. In others, you may be able to use multiple methods, such as delivering a prepared case extemporaneously but then impromptu delivery by generating responses your co-arguer's case on the spot and manuscript delivery by referencing the refutation briefs you created based on the advice in Chapter 8. But in most situations, you'll need to decide for yourself how you will deliver your arguments. Box 11.3 offers some guidelines to assist your decision-making. As you can see from the box, each method has trade-offs with the others that you need to weigh.

The purpose of selecting a delivery method is to ensure that your oral communication accomplishes your primary goals for arguing in the first place. In this effort, it's important to also consider the three elements of delivery—eye contact, vocal quality, and movement and gestures—that can enhance or detract from your argumentation.

Elements of Delivery

Eye Contact

In U.S. and European culture, oral communication should be accompanied by eye contact regardless of the status or power differential between communicants. Why is this? We tend to believe that eye contact fosters warmth, trust, and identification between speaker and audience. It is also more interesting for the audience; people are less likely to tune you out or distract themselves with their phones if you are looking right at them.

Despite the importance of eye contact, it can be difficult to find the right amount. If you have too little eye contact, you might appear dishonest, distracted, or disrespectful. Not looking at your audience at all (such as reading from a manuscript or looking at the floor) is an extreme case of poor eye contact but it might also involve quick glances between long stretches of looking at your notes or scanning the audience quickly without actually connecting with individuals. Also keep in mind that, when it comes to eye contact, there can be too much of a good thing; if you have too much eye contact, you may seem

BOX 11.3: CHOOSING DELIVERY METHODS

Use the table below to select a delivery method based on the important qualities to your oral delivery. *The options with a check mark are best if...*

	Impromptu	Manuscript	Memorized	Extemp.
You have time to prepare	x	✓	✓	✓
You are unable or unwilling to use notes	✓	x	✓	✓
You want strong eye contact and delivery	✓	x	✓	✓
You want to use specific words you've chosen	x	✓	✓	x
You want to be flexible	✓	x	x	✓
You want to sound natural	✓	x	x	✓

intimidating, insensitive, or just plain creepy. As a general rule, speakers should look at each audience member, engage him or her for 1 to 2 seconds, and then move to the next person.

Vocal Quality

Vocal quality is a second element of delivery that impacts audience perception. Vocal quality is a broad category that includes a number of features:

- **Rate**: How fast you speak

- **Volume**: How loud you speak

- **Pitch**: How high you speak

- **Variety**: How you fluctuate the above features

- **Articulation**: How clearly you speak each word

- **Pronunciation**: How you emphasize the syllables in words

- **Pauses**: How you use silent and vocalized breaks in the flow of your delivery

Because each debate situation is different, there's not a single vocal quality that will appeal to every audience. Some situations may call for a firm, low voice while others may demand a softer and higher pitched voice. Some situations may require you to speak loudly to be heard before a crowd of hundreds while others may require you to talk with those right next to you. Some situations may require you speak your ideas slowly so the audience can follow along while others may lend themselves to a fast rate of speech that builds momentum and energy. And, all of the above situations likely require variation in the vocal features to make the presentation natural and engaging for the audience.

Despite this variance, we know that audiences respond to confident vocal delivery, marked by clear articulation, proper pronunciation, and fluency with limited if any vocalized pauses. Mali's poem at the introduction of the chapter emphasized how vocal delivery should avoid verbal fillers and raising the pitch at the end of sentences because they undercut the audience's perception of you as a confident speaker.

Audiences also respond to passionate but measured delivery that demonstrates personal commitment but avoids making you appear aggressive or wild. Learn from the mistake Howard Dean made when campaigning for president during the 2004 Democratic primary; he showed his passion with a verbal yell meant to energize the crowd but it ended up sinking his candidacy for suggesting he was unable to control his emotions. Experiencing arguments through television and amplification devices (such as microphones) means that the previous need for speakers to project their voice when speaking to crowds is now alienating or aggressive rather than a sign of authority.

Finally, audiences respond to natural, conversational delivery. It is usually obvious when someone is inauthentic or performing a prepared message. Instead, your vocal quality should be natural and represent who you are. This doesn't mean you should be casual every time you orally deliver arguments; a formal presentation should certainly sound different from your conversation with friends. Rather, you shouldn't perform a pitch, volume, or rate of speech beyond your normal vocal range.

The above guidelines offer a starting point for thinking about how to use your vocal quality when orally delivering your arguments. The final element of delivery worth noting is the use of your body.

Movement and Gestures

Were you to deliver your arguments orally on the radio or a podcast, then movement and gestures are irrelevant. When your physical presence is part of oral delivery, however, movement and gestures can be impactful. While each person normally has an idiosyncratic pattern of gesturing, you can train yourself to punctuate and emphasize points you want to make through movement and gestures.

A basic guideline is to avoid distracting behavior. Fidgeting with a pen, pacing back and forth, playing with your hair, shifting your weight from side to side, touching your face, putting hands in pockets, and crinkling your notes are all things that can distract audience members and detract from your argumentation. In some ways, it would be better to stand with feet planted and arms at your sides than engage in those behaviors. Once you have control over your body, you can then add natural gestures and movement to highlight the points you want to make.

To relate the above elements of delivery—eye contact, vocal quality, and movement and gestures—to yourself, reflect on the questions in the Find Your Voice feature. The more you consider how to utilize effective delivery techniques, the stronger your argumentation skills can become.

FIND YOUR VOICE
ORAL DELIVERY

Take some time to diagnose your own delivery strengths and weaknesses: On what elements of delivery are you naturally strong? What are some ways you could harness these strengths in your oral argumentation? On what elements are you naturally weak? What are concrete steps you can take to improve these elements? Given that you will often engage in oral argumentation and debate, you should hone delivery skills to enhance your leadership, credibility, and success.

Summary

This chapter has considered how audience adaptation, style, and oral delivery each contribute to cogent argumentation. Audience adaptation involves analyzing demographics, psychographics, and situational factors and using the insights from the analysis to adjust your arguments. Style represents the distinctive quality of an argument's content when arguers choose which words to use and which figures of speech to employ. Style should strive for clarity, connection, and creativity. Finally, oral delivery involves the choices arguers make in how to speak their arguments, including the method of delivery they use and how they incorporate eye contact, vocal delivery, and movement and gestures. Using the principles outlined in this chapter will help you communicate arguments that resonate with your audience and express your individuality.

Application Exercises

Practicing Audience Adaptation: Suppose you're hungry and want to convince someone to give you $5 for a fast food meal. How could you adapt your arguments—specifically the reasons you offer—to appeal to the interests, motivations, values, etc. of the following audiences in order to convince them to give you the money:

- Your parent, guardian, or sibling

- Your best friend

- Your social media followers

- A random female stranger aged approximately 40

- A random male stranger aged approximately 22

HINT: For this exercise, make sure you are ethical in your argumentation (e.g., don't lie about what you will do with the money) and keep in mind that you are asking for a gift of $5, not a loan you will pay back.

Pulling the Pieces Together: Locate a video or transcript of Malcolm X's debate at Oxford Union on December 3, 1964, addressing the proposition that "Extremism in the defense of liberty is no vice; moderation in the pursuit of justice is no virtue" (a quotation taken from Barry Goldwater's 1964 presidential nomination acceptance speech). Apply the guidelines in this chapter to Malcolm X's arguments:

1. How well does Malcolm X *adapt to his British audience* and follow decorum? What are examples of effective adaptation? What are examples of places he could have adapted more?

2. How well does Malcolm X *use style* for clarity, connection, and creativity? What word choices stand out as significant and why? What figures of speech, if any, seem effective or ineffective in achieving his goals?

3. If you watched a video of his debate, how well does Malcolm X *deliver* his arguments? What method of delivery does he use and was this the best choice given the debate situation? What features of delivery are strong and what features need improvement?

4. What strategies and devices from Malcolm X's debating could you emulate in your own argumentation?

Key Terms

Audience Analysis 239
Audience Adaptation 239
Demographics 240
Psychographics 240
Situational Factors 241
Style 245

Verbal Hedge 246
Semantic Triangle 246
Referent 246
Symbol 246
Reference 246
Figures of Speech 248

Impromptu 252
Manuscript 253
Memorized 253
Extemporaneous 253

Endnotes

1. Taylor Mali, "Totally Like Whatever, You Know?" *Taylor Mali*, 2002, https://taylormali.com/poems/totally-like-whatever-you-know.

2. Victor Luckerson, "Here's How Facebook's News Feed Actually Works," *Time*, July 9, 2015, http://time.com/collection-post/3950525/facebook-news-feed-algorithm.

3. David G. Levasseur and Diana B. Carlin, "Egocentric Argument and the Public Sphere: Citizen Deliberations on Public Policy and Policymakers," *Rhetoric & Public Affairs* 4 (2001): 407-431; Diana B. Carlin, Dan Schill, David G. Levasseur, and Anthony S. King, "The Post-9/11 Public Sphere: Citizen Talk about the 2004 Presidential Debates," *Rhetoric & Public Affairs* 8 (2005): 617-638.

4. "ZIP Code Look-Up," *Claritas MyBestSegments*, https://segmentationsolutions.nielsen.com/mybestsegments/Default.jsp?ID=20&menuOption=ziplookup&pageName=ZIP%2BCode%2BLookup; "Discover Community Lifestyle and Demographic Information," *Esri*, http://www.esri.com/data/esri_data/ziptapestry.

5. Zach Wahls, *My Two Moms: Lessons of Love, Strength, and What Makes a Family* (New York: Gotham Books, 2012), 4-5.

6. Zach Wahls, "Zach Wahls Speaks About Family," *Iowa House Democrats*, YouTube

video, 3:00, February 1, 2011, https://youtu.be/FSQQK2Vuf9Q.

7. Steve Landsburg, "Hawkeye Talk," *The Big Questions* (blog), February 4, 2011, http://www.thebigquestions.com/2011/02/04/hawkeye-talk.

8. *Harry Potter and the Deathly Hallows, Part 2*, directed by David Yates (2011; Burbank, CA: Warner Home Video, 2011), Blu-ray Disc.

9. C. K. Ogden and I. A. Richards, *The Meaning of Meaning: A Study of the Influence of Language Upon Thought and of the Science of Symbolism* (New York: Harcourt Brace, 1923), 11.

10. Chris Graythen/Agence France Press/Getty Images, quoted in Van Jones, "Black People 'Loot' Food . . . White People 'Find' Food," *The Blog, Huffington Post*, September 1, 2005, https://www.huffingtonpost.com/van-jones/black-people-loot-food-wh_b_6614.html; Originally: Chris Graythen/Agence France Press/Getty Images, "Two residents wade through . . .," Image, *Yahoo News Photo*, August 30, 2005, http://news.yahoo.com/photo/050830/photos_ts_afp/050830071810_shxwaoma_photo1.

11. Dave Martin/Associated Press, "A young man walks through . . .," Image, *Yahoo News Photo*, August 30, 2005, https://web.archive.org/web/20050908081725/http://news.yahoo.com/photo/050830/480/ladm10208301530.

12. Jones, "Black People 'Loot' Food . . . White People 'Find' Food."

13. Kenneth Burke, *A Rhetoric of Motives*, (Berkeley, University of California Press, 1969), 43.

14. Barack Obama, quoted in Julian Pacquet, "President Embraces ObamaCare Label," *The Hill*, October 6, 2011, http://thehill.com/policy/healthcare/185877-president-embraces-obamacare-label.

15. Mary Fisher, "A Whisper of AIDS (August 19, 1992)," in *Words of a Century: The Top 100 American Speeches, 1900-1999*, ed. Stephen E. Lucas and Martin J. Medhurst (New York: Oxford University Press, 2008), 645.

16. "America's Top Fears 2017: Chapman University Survey of American Fears," *Wilkinson College of Arts, Humanities, and Social Sciences*, October 11, 2017, https://blogs.chapman.edu/wilkinson/2017/10/11/americas-top-fears-2017.

17. Sherry Turkle, *Reclaiming Conversation: The Power of Talk in a Digital Age* (New York: Penguin Press, 2015), 107.

18. Dale Hample et al., "Face-to-Face Arguing Is an Emotional Experience: Triangulating Methodologies and Early Findings," *Argumentation and Advocacy* 42 (2005): 74-93.

19. Juliann Cortese and Mihye Seo, "The Role of Social Presence in Opinion Expression during FtF and CMC Discussions," *Communication Research Reports* 29 (2012): 44-53.Box 11.1: Audience Considerations

12

FORMATS FOR EVERYDAY PUBLIC ARGUMENTATION

Following the tragic shooting at Sandy Hook Elementary School in December 2012, President Obama's administration launched an advocacy campaign, called "Now Is the Time," to tackle gun violence.[1] One significant facet addressed the stigma of mental health, promising to "launch a national conversation to increase understanding about mental health: The sense of shame and secrecy associated with mental illness prevents too many people from seeking help."[2] Kathleen Sebelius, Secretary of the U.S. Department of Health and Human Services (HHS), previewed this new initiative through an op-ed article in *USA Today* and implored her national audience to "bring mental illness out of the shadows" by participating in "a national dialogue on mental health."[3]

As part of this campaign, HHS overhauled the mentalhealth.gov website. Previously, the site prioritized technical sphere argumentation by emphasizing expert research on mental health. The redesign prioritized personal and public sphere argumentation by emphasizing how citizens can address the challenges of mental illness in their individual lives and their communities.[4] This is evident in the changing slogan of the website alone, from "Transforming the understanding and treatment of mental illness through research" to "Let's talk about it."[5] Individuals were also able to share their own stories of hope and recovery through online text and videos.[6]

The website also provided a platform for people in communities across the United States to hold conversations—or public deliberations—about promoting mental health and share resources.[7] This project emphasized the way that knowledge is formed through community debate and the sharing of personal experiences.[8]

I offer this example because it involved op-eds, online platforms, and public deliberations as everyday sites for argumentation—the very three formats we'll explore in this chapter. When we imagine debate and argumentation, we often envision an arguer speaking to an identifiable audience or a debate between two or more co-arguers in the same location. Nevertheless, the public argumentation you experience comes in multiple formats and occurs for many different reasons. By the end of this chapter, you should be able to use op-eds and letters to the editor, public online argumentation, and public deliberations by understanding the what, how, and why of each of them.

OP-EDS AND LETTERS TO THE EDITOR

What It Is: Op-Ed and Letter to the Editor Formats

Newspaper articles constitute one of the most traditional yet impactful modes of communicating public argumentation in the United States. Since before the nation even declared independence from Britain, people used newspapers to advance argumentative cases.[9] In the present day, everyday arguers still have the opportunity to publish their arguments through op-eds or letters to the editor. In fact, op-eds have the power to propel controversy about contemporary issues. Consider Ross Douthat's 2018 article, "The Redistribution of Sex,"[10] which some argued validated the incel, or involuntary celibate, movement (a movement of primarily white men "who are deeply suspicious and disparaging of women, whom they blame for denying them their right to sexual intercourse").[11] Op-eds are also a powerful way to bring attention to significant problems, which explains why many celebrities—from Taylor Swift to Tom Hanks to Angelina Jolie to George Clooney—have used op-eds to communicate their arguments.[12]

OP-ED: An argumentative newspaper article that communicates an opinion attributed to the individual author

An **op-ed** is an opinion piece advocating a proposition of the author's choosing. An op-ed differs from an **editorial** in that an editorial represents the official opinion of the newspaper's editorial board whereas an op-ed represents the viewpoint of the individual author. A **letter to the editor** (what we'll just call "letters") is a response to someone else's article, usually fewer than 500 words. Letters are the print-version equivalent of the comments section, although they have higher content requirements since the physical limits of the newspaper page mean that not all letters will be published.

EDITORIAL: An argumentative newspaper article that communicates an opinion attributed to the newspaper's editorial board

Op-eds and letters run in both print and online versions of the newspaper and follow the same general format and standard. The same is true of many online-only news and blog sites, such as *Scary Mommy* (which we encountered in Chapter 1) or the *Huffington Post*, that model the opinion pages of a newspaper. That is, even though some letters are published online, they should use the style described here rather than in the subsequent section about online argumentation.

LETTER TO THE EDITOR: An argumentative newspaper article that communicates an opinion in response to another person's article

How You Do It: Op-Ed and Letter to the Editor Style

Although op-eds differ from letters in length and purpose, they both require focus and word economy to make your case in an engaging fashion. Both formats are also part of a broader debate situation insofar as they support or oppose a proposition (serving as the article's thesis) and advance arguments concerning issues relevant to the controversy. Op-eds and letters, although opinionated, must advance cogent arguments adapted to the audience and based on verifiable information.

Nevertheless, the public sphere nature of op-eds and letters means that they have less stringent requirements for consulting and citing research when compared to argumentation in technical spheres such as classrooms, board rooms, or academic journals. In many cases, they cite other articles and online documents and use hyperlinks to directly reference those sources.

An op-ed or letter follows generally the same process of case building described in Chapter 7 but some elements of this written advocacy require more attention than other formats. In particular, structure, style, and audience adaptation are more important considerations for op-eds and letters than for other forms of advocacy. Stylistically, you need to determine the tone you want to use (e.g., matter-of-fact or aggressive) and be sure to generate a creative title; if you don't title your article, the newspaper editor will do so for you with a title that probably will not match what you envisioned. It's not enough to just go through the motions of writing an op-ed or letter. You should also convey your passion and energy in the article.

This task can be challenging for some people, especially those who are used to writing academic papers or business memos. Here are some tips to facilitate your advocacy through op-eds and letters:

- **Use your strengths.** As we discussed in Chapter 11, your style should be adapted to your strengths. Your writing should make the argumentative content come alive through narratives, figures of speech, wit, and other devices that produce an engaging read.

- **Don't get mired in explaining the proposition.** The meaning of the proposition is important but we can sometimes focus here at the expense of the arguments affirming or opposing it. Especially when advocating policy propositions, it's tempting to explain the plan in substantial detail. Doing so, however, is much less interesting and persuasive than the solvency and advantages of the proposition.

- **Emphasize functions and benefits of your advocacy.** People, as largely self-interested beings, want to know what's in it for them. Thus, tailor your arguments to the functions and benefits of your advocacy by demonstrating what your audience stands to gain from accepting your proposition.

- **Use an economy of words but also add style to inspire.** You will need to be concise in your argumentation, but you don't want to be so direct that there's nothing to interest the audience. Effective op-eds and letters find the right balance between stylistically rich and focused argumentation.

The above tips are just some of the guidelines you should follow in constructing op-eds and letters. Nevertheless, just as training in public speaking has historically been done by emulating great speakers, the best way to learn this style of advocacy is to model others. Read others' op-eds and, as you do, pay attention to the features that stand out to you as particularly cogent to use in your own writing. Along those lines, the Build Your Skill prompt invites you to evaluate an opinion article you've already encountered.

Why You Should Do It: Op-Ed and Letter to the Editor Benefits

Writing an op-ed or letter can be valuable for a number of personal, professional, and public reasons. Here are some of the benefits you might gain from participating in this format of everyday argumentation:

- **Affecting change in society**. Writing articles on significant topics is one way to produce societal change. In some cases, you might address local concerns through a community newspaper. In other cases, you might tackle state or national problems in a paper with wider readership. Some of the examples earlier show this potential.

BUILD YOUR SKILL
EVALUATING AN OP-ED

Evaluate Maria Guido's *Scary Mommy* op-ed in Chapter 1 using the guidelines above to answer the following questions:

1. How well did Guido emphasize the reasons for accepting the proposition, particularly as adapted to the audience's interests, values, etc.?

2. How well did Guido include concise but engaging content?

3. Did Guido's title effectively pique your interest and capture the main gist of the article?

4. What are the major strengths of the article and what major weaknesses would you change?

- **Showcasing your expertise and experience.** In addition to creating change, op-eds and letters emphasize your expertise or experience. By addressing topics related to your personal interests, op-eds and letters are an empowering format for communicating argumentation.

- **Being taken seriously.** Whereas you could argue through the comments feature on a website or by creating your own blog (as we'll discuss in the next section), audience members will take your argumentation more seriously in an op-ed or letter because they know that it is a more rigorous process to be published. This gives your arguments a wider impact.

- **Reaching numerous demographics.** Whereas online forums tend to be narrowly drawn, focusing on niche interests, newspapers speak to a more general readership. Writing an op-ed or letter, then, enables you to reach a diverse audience. And, newspapers are finding ways to adapt to the online environment despite concerns that they are a dying mode of communication in the digital age.

FIND YOUR VOICE
OP-EDS AND LETTERS

Have you ever written an op-ed or letter? Why have or haven't you? Rather than discounting them as antiquated modes of argumentation, consider why you might write one and where you might submit it for publication. Chances are there is a local or regional paper in your community or at your school that has an opinion section. Depending on your goals, op-eds and letters may be a productive mode of argumentation.

While there are numerous benefits to pursuing this argumentation format, you may face some challenges in the process. We'll discuss three significant ones here. First, newspaper editors serve as gatekeepers who decide what information is "newsworthy" or merits publication. Whereas the editorial process adds legitimacy, getting through the gate can sometimes be challenging; not every submitted article will be published, and it is possible that you'll be rejected more than once. This can be demoralizing, especially if you've put in substantial time crafting your arguments. You need to decide whether the increased credibility and reach of your published article is worth the potential rejection.

A second, related challenge is space. Op-eds and letters often have strict word limits that constrain your options. For instance, *The Washington Post* limits op-eds to 800 words, enough for maybe one or two cogent arguments on a topic, and only 200 words for a letter.[13] *The New York Times* is not much better, allowing up to 1,200 words for op-eds.[14] The space constraint may be particularly noticeable in comparison to other modes of everyday public argumentation. If you create your own blog, there's no limit to the number of words you include (see Mr. Money Mustache's full post from Chapter 9, for instance). Similarly, if you have a face-to-face debate, you get to set the parameters and could even go for a filibuster, talking all night and into the day. Thus, the space limitations for op-eds and letters may feel restrictive.

The final challenge to argumentation through op-eds and letters is significance. Even though they have more credibility than other outlets and even though they have a built-in readership that you won't need to generate yourself, the opinion page still involves a lot of clutter competing against others and is often buried in the middle section of the paper. Op-eds rarely go "viral"—although they do occasionally find circulation on Facebook and Twitter—and those that do tend to be authored by people who are experts or widely known.

Despite the challenges, writing op-eds and letters can be a rewarding opportunity to communicate your voice and generate change in your community. They provide a historically tested format for argumentation in everyday life, especially when compared to public online argumentation, the next format we'll consider.

PUBLIC ONLINE ARGUMENTATION

What It Is: Public Online Argumentation Formats

The boundaries of public online argumentation are harder to define than op-eds and letters because the Internet is so expansive and diverse. Our label, **public online argumentation**, refers to argumentation that exists exclusively online and is communicated through public websites. The word "public" in the definition requires the site to enable but not require open access. Thus, sites that have privacy settings allowing you to block non-followers/friends (e.g., Twitter, Instagram, Facebook, YouTube, Reddit) would still be sites for public online argumentation because they have the option to disable those settings for open access. However, sites that require membership to the site or group (e.g., a class discussion board through an online platform like Canvas, Moodle, or Blackboard) would be excluded from public online argumentation because they are only accessible to subscribers and members rather than the general public. Even with this definition, there are still dozens of different sites you might use for public online argumentation, both to generate your own content and to respond to the content of others.

PUBLIC ONLINE ARGUMENTATION: Argumentation on sites that are exclusively online and that enable open access

Just as the sites for public online argumentation are diverse, so too are the forms of engagement. Here are some of the most common forms:

- *Blog/Vlog:* A blog, short for "weblog," is a website featuring frequently updated commentary and narration. A vlog, short for video blog, is essentially a blog in video format. Because blogs started as digital journals or diaries, entries are organized chronologically, and the content for a blog or vlog tends to be generated by one or a few people. Their length, layout, and structure frequently lack restrictions or rules and are thus largely user-generated. For example, Greg Mankiw's case for eliminating the penny in Chapter 7 and Mr. Money Mustache's case against Bitcoin in Chapter 9 differed substantially in terms of scope and format even though both came from individually maintained blogs.

- *Post:* A post refers to user-generated content shared through a particular web platform. Blogs do involve posts, but posts are also a feature of many additional sites ranging from social media to informational news sites. The length, layout, and structure of posts are constrained by each particular site. James Harrison's Instagram photo about participation trophies from Chapter 4 is an example of a post as are Donald Trump's tweets from Chapter 8.

- *Forum:* A forum or discussion board enables people to engage in non-synchronous conversation or argumentation. Forums are usually dedicated to a particular topic or sub-topic. General forum sites, such as Reddit, include a variety of sub-topics but there are also more niche forum sites, such as RebelScum.com (a forum for Star Wars collectors), that cater to specific interests. Forums have threads that help organize the content into sub-topics or categories. Change My View, which we discussed in Chapter 3, is one forum you've encountered.

- *Chat:* A chat is similar to a forum in layout except it enables people to engage in synchronous, real-time conversation. Chats are usually dedicated to special interests but there are also general chat sites. You're probably familiar with instant messaging or text messaging as forms of chat but they're private nature excludes them from consideration here.

- *Comments:* Comments are a kind of post but they are designed as a response to someone else's original post and their content is constrained in this regard. Many different kinds of sites, from blogs to social media to informational sites like ESPN, provide the option for comments.

FIND YOUR VOICE
PUBLIC ONLINE ARGUMENTATION

Reflect on your online argumentation: What sites and modes of public online argumentation do you commonly use? What motivates you to read and/ or participate through those sites? Do you tend to generate your own arguments, engage the arguments of others, or both? What characterizes your style of argumentation there, as compared to offline formats for argumentation? The more you monitor when, how, and why you engage online, the more productive it can become.

How You Do It: Public Online Argumentation Style

The diversity of public online argumentation makes it difficult to clearly define its style. In fact, it sometimes seems like anything goes in an online environment. It is also true that the practices for argumentation on one site, such as Facebook, may differ substantially from the practices on another, such as Instagram or YikYak. In fact, a Google search can yield various etiquette guides for the major social media sites, such as the "34 Unwritten Rules of Facebook" or the "13 Golden Rules of Twitter."[15]

Nevertheless, a few features do distinguish the style of public online argumentation from other forms of everyday argumentation. First, public online argumentation tends to be shorter, often providing a single support and claim. This is often by choice rather than necessity, presuming that people are less likely to read and engage material if it is longer. Thus, *The New York Times* limit of 1,200 words for op-eds seems enormous compared to Twitter's iconic 140-character limit (now 280), which afforded approximately 30 words to make your case.[16] Additionally, social media and our fast-paced information environment has made brevity a virtue. Telling someone that his or her email is too long, for instance, is sometimes a justifiable defense for simply not reading it. Creating "tl;dr" summaries at the start or end of posts converts complex cases into simplified soundbites. This also helps explain why Donald Trump Jr.'s tweet about Skittles from the start of Chapter 10 included an image (it didn't count against the 140 characters) and offered a single analogy argument.

Even though public online argumentation tends to be briefer, it also tends to be less organized and more stream-of-consciousness. When posting arguments online, people often write content as it occurs to them without taking time to edit it into an organized case. Poor spelling and grammar are more common in public online argumentation than in more formal modes such as op-eds. As a result, public online argumentation is often more challenging to interpret in relation to claim and support structures. James Harrison's Instagram post about participation trophies illustrates this style feature; it was challenging to diagram the post in Chapter 4 because he didn't argue in a clear case structure like you might find in op-eds and letters.

Finally, public online argumentation is hypertextual. The prefix, "hyper," in hypertext means that the text is overactive. It refers to how online communication lacks a definitive start or end because the links to other communication expand the text. You've probably seen this potential anytime you've gotten sucked into Facebook or other sites where you click away on links or scroll through a never-ending feed. This quality is unique to online communication because print and televisual messages have clear boundaries and involve a different mode of interaction. Even choose-your-own-adventure books are constrained by the start and end constructed by the author.

The hypertextual nature of online argumentation means that arguers are able to reference a wealth of information through hyperlinks. At the same time, public online argumentation tends to use the loosest standards for quality information. In Chapter 5, we explored how online information is often low quality and people may not take much time to research topics beyond a basic Google search. Thus, while online argumentation can link to a variety of places—relying on material from other sites to develop the arguments—those places may not be credible or dependable.

When creating your own public online argumentation, you should heed the following guidelines:

- **Choose your sites carefully.** Twitter is good for brief statements. Instagram is good for sharing photos and captions. Facebook is good for connecting with people on a personal level. LinkedIn is good for connecting with people on a professional level. Knowing the value and focus of these sites (and others) will help you argue through social media in a more productive fashion rather than trying to force each site to be something it isn't.

- **Follow the rules.** Many legitimate sites for public online argumentation will have clearly defined rules for appropriate conduct. Numerous sub-reddits, for instance, concretely define the format and content allowed in a post. Additionally, Facebook has a list of Rights and Responsibilities that you must heed.[17] If you violate the rules, your post will likely be deleted, and, if you break the rules numerous times, you might be banned altogether.

- **Be ethical and accountable.** An argumentation tactic isn't ethical just because there isn't a rule forbidding it. A third guideline then is to be ethical and accountable. Whenever you post something anonymously, ask yourself if you would stand by it were your name attached (after all, your Internet service provider knows it was you). Whenever you post something you think is "private" (e.g., a tweet in a protected account or a text message to a single person or a Snapchat message that you are certain will disappear after a few seconds), ask yourself if you would stand by it if it were screenshotted and went public. We have the feeling that we're alone when we engage in online argumentation but that can't be farther from the truth, a potentially dangerous combination that could impact your everyday life.

- **Be cautious and use critical thinking.** Even if you personally use the most ethical public online argumentation, other people will not. Research shows that people are less authentic in online conversation, especially because they tend to view social media as a performance that illustrates their best selves, and some people will intentionally manipulate others to get their way.[18] The solution is not to sink to their level or disengage from online argumentation entirely but to use caution and critical thinking. The more vigilant you are and the more you research information, the more you can impact the overall quality of the conversation.

- **Stop and reflect to avoid emotional and personal responses.** Just as you may sometimes be the victim of online harassment, you may also be the perpetrator. This often happens when we write a post quickly and submit it as soon as possible. We often say things in the heat of the moment because we allow our emotions to cloud our judgment or because we take things personally. There can be strong personal and professional consequences for this; I'm sure you could easily find a dozen examples of people who were scorned, fired, or arrested for things they posted online. Because you are publicly communicating your ideas, you should stop and reflect to avoid saying something you'll later regret and being another example of online shaming. Also keep in mind that the higher quantity of posts, the lower impact for each post. People who overshare or post too frequently actually undermine the force of any given message. Thus, the more you exercise restraint, the more powerful and effective your argumentation can become.

BUILD YOUR SKILL
EVALUATING TWEETS

Evaluate Adria Richards's tweets in Chapter 3 and Donald Trump's tweets in Chapter 8 using the guidelines above. In particular, consider the following questions:

1. Should the arguers have used Twitter to communicate their arguments or would a different forum have been more appropriate?

2. How well did the arguers follow the (explicit and implicit) rules of Twitter?

3. How well did the arguers avoid emotional and personal responses?

4. What are the major strengths of the tweets, and what major weaknesses would you change?

Why You Should Do It: Public Online Argumentation Benefits

Given the cautions of the previous section, it may seem best to avoid online public argumentation entirely, but, in today's society, such argumentation is almost a necessity. Nevertheless, don't just do it because everyone else is. Instead, reflect on the benefits of engagement and choose your sites for engagement carefully based on what you hope to accomplish. At a general level, here are some benefits of public online argumentation as compared to other formats:

- **Communicating immediately.** Very few forms of *public* communication are as immediate as online communication. If you wanted to get an audience for a public speech, for instance, you'd need to advertise it weeks ahead of time and secure a space. If you wanted to get an audience for an op-ed, you'd need to submit it and get editorial approval. If you wanted to buy a TV advertisement slot, you'd need to create the ad well in advance. But, if you wanted to post an online video advertisement to YouTube, you can do so virtually in real time, enabling efficiency and productivity. Nevertheless, this can be a double-edged sword, allowing quick communication but also potentially undermining its quality.[19]

- **Arguing on your own terms.** There is little cost or barrier to entry for public online argumentation. It is true that you must have Internet access (something you shouldn't take for granted), but that's about it. There are also few gatekeepers apart from occasional moderators who must approve posts. This means you are largely in control of your own argumentation, and, on some sites, there is no one to edit or censor you. Finally, some people feel more comfortable and safe arguing online because they are removed from the other participants and, in some cases, anonymous.[20] This freedom can be very beneficial, especially compared to less accessible modes of argumentation such as op-eds, books, or public speaking.

- **Fostering relationships with people.** Many opportunities for public online argumentation are through social media, which connect the arguer to others. Consequently, public online argumentation can help you forge relationships with others that extend beyond the communicative exchange. Friend circles, followers, connections, and the like are all ways that online argumentation emphasizes relationships as a fundamental feature of engagement. In some cases, people may form deep bonds despite never having met or orally spoken to one another.

- **Engaging people you might not otherwise.** Not only does public online argumentation foster relationships but you can also encounter people you otherwise would not meet. You can argue with someone on a different continent or from a different culture, expanding your horizons. You can also argue with people who believe the same thing as you, providing encouragement and security. Especially for those who may be marginalized in their physical community, finding a digital community could provide safety and comfort. All of this, of course, is possible in face-to-face interactions but it is harder to achieve and limited by geography.

As with other public argumentation formats, online argumentation presents its own set of challenges. The discussion so far has already hinted at a few of them, but we'll discuss three explicitly. First is the challenge of disembodiment. Because electronic communication is disconnected from physical bodies, it means that people are unable to respond to feedback and cues from co-arguers and audience members. When you see someone become upset or hear them fall silent in response to your argumentation, you might restrain yourself or seek to clarify but you don't have that luxury in online environments.[21] Additionally, disembodiment means that people can be anyone they want to be. People are often anonymous arguing behind generic screennames and avatars and can also fabricate identities that don't match their "real" person. These factors may limit the quality and effectiveness of online argumentation.

INTERNET TROLL:
A person who intentionally employs non-cogent arguments

Disembodiment relates to a second challenge: trolls.[22] A **troll**, according to the *Oxford English Dictionary*, is "a person who posts deliberately erroneous or antagonistic messages to a newsgroup or similar forum with the intention of eliciting a hostile or corrective response."[23] Trolls are particularly relevant to argumentation because trolling frequently involves the use of non-cogent arguments (fallacies, *ad hominem* attacks, etc.) to rile up participants. You likely have encountered trolls at some point in your online life and have seen how they can undermine productive discourse. According to one study in 2014, 70 percent of 18 to 24-year-olds had experienced some form of online harassment.[24] Unfortunately, the incentives of power and prestige attached to online participation promote trolling and, thus, experts believe the problem is likely to persist.[25] As Joel Stein explained in *Time* magazine, "factors like anonymity, invisibility, a lack of authority and not communicating in real time strip away the mores society spent millennia building."[26] The best solution in such situations is to just ignore trolls, blocking them as appropriate.[27]

The third and final challenge is that of audience. Even if the content is cogent and troll-free, you aren't guaranteed a readership. There is so much clutter in cyberspace that not all of your Twitter followers or Facebook friends will even see your posts, let alone read and consider them. Thus, public online argumentation provides the *potential* for massive reach—the holy grail of going viral—but the actuality is much smaller in most cases.

Although there are clear risks to public online argumentation, people are likely to use it as a go-to format for argumentation because of the benefits and because it requires few skills and resources. It ultimately provides a platform for many people who might otherwise lack the opportunity or courage to argue.

PUBLIC DELIBERATION

What It Is: Public Deliberation Format

Public deliberation, the third format for everyday argumentation we'll address, is probably the most unfamiliar to you. This is because deliberation happens under specific conditions that strive for productive conversation. The National Coalition for Dialogue and Deliberation defines deliberation as "the kind of reasoning and talking we do when a difficult decision has to be made, a great deal is at stake, and there are competing options or approaches we might take. At the heart of deliberation is weighing possible actions and decisions carefully by examining their costs and consequences in light of what is most valuable to us."[28] Deliberation relies on argumentation to better understand the problem, explore possible solutions, and decide courses of action. Although public deliberation is designed for community problem-solving in public spheres, the lessons here apply to non-public deliberation in professional contexts, such as organizational meetings.

But deliberation is not appropriate for every single problem that exists; rather, it best addresses "**wicked problems.**" The adjective, wicked, refers to problems that are particularly vicious or tricky because they defy a single, easy solution taken by a single agent. Wicked problems thus require the effort of multiple stakeholders and have a range of options with their own advantages and disadvantages.[29] By stakeholder, we mean those who have a vested interest in and are impacted by the problem and any actions to address it.

For instance, healthcare in the United States is a wicked problem because as soon as one approach was implemented (the Affordable Care Act), it generated another set of concerns and some stakeholders who felt it was the wrong approach called on other agents (state governments, private corporations, the judicial system, etc.) to take action. Declining profits in a company is another example of a wicked problem because numerous factors, from sales and marketing to employee wages and benefits to electricity use, impact profits and there is not a magic potion or single actor that can easily fix the problem. Use the Find Your Voice feature to consider wicked problems in your experience. Because we can't easily address wicked problems, slowing down to discuss them in detail can help ensure we know what's gained and lost with each viable approach to it. Thus, wicked problems are ripe for the process of deliberation.

In the United States, public deliberations occur in communities and organizations across the country. The example at the start of this chapter about the national conversation on mental health is just one example of a public deliberation initiative. The National

PUBLIC DELIBERATION: Argumentation aimed at managing a wicked problem by weighing advantages and disadvantages to various approaches

WICKED PROBLEM: A problem that defies easy solution and has multiple viable approaches, each with advantages and disadvantages

FIND YOUR VOICE
WICKED PROBLEMS

Using the definition of wicked problems, brainstorm a significant wicked problem from your everyday life (it can be related to any sphere or facet of life). What makes it a *wicked* problem rather than a *normal* problem? What potential approaches to the problem come to mind? Were you to convene a deliberation for it, which stakeholders would you want to participate? Keep this wicked problem in mind as a real-life site for deliberation while you read through the discussion of deliberation below.

Issues Forums Institute (NIFI) is a frontrunner in promoting the practice of public deliberation, having generated a variety of framing guides that outline various approaches to a single wicked problem that communities can request to convene their own community deliberations.

Some U.S. states have also experimented with public deliberation in relation to ballot initiatives. For example, for the Oregon's Citizens' Initiative Review Commission (CIRC), "a panel of randomly-selected and demographically-balanced voters is brought together from across the state to fairly evaluate a ballot measure. The panel hears directly from campaigns for and against the measure and calls upon policy experts during the multi-day public review."[30] Once the panelists have learned from the various stakeholders, they create a pamphlet with important facts as well as arguments for and against the ballot initiative. This pamphlet, created through the process of public deliberation, is subsequently distributed to all voters in the state to assist their decision making.

Both the NIFI and CIRC promote formats of everyday argumentation that look quite different from a typical debate. Whereas a debate is organized around a single proposition and is designed to persuade an audience, deliberation is useful for generating options and considering which solution, among many, is the best approach. Additionally, participants in a deliberation serve as arguers, co-arguers, and audience members; it's expected that everyone will speak and listen. This is because deliberation strives to empower the audience to make an informed determination of how best to proceed.

While there are dozens of different models for public dialogue and deliberation,[31] our focus in this section will be on the NIFI model. The NIFI model is organized around a framing guide that explains a concrete problem and offers three to five possible approaches to addressing it. The approaches are worded generally to encompass many possible agents and actions rather than focusing on clearly defined policy propositions. This enables creativity from the participants to envision multiple concrete actions that might fall beneath each general approach.

The deliberation itself involves small groups of people (usually no more than 12) systematically discussing the various approaches and using supporting materials from the framing guide and personal experiences. A single, deliberative event will have multiple tables of face-to-face conversations, each with a facilitator who leads the participants through it and a notetaker who records the ideas for reporting back to the relevant stakeholders. Facilitators are not speakers in a traditional sense but rather they ask questions to prompt the participants' engagement with the problem and the various approaches to it.

Box 12.1 outlines the general format for a NIFI-sponsored, deliberative forum. As you can see there, a deliberation commonly begins with a welcome and discussion of the ground rules for argumentation. These rules usually ensure everyone has an opportunity to participate and that the arguments follow particular ethical guidelines. Because deliberations are about empowering community members, the next step is often to discuss personal stakes in the problem. Participants explain how they are connected to the problem, what motivated them to participate in the deliberation, and what they hope to accomplish. This helps foster investment in the process and lets the facilitator better understand the interests of the participants.

The heart of the deliberation is stages three to five, when the participants systematically explore the advantages, disadvantages, trade-offs, and values of each approach. Since there is no perfect solution, the participants need to think carefully about what drawbacks they are willing to accept. For example, were you to deliberate about the wicked problem of climate change, you would need to decide how willing you are to change your lifestyle now by paying more for sustainable goods or giving up convenience to reduce the negative impacts of climate change. This is an example of a trade-off that puts numerous values—financial wellbeing, convenience, security, and safety—in conflict. While all are desirable in theory, deliberation encourages participants to rank them in concrete rather than abstract terms by finding common ground and learning from each other's knowledge.

After the participants have discussed the approaches, the facilitator will then conclude the deliberation and, as appropriate, encourage the participants to generate action steps. Action might involve wholesale implementation of one of the approaches but often participants call for baby steps, such as putting together a task force to study implementing an approach or encouraging future research on the causes of the problem. Finally, the participants report their conclusions to the other people at the deliberation and facilitators often compile a written report to distribute to relevant stakeholders.

The Everyday Life Example in this chapter illustrates what framing a public deliberation might look like. The U.S. Substance Abuse and Mental Health Services Administration (SAMHSA) created this framework in 2013 for the mental health deliberations discussed at the start of the chapter. The guide offered five approaches or "views" in

BOX 12.1: PUBLIC DELIBERATION STRUCTURE

1. Welcome and ground rules

2. Personal stakes or investment in the problem

3. Discussion of approach 1

4. Discussion of approach 2

5. Discussion of approach 3

6. Wrap-up and action steps

7. Reporting out

Everyday Life Example 12.1

SAMHSA, Community Conversations about Mental Health Discussion Guide, 2013[33]

1 **View 1: Reduce negative attitudes and raise awareness about the importance of mental health and**
2 **wellness**

3 *According to this view*, we should promote mental health as a key component of overall health and
4 wellness. This will help make it more acceptable to talk about mental health and seek help if needed.
5 We cannot improve the mental health of young people if we do not improve how people view mental
6 health and mental illness, promote acceptance, eliminate misperceptions, and reduce negative
7 attitudes associated with mental illnesses. By making health and wellness an inspiring, positive goal for
8 individuals and communities, we can create an environment that supports the changes we seek.

9 **View 2: Support people in our community in mental health crisis situations**

10 *According to this view*, we can teach others how to respond to people in crisis and provide responders
11 with the knowledge and skills to address their needs. When family members, loved ones, friends,
12 neighbors, and community members learn how to be helpful when a young person is going through
13 a difficult time, they can help that young person avoid isolation and engage in the solution. The entire
14 community benefits when first responders, schools, health care providers, parents, and peers know
15 how to engage a young person in crisis. This will help provide supports to people who are experiencing
16 these conditions for the first time, help build greater understanding and acceptance in the community,
17 and reduce crisis situations associated with mental illnesses.

18 **View 3: Help young people access local mental health supports and services to meet their needs**

19 *According to this view*, we can help young people and their families access mental health supports and
20 services when they need them. Many different kinds of groups can be involved: public, private, nonprofit,
21 and faith-based. Multiple youth-serving systems can work together to meet the needs of young people
22 and their families, including schools, law enforcement, child care providers, and others. Efforts between
23 systems need to be coordinated, and families and young people should be engaged in deciding how services
24 are provided. We also need to harness the power of youth and families to help one another by strengthening
25 peer-to-peer and family supports and resources in the community. To support and sustain these efforts, we
26 need to look for ways to take advantage of existing resources in the community.

27 **View 4: Build connections throughout the community**

28 *According to this view*, implementing multiple strategies will require us to mobilize all the different
29 resources in our community. Other youth-serving systems (juvenile justice, child welfare, early
30 childhood), schools, health care providers, civic groups, individual volunteers, and many other people
31 and organizations can all pitch in. By working together, we will also build the social connections that
32 promote positive mental health. Research shows that the largest risk factor for serious illness is lack
33 of social connectedness. By focusing on this issue, we can strengthen our community and help address
34 health and mental health in many ways.

35 **View 5: Help youth, families, and communities promote mental health and prevent or delay the onset**
36 **of mental illnesses**

37 *According to this view*, we must focus efforts on activities that promote mental health and prevent
38 the development of mental illness. We need to focus on interventions designed to prevent or delay
39 the onset of mental illness or substance use disorders. Child development and early life experiences
40 are important, and we can help young children who are at risk of developing mental, emotional, and
41 behavioral problems. We need to look for sustainable ways to support the needs of children and youth
42 through prevention programs, early intervention strategies, and other activities that promote healthy
43 childhood development and create positive learning experiences.

Source: Substance Abuse and Mental Health Services Administration, Community Conversations About Mental Health Discussion Guide, HHS Publication No. SMA-13-4765, Substance Abuse and Mental Health Services Administration, 2013, 6, https://store.samhsa .gov/shin/con-tent//SMA13-4764/SMA13-4764.pdf.

response to the framing question, "How can we best support the mental health of young people?"[32] The explanation offers a general synopsis of the five views, but it does not indicate their advantages and disadvantages. Keep in mind, though, that this framework is a small piece of a much longer discussion guide.

As you read over the framework, consider whether the five views offer a viable agenda for discussion and argumentation: Do they represent broad approaches to the problem to spur conversation rather than narrowly focused policy propositions? Do they prompt consideration of productive trade-offs? If so, what are the key trade-offs? Do they overlap in unproductive ways? Are any views missing from the list? Are five views the right number, too many, or too few?

SAMHSA's framework is a useful starting point for a conversation on the topic of mental health because it addresses a clear wicked problem and encourages the participants in the deliberation to identify the best way to allocate resources in tackling it: prevention, treatment, response capacity, etc. The views also represent general approaches rather than concrete actions, enabling participants to consider how individuals, corporations, organizations, and government entities might all play a role in addressing mental health among youth.

However, five views are likely too many for a productive deliberation because they limit the focus of the participants. In this particular case, the five views could have been condensed into three or four to make the discussion more manageable. Views one and five, for instance, both seem to emphasize actions that reduce the stigma of mental illness, thereby ensuring that people take active steps toward mental health (lines 4-7, 41-43). Eliminating this overlap would help focus the conversation. Despite this shortcoming, this example illustrates how a deliberation uses argumentation to address a problem in a fundamentally different way than a traditional debate between two sides.

Even though deliberation is a rare form of everyday argumentation, you may be in deliberative settings more often than you realize. Learning about deliberation is not only useful for structured conversations in public life but also for leading and participating in conversations about wicked problems in your personal and professional lives. Workplaces and organizations might use deliberation at meetings to ensure all participants have a voice and that all options get fair consideration. Your family might use deliberation if it has to make a challenging decision about how to spend its money. An organization to which you belong might use deliberation if it is deciding on an activity or fundraiser to organize. In these situations, deliberation strategies are relevant to everyday life. And since the argumentative strategies in these situations often differ from debate, let's explore this style of argumentation.

How You Do It: Public Deliberation Style

Our discussion of public deliberation style will focus at two levels: style as facilitator and style as participant. It is probable that you'll participate in deliberations more often than you'll facilitate them, but there are often opportunities for facilitative leadership in group settings (particularly the workplace)[34] so it's important to be prepared for both situations. We'll first address facilitation before turning to participation.

Facilitating Public Deliberation

Public deliberation facilitators are usually concerned more with the quality of the process than the content or outcome. If you have ever run an organizational meeting, you likely understand that this means facilitators believe the best decision will be made if certain conditions for discussion are furnished and followed. We'll explore four important conditions here:

1. **Neutral framing.** Good facilitation begins with a good framework that outlines the options neutrally. The mental health framework in the Everyday Life Example illustrated this neutral approach insofar as it did not imply a "right" or "best" view. Recall that participants in the deliberation should reach a decision based on weighing the information and trade-offs. This is one substantial difference from a debate because debaters tend to be invested in a particular outcome or proposition.

2. **Probing and focused questions**. Facilitators should prepare a variety of questions to help participants interrogate the approaches to solving the problem. Vague questions like "What do you think of approach 1" don't focus mental energy because the responses could veer in multiple directions. Rather, more directed questions like "What about approach 1 don't you like?" or "How does approach 1 promote things of value to you?" are more useful.

3. **Equal involvement**. Effective facilitation promotes equal involvement among all participants and for all options. If one person dominates the discussion, it hampers shared decision making. If some people are not invested or involved, it limits the perspectives that are heard. If some options get more time than others, it prevents full and fair consideration of the choices. Creating balance between participants and options ensures the best outcome of a deliberation.

4. **Accountability**. Finally, good facilitators, like good arguers, promote accountability and take responsibility for the outcomes of the deliberation. As we discussed in the context of online argumentation, the lack of accountability often leads to trolling, personal attacks, and conflict. Conversely, deliberation promotes personal responsibility for the quality of discourse and the outcome of the deliberation. As a facilitator, accountability means in part that you have a purpose for convening the deliberation and that you report the results to stakeholders. When facilitators model accountability, they encourage it from participants as well.

Creating these conditions for deliberation ideally fosters a comfortable space for participants to share honestly and to feel invested in making a difference.

Participating in Public Deliberation

Whereas facilitators are unlikely to advance arguments apart from establishing the significance of the problem and the importance of solving it, participants in a public deliberation should offer cogent arguments when discussing the various approaches. And even though facilitators guide the conversation, participants share responsibility for the outcome. If participants use a competitive or manipulative stance, rely on bad information, or don't follow the lead of the facilitator, they may undermine the overall quality of the discussion.

A few features distinguish argumentation in a public deliberation from other formats. First, argumentation often starts with but can't be limited to personal experience. This is quite different from the role of personal experience in op-eds, letters, and online argumentation. For op-eds and letters, personal experience is an ancillary feature that may be supplemental support for a broader claim. For public online argumentation, personal experience often drives the content, and people are unwilling to take the perspective of others. However, deliberation balances personal experience with other considerations. It begins with personal stakes but the conversation will eventually need to consider if people's experiences are representative of most and, in cases where they aren't, how to weigh different people's experiences.

A second quality of argumentation in public deliberation is the promotion of communal knowledge. Communal knowledge is the idea that we all arrive at a stronger understanding of something when we share information rather than withholding it to have an upper hand. This is why it's so significant that participants in a deliberation are both arguer and audience member; they are invested in solving the problem and, thus, should be invested in learning from one another to reach the best outcome. When you participate in a deliberative discussion, you may have a preferred outcome but you also recognize that you don't know everything about the topic. Sometimes we may dispute facts in a deliberation but this is all part of the process of reaching a decision. Thus, unlike the tendency during a debate to defend our side to the bitter end, deliberation involves sharing information and personal growth.

Below are some tips to guide your involvement in deliberations. It should be evident that deliberation requires you to participate and listen in unfamiliar ways.

1. **Be honest**. We may often perform in communication settings by saying what we think other want to hear. In a deliberation, however, honesty is necessary to fostering community and arriving at satisfying outcomes for everyone.

2. **Be open-minded**. Even if you are strongly supportive of a particular outcome or stance, you should try to learn from others and take different people's perspectives. Being open-minded allows you to be a full participant in the process.

3. **Use active listening**. Both facilitators and participants need to use active listening. It's often tempting while others are speaking to be thinking of the next thing to say or the argument you want to advance but doing so will dilute the quality of the discussion and you may find that your own arguments are not addressing the conversation as it evolves.

4. **Take ownership**. While deliberation facilitators are invested in the process, the participants are invested in the outcome. Thus, as a participant, it's important to take ownership over the quality of the outcome by putting forth a good faith effort to find the best solution.

Why You Should Do It: Public Deliberation Benefits

Although public deliberation is not as common as other formats for argumentation, it is a useful mode for resolving wicked problems. Box 12.2 cites the benefits of public deliberation that the NIFI has identified, all related to the outcomes of the deliberation.

BOX 12.2: OUTCOMES OF PUBLIC DELIBERATION

From the National Issues Forums Institute:[35]

1. Deeper understanding of the issue and the tensions within it

2. Insight and awareness into different points of view

3. Which tradeoffs your group is willing to accept—or not

4. A starting point for citizen action, both individual and collective

5. Effective guidance for policymakers

Beyond the ability to resolve problems, there are numerous additional benefits to public deliberation:

- **Forming and strengthening relationships**. Because deliberation involves sharing with and learning from others, it is a fundamentally communal process. Thus, deliberation can help you better understand people in your community and, in turn, strengthen your relationships with them. This benefit is harder to achieve in a traditional debate model of op-eds and public online argumentation because the focus there is more on your own stance and you don't have a built-in process to promote understanding of other people's perspectives.

- **Increasing commitment and action**. People who feel they contribute to the process of solving problems show stronger trust and commitment, even if they disagree with the outcome, than if they were not part of the process.[36] You can likely understand this if you consider scenarios in which rules were imposed on you by others versus scenarios in which you and others generated rules together. Because public participation fosters commitment, it makes sense that some communities use deliberation when deciding how to manage public services, such as the deliberations in the United Kingdom on Brexit or how to fund the National Health Service.[37]

- **Generating communal knowledge**. Communal knowledge, which we discussed earlier, is another benefit of participating in deliberation. We tend to view argumentation as goal-oriented, which is often understandable, but we shouldn't underestimate the importance of outcomes related to knowledge. Thus, even if a deliberative discussion fails to spur action (see the challenges below), the formation of communal knowledge is itself a valuable end for improving community life. Such outcomes are harder to achieve through adversarial formats of argumentation that don't focus on sharing and learning.

- **Developing leadership skills**. Finally, deliberation helps you hone arguing, facilitating, and notetaking skills that can enhance your leadership ability. As we've discussed, deliberation flexes different argument muscles than other formats due to its unique style. Facilitation and notetaking skills are an especially valuable benefit to participating in public deliberation because, as we discussed earlier, they are transportable to situations in which you must lead a group in problem-solving.

As with the previous formats for everyday argumentation, public deliberation involves challenges. One substantial obstacle to deliberative efficacy is getting people to show up and participate. Unless there are incentives for attending a deliberation, the people who show up tend to be those who are strongly invested in one of the approaches or those who are generally active in the community. These are valuable people to have at the table but they aren't necessarily representative of all community members. Thus, facilitators need to be quite active in generating advance interest and/or ensuring that participants take the perspective of stakeholders who aren't present.

A second challenge to deliberation is that it may oversimplify complex problems and solutions.[38] For example, facilitators might offer two advantages and two disadvantages to each approach in order to create balance and neutrality but doing so might overlook actual differences between the approaches (it's possible that one approach has substantially more benefits than the others). Additionally, it's often the case that approaches get reduced to a single action and agent (often local or national government), rather than allowing participants to think outside the box and generate creative solutions. This is why effective facilitators allow space for people to exceed the boundaries of the original framing and encourage deep rather than surface-level engagement with the approaches.

A final challenge to public deliberation, as opposed to debate, is that the end does not translate easily into action. Whereas debates often end in "yes" or "no" vote on a pre-determined proposition, deliberation is more open-ended and relies more on the initiative of the participants to move forward. Additionally, in a group setting, it is common for social loafing to occur, in which people avoid responsibility for solving the problem because they assume others will do so. This latter reason is often cited by students who despise group work in classes. As you can imagine, loafing can become a more significant hurdle when it scales up to solving problems in the local community. Facilitators can try to combat this through focused discussion of next steps and by inspiring participants to take ownership.

Despite these challenges, deliberation serves as a valuable format for everyday argumentation when there are wicked problems that demand the attention and energy of multiple stakeholders. Those interested in using deliberation can find a wealth of online resources to help them convene and facilitate deliberative events in their own communities.[39]

Summary

This chapter has explored three possible formats for argumentation that you can employ in your everyday life: op-eds and letters, public online argumentation, and public deliberation. The goal has been to give you a taste of each, keeping in mind that the discussion here has not been an exhaustive primer on how to do it. Op-eds and letters are a useful way to communicate your arguments with legitimacy and reach. Online argumentation is a useful way to communicate your arguments with efficiency and freedom. And, public deliberation is a useful way to communicate your arguments with empathy and impact. Providing these options for argumentation has hopefully put you in a better position to choose the right format and audience for your arguments in everyday life.

Application Exercises

Evaluating Op-Eds: Find three op-eds on the same controversial topic using a newspaper research database or going to different news websites. Read all three and evaluate them using the guidelines in this chapter:

1. Identify the thesis/proposition for each article and compare and contrast them for clarity and scope.

2. Compare and contrast how well the articles avoid getting mired in explaining the proposition.

3. Compare and contrast how well the articles emphasize the benefits and features of the proposition, assessing the major kinds of argument in the articles and the quality of support and warrants.

4. Compare and contrast how well the articles use style and an economy of words.

5. Compare and contrast the quality of the headlines and hooks (first sentences) in the articles.

Extra Credit: Also follow Steps 3 and 4 in evaluating the public comments to the op-eds.

Understanding Framing for Public Deliberation: Look over three NIFI framing guides at https://www.nifi.org/en/issue-guides and consider the following questions:

1. What do the various topics have in common? Why is each of them a "wicked problem" appropriate for public deliberation?

2. For each framing guide, are the approaches clearly defined, feasible, and neutral?

3. For each framing guide, are there any viable approaches that are missing and should be included in the framing? Are there any approaches that overlap and should be combined?

4. Were you to participate in a deliberation on each of the topics, what major hurdles to understanding and action do you anticipate will arise?

Key Terms

Op-ed 262
Editorial 262
Letter to the Editor 262

Public Online
  Argumentation 265
Internet Troll 270

Public Deliberation 271
Wicked Problem 271

Endnotes

1. "Now is the Time to Do Something about Gun Violence," *The White House*, 2013, https://web.archive.org/web/20130121192924/http://www.whitehouse.gov/issues/preventing-gun-violence.

2. "Now Is the Time: The President's Plan to Protect Our Children and Our Community by Reducing Gun Violence," *The White House*, January 16, 2013, 15, https://web.archive.org/web/20130117094055/http://www.whitehouse.gov/sites/default/files/docs/wh_now_is_the_time_full.pdf.

3. Kathleen Sebelius, "Sebelius: Bring Mental Illness Out of the Shadows," *USA Today*, February 4, 2013, http://www.usatoday.com/story/opinion/2013/02/04/kathleen-sebelius-on-mental-health-care/1890859.

4. Sara A. Mehltretter Drury and Jeffrey P. Mehltretter Drury, "Engagement through the Oval Office: Presidential Rhetoric as Civic Education," in *Civic Education in the Twenty-First Century: A Multi-Dimensional Inquiry*, ed. Michael T. Rogers and Donald Gooch (Lanham, MD: Lexington Books, 2015).

5. "National Institute of Mental Health," *The White House*, November 1, 2012, https://web.archive.org/web/20121101093601/http://mentalhealth.gov/; "MentalHealth.gov," *The White House*, June 3, 2013, https://web.archive.org/web/20130603231044/http://www.mentalhealth.gov/.

6. "Stories of Hope and Recovery," *The White House*, June 3, 2013, https://web.archive.org/web/20130608081514/http://www.mentalhealth.gov/talk/recovery/index.html.

7. "Conversations in Your Community," *The White House*, June 3, 2013, https://web.archive.org/web/20130615024430/http://www.mentalhealth.gov/talk/community-conversation/index.html; Creating Community Solutions,

"Statement of Purpose," 2013, https://web.archive.org/web/20130817034947/http://www.creatingcommunitysolutions.org:80/about.

8. Drury and Drury, "Engagement through the Oval Office," 174.

9. Mel Laracey, *Presidents and the People: The Partisan Story of Going Public* (College Station, TX: Texas A&M University Press, 2002).

10. Ross Douthat, "The Redistribution of Sex," *The New York Times*, May 2, 2018, https://www.nytimes.com/2018/05/02/opinion/incels-sex-robots-redistribution.html.

11. Niraj Chokshi, "What Is an Incel? A Term Used by the Toronto Van Attack Suspect, Explained," *The New York Times*, April 24, 2018, https://www.nytimes.com/2018/04/24/world/canada/incel-reddit-meaning-rebellion.html. For an overview of the controversy, see Molly Roberts, "What Ross Douthat Got Wrong about Incels," *The Washington Post*, May 4, 2018, https://www.washingtonpost.com/blogs/post-partisan/wp/2018/05/04/incels-sex-robots-and-what-ross-douthat-got-wrong.

12. Taylor Swift, "For Taylor Swift, the Future of Music Is a Love Story," *The Wall Street Journal*, July 7, 2014, https://www.wsj.com/articles/for-taylor-swift-the-future-of-music-is-a-love-story-1404763219; Tom Hanks, "I Owe It All to Community College," *The New York Times*, January 14, 2015, https://www.nytimes.com/2015/01/14/opinion/tom-hanks-on-his-two-years-at-chabot-college.html; Angelina Jolie, "My Medical Choice," *The New York Times*, May 14, 2013, https://www.nytimes.com/2013/05/14/opinion/my-medical-choice.html; George Clooney, "George Clooney on Sudan's Rape of Darfur," *The New York Times*, February 25, 2015, https://www.nytimes.com/2015/02/26/opinion/

george-clooney-on-sudans-rape-of-darfur .html. For additional examples, see Maria Yagoda, "James Franco and 9 Other Celebs Who've Penned Op-Eds," *People*, March 24, 2015, https://people.com/celebrity/james-franco-writes-mcdonalds-op-ed-celebrity-op-eds.

13. "Submit an Op-Ed," *The Washington Post*, https://www.washingtonpost.com/opinions/submit-an-op-ed; "Submit a Letter to the Editor," *The Washington Post*, https://www.washingtonpost.com/opinions/letter-to-the-editor.

14. "How to Submit an Op-Ed Article," *The New York Times*, https://www.nytimes.com/content/help/site/editorial/op-ed/op-ed.html.

15. Laura Jones, "34 Unwritten Rules of Facebook," *The Daily Touch*, February 4, 2014, https://web.archive.org/web/*/https://www.thedailytouch.com/lauraj/34-unwritten-rules-of-facebook; Darren Rovell, "My 13 Golden Rules of Twitter," *CNBC*, January 11, 2011, https://www.cnbc.com/id/40853842.

16. The 30 words is estimated from research that found an average of 4.8 characters per word on Twitter. Lauren Dugan, "Linguistics Professor Finds Average Word Length in a Tweet Is Longer Than in Shakespeare," *Adweek*, October 31, 2011, http://www.adweek.com/digital/linguistics-professor-finds-average-word-length-in-a-tweet-is-longer-than-in-shakespeare.

17. Britney Fitzgerald, "The Facebook 10 Commandments: Break These Rules and End Up in Social Media Purgatory," *Huffington Post*, August 30, 2012, http://www.huffingtonpost.co.uk/entry/facebook-ten-commandments_n_1819699;

18. Sherry Turkle, *Reclaiming Conversation: The Power of Talk in a Digital Age* (New York: Penguin Press, 2015); John W. Jordan, "A Virtual Death and a Real Dilemma: Identity, Trust, and Community in Cyberspace," *Southern Communication Journal* 70 (2005): 200-218.

19. Patrick Freyne, "Why Do We Argue Online?" *Irish Times*, July 24, 2015, https://www.irishtimes.com/culture/tv-radio-web/why-do-we-argue-online-1.2295986.

20. Jennifer Stromer-Galley, "New Voices in the Public Sphere: A Comparative Analysis of Interpersonal and Online Political Talk," *Javnost—The Public* 9 (2002): 23-41.

21. Freyne, "Why Do We Argue Online?"

22. Suzanne Moore, "Does Free Speech Give Us the Right to Anonymously Troll Strangers?" *The Guardian*, October 6, 2014, https://www.theguardian.com/commentisfree/2014/oct/06/free-speech-anonymously-troll-strangers-mccann-dossier.

23. *Oxford English Dictionary*, 3rd edition, s.v. "troll, n.," "Draft Additions March 2006."

24. Maeve Duggan, "Online Harassment," *Pew Research Center*, October 22, 2014, http://www.pewinternet.org/2014/10/22/online-harassment.

25. Lee Rainie, Janna Anderson, and Jonathan Albright, "The Future of Free Speech, Trolls, Anonymity, and Fake News Online," *Pew Research Center*, March 29, 2017, http://www.pewinternet.org/2017/03/29/the-future-of-free-speech-trolls-anonymity-and-fake-news-online.

26. Joel Stein, "How Trolls Are Ruining the Internet," *TIME*, August 18, 2016, http://time.com/4457110/internet-trolls.

27. Susan Herring et al., "Searching for Safety Online: Managing 'Trolling' in a Feminist Forum," *The Information Society* 18 (2002): 381.

28. Sandy Heierbacher, "NCDD Project Report for the Kettering Foundation," *National Coalition for Dialogue and Deliberation*,

October 19, 2009, http://www.ncdd.org/main/wp-content/uploads/2010/03/Heierbacher-KetteringReport_PDF.pdf, 3.

29. Horst W. J. Rittel and Melvin W. Webber, "Dilemmas in a General Theory of Planning," *Policy Sciences* 4 (1973): 155-169.

30. "What is the CIRC?" *Citizens' Initiative Review Commission*, State of Oregon, https://web.archive.org/web/20170708002754/http://www.oregon.gov/circ/Pages/index.aspx.

31. "D&D Methods," Resource Center, *National Coalition for Dialogue and Deliberation*, http://ncdd.org/rc/item/category/dd-methods.

32. Substance Abuse and Mental Health Services Administration, *Community Conversations About Mental Health Discussion Guide*, HHS Publication No. SMA-13-4765, Substance Abuse and Mental Health Services Administration, 2013, 6, https://store.samhsa.gov/shin/content//SMA13-4764/SMA13-4764.pdf.

33. Substance Abuse and Mental Health Services Administration, *Community Conversations About Mental Health Discussion Guide*, 7-8.

34. Jeffrey Cufaude, "The Art of Facilitative Leadership: Maximizing Others' Contributions," *The Systems Thinker* 15.10 (2004/2005): 2-5.

35. "The Forum and the Framework: You Can't Have One Without the Other," *The National Issues Forums Institute*, 2014, https://www.nifi.org/en/about.

36. For more about deliberation and trust, see Robert Asen, "Deliberation and Trust," *Argumentation and Advocacy* 50 (2013): 2-17.

37. Amy Galea, et al., "How Should We Pay for Health Care in Future? Results of Deliberative Events with the Public," *The King's Fund*, April 2013, https://www.kingsfund.org.uk/sites/default/files/field/field_publication_file/how-should-we-pay-for-health-care-in-future-kingsfund-apr13.pdf; "Citizens' Assembly on Brexit," *Involve*, 2017, https://www.involve.org.uk/programmes/citizens-assembly-on-brexit.

38. Martín Carcasson and Leah Sprain, "Beyond Problem Solving: Reconceptualizing the Work of Public Deliberation as Deliberative Inquiry," *Communication Theory* 26 (2016): 47-48.

39. For example, see: "Resource Center," *National Coalition for Dialogue and Deliberation*, 2017, http://ncdd.org/rc; "For Moderators," *National Issues Forums Institute*, 2014, https://www.nifi.org/en/moderators; "Resources," *Creating Community Solutions*, https://web.archive.org/web/20130608115406/http://www.creatingcommunitysolutions.org/resources.

APPENDIX I
Formats for Academic and Competitive Debate

Our focus throughout the book has been argumentation in everyday life, but this appendix explores formal and competitive opportunities for argumentation that exist through debate societies at the collegiate level. These societies are part of numerous technical spheres operating around the country—policy, parliamentary, Lincoln-Douglas, British parliamentary, town hall, moot court, mock trial, and others—that each have concrete and idiosyncratic procedures for arguing. Some of the rules, such as establishing time limits, are understandable and familiar. Others, such as guidelines for how to begin your speech or when you are able to ask questions of your co-arguers, are more distinctive.

Learning formats for competitive debate can help you hone your speaking, critical thinking, and argumentation skills. The formats also add the thrill of competition and face-to-face argumentation that motivates you to find your voice and grow in confidence. These are desirable outcomes for anyone, even those who already have a strong public speaking presence. Additionally, the formats offer adaptable frameworks you can use to stage public debates in your own communities.

This appendix covers the formats, norms, and benefits of three of the most common modes of academic debate: parliamentary debate, policy debate, and moot court. Competitive circuits for these modes are available coast to coast in the United States, at both the high school and collegiate levels, and many debate courses utilize the formats for classroom debates and exercises. We'll focus on the collegiate versions of each but bear in mind that the formats and rules described here may not always apply. By the end of this appendix, you should understand the what, how, and why of parliamentary debate, policy debate, and moot court.

Before turning to our first format, there are a few common terms worth defining. We'll be discussing what it is like to participate in *tournament* debating, in which teams from different colleges and universities meet at a specific site or virtually to compete against each other and determine the best team. A *team* is a pair of students representing its school (debaters compete individually in some formats and, on rare occasion, there may be a team comprised of students from different schools). Much like athletics, debate tournaments feature novice, junior varsity, and varsity divisions with strict eligibility requirements.

At a typical tournament, debaters will compete in four to eight preliminary rounds, alternating sides, before elimination rounds. A *debate round* is an individual debate comprising a series of oral speeches following an established format. This means that a single team will compete against four to eight other collegiate teams at any given tournament. Debaters in each round are evaluated by one to three *judges*, representing coaches of other schools' teams or hired laypeople. The judges evaluate the individual speakers (assigning speaker points to determine the best advocate) as well as declaring a winner of each debate. Teams that perform well in the preliminary rounds move on to the elimination rounds where a winner is determined through single-elimination bracket competition (the size of the bracket will depend on the total number of teams in the competition).

PARLIAMENTARY DEBATE

What It Is: Parliamentary Debate Format

Parliamentary debate is named and modeled after the British House of Commons in Parliament. It features two debaters representing the Government (the Prime Minister, or PM, and Member of Government, or MG) and two debaters representing the Opposition (the Leader of Opposition, or LO, and Member of Opposition, or MO) who debate a proposition across six speeches before a judge (called the Speaker of the House, or just Speaker). Our exploration of parliamentary debate will address the debate's format, style, and value.

In the United States, the two largest organizations that sponsor competitive parliamentary debate are the National Parliamentary Debate Association (NPDA) and the American Parliamentary Debate Association (APDA).[1] Debate tournaments sponsored by these organizations feature a different proposition every round. They could be fact, value, or policy propositions, but they are frequently related to public controversies and current events. The Government team must affirm the proposition, and the Opposition team must oppose the proposition regardless of their personal beliefs.

After the proposition is announced for a debate round, the teams have 15 to 20 minutes to prepare. During this time, the debaters outline a case for their side and anticipate the other side's arguments. Because of the limited preparation time, formal research is not permissible in the debate. Instead, arguers must draw upon common knowledge and directly contest the truth of factual information in the debate.

The debate structure involves six speeches of varying lengths. Table AI.1 offers a model of a debate round at a typical tournament. As you can see, the PM and LO speak twice and the MG and MO speak once. The debate is 40 minutes of speaking time from start of finish, evenly divided between the two sides. The Government team has the opportunity to begin and end the debate but it does mean, then, that there are 10 minutes of uninterrupted opposition argumentation across the MOC and LOR speeches. Between speeches, there is little to no preparation time; the expectation is that speakers will stand and deliver when it is their turn.

The columns in Table AI.1 outlines the major expectations for the various speeches. The material there echoes the content for case and argument construction from Chapters 4 through 7 and tools of refutation from Chapters 8 through 10. The first four speeches of the debate are called "constructive" speeches because arguers are able to construct new arguments in them. The final two speeches are called rebuttal speeches because arguers are limited to the existing arguments and wrapping up the debate (with the one exception of the PMR addressing arguments first raised in the MOC). However, arguers may provide new support, analysis, examples, etc. for their already existing claims in order to clarify and enhance their case.

TABLE AI.1 ■ Structure for Parliamentary Debate*					
Prime Minister Constructive (PMC)	**Leader of Opposition Constructive (LOC)**	**Member of Government Constructive (MGC)**	**Member of Opposition Constructive (MOC)**	**LO Rebuttal (LOR)**	**PM Rebuttal (PMR)**
7 min.	8 min.	8 min.	8 min.	4 min.	5 min.
A. Explain team's perspective toward the proposition B. Define terms & establish criteria (as appropriate) C. Present *case*: Well-developed arguments for the proposition using tools from Chapters 5-7	A. Explain team's perspective toward the proposition B. Either accept PM's definitions/criteria or present counter-definitions/criteria and reasons to prefer C. Present *case*: Well-developed arguments against the proposition using tools from Chapters 5-7 D. Present *refutation*: Well-developed responses to PM's arguments using tools from Chapters 8-10	A. Extend & defend *case*: further develop reasons, restate ignored arguments, and/or respond to LO's refutations. As time permits, develop new arguments using tools from Chapters 5-7 B. Present *refutation*: Well-developed responses to LO's arguments using tools from Chapters 8-10	A. Extend & defend *case*: further develop reasons, restate ignored arguments, and/or respond to MG's refutations. As time permits, develop new arguments using tools from Chapters 5-7 B. Present *refutation*: Well-developed responses to MG's arguments using tools from Chapters 8-10	A. Usually begin with refuting co-arguer's strongest arguments B. Address your team's arguments on the proposition C. Conclude the debate by weighing the competing *issues* for the audience, using tools from Chapter 8 **Rebuttals must focus on *existing* or *established* arguments in the debate. "New" arguments prevent you from meeting your responsibilities and the Speaker or your co-arguers may raise a point of order on account of abuse.**	

*All speeches should have a formal introduction and conclusion in addition to the content included in the columns here.

During a debate, the teams may raise Points of Information, Points of Order, and Points of Personal Privilege. **Points of Information (PI)** are questions you ask a member of the opposing team during his or her speech to gain further information. A debater may request a PI between the first and last minute of a co-arguer's constructive speech. The first and last minute of each constructive speech and the entirety of the rebuttal speeches are called "protected time" and cannot be interrupted for PIs.

A debater signals a PI by saying "Point of Information," usually accompanied by standing up. The speaker has the discretion of whether to accept or refuse the PI. Asking

POINT OF INFORMATION: A question an arguer asks during the unprotected time of a speech by the opposing team

and answering PIs is part of the strategy of parliamentary debate. For the arguer, accepting too many will take precious time from your own argumentation (the clock keeps running during the question and answer) but refusing too many will harm your credibility and provide your co-arguers some benefit of the doubt. For the questioner, asking too few PIs makes you look weak and uninterested but asking too many makes you appear aggressive and mean spirited.

Arguers commonly accept three PIs during a speech and make a questioner wait until they are finished with a point before accepting them. Questioners usually ask one to two PIs during each of his or her co-arguer's speeches (or two to four questions as a team per speech). As you can imagine, PIs make parliamentary debate exciting as advocates spar over challenging questions that seek information, identify contradictions, point out misinformation, or preview their own arguments. Keep in mind that PIs must be phrased as questions but don't you agree that a lot of arguing can be done through questions?

POINT OF ORDER: An arguer's allegation that a member of the opposing team has violated the rules

Whereas PIs are part of the strategy of the debate, **Points of Order (PO)** are a more serious matter because they accuse the opposing team of violating the rules of the debate. If you think a member of your opposing team has broken the rules at any time, you state "Point of Order." At that point, the Speaker will stop the clock and ask you to explain (but not argue) the rule and the violation. The Speaker may ask the accused to explain his or her perspective and will offer an immediate ruling, either accepting, rejecting, or taking under consideration the PO. POs are reserved for actions that harm the fairness of the debate. For instance, a new argument in a rebuttal speech would likely trigger a PO, as would a speaker egregiously exceeding the speaking time, drawing upon prohibited research, or asking a PI during protected time (to name a few).

POINT OF PERSONAL PRIVILEGE: An arguer's allegation that a member of the opposing team has offended or misrepresented him or her

A **Point of Personal Privilege (PPP)** is more similar to POs than PIs. Whereas POs focus on the rules of the debate, PPPs address situations in which a debater believes a member of the opposing team has engaged in insulting behavior or seriously misrepresented his or her arguments. The procedure for handling a PPP mirrors that of a PO. Because PPPs are serious allegations, you should only raise them if there is clear and significant misconduct. In fact, debaters who raise specious PPPs may themselves be penalized by the Speaker.

It should be clear to this point that parliamentary debate has many guidelines in place to foster robust debate, ensure equity between the two sides, and provide recourse in the case of transgressions.

How You Do It: Parliamentary Debate Style

Parliamentary debate emphasizes a strong balance between content and delivery; arguers should present the kind of organized and cogent arguments we've discussed throughout the book and they should speak with the effective delivery techniques outlined in Chapter 11. More specifically, parliamentary debate relies on a few stylistic guidelines:

- **Be respectful of your co-arguers.** Like the House of Commons on which it's modeled, parliamentary debate involves a respect for your co-arguers. You should be cordial toward them and recognize common ground when appropriate. A competitive stance will not get you very far with the Speaker in most parliamentary debates, especially if you are rude toward or dismissive of your co-arguer's arguments.

- **Be witty.** "Wit" is used here intentionally rather than "humor." Whereas humor can come in many guises, wit is more apt to this mode of debate. We say something is witty or someone has a "quick wit" when the speaker uses words with cleverness to create humor. One liners, snappy comebacks, and puns (within the confines of appropriate conduct) often ingratiate yourself with the other team and the Speaker while demonstrating your ability to think on your feet.

- **Be organized.** Parliamentary debate style requires an arguer to be organized by using a clear and appropriate case structure (see Chapter 7). It also requires arguers to lead the audience through their argumentation with signposts (phrases like, "first," "second," "next," etc.) and to explain how ideas connect back to the overall proposition. Even the most cogent arguments will fail when argued haphazardly.

- **Be prepared for heckling**. Audience members and co-arguers are given the right to heckle the debaters in a respectful manner. Often, it takes the form of knocking on the table to support something or calling out words and phrases (such as "here here!" or "for shame!") to communicate a reaction. While arguers won't be shouted down, they should be prepared for the audience to remind them that they need to appropriately adapt their arguments.

The above explanation addresses the activity in broad strokes, overlooking much of the jargon and strategy. If you wish to participate in the formal activity, you would need to consult the rules and a formal guide document for parliamentary debate.[2] Why might you participate? Let's consider the major skill benefits.

Why You Should Do It: Parliamentary Debate Benefits[3]

While all competitive debate activities are useful for cultivating different skills, parliamentary debate emphasizes the following three main skills:

- **Effective public speaking.** This format of debate requires you to effectively articulate your ideas and look nice while doing so (most parliamentary debaters, both men and women, wear suits at tournaments). Thus, parliamentary debate is one of the best activities to help you effectively speak in an impromptu fashion. You will encounter many other people who have different speaking styles from you, helping you to learn from others and hone your skills.

- **Improvisation and thinking on your feet**. The unpredictable nature of parliamentary debate requires you to improvise your argumentation. The inability to script out everything in advance and the requirement to respond immediately to your co-arguer's arguments means that you will quickly learn to think on your feet and draw upon the argumentation patterns we discussed earlier in the book.

- **Well-rounded knowledge.** The research prohibition in parliamentary debate means that those who wish to succeed in the activity must keep abreast of current affairs and cultivate well-rounded knowledge. Since empirical examples, famous figures, and current controversies all play a part in parliamentary debate, participants will build up their store of knowledge over time.

In sum, people who wish to learn debate skills similar to what they see in campaign debates would be wise to pursue parliamentary debate as an activity. It helps you cultivate a strong speaking voice, confidence, and well-rounded knowledge for use in any context.

POLICY DEBATE

What It Is: Policy Debate Format

Policy debate is focused solely on policy propositions, or considering desirable courses of action to resolve public controversies. The side favoring the proposition, called the affirmative team (comprised of the first and second affirmative speakers), debates against the negative team (comprised of first and second negative speakers) across eight speeches.

In the United States, the American Forensic Association (AFA), through the National Debate Tournament (NDT), and the Cross Examination Debate Association (CEDA) are the two largest sponsors of competitive policy debate.[4] Whereas parliamentary debate addresses a different proposition every round, policy debate addresses the same proposition for an entire school year, enabling depth of engagement with the topic.

The annual proposition for policy debate is worded generally so that each team when advocating the affirmative side will argue a specific plan that falls within the jurisdiction of and affirms the general proposition. For instance, the 2017-2018 topic was "Resolved: The United States Federal Government should establish national health insurance in the United States." When a team is arguing the affirmative side at a tournament, it would advocate a specific national health insurance plan and argue that this plan would bring about advantageous effects beyond the *status quo*. When arguing the negative side at a tournament, teams must be prepared to argue disadvantages to any possible plan that would fit underneath the broad resolution and, if they chose to offer a counterplan, it must *not* affirm the resolution that the United States Federal Government should establish national health insurance in the United States.

Because the same topic is debated all year, teams amass substantial research that they access during the debates to support their claims. In fact, debaters will support claims by reading passages directly from articles, books, or websites. Consequently, refutation in a debate will often address two major elements: the causal connection between the plan and its consequences and the quality of the cited research.

The debate itself includes eight speeches, four constructive speeches of the same length and four rebuttal speeches of the same length. Table AI.2 illustrates a typical policy debate round. The table does not indicate that each team is also given up to 10 minutes of total preparation time to use prior to their speeches. This means that a complete debate takes approximately 90 minutes, with 72 minutes of speaking time divided

TABLE AI.2 ■ Structure for Policy Debate*

1st Affirmative Speaker Constructive (1AC)	CX	1st Negative Speaker Constructive (1NC)	CX	2nd Affirmative Speaker Constructive (2AC)	CX	2nd Negative Speaker Constructive (2NC)	CX	1NR	1AR	2NR	2AR
9 min.	3 min.	9 min.	3 min.	9 min.	3 min.	9 min.	3 min.	6 min.	6 min.	6 min.	6 min.
A. Explain team's perspective toward the proposition B. Present *case*: Well-developed arguments following *stock issues* structure and using tools from Chapters 5-7	2nd Neg.	A. Explain team's perspective toward the proposition B. Challenge *topicality* of affirmative case (as appropriate) C. Present *case*: Well-developed *disadvantages* (and *counterplan*) using tools from Chapters 5-7 D. Present *refutation*: Well-developed responses to 1AC arguments using tools from Chapters 8-10	1st Aff.	A. Extend & defend *case*: further develop reasons, restate ignored arguments, and/or respond to 1NC's refutations. As time permits, develop new advantages using tools from Chapters 5-7 B. Present *refutation*: Well-developed responses to 1NC's arguments using tools from Chapters 8-10	1st Neg.	A. Extend & defend *case*: further develop reasons, restate ignored arguments, and/or respond to 2AC's refutations. As time permits, develop new disadvantages using tools from Chapters 5-7 B. Present *refutation*: Well-developed responses to 2AC's arguments using tools from Chapters 8-10	2nd Aff.	A. Usually begin with refuting co-arguer's strongest arguments B. Address your team's arguments on the proposition C. Conclude the debate by weighing the competing *issues* for the audience, using tools from Chapter 8 **Rebuttals must focus on *existing* or *established* arguments in the debate. "New" arguments prevent you from meeting your responsibilities and the judge or your co-arguers may discredit them on account of abuse.**			

*All speeches should have a formal introduction and conclusion in addition to the content included in the columns here.

equally across the two teams. As with parliamentary debate, the team affirming the proposition begins and ends the debate, affording a 15-minute "negative block" comprised of the 2NC and 1NR.

The speech expectations in the columns of Table AI.2 are nearly identical to those for parliamentary debate, except that the cases exclusively use the tools for policy debate outlined in Chapter 7. Each constructive speech is separated by three minutes of cross examination (often abbreviated as CX), in which the speaker identified in the column asks questions of his or her co-arguer. Rather than Points of Information interrupting a co-arguer's speech, policy debate only allows questions during cross examination. The argumentative strategy is similar to PIs but CX provides your debate partner additional preparation time for his or her speech rather than interrupting your co-arguer's.

Whereas points of order and personal privilege stop the clock in a parliamentary debate, there is no such thing in a policy debate. If rules are violated or people are insulted, that becomes part of the debate itself in which the opposing team would make the case that the other team's performance has been offensive, unfair, or harmed the educational value of the debate. The most common rule transgression that debaters argue is called **topicality**. A topicality argument alleges that the affirmative plan falls outside the scope of the proposition and, thus, the affirmative team has not met its burden to affirm the proposition.

TOPICALITY:
Arguing that the affirmative plan is outside the scope of the wording of the proposition

Because research is so important to policy debate and because everything must be argued explicitly on the clock, the style of debate differs substantially from parliamentary debate.

How You Do It: Policy Debate Style

Policy debate prioritizes content over delivery. It is not uncommon for debaters to wear casual clothes and to read their support directly from the page without eye contact or vocal variation. Here are some of the unique qualities of policy debate style:

- **Be quick**. Because debaters hope to say as much as they can in their allotted time, policy debate is characterized by fast talking. Training often includes practicing how to talk as fast as you can in a clear and articulate manner. Quickness also means that policy debaters take argumentative shortcuts, such as referring to arguments by labels (e.g., "Economy disad" to refer to the argument establishing a disadvantage that the affirmative team's plan would harm the economy) or even numbers from an outline (e.g. "Carry across point A.2., which my opponent dropped"). Policy debate also involves a "spread offense," a term borrowed from American football, in which an arguer attempts to provide more content than his or her co-arguer can address in the allotted time. Given this speed, judges for policy debate tend to be specialized and capable of following the jargon.

- **Be prepared with research**. You could not win a formal policy debate without research (commonly called "evidence"). The expectation of the activity is that you base your claims on credible people that you cite explicitly. For instance, you might demonstrate that climate change is a growing concern by reading a selection from the Intergovernmental Panel on Climate Change's most recent report. In a policy debate, it would sound like this: "Climate change is a threat to civilization as we know it. IPCC, 2013. [excerpt from IPCC report]." This would be called a "card" that your co-arguers might then ask to see for the full citation details.

- **Be organized**. The speed at which policy debaters argue means that they often rely on systematic outlines of arguments. Whereas parliamentary debaters tend to use a prose format offering eloquent analysis for their points, policy debaters tend to be more direct in identifying claims and then providing cited research as support. As noted earlier, policy debaters commonly enumerate each claim and support in outline structure using letter and number combinations to help the co-arguers and judge follow along.

- **Be aggressive**. Compared to parliamentary debaters, policy debaters tend to be more aggressive and disrespectful toward their co-arguers, viewing them as opponents to be conquered. Driven by a desire to win within the confines of the rules, policy debaters are often ruthless even when facing much weaker competition. The biggest boon of policy debate is a dropped argument that debaters can then inflate into a significant impact, exploiting weakness in their favor. This approach to argumentation means that strategy is as important to policy debate as cogent arguments.

Success in this format would require familiarity with the rules and more specialized training than discussed above.[5] If policy debate is a dog-eat-dog world, you might think it odd that anyone would choose to participate. So, let's turn to the value of this format.

Why You Should Do It: Policy Debate Benefits

Policy debate emphasizes some skills to a higher degree than other formats of competitive debate:

- **Improvisation and thinking on your feet**. Like parliamentary debate, policy debate emphasizes your ability to improvise. For policy debate, this skill is particularly focused on understanding and adapting your strategy as the debate develops and the ability to see the big picture of the debate. Although debaters are given preparation time, much of this is spent locating research in the organized file systems. Thus, you need to be able to make split-second decisions about where to focus your argumentative efforts.

- **Efficiently find and process research**. Because research is fundamental to this format of debate, it requires you to make sense of a lot of information very quickly. As part of the research process, a skilled debater will have strong familiarity with newspaper databases. It is also common for debaters to be able to "read" an entire book in less than an hour by looking for very precise things to help their arguments. In the debate itself, arguers need to be able to make sense of the research provided by the other team and quickly respond.

- **Developing depth of knowledge**. Whereas parliamentary debate requires general knowledge adaptable to any proposition that might arise, policy debate's use of a single proposition leads to the exact opposite: cultivating depth of knowledge on the topic. Students who participated in competitive policy debate during the 2017-2018 academic year learned a lot about health care in the United States. This provides expertise for the participants as they develop a store of knowledge to use in the real world.

If you like a fast-paced, analytical environment based on research and reasoning, then policy debate may be a viable activity for you. It is particularly useful for those who might be interested in a career in government, politics, and policymaking.

A NOTE ABOUT NOTETAKING (OR "FLOWING")

FLOWING: Writing down arguments from a debate in column sequence by placing responses beside the argument to which they respond

Before turning to the final format of debate, we'll discuss the process of notetaking, called **flowing**, that debaters use in parliamentary and policy debate. Because a debate round can be a messy and lively affair, it's important to efficiently take notes on what arguers say. To flow a debate, you would divide the paper into the column structure you saw in Tables AI.1 and AI.2 and track the first speaker's arguments vertically down the column and onto a new page as needed. Why do you do this? Because you would place the next speaker's responses to those arguments beside them in the succeeding column, the responses to those responses in the next column, and so forth. You've created a flow of the debate that visually demonstrates where there is substantial clash and where there are dropped arguments.

A few things will help you more successfully flow a debate. First, speakers should be organized in their argumentation to indicate which argument they are addressing and exactly how ideas relate to one another. Second, notetakers should avoid full sentences and use shorthand symbols to represent fuller ideas. You should come up with a system that makes sense to you and that you can understand when you look at your flow. Box AI.1 identifies some common symbols used in debate flows. Third, notetakers should make sure they write down both the claim *and* support for the argument, including citations when possible. Without all the details, they will be unable to effectively utilize the ARG conditions to evaluate the arguments.

For instance, we could take Table 10.1 from Chapter 10 that tracked the comments to Mr. Money Mustache's blog post and infuse shorthand into it, creating Table AI.3. There, you can see that shorthand saves substantial space by truncating the complex, full-sentence ideas into brief phrases that signal a broader argumentative idea. The flow also shows where the clash was weak and where it was strong.

Like arguing more generally, it can take a lot of time and practice to cultivate the skill of flowing but doing so makes you a more efficient notetaker in all contexts and helps you quickly organize ideas into clear argument structures and patterns.

TABLE AI.3 ■ Flow of the Mr. Money Mustache Discussion Thread [Lp1]

Commenter's Case	First Response	Subsequent Responses to Responses					
		Tawcan	**Vijay**	**Jacob** / **Andreas**	**Vijay**	**Mark**	**Vijay**
Tawcan 1. BC* wastes energy	**Vijay** 1. BC mining < 1% of all energy 1. banks + media mislead 2. CNBC, 2017	1. CO_2 pollution a. BC elec. = 3.3 m homes b. China BC mining uses coal	a. move to renewables	1. Ø likely a. ↓ energy $ → mining **Andreas** 2. Farms Ø give $ a. energy rates < 36 TW demand	1. Do all world $ use < energy than BC?	1. BC C02 is 500-30,000 times > U.S. Dollar	** ↑ a. Rest of world? 1. BC is universal$, Ø U.S. b. No source
Thaitum a. BC invest Ø mistake 1. $28,000 → $500,000	**Ben** a. Get out now 1. You gambled + won 2. Not repeatable						
Lily a. BC = speculation, ≠ asset 1. ≈ gold & MIL's Beanie Babies	**Justin** b. Gold ≠ speculation, = commodity 1. ≈ corn, coffee, cr wheat 2. Gold $ stable 3. Stock index funds > speculation than gold						

*"BC" stands for "Bitcoin." In a flow, it wouldn't make sense to write out Bitcoin every time someone mentioned it.

**An arrow from one column to the next means that the argument is granted and/or reiterated ("carried across") by an arguer.

BOX AI.1: SHORTHAND SYMBOLS FOR FLOWING

Symbol	Meaning	Symbol	Meaning
b/c	Because	= ≠	Is and is not
→	Leads to, causes	≈ ≉	Similar to, almost and is not similar to, not almost
↑↓	Increases, improve, high and decreases, worsen, low	♂	Men, males, masculine
Ø	Not, nothing, no	♀	Women, females, feminine
+	And, also, additionally	Δ	Change
<>	Lesser, weaker and greater, stronger	$	Money, cost, funding

MOOT COURT

What It Is: Moot Court Format

Moot court is the final competitive debate format we'll consider in this chapter. Whereas the previous two types of debate focus on personal and political issues, moot court addresses legal issues in a technical sphere. Specifically, this format mimics oral arguments at the appellate level in the U.S. court system.

The appellate court (or court of appeals) represents a different process of judgment than the trial court. When someone is accused of a crime or sued by someone else in the United States, the case may go to trial court (or it may be settled out of court). At the trial level, the prosecution and the defense both make arguments based on admitted evidence about the accused's guilt or lack thereof. When all evidence is presented and all witnesses have been heard, the judge or jury renders a verdict. If the losing side believes the verdict was based on legal error—not merely disagreeing with it—the lawyer(s) representing that side has the right to appeal the ruling. An appeal is entered in writing to the appropriate appellate court at the local, state, or federal level, which has their own judges and procedures. The submitted document, called a **legal brief**, addresses the legal issues and develops arguments based on **precedent,** or existing court rulings and laws as they guide

LEGAL BRIEF: A written case that argues whether the lower court erred in its ruling

PRECEDENT: Prior court opinions and existing law

the current dispute. Once the appeal is filed, the other side will have the opportunity to also respond in writing, followed by a reply brief from the side appealing the lower court's ruling. Those who submit the appeal are called the **petitioner** or **appellant** and those defending the lower court's ruling are called the **respondent** or **appellee**.

In most cases, the appellate judges will rule on the written briefs. However, for cases that are particularly challenging, judges may request oral arguments to ask questions of the lawyers and discuss the issues in more depth. Moot court mimics these oral arguments by asking students to play the role of appellate counselors (or lawyers) in arguing their cases. Moot court relies on prewritten briefs so that the participants can focus on their oral argumentation skills rather than their ability to research and write legal briefs.

In the United States, the major collegiate sponsor of moot court is the American Moot Court Association[6] but schools commonly host competitions for current students and instructors might incorporate moot court activities into classes. This means that the format may differ depending on the specific hosting institution. That said, often the cases are simulated to be before the U.S. Supreme Court and the judges tend to be lawyers or coaches. Because it's technical sphere argumentation, judging requires people with strong familiarity with the procedures and argumentative norms.

The format for moot court is quite distinct from the other two types of debate. One major difference is that each side speaks in a single block of time with the opportunity for the petitioner to deliver a rebuttal speech. Most oral arguments total 40 or 60 minutes, divided evenly among both sides. The petitioners speak first followed by the respondents followed by an optional petitioner rebuttal. Table AI.4 offers an overview of a typical oral argument. You'll notice each column indicates two times. The first number is for a 40-minute oral argument, and the second is for a 60-minute oral argument.

Because the speaking doesn't alternate between sides, this means that each speaker is responsible for different issues and arguments than his or her co-counsel. As a result, each speech uses the same basic structure: introduction, facts of the case, arguments, and conclusion. The first statement of each speech follows a very precise format: "May it please the court, my name is _____, and I represent _____, the [Petitioner/Respondent] in this appeal." If a petitioner is reserving rebuttal time, now would be the time to request it unless the bailiff or judge asks in advance of the speech. Then, all speakers should identify the major issues in the debate (i.e., the reason for the oral arguments in the first place) before previewing their case.

The conclusion of the speech also follows a technical formula. An effective conclusion will summarize the main points and then end with a request (sometimes called a prayer) stating your ultimate aim: "We respectfully request that you [reverse/affirm] the lower court's ruling." If time expires before arguers get here, they must ask the chief judge for permission to continue: "I see that my time has expired. May I conclude my point?" If granted (it usually is), then they should quickly wrap up by finishing the point, skipping the summary, and going right to the request.

The middle stage of each speech is dedicated to organized development of the arguments, using precedent as support. Because the briefs are already written for the

PETITIONER/ APPELLANT: The party appealing the lower court's ruling

RESPONDENT/ APPELLEE: The party defending the lower court's ruling

TABLE AI.4 ■ Structure for Moot Court Oral Argument*				
First Petitioner	**Second Petitioner**	**First Respondent**	**Second Respondent**	**Petitioner Rebuttal**
7-10 min./ 10-15 min.	**7-10 min./ 10-15 min.**	**10 min./ 15 min.**	**10 min./ 15 min.**	**0-3 min./ 0-5 min.**
A. Introduction	A. Introduction	A. Introduction	A. Introduction	A. Introduction
B. Briefly review facts (as appropriate)	B. Briefly review facts (as appropriate)	B. Briefly review facts (as appropriate)	B. Briefly review facts (as appropriate)	B. Refute respondents' strongest arguments
C. Present *case*: Well-developed arguments on the relevant issue(s) citing precedent and using tools from Chapters 5-7	C. Present *case*: Well-developed arguments on the relevant issue(s) citing precedent and using tools from Chapters 5-7	C. Present *case*: Well-developed arguments on the relevant issue(s) citing precedent and using tools from Chapters 5-7	C. Present *case*: Well-developed arguments on the relevant issue(s) citing precedent and using tools from Chapters 5-7	B. Address your team's arguments C. Reiterate major issues and conclude with why your appeal is justified
D. Present *pre-emptions* (as appropriate) on the same issue(s) using tools from Chapters 8-10	D. Present *pre-emptions* (as appropriate) on the same issue(s) using tools from Chapters 8-10	D. Present *refutations* on the same issue(s) using tools from Chapters 8-10	D. Present *refutations* on the same issue(s) using tools from Chapters 8-10	**Rebuttal must focus on *existing* or *established* arguments in the debate. "New" arguments prevent you from meeting your responsibilities and the judges may shut down new lines of argument.**
E. Conclusion & Request	E. Conclusion & Request	E. Conclusion & Request	E. Conclusion & Request	

advocate, preparation tends to turn inward to learning the issues and precedent rather than outward toward researching the topic or crafting your own arguments. That is, the argumentative skill of moot court is not in generating arguments per se but in translating the written arguments to an oral format and being able to respond to challenging questions.

Although speakers are responsible primarily for their own issues, they must be prepared to argue all issues in the debate and be consistent with their co-counsel. This is because the judges in moot court will interrupt the speaker at any point to ask him or her pertinent questions to resolving the case. As with parliamentary debate, the clock keeps running while you're handling questions but, unlike parliamentary debate, you can't refuse a question. In moot court, the questioners have more power than you and, thus, you must be deferential to them even if they ask you about a topic for which you're unprepared. The questions usually seek clarity about particular points from the briefs but it's not uncommon for judges to offer hypotheticals and counterfactuals to test ideas.

How You Do It: Moot Court Style

The power difference between speaker and judge means that moot court has quite a different style compared to parliamentary or policy debate. However, as with parliamentary debate, the focus is on cogent arguments *and* effective oral delivery. Here are some more concrete guidelines:

- **Be decorous**. To be decorous means you follow decorum, or the appropriate expectations for the sphere. In this sphere, you must be respectful to the judges by referring to them as "Your Honor," not interrupting their questions, and avoiding humor as much as possible. You should also follow the proper structure described in the previous section, using time wisely and asking for permission to go over your time limit. Respect here will get you a long way whereas a lack of it may leave you in contempt of court and undermine your case.

- **Be focused (on the law)**. One common misstep of beginning moot court advocates is to get bogged down in the facts of the case at the expense of precedent. Your job is to address the alleged legal errors in the ruling, not retry the case in a different court. One way to ensure focus is to be organized with clear arguments from classification: start with a claim about the legal error, explain what the law says, and then apply the law to the current situation/case. Beyond structuring your own arguments, use judge questions to refocus on your case. If a question misses the point, find a polite way to say as much and return to your prepared argumentation.

- **Be extemporaneous and flexible**. You can't know for certain how a judge will respond to your arguments so you must prepare for a variety of questions. There's also no protected time in your speech so questions can come at any point. Judges will not approve if you are too reliant on your notes and they will try to get you off script. To help this flexibility, you will want *at most* an outline in bullet points of your main arguments and a list of relevant precedent with a brief summary of each.

- **Be confident**. Finally, you should be confident (but not arrogant) in your delivery. The more you believe that your side is on the side of justice, the more your judges may believe you as well. If you waver or show a lack of knowledge, you can easily sink your case. Confidence is easier when arguing your prepared case than when answering unpredictable questions from the judges so, to help your preparation and confidence, use the tips for answering questions in Box AI.2.

BOX AI.2: TIPS FOR ANSWERING JUDGE QUESTIONS

1. Let the judge finish asking the question before answering. Interrupting will harm your credibility or may cause you to miss important information.

2. In general, only ask a judge to repeat or clarify a question if absolutely necessary. It may be tempting to ask this to buy time but doing so may make you look unprepared or, worse, incompetent.

3. Since eye contact matters, do not write notes unless there are multiple parts. Look the judge in the eye and answer directly.

4. Answer with "yes," "no," or "it depends" and only then, as appropriate, explain your answer with arguments. This will show the judges you are focused and not trying to evade their questions.

5. Don't dwell on any single question too long and avoid the rabbit hole. Judges will try to trap you or get you to play on their terms. To avoid this, tie your answers back to your prepared case and get yourself back on track.

As with the other formats, the above description of moot court is in general terms and glosses over many of the formal rules and procedures in place that you would want to study to succeed.[7] Learning this style of debate can, as you will see, be very valuable.

Why You Should Do It: Moot Court Benefits

Participation in moot court offers numerous benefits, especially for those interested in and excited by the law:

- **Improvisation and thinking on your feet.** Like the other two formats, moot court also hones your ability to think on your feet and improvise because you will need to respond to the judges' questions in the moment. You can't expect that everything will go according to plan, and thus you must prepare for many contingencies.

- **Anticipating and answering questions.** Whereas all formats of debate sharpen your improvisational argumentation, moot court more strongly emphasizes your capacity to anticipate and answer questions. In fact, training for moot court often focuses less on communicating your prepared arguments and more on how to effectively answer potential questions. This is a useful skill to have, especially for your professional life (interviewing for a job, defending a presentation to co-workers, etc.).

- **Understanding legal processes.** Since preparation for moot court is about learning the legal issues outlined in the briefs, you will develop a strong grasp of the processes and concepts undergirding the particular moot court problem. Understanding these complex legal arguments may, in turn, inform your engagement in public and personal sphere argumentation. If you have a stronger understanding of your rights, for instance, you can more easily protect them in the future.

If you are excited by legal controversies and strive to improve your ability to answer challenging questions about a complex problem, moot court might be a great activity for you. Especially for those considering a career in law, moot court offers vital experience.

Box AI.3 summarizes the focus and style of each. Parliamentary debate addresses a variety of topics and emphasizes limited preparation in generating organized cases and effective refutations. Policy debate addresses the effectiveness of policy solutions to public problems and emphasizes researched argumentation and strategic refutation. Moot court addresses the application of precedent to current legal controversies and emphasizes organized argumentation and the ability to effectively answer judge questions. Each kind of debate is unique in terms of the format, rules, style, and benefits. You should consider if and how any of the activities might be right for you.

BOX AI.3: SUMMARY OF COMPETITIVE DEBATE ACTIVITIES

Activity	Topics	Style
Parliamentary Debate	Personal & Public	Oral delivery of arguments using common knowledge with limited preparation
Policy Debate	Public Policy	Oral delivery of arguments using high quality research about a single topic area
Moot Court	Legal	Oral delivery of arguments using legal precedent as it helps explain and resolve the current controversy

Key Terms

Parliamentary Debate 280	Policy Debate 284	Legal Brief 290
Point of Information 281	Topicality 286	Precedent 290
Point of Order 282	Flowing 288	Petitioner/Appellant 291
Point of Personal Privilege 282	Moot Court 290	Respondent/Appellee 291

Endnotes

1. National Parliamentary Debate Association, 2017, https://www.parlidebate.org; American Parliamentary Debate Association, 2016, http://apdaweb.org.

2. National Parliamentary Debate Association, "NPDA Rules," NPDA, June 2008, https://www.parlidebate.org/npda-rules.

3. I determined the benefits of participating in the various forms of competitive debate from my first-hand experience judging each of them and seeing students' progress over time.

4. "NDT Charter," *American Forensic Association*, 2017, http://www.americanforensicsassoc.org/ndt-charter; Cross Examination Debate Association, 2017, http://www.cedadebate.org.

5. "Learn to Debate," *Debate Central*, University of Vermont, http://debate.uvm.edu/learndebate.html.

6. American Moot Court Association, 2017, http://www.amcamootcourt.org.

7. American Moot Court Association, "AMCA Rules," August 1, 2017, https://storage.googleapis.com/wzukusers/user-28362831/documents/59a064fbd1240wogx4lP/AMCA%20Rules-revised%20August%201%202017.pdf.

APPENDIX II
Answers to Build Your Skill Prompts

Chapter 1

Build Your Skill: Spheres of Argument

Answers will vary

Chapter 2

Build Your Skill: Identifying Propositions

Answers will vary

Build Your Skill: Testing Policy Propositions

The numbers refer to the criteria each proposition violates:

    A. *2, 3*

    B. *4, 6*

    C. *1, 4*

    D. *5*

    E. *3, 4*

    F. *6, 3 (unless it's not too late)*

Chapter 3

Build Your Skill: Exploring Ethical Guidelines

Answers will vary but here are some violations you might identify:

    A. *Respect, Courage*

    B. *Honesty, Accountability*

    C. *Respect, Accountability*

Chapter 4

Build Your Skill: Using Argument Cues

*Cues are indicated by **bolded underlining***

A. **Lou Gehrig, Farewell, July 4, 1939:** *"Fans, for the past two weeks you have been reading about the bad break I got. **Yet** today I consider myself the luckiest man on the face of this earth. I have been in ballparks for seventeen years and have never received anything but kindness and encouragement from you fans."*

B. **Barack Obama, Remarks on the Situation in Syria, August 31, 2013:** *"Our military has positioned assets in the region. The Chairman of the Joint Chiefs has informed me that we are prepared to strike whenever we choose. **Moreover**, the Chairman has indicated to me that our capacity to execute this mission is not time-sensitive; it will be effective tomorrow, or next week, or one month from now. And I'm prepared to give that order. **But** having made my decision as Commander-in-Chief based on what I am convinced is our national security interests, I'm **also** mindful that I'm the President of the world's oldest constitutional democracy. I've long believed that our power is rooted not just in our military might, but in our example as a government of the people, by the people, and for the people. **And that's why** I've made a second decision: I will seek authorization for the use of force from the American people's representatives in Congress."*

C. **Meryl Streep, Golden Globe Acceptance Speech, January 7, 2017:** *"We need the principled press, to hold power to account, to call them on the carpet for every outrage. **That's why** our founders enshrined the press and its freedoms in our constitution. **So** I only asked the famously well-heeled Hollywood Foreign Press and all of us in our community to join me in supporting the Committee to Protect Journalists, **because** we're gonna need them going forward, **and** they'll need us to safeguard the truth."*

Build Your Skill: Unstated Warrants and Assumptions

A. *Warrant: "The right to own guns (the Second Amendment) applies to assault rifles."*

Some Assumptions: The audience ("us") is comprised of U.S. citizens; The Supreme Court in 1997 correctly interpreted the Second Amendment in DC v. Heller; The current Supreme Court will maintain the precedent established in DC v. Heller; the 1994 assault rifle ban was also unconstitutional

B. *Warrant: "God caused my success."*

Some Assumptions: God exists; God has provided you grace; you are successful

C. *Warrant: "Someone who has lied before will lie again."*

Some Assumptions: Omitting information ("not tell you he was out partying") is the same as a lie; Lying is an innate trait of a person's character

Application Exercise: Creating Argument Diagrams

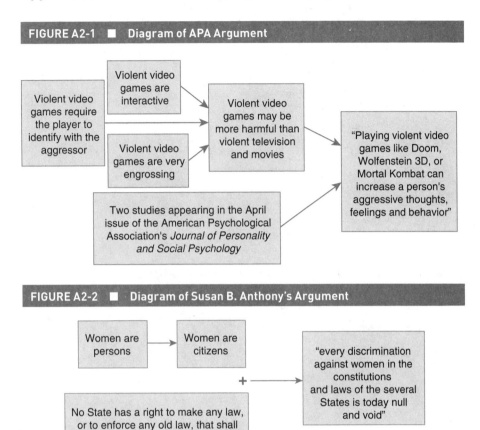

FIGURE A2-1 ■ Diagram of APA Argument

Violent video games require the player to identify with the aggressor

Violent video games are interactive

Violent video games are very engrossing

Violent video games may be more harmful than violent television and movies

Two studies appearing in the April issue of the American Psychological Association's *Journal of Personality and Social Psychology*

"Playing violent video games like Doom, Wolfenstein 3D, or Mortal Kombat can increase a person's aggressive thoughts, feelings and behavior"

FIGURE A2-2 ■ Diagram of Susan B. Anthony's Argument

Women are persons

Women are citizens

No State has a right to make any law, or to enforce any old law, that shall abridge their privileges or immunities

+

"every discrimination against women in the constitutions and laws of the several States is today null and void"

Chapter 5

Build Your Skill: Evaluating Statistics

A. *Weak: It indicates scale and units of statistic, relates it to the audience, uses the best measure, and uses them sparingly but cites no source. This last point is enough to make it weak.*

B. *Strong-ish: Cites the source for the statistic, indicates units and scale, uses the best measure, relates it to audience, and uses them sparingly. Trump did fudge the number, though, claiming it cost over $17 million but the report indicated that it cost almost $17 million ($16.7 to be exact). Associated Press, "The Latest: Russia Investigation's Costs Hit $16 Million," May 31, 2018, https://apnews. com/473d5e2b989b47789f0a97f9fb3f2a54/The-Latest:-Russia-investigation's-costs- hit-$16-million*

C. *Weak: It uses the best measure (supposedly) and indicates units but doesn't indicate scale, doesn't relate statistics to the audience, doesn't use them sparingly, and provides no source. Failure to relate it to the audience is particularly important for the assessment of this example.*

Chapter 6

Build Your Skill: Kinds of Cause

A. *Contributory*

B. *Sufficient*

C. *Necessary*

D. *Necessary*

E. *Necessary and Sufficient*

Chapter 7

Build Your Skill: Assessing Stock Issues

Stock Issues (the numbers refer to the lines in the case):

Significant Harm: 4-5

Inherency: 5-6

Plan: 2, 9

Solvency and Advantages: 3-4, 6-8, 10.

Assessments of the stock issues will vary

Chapter 8

Build Your Skill: Generating Refutation

Answers will vary. The answers below are possible refutations to illustrate options:

A. Rejection: *I don't have unprotected sex.*

Mitigation: *Unprotected sex on its own isn't enough for pregnancy.*

Turning: *My partner and I want to get pregnant.*

Transcendence [provide additional content]: *My partner and I use oral contraceptive.*

B. Rejection: *Companies don't exploit Christmas.*

Mitigation: *Just because a company profits from something, that doesn't make it a capitalist conspiracy.*

Turning: Capitalism is beneficial, not dangerous, to society.

Transcendence [reductio ad absurdum]: If Santa Claus is a capitalist plot, so is Thanksgiving, the 4th of July, Memorial Day, and all other holidays.

C. Rejection: You're not actually falling.

Mitigation: Your falling was not because you were going too fast.

Turning: Falling is a good thing.

Transcendence [provide additional content]: Your ride has training wheels to prevent you from falling.

Chapter 9

Build Your Skill: Considering Statistical Relevance

Statistic 2 is the more relevant statistic to use because it is tailored to your specific town. Although it doesn't demonstrate the "significance" as strongly as Statistic 1, it is more relevant. In using it, you might need to qualify your claim (e.g., some people in your town suffer from poverty).

Build Your Skill: Evaluating Cogency

1:

A. *Grounds*

B. *Acceptability*

C. *Relevance*

2:

A. *Relevance*

B. *Grounds*

C. *Acceptability*

Chapter 10

Build Your Skill: ARC Conditions & Argument Types

The weakest condition for each argument is debatable but the answers below represent the likeliest conclusion based on reasoned analysis in parentheses.

A. *Causal Argument Weakest Condition: G condition (people enjoying life may result in a more pleasant world but there are many rebuttals that might prevent that)*

B. *Authority Argument Weakest Condition: R condition (Twenty One Pilots is likely not a relevant authority on life)*

C. *Classification Argument Weakest Condition: A condition (the definition of "to live" is likely too limited)*

D. *Generalization Argument Weakest Condition: R condition (you and your friends are likely not representative of all people)*

E. *Sign Argument Weakest Condition: R condition (death's unpredictability is likely not a strong indicator that people should enjoy life)*

F. *Analogy Argument Weakest Condition: G condition (there are likely more differences than similarities between living life and prison/liberation)*

Chapter 11

Build Your Skill: Identifying Style

Alliteration, Metaphor, Antithesis, Parallelism

Chapter 12

Build Your Skill: Evaluating an Op-Ed

Answers will vary

Build Your Skill: Evaluating Tweets

Answers will vary

APPENDIX III
Glossary

ACCEPTABILITY: The degree to which the audience finds the support reasonably permissible in a debate.

ADVANTAGES: Positive consequences of enacting the plan in addition to solving the harm.

ANTICIPATION: Examining the proposition from your co-arguers' perspectives.

APPELLANT: See "petitioner."

APPELLEE: See "respondent."

ARGUMENT: A claim advanced by support.

ARGUMENT BRIEF: An easy to reference document, often organized around a particular issue, including the major arguments you may need to advance.

ARGUMENT CHAIN: The claim of one argument supports a subsequent claim.

ARGUMENT CUE: A verbal or structural indicator of the relationship between two or more statements in an argument.

ARGUMENT DIAGRAM: A graphic representation of the sequence of argumentative statements from support(s) to claim(s).

ARGUMENT FROM ANALOGY: An argument extending what is true of a known case to an unknown case.

ARGUMENT FROM AUTHORITY: An argument concluding that something is true based on the expertise of the source.

ARGUMENT FROM CAUSE: An argument claiming that one or more elements are an influencing factor for another.

ARGUMENT FROM CLASSIFICATION: An argument claiming that a general statement of definition, rule, or principle applies to one or a few instances under that general statement's jurisdiction.

ARGUMENT FROM CONSEQUENCE: An argument claiming that a hypothetical cause will produce an anticipated effect.

ARGUMENT FROM GENERALIZATION: An argument claiming that what is true of the sample is likely true of the target category.

ARGUMENT FROM PARALLEL CASE: An argument extending what is true of a known, empirical case to an unknown, related case.

ARGUMENT FROM SIGN: An argument claiming that observable signs indicate the existence of some condition or state of affairs.

ARGUMENT SPHERE: A metaphoric realm of argumentation characterized by predictable patterns.

ARGUMENTATION: The process of forming and communicating arguments.

ARGUMENTATION ETHICS: Guidelines for moral conduct in argumentation

ARGUMENTATION STANCE: An arguer's attitude and intention toward co-arguers and audiences.

AUDIENCE: The people to whom arguers speak and from whom arguers seek assent.

AUDIENCE ANALYSIS: Deliberate consideration of the audience's composition, beliefs, and interests in relation to the debate situation.

AUDIENCE ADAPTATION: Adjusting argumentation to the audience to achieve the arguer's goal.

BACKING: Support for the warrant of an argument.

BURDEN OF PROOF: An arguer's responsibility to demonstrate a sufficient case on the proposition.

CASE: A strategic and comprehensive series of argument chains that an arguer communicates on a proposition.

CATEGORY: The entire category represented by the sample.

CLAIM: A statement that you want your audience to accept.

CLASH: Arguing the same issues as your co-arguer(s) in a debate.

CO-ARGUER: The people with whom arguers exchange arguments.

COGENT: Rationally persuasive.

COMPETITIVE STANCE: Arguers pursue self-interest by overpowering their co-arguer(s) and audience(s).

CONTROVERSY: Prolonged argumentation at the societal level spanning space and time.

CONVERGENT SUPPORT: Two or more support statements that independently warrant the claim.

COOPERATIVE STANCE: Arguers pursue mutual-interest by treating their co-arguer(s) and audience(s) as equals.

COUNTERPLAN: An alternative plan to the proposition that solves the harm and avoids one or more of the disadvantages.

CREDIBILITY: The arguer's competence and character.

CRITICAL THINKING: Active, persistent, and careful consideration of arguments.

DEBATE: The exchange of arguments on a topic.

THE DEBATE SITUATION: The interaction of arguments addressing issues relevant to a proposition about a controversy.

DEFINITION: The dictionary or cultural meaning attached to something.

DEMOGRAPHICS: The audience's composition based on its various qualities.

DISADVANTAGES: Negative consequences of enacting the plan.

EDITORIAL: An argumentative newspaper article that communicates an opinion attributed to the newspaper's editorial board

EXAMPLE: A single instance or case used for illustration purposes.

EXTEMPORANEOUS: Oral delivery from prepared outline of ideas (rather than complete script) that may use key words or bullet points.

FACT: Empirical or descriptive information widely accepted as true.

FACT CLAIM: A descriptive claim characterizing truth or falsity.

FALLACY: A logical error.

FALSE ANALOGY: A non-cogent argument that reaches a claim by comparing two fundamentally dissimilar cases.

FLOWING: Writing down arguments from a debate in column sequence by placing responses beside the argument to which they respond.

FORMAL LOGIC: The study of argument forms for validity.

FUNDAMENTAL ATTRIBUTION ERROR (FALLACY): A potentially non-cogent argument that claims a person's internal factors (character, personality, attitudes, etc.) are the cause for that person's behavior.

GROUNDS: The degree to which the support is sufficient to justify the claim.

HASTY GENERALIZATION (FALLACY): A non-cogent argument that reaches a claim from a small or unrepresentative sample.

IMPACT: A statement explaining the ultimate consequence of the advantage or disadvantage.

IMPROMPTU: Oral delivery from short preparation time and limited notes.

INHERENCY: The structures and/or attitudes in the present system that (help) produce and perpetuate the significant harm.

ISSUE: A neutral yes/no question representing a point of disagreement on a proposition.

LEGAL BRIEF: A written case that argues whether the lower court erred in its ruling.

LETTER TO THE EDITOR: An argumentative newspaper article that communicates an opinion in response to another person's article

LINK: A statement explaining how the plan connects to the advantage or disadvantage.

LINKED SUPPORT: Two or more support statements that are both required to warrant the claim.

MANIPULATIVE STANCE: Arguers pursue self-interest by deceiving their co-arguer(s) and audience(s).

MANUSCRIPT: Oral delivery from a fully prepared script.

MEMORIZED: Oral delivery from recall of a fully prepared script committed to memory.

NET BENEFITS: Resolving a policy debate by weighing advantages vs. disadvantages of the proposition.

OP-ED: An argumentative newspaper article that communicates an opinion attributed to the individual author

PERSONAL SPHERE: A realm characterized by informal argumentation of limited scope among individuals.

PETITIONER: The party appealing the lower court's ruling.

PLAN: The proposition and any provisions relevant to enacting it.

POINT OF INFORMATION: A question an arguer asks during the unprotected time of a speech by the opposing team.

POINT OF ORDER: An arguer's allegation that a member of the opposing team has violated the rules.

POINT OF PERSONAL PRIVILEGE: An arguer's allegation that a member of the opposing team has offended or misrepresented him or her.

POLICY CLAIM: A deliberative claim proposing some agent take some action.

POST HOC (FALLACY): A non-cogent argument that erroneously claims an effect after some cause is because of that cause.

PRECEDENT: Prior court opinions and existing law.

PREEMPTION: Raising and refuting an anticipated argument.

PREPONDERANCE OF EVIDENCE: Resolving a fact debate by weighing the superiority of evidence for and against the proposition.

PRESUMPTION: The expected outcome of a proposition absent a debate.

PRINCIPLE: A truth or belief that guides one's (moral) conduct.

PROPOSITION: The main claim over which an entire debate occurs.

PSYCHOGRAPHICS: The audience's composition based on its mental characteristics.

PUBLIC DELIBERATION: Argumentation aimed at managing a wicked problem by weighing advantages and disadvantages to various approaches.

PUBLIC ONLINE ARGUMENTATION: Argumentation on sites that are exclusively online and that enable open access.

PUBLIC SPHERE: A realm characterized by community-oriented argumentation of societal scope.

QUALIFIER: A word of phrase indicating the force of the claim.

REBUTTAL: Conditions in which the warrant does not apply.

REFERENCE: The general concept of the symbol and referent.

REFERENT: A thing about which we want to communicate.

REFUTATION: The process of articulating flaws in the logic of your co-arguer's arguments.

RELEVANCE: The degree to which the support has bearing on the claim.

RESOLUTION: See "proposition."

RESPONDENT: The party defending the lower court's ruling.

SAMPLE: The group of examples from which the support is derived.

SIGNIFICANT HARM: The harm, problem, or defect in the status quo motivating policy change.

SINGLE CAUSE (FALLACY): A non-cogent argument that erroneously claims an effect of a complex situation is the result of a single cause.

SITUATIONAL FACTORS: The audience's characteristics based on the debate situation.

SLIPPERY SLOPE (FALLACY): A non-cogent argument that erroneously claims a single cause will produce an inevitable series of events leading to an extreme consequence.

SOLVENCY: How the plan solves the harm (and/or inherency).

STATISTIC: A numerical representation of information.

STOCK ISSUES: The primary issues arguers must address to justify a policy proposition. See "significant harm," "inherency," "plan," "solvency," and "advantages."

STRATEGIC CONCESSION: Intentionally granting a co-arguer's claim.

STYLE: The arguer's use of figures of speech and word choice.

SUPPORT: The reason(s) for a claim.

SYMBOL: The communicated thing that stands for or represents the referent.

TECHNICAL SPHERE: A realm characterized by formal argumentation within a specialized community.

TESTIMONY: Other people's words or ideas.

TOPICALITY: Arguing that the affirmative plan is outside the scope of the wording of the proposition.

TROLL: A person who intentionally employs non-cogent arguments.

UNSTATED ASSUMPTION: An idea or belief implied by the stated elements of an argument.

VALUE CLAIM: An evaluative claim asserting a judgment about something.

VALUE CRITERION: Resolving a value debate by weighing the application of the criteria defining the value for and against the proposition.

VALUES: Things of worth to a person or community.

WARRANT: The inferential statement that justifies the claim on the basis on the support.

WICKED PROBLEM: A problem that defies easy solution and has multiple viable approaches, each with advantages and disadvantages.

INDEX

ABOUT THE AUTHOR

Jeffrey P. Mehltretter Drury (PhD, University of Wisconsin-Madison; MA and BA, Northern Illinois University) is an Associate Professor of Rhetoric at Wabash College, an all-male liberal arts college in Crawfordsville, Indiana. As an undergraduate student, Drury competed in intercollegiate policy debate for four years before coaching the team as a master's student. Since 2003, Drury has taught courses in argumentation and debate at four different institutions. His research, which considers representations of self and others in political argumentation, has appeared in journals such as the *Western Journal of Communication*, the *Journal of Contemporary Rhetoric*, and *Voices of Democracy*. In 2014, he authored *Speaking with the People's Voice* (Texas A&M University Press), an analysis of the argumentative forms modern U.S. presidents use when they invoke public opinion in their nationally televised speeches.